RADIO

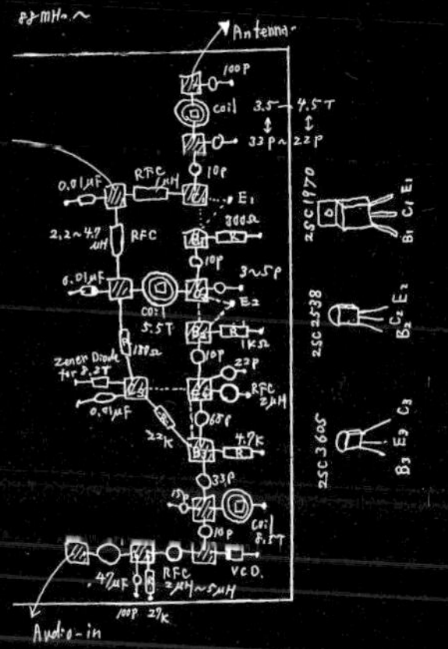

Antenna
100P
coil
3.5~4.5T
33P~22P
10P
RFC
E1
0.01μF
2.2~4.7μH
RFC
300Ω
10P
3~5P
E2
coil
5.5T
1KΩ
Zener Diode
10P
22P
RFC
2μH
0.01μF
68P
4.7K
22K
33P
10P
VCO
RFC
2μH~5μH
Audio-in
100P
27K
2SC1970
B1 C1 E1
2SC2538
B2 C2 E2
2SC3605
B3 E3 C3

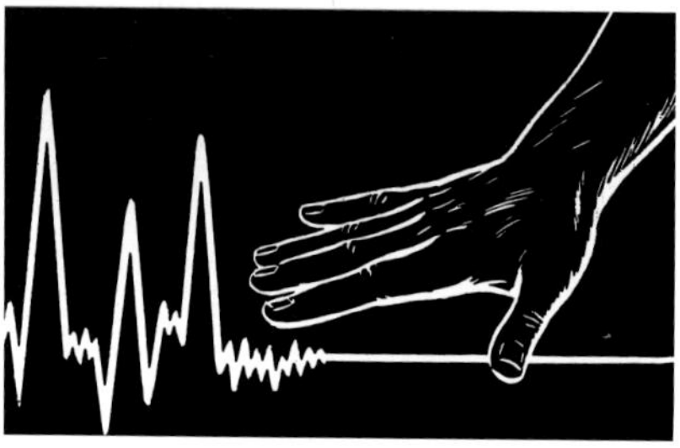

rethink

RADIO

r e t h i n k

art, sound and transmission

Edited by
Daina Augaitis
and Dan Lander

Walter Phillips Gallery

Walter Phillips Gallery
The Banff Centre for the Arts
Box 1020–14
Banff, Alberta
Canada TOL OCO
(403) 762-6281

The Banff Centre
for the Arts

Canadian Cataloguing in Publication Data
Main entry under title:

Radio rethink

Includes biographical references and index.
ISBN 0-920159-66-4
1. Radio art – Canada. 2. Radio and the arts – Canada. I. Augaitis, Daina.
II. Lander, Dan 1953–. III. Walter Phillips Gallery.
NX513.A1R32 1944 700 C94-910057-9

Editing, Production and Design: Mary Anne Moser
Production and Design Assistant: Mary Squario
Printing: Sundog Printing Limited
Cover photo: Monte Greenshields and Cheryl Bellows
Radio schematic on cover and page *i*: courtesy Tetsuo Kogawa
Graphics on page *ii*: courtesy Tim Westbury

Contents

Acknowledgements

The Banff Centre for the Arts has initiated several projects to explore and develop the possibilities of radio as a medium for artistic activity. The first manifestations of radio activity, under the name of RADIA 89.9 FM and primarily through the efforts of Al Mattes and Claude Schryer, underscored the potential of the laboratory conditions that permitted an amazing diversity of content and technique. This legacy precedes *Radio Rethink,* a project organized by the Walter Phillips Gallery in January through March of 1992, intended as a sustained and focused examination of radio produced as a means of transmission, communication and exploration by artists. In all of its manifestations – a radio "station" airing radio art programming and live events; commissions of new works by artists in residence; a chronological research project on a select history of radio art in Canada; a gallery exhibition; a compact disc compilation; and this publication – *Radio Rethink* was made possible only through the enthusiasm and support of many individuals and organizations. We acknowledge and express gratitude to all, and mention some by name.

The excitement that pervaded *Radio Rethink* was generated primarily by a core group of artists invited to create new radio works while in residence at the Banff Centre: Hank Bull, Leonard Fisher with Archer Pechawis, Rita McKeough, Christof Migone, Rober Racine, Patrick Ready, Colette Urban and Hildegard Westerkamp. It was both an honour and a great pleasure to work with all of them. These artists were simultaneously part of an Art Studio residency shaped by consultants Bernie Miller and Jeanne Randolph entitled "Technology, Rhetoric and Utopia," where over twenty artists came together to create their art and develop the thematic context. The Art Studio, under the guidance of artistic director Lorne Falk, and the Media Arts program, headed during this period by artistic director Vern Hume with Kevin Elliot responsible for audio, were all generous collaborators in critical aspects of the project.

The week-long symposium brought excitement and debate to the airwaves with presentations by the commissioned artists as well as talks, performances or workshops by Frances Dyson, Deborah Esch, Guillermo Gómez-Peña and Coco Fusco, Heidi Grundmann, Douglas Kahn, Tetsuo Kogawa, Dan Lander, Tom Moylan, Jeanne Randolph and Kim Sawchuk. Further radio manifestations over a two-month period were provided by Robert Adrian X, Guy Brett, Don Buchla, Mary Bull, Allison Cameron, Alan Conter, Mike Ewanus, FASTWÜRMS, Nancy Froehlick, Sally Garen, Jeff Gilman, David Gutnick, Gay Jackson, Kaolin and the Eutectics from the Ceramics program, Music program musicians, Neil MacInnis, Doug Melnyk, Robert Normandeau, Sheilagh O'Leary, Claire Paquet, Suzanne Paquet, Winfried Ritsch, Jocelyn Robert, Claude Schryer, Pauline See, Barbara Todd, Janice Williamson and many other members of the community, and artists in residence at that time.

Radio by its very nature is an ephemeral medium; however, it takes a transmitter, miles of audio cable, lots of people, equipment, paperwork and money to allow sound to emerge from the radio speaker at the other end. Very special appreciation is extended to Michael Young, representative for Yamaha Canada Music Ltd., who supported the project with a generous donation of Yamaha audio equipment; Colin Griffiths, production coordinator and programmer who, on this as well as previous manifestations of RADIA, enthusiastically fulfilled the instrumental role of configuring and sustaining the multifaceted aspects of radio transmission, this time together with associate Tim Westbury; and Mimmo Maiolo, gallery preparator, who magically transformed a gallery into a radio "station." Walter Phillips Gallery staff were most important to the success of the project: registrar Deborah Cameron, curator Sylvie Gilbert, gallery technician Sally Garen, Visual Arts assistant manager Pauline Martin, Visual Arts administrative assistant Wendy Robinson, publications editor Mary Anne Moser, gallery attendant Mary Squario and project intern Mike Ewanus were key players. Equally critical to the project were the ideas and/or work of Banff Centre staff and associates: Ingrid Bachmann, Jack Butler, Michael Century, Colin Funk, Inge Gaida, Bob Knowlden,

Maureen Lee, Frank Lockwood, Douglas MacLeod, Woodrow MacPhail, Mark Richardson, Chris Segnitz, Doug Smith, Phillip Strong, Paul Sylvestre, Dan Thorburn, Ben West, the Buildings and Grounds electricians, Jon Bjorgum and Communications staff.

Like the medium itself, radio art activity in this country is largely ephemeral, its documentation is sporadic. We undertook research to begin a compilation of selected Canadian radio events, projects, broadcasts and programs related to contemporary art, which is published in a separate volume simultaneously with this book. Coordinated and edited by Dan Lander, he was aided in research by Hank Bull, Boris Chassagne, Colin Griffiths, Gerry Kisil, Michael Toppings and Tim Westbury.

A compact disc composed of selected portions of the commissioned radio works produced for *Radio Rethink* is also released concurrently as a companion to this book. Edited by Dan Lander, it has been produced with the coordination of Jean-François Denis of Imprintes Digitales.

We are very grateful to all the writers who put their ideas, energy and cooperation into this project. In addition to the artists who wrote about their own work, and the symposium speakers whose texts are included here, deep appreciation is extended to Jody Berland, Margaretta D'Arcy, Friedrich Kittler, Rob Kozinuk, Richard Kriesche, Carol Laing, Paula Levine, Tim Westbury, Gregory Whitehead, Paul Wong; as well as *Public* and Museum moderner Kunst Stiftung Ludwig Wien who granted permission for reprints; and Anna Lausch and Gosia Nowaczyk for translations. Photographs by Cheryl Bellows, John Blake, Monte Greenshields and Don Lee along with others who are credited in the book, as well as those who loaned photo material – the artists, Canadian Marconi Company, CN Information Services, and National Archives of Canada – add to the visual appeal. Additional support for copy editing from Helga Pakasaar and Tim Westbury is also acknowledged.

This book has been a two-year project of the gallery's publications editor, Mary Anne Moser, and her energetic, constructive and astute contributions are fundamental components to the material contained within. Whether collaborating editorially with the contributors, creating the book's design, or overseeing its production, her integrity and commitment to the ideas of artists and writers alike make this book a pleasure to read. Her work has been ably supported by publications assistant, Mary Squario.

No project of this scope can come to fruition without the generous support of funding agencies and companies. In addition to the assistance provided by Yamaha Canada Music Ltd., this project received support from the Alberta Foundation for the Arts and the Canada Council – the Exhibition Assistance Program and Program Assistance to Public Art Museums and Galleries of the Visual Arts Section, and the Media Arts Section. Canada Council's contribution to contemporary art practice is critical to many artists and institutions in this country and we are grateful for this support.

Since the day I asked Dan Lander to join me in curating this project, he has been an enthusiastic and committed collaborator in planning and executing *Radio Rethink*. His wealth of ideas and experience have been integrated with my own in a very fruitful working relationship.

Daina Augaitis
Director, Visual Arts
Chief Curator, Walter Phillips Gallery

This project was made possible with the support of
YAMAHA CANADA MUSIC LTD. MUSIQUE LTÉE.

Photo Monte Greenshields

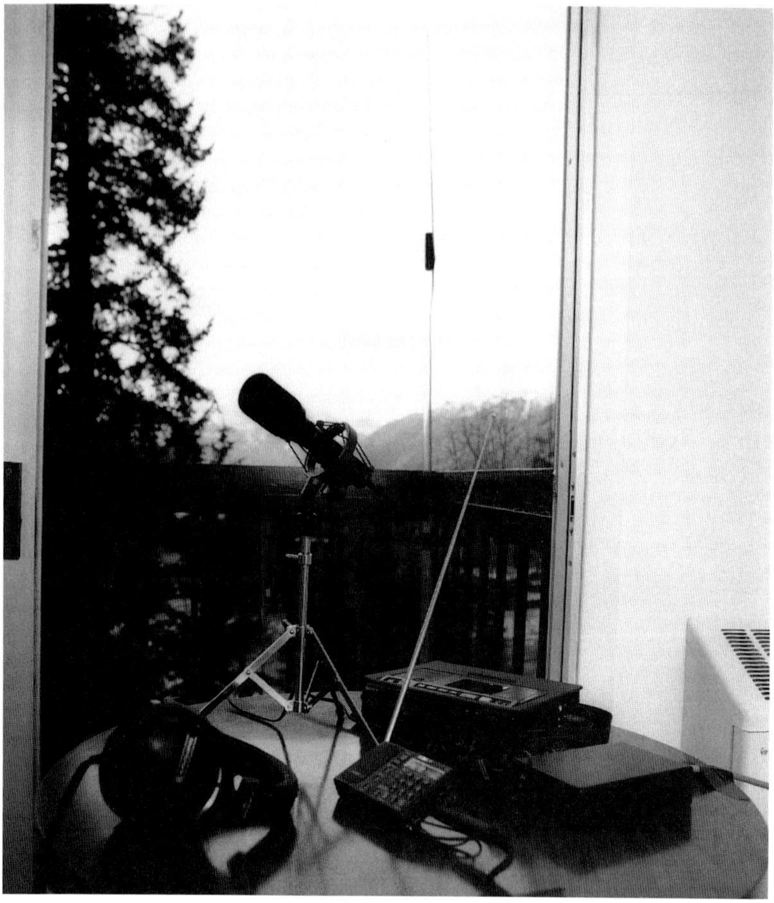

Mini-FM station installed in artist's room during *Radio Rethink*

Introduction

Daina Augaitis and Mary Anne Moser

In a six hundred-channel universe, it may seem unusual to consider radio as a medium for critical intervention in today's cultures. However, as a tool and forum, artists are using radio in ways that illuminate a profound and significant set of questions about community, technology and domination, to name a few. Though complex, these concepts are addressed in artistic practices that present themselves through serious as well as humourous means. After all, radio no longer appears as the seductive medium that it once was and artists, in choosing this form, have adopted strategies that not only acknowledge radio's weighty cultural history but also lay claim to the power of aurality in human experience. While radio's successor, television, has generally attempted to reach broad audiences through its programming, radio has often paid greater attention to questions of local context. It is in such niches and cracks of mass media's mortar that many artists locate their work.

Radio's role in the development of nationhood, in Canada at least but in other countries as well, casts a specific hue on practices that take up radio as a medium for artworks. While many have upheld radio's significant impact in articulating Canadian identity, nevertheless, a predominant feature of radio art is a resistance against state regulation of the airwaves and the many subtle and overt levels of control that have resulted. Not only is government censorship an issue, so too is corporate power. Even with, for example, six hundred channels to choose from, content may still be driven by powerful commercial interests that determine many of the prescribed formats of AM and FM radio. One of the goals of many radio artists is to challenge the half-hour format, the packaged radio voice, and other devices that have developed in tandem with consumerism.

It has been argued that although cultural specificity in terms of content are positive developments, it will change little about the fact that radio and television are unidirectional. Once again, the medium is the message. Related to this are issues about community and the role of radio in shaping or facilitating a community voice – which leads to the still relevant litany of questions: who is speaking for whom, why and with what consequences?

All of these questions culminate in Japanese activist Tetsuo Kogawa's essay in this volume when he asks, "What ends in radio?" As he charts out, there is a role for radio within a community that is shaped by and functions for its participants and breaks from the unidirectional voice of authority. His position, gleaned from involvement in the theory and practice of emancipatory social movements, finds a striking correspondence in a women's pirate radio movement halfway around the globe. One of the organizers, Margaretta D'Arcy, describes a similar attitude toward the role of radio technologies regarding community, with an emphasis on the participation of women.

Radio projects such as Kogawa's and D'Arcy's are called "free radio" or "pirate" because they are not licensed by the regulatory body of Japan and Ireland respectively. However, extremely low-watt transmissions are not at the same time illegal if they do not exceed output levels determined by the state. Given this window of opportunity, a community can be created around a low-watt transmitter that is so limited in size that listeners are most likely to be producers as well.

The arrival of a radio transmitter at the Banff Centre in the late 1980s kindled the formation of just such a community and triggered a series of projects that eventually led to *Radio Rethink*. At the time the transmitter was acquired, artists were keen to engage in an opportunity to create work outside some of the existing definitions of art production and to develop new audiences. Responding to emerging desires for community involvement and increasingly blurred distinctions between artist and non-artist, a group of workers at the Banff Centre decided to start an informal radio "station." This coincided with the Centre's decision to install radios in all of the residence bedrooms. After patching a microphone into a mixer, connecting it to a ten-watt, mono-FM transmitter housed in a small metal box nearby and running a cable to a dipole antenna on the roof,

Installation detail showing the radio hats used for Colette Urban's *It's On Your Head, It's In Your Head* (1992)

Photo Monte Greenshields

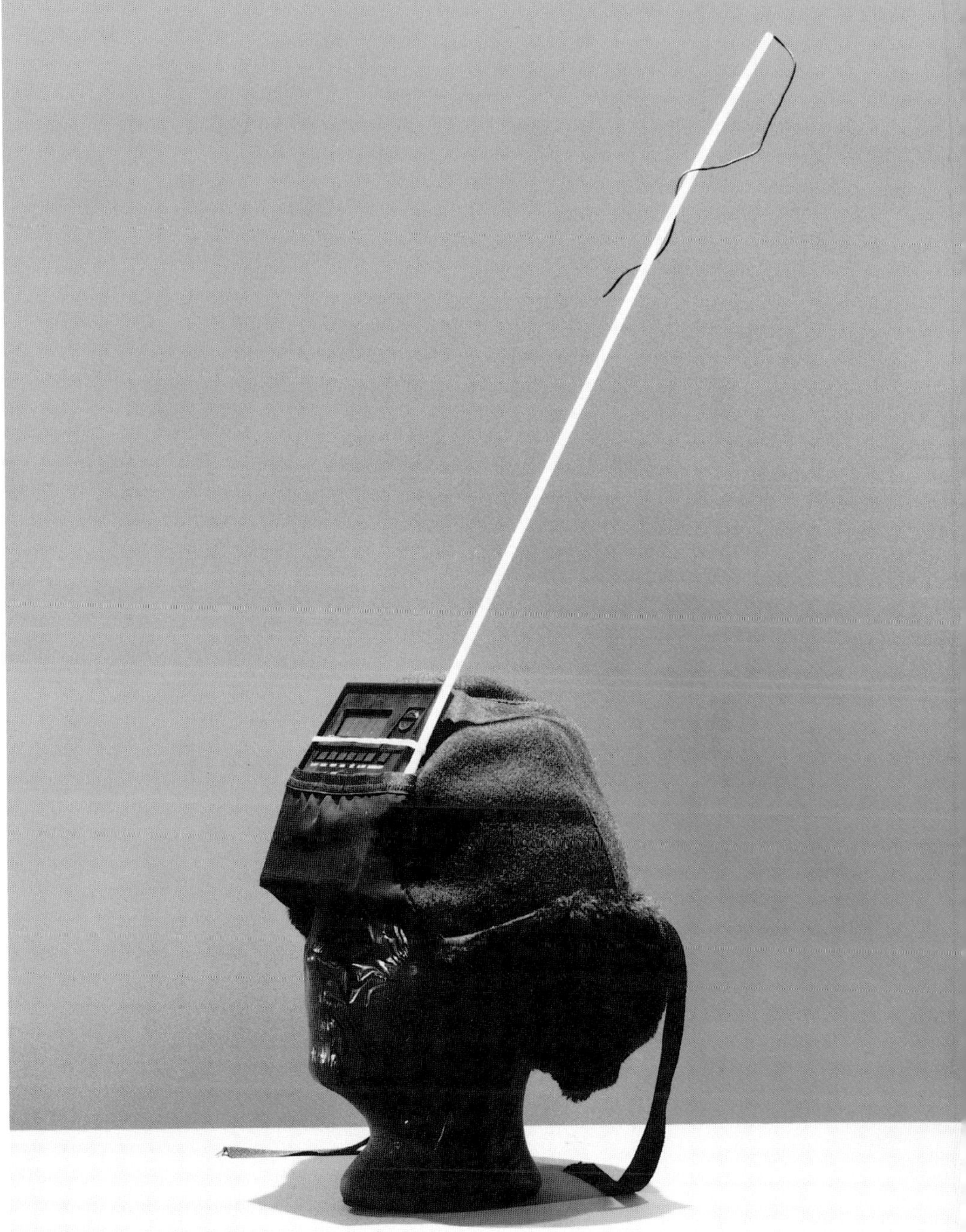

RADIA 89.9 was created. The programming that developed was an admixture of expressions, broadcast intermittently. The station went to air for weeks at a time, guided by the leadership of various people during several specific projects. Many questions were considered during this exploratory period, such as the consequences of dead air, perceptions of audience, distinctions between radio art and alternative programming, whether any intervention was art, and how sculpture, installation, performance and other time-based arts related to what was being created for radio. *Radio Rethink* was a concentrated focus on many of these issues, bringing together an array of pre-recorded projects, live works and interactive pieces for radio. It is also significant that it was undertaken by a contemporary art gallery, challenging the prescribed limits of the white cube and embracing a participatory and process-oriented activity in its space.

The questions about radio art's parameters have been far from answered as the artworks, essays and writings in this book reveal, however, there are many inspirational directions to consider as this medium is examined by artists and theorists. As a book, *Radio Rethink: Art, Sound and Transmission* assembles art practices and readings using radio as a focus to consider changing artist and audience relationships, and shifts in the politics of power. The resulting publication both addresses and exemplifies these issues that demand scrutiny if, to follow Kogawa's lead on "what ends in radio,"

> the end suggests the completion and the place in which the whole of history is gathered in its most extreme possibility.[1]

Artworks for *Radio Rethink* have been commissioned from Hank Bull, Leonard Fisher, Rita McKeough, Christof Migone, Rober Racine, Patrick Ready, Colette Urban and Hildegard Westerkamp. The writings in this book – by or on the artists – present their art practices and the issues that they raise in multiple and often idiosyncratic expressions of the not-so-dominant radio voice. Among the texts by artists is a letter from one of the earlier participants in radio at the Banff Centre, Hank Bull, a long-time director at the Western Front artist centre in Vancouver. He returned to Banff for *Radio Rethink* to further explore radio's ability to communicate, which included a collaboration with Patrick Ready, his co-host on the *The HP Show* on Vancouver Co-op Radio for over eight years. An engaging history of this experimental program and the meaning of collaboration are included, in which the specific interests of Bull and Ready as well as the Vancouver context for artmaking in the 1960s and 1970s are poignantly revealed. Ready's interests in the physical aspects of radio are manifest very concretely in the installation he created for the *Radio Rethink* exhibition, *Radio and Beans*. Dan Lander elaborates on this electromagnetic experiment and its ecological repercussions.

Colette Urban's piece for radio brings in sculptural and performance components that complicate readings of radio as an art and communications medium. Her artistic concerns and integral treatment of the audience in the conception of this seven-day collaborative work are incorporated into a description of the project by Tim Westbury, one of seven performers who themselves became "radio (re)transmitters." In another radio work involving an installation with viewer interactivity, Christof Migone also explores the relationship of transmitter, receiver and audience, more specifically, the unstable intimacy that can take hold in the relationship between radio host and listener. Constructing imaginary texts based on elements of actual conversations, his writing retains an aura of anonymity, and is steeped in interrogation and guilt – reinforced by the role of the confessional booth which housed the installation.

As a visitor to Banff, Hildegard Westerkamp creates a sound portrait of Banff for broadcast. The anonymous natural sounds in her soundwalks convey her interest in experiential listening and acoustic ecology. As she explains in her essay, her practice has long focused on creating a "radio that listens" by broadcasting soundscapes that listeners' experience in their daily lives. The aural world created by Rober Racine also highlights the often unheard sound created by one common activity: handwriting. Inviting a range of people to sign their names for a duration of two minutes, Racine transforms this very personal statement into another realm where the personality emerges through the rhythmic intonations of aggression, compassion, enthusiasm, calm. In her multilayered operatic work for radio, Rita McKeough takes the listener to a point past the pain after leaving an abusive situation. Performed with two other singers, this piece makes suffering and healing present in the public space of radio, thus continuing McKeough's social concerns which are expressed poetically within Paula Levine's essay. Leonard Fisher's art practice and his piece for *Radio Rethink* are presented here in conversation with Paul Wong who introduces Fisher's work in the context of his political concerns. "*Earth Police* is a concept I have been mulling over as a

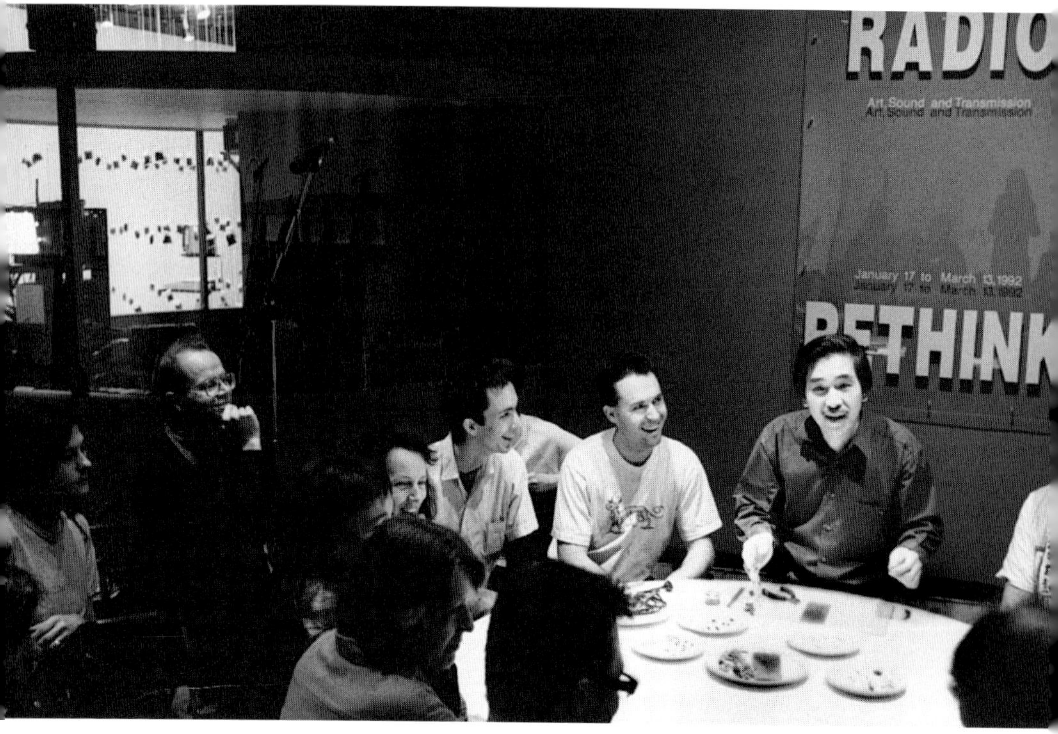

Tetsuo Kogawa's workshop demonstrating how to build a one-watt FM transmitter at the Walter Phillips Gallery

conceptual explanation of what aboriginal people are doing right now in the defense of their homelands and territories," Fisher explains.

As part of the *Radio Rethink* project, a symposium was organized to provide background, context and critical discussion around radio art histories and practices. In addition to the broadcast, performance and installation of artists' works, presentations were made by Frances Dyson, Coco Fusco and Guillermo Gómez-Peña, Heidi Grundmann, Douglas Kahn, Tetsuo Kogawa and Kim Sawchuk. The essays published here by these writers are versions of their presentations adapted for publication. However, as is often the case, the published version differs considerably from the events that transpired in Banff. Coco Fusco and Guillermo Gómez-Peña, for example, created a performative space with candles, arranged seating and accentuated voices in combination with the presentation of theoretical issues around the representation of cultural diversity in the media. A conversation describing their motivations for using radio to

Photo Cheryl Bellows

represent hybridity in a public domain is accompanied by a radio script from *The Year of the White Bear*. Kim Sawchuk's essay was performed, rather than presented, with two collaborators, slide projections, live and recorded radio components, in a prepared performative space. Starting from the premise that "identity is not a fact, it's an act," she weaves the construction of her own identity into an examination of the pirate as an enabling metaphor for viewing women's relationship to technology. Tetsuo Kogawa conducted a workshop in Banff on how to build a one-watt FM transmitter. The instructions have been prepared for publication by Rob Kozinuk to accompany Kogawa's essay on his involvement in the mini-FM movement in Japan in which he raises important questions about the relevance of the term "free radio" in contemporary culture.

Many of the artworks and essays in this book level a critique of dominant radio practice that to some extent is based on its cultural hegemony. In a thorough and well-researched argument, Frances Dyson traces the roots of this domination through schools of philosophy and religion. While the dominant radio voice may seem to appear with the advent of radio, she explains how it brings with it "a host of characteristics that connect it to the deepest symbolic and epistemological structures governing thought, speech and media in western culture." Incorporating ideas from radio art's Futurist antecedents, Heidi Grundmann presents her insights on the factors that motivate many contemporary radio artists working in Europe. She writes: "The traditional meaning of concepts such as the author, the piece/work of art, the original, the object, the medium, and so on, are constantly and consciously challenged by the practices of those artists who confront the conditions of postindustrial society and situate their work in the immaterial space of new communications technologies." The artists of the avant-garde and their legacy on contemporary practice is the focus of Douglas Kahn's detailed overview of radio projects, some of which were never realized. To move beyond restrictive genres that still contain art practices, Kahn suggests that "because space is the place in new audio technologies, there is no reason not to nest one space in another, or move one through several, in both a sustained or immediately disappearing way and then bring the whole conglomeration into a cipher which finds itself nested or moving somewhere."

Additional essays have been commissioned or reprinted such as the text by Margaretta D'Arcy, mentioned earlier, who takes up a pirate radio project to create a women's radio station. D'Arcy suggests in her text that one of the reasons for the exclusion of women from existing radio stations is that they do not accommodate the hours that she, as a mother, must keep. The artworks of three women who are active radio artists are digested by Carol Laing in her flavourful text in which she writes back to the artists. Laing's consideration of rhetoric, desire and mimicry around these works is an honest and open approach to ways in which one might respond to artworks and, in the process, takes a step toward the exchange of information rather than the unidirectional delivery of information – be it on radio or in letters. Digestive systems, bodily systems, the radiobody, are the subjects of Gregory Whitehead's article, revised for publication here. In his description, "the radiobody is a strange and unruly composite of opposites: speaking to everyone abstractly but no one in particular; ubiquitous, but fading without a trace; forever crossing boundaries but with uncertain destination; capable of intimate communion but charged with enough power to trigger sudden destruction." Like Kogawa, Jody Berland re-examines radio as a medium for artists now that it appears to be "old-fashioned." This status, she argues, renders radio as "a subject of innovative expression, rather than a site for innovative communication. But this supposes we have fully comprehended and indeed exhausted radio. In reality we have barely begun." Her observations on the political origins of radio point to the confluence of radiophonic space and the concept of nation.

Two texts that were first published in German have been translated for inclusion here. Friedrich Kittler surveys the impact of philosophical shifts in thinking on the changing role and perception of radio in society. Contrary to Kogawa and Berland, he refers to military and industrial uses of radio and the decline of radio in the midst of the telecommunications revolution. Richard Kriesche unravels stimulating observations of changing media and their social functions through his poetic writing that covers topics such as the car radio, perspective, radioman, infinity, noise, speed and the dead data background.

The vastly different writings in this book – ranging from fictional to descriptive, political to whimsical, scholarly to conversational – convey the breadth of the field of radio art and related artistic practices emerging in the 1990s. Perhaps this range embodies the politics informing many of these contributions, one that strives to dismantle fixed representations of genres, cultural identities and genders. Perhaps it is also responding to a moment in the specific history of radio as an aspect of artistic production, a background that Dan Lander surveys in his essay.

Photo John Blake

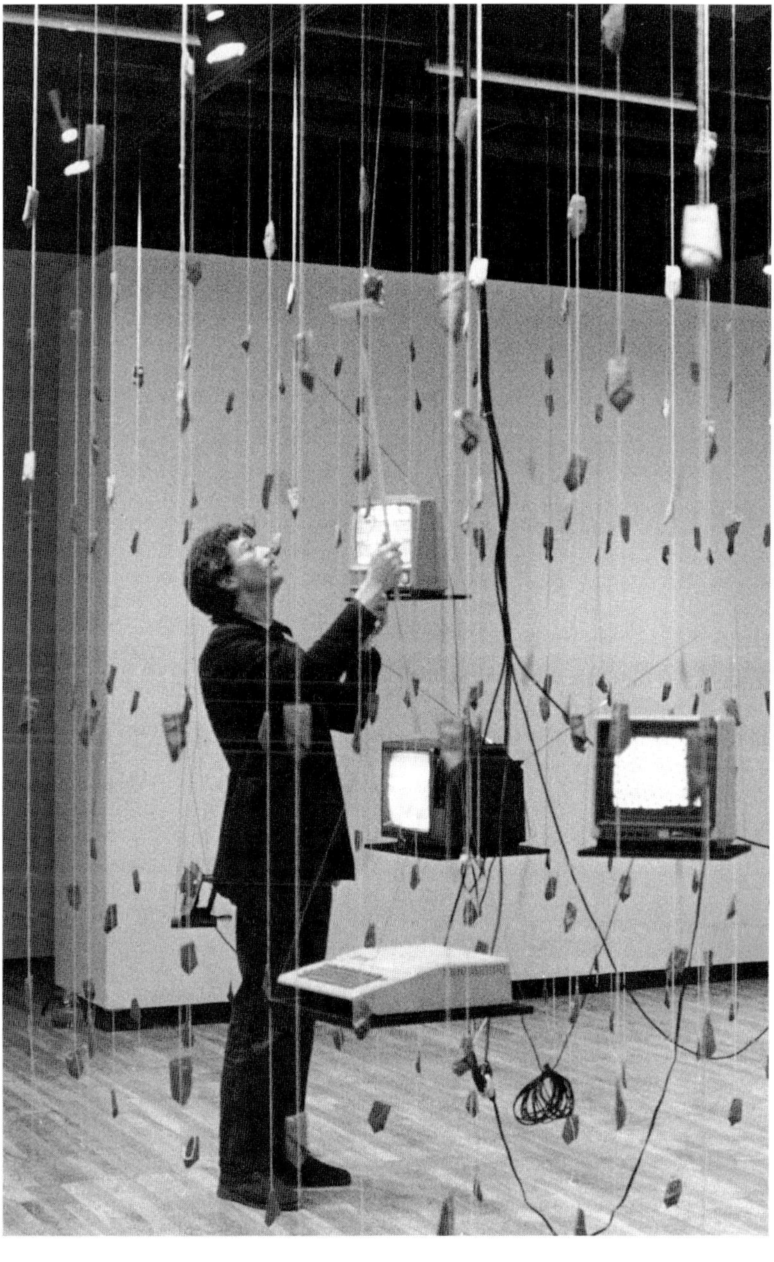

Patrick Ready watering the mung beans in his installation *Radio and Beans* (1992) at the Walter Phillips Gallery

Published in conjunction with this volume is a compact disc of selected radio artworks, commissioned and produced during the *Radio Rethink* exhibition, and an overview of Canadian activity titled *Selected Survey of Radio Art in Canada 1967–1992*. Together, the CD, survey and this anthology of writings create a body of information that addresses some of the issues that are important to understanding cultural practices today. The ideas in this book point to the exciting potential radio has as an artistic medium that, as Kriesche suggests, calls art back to its social reality.

Notes

1 Martin Heidegger, *On Time and Being*, trans. Joan Stambaugh (New York: Harper Collins, 1972), 56–57.

Radiocasting: Musings on Radio and Art

Dan Lander

INTRODUCTION

Although historical and contemporary artistic and theoretical discourse regarding radio art is scant to say the least, there has been, and continues to be, audible evidence of artists and writers whose considerations on the subject begin to shape a theoretical body. The combination of influences shaping this history sheds valuable light on radio art practices today, as there appears to be a clear relationship between early explorations and more recent theoretical considerations. From the beginning, artists were prone to considering radio as a material as opposed to merely a distribution apparatus, as is evident in the writings of Bertolt Brecht, F. T. Marinetti and others. However, when compared to the other arts, namely the visual, there is a marked absence of historical radio artworks and theoretical writings. There are many factors which contribute to this absence including the prominence of the visual over the aural, industrial impositions, the practice of transposing other media onto a radiophonic space, the lack of an autonomous theory of sound and, finally, a generalized disengagement with the spatial and temporal shift brought about by the new electronic technologies. In addition, radio artists have had to confront the regulation of content, political and conceptual, that follows with state regulation of the airwaves. The development of, and desire for, new modes of production and interpretation that artists have expressed over the years has not always materialized as a result of these imposed restrictions. This essay attempts to explore some of the reasons for the historical discontinuity regarding radio art and, at the same time, points to the relevance of the theoretical groundwork that has been laid.

A GAP

> There is no history of a self-described and autonomous [sound] art in the way one might think of the history of sculpture, no façade of a purposeful unity and linear continuity, no ongoing biographical intrigues and libidinal exchanges of influence. As a historical object, sound [and radio art], cannot furnish a good story or consistent cast of characters nor can it validate any ersatz notions of progress or generational maturity. The history is scattered, fleeting and highly mediated – it is as poor an object in any respect as sound itself.[1]

In 1936, Rudolph Arnheim contemplated in his book, *Radio*, the possibilities for what he perceived to be a new form of art, born from the invention of the wireless, a phenomenon that by 1933 had already provided Europe with 235 radio stations and a "wireless police"[2] based in Brussels. He discussed a range of ontological and conceptual considerations with topic headings such as "A new art of sound," "Voices without bodies," "The hermit at the loudspeaker" and "Armaments in the ether." His ruminations on the order of the senses are most relevant when considering the gap in historical, theoretical and practical developments of an art of radio.

> The eye alone gives a complete picture of the world, but the ear alone gives an incomplete one . . . The essence of broadcasting consists just in the fact that it alone offers unity by aural means . . . the essence of an event, a process of thought, a representation . . . The sensory preponderance of the visual over the aural in our life is so great that it is difficult to get used to considering the aural world as more than just a transition to the visual world. Thus there is a widespread fixed opinion as to the task of the wireless.[3]

Arnheim's observations point to one of the major contributing factors that has stifled the development of radio art: a hierarchy of the senses which installs sight at the top of the perceptual ladder. It *is* the gaze that has preoccupied theoretical ruminations in western art discourse. While there now exists a massive body of deliberations on the ontology of the image, representational strategies, stasis, objecthood, perspective, body/object relations, performative tactics and the resultant consumptive transactions that accompany the digestion of the visual arts, an autonomous language suited to the task of developing a discourse on non-objecthood, the time-active and the de-localized reality of media forms such as radio art remains elusive. As Peter Weibel has stated, this deficiency is nothing less than striking:

> If we take an inquisitive look at the aesthetical conceptions during the last two centuries, it is striking that they are based on the ontology of the image, upon a static world-picture, that inadvertently ignores, makes impossible, the essence of media art; its dynamics, immateriality and time related form.[4]

Other factors have also contributed to the underdevelopment of an art of radio. This includes the imposition of a borrowed musical discourse[5] applied to all sound phenomenon, stripping away any social and/or cultural referentiality, thus creating a situation in which aurality in general is perceived as music, as if the origin, context and phenomenology of any given sound or noise can be measured only by its contribution to a renovation of western art music. Radio art requires a consistent body of research and practice that concentrates on sound at its point of signification, not a literal rendering which will collapse into cliché, but a sensitivity to the ways in which meaning in sound circulates, dissipates and re-emerges. The development of an autonomous body of theory and practice regarding aural referentiality – in particular as it relates to radio and electronic media – will contribute to a better understanding of the role that radio art plays in the articulation of social and cultural ideas.

Impeding the development of an art of radio, above and beyond a complete consideration of aural signification, is the fact that artists have not had easy access to the airwaves, as the radio apparatus itself has historically been consigned to the control of state and corporate interests, in a bogus effort to protect the general well being of the public. Radio, and other electronic and digital technologies, are derived from military research and development, sought primarily as weapons of destruction and social control. The military-industrial lineage of the radio apparatus itself presents artists with a particular challenge: how to circumvent the all-prevailing influence of these violent roots and how to minimize the likelihood that their ideas will be subsumed and co-opted by these power structures. When considering radio *as* art (and this pertains to electronic media communications in general) most practitioners have grown to accept a level of control and censorship that is not normally tolerated with forms of artistic and cultural expression such as painting and literature. Given the restraints applied to the medium (broadcast quality, balanced programming, congruent appeal, enforced programmatic assumptions, marketing research, the trained voice, restrictions to access, uniform time allocations, technical specifications, licensing regulations, to name a few) there is little room for the complex and idiosyncratic forms of expression that we experience in day-to-day cultural and social transactions. These restrictions make radio art distinct from what is generally considered to be a form of autonomous artmaking, placing the radio artist in a quasi-industrial relationship with the medium.[6]

For those who wish to autonomously express themselves through the medium of radio, a barrier exists that is now so firmly entrenched it represents a crisis of democracy and freedom of expression. Without the usual cultural support systems provided for other forms of expression, radio artists are left to their own devices. The education provided regarding media in general is one-sided and deficient. The majority of media literacy programs concentrate on the development of analytical listening skills only, while denying any actual production experience. In other words, literacy is a two-way street in which reading (as in listening), and writing (as in producing) play equal roles in the development of expression and comprehension. To offer children, for instance, only a discourse of reading we deny them a child's artistic engagement with radio and all that implies. In addition, it is the mainstream radio model that dominates the context of the majority of production and reception. However, if one is to seek out alternative approaches, ones that point to alternative modes of expression, it is to the documented historical artistic ideas and activities that we must turn.

PRECEDENCE

> New technological space has been at one and the same time a new horizon and a closure, an intoxicating possibility and a dangerous suppression of something just beginning to happen.[7]

Given the complexity of the historical developments of radio as industry, radio as military weapon, it is no wonder that artists have had a difficult time in creating autonomous works and contingent theoretical histories. However, although the odds were, and are, stacked in favour of a radio that is controlled, aimed as if a missile, devoid of any real communicative properties, there continues to be artists who have developed complex relationships to the medium. One of the earliest of such artists was Russian avant-garde poet Velimir Khlebnikov,[8] whose poetry was "aimed at revealing the primeval meaning of existing word roots, expressed through consonantal sounds rather than conventional semantics," creating "a universal language based on similar-sounding roots."[9] In 1921, Khlebnikov wrote a manifesto entitled "The Radio of the Future":

> The Radio of the Future – the central tree of our consciousness – will inaugurate new ways to cope with our endless undertakings and will unite all mankind [sic].
>
> The main Radio station, that stronghold of steel, where clouds of wires cluster like strands of hair, will surely be protected by a sign with a skull and crossbones and the familiar word "Danger," since the least disruption of Radio operations would produce a mental blackout over the entire country, a temporary loss of consciousness.[10]

Khlebnikov considers radio as a kind of billboard, an agit-prop device that can inform, educate and unify all people. His somewhat prophetic understanding of how new media would affect the collective consciousness of humankind by its global presence, is mirrored in a later manifesto written by the Italian Futurists Filippo Tommaso Marinetti and Pino Masnata. *La Radia*,[11] written in 1933, borrowed from Marinetti's earlier notion of *parole in libertà* (words-in-freedom). The basis for his idea was "that the elements central to the logical linguistic structure (conjunctions, adverbs, adjectives, verbal conjugations and punctuation marks) had to be eliminated to reduce language to its essential parts."[12] Words that were now "liberated" from their original syntax could be juxtaposed by analogy, creating what Marinetti called a *wireless imagination*. The manifesto, prefaced with a general Futurist overview, details what "La Radia Must Not Be . . . theatre because radio has killed the theatre already defeated by sound cinema," what "La Radia Abolishes . . . time" and "unity of action," and what "La Radia Shall Be:"

3 The immensification of space No longer visible and frameable the stage becomes universal and cosmic

6 A pure organism of radio sensations

7 An art without time or space without yesterday or tomorrow The possibility of receiving broadcast stations situated in various time zones and the lack of light will destroy the hours of the day and night The reception and amplification of the light and the voices of the past with thermoionic values will destroy time

17 The utilization of interference between stations and of the birth and evanescence of the sounds[13]

La Radia signals a clear understanding of the implications inherent in the ability of new technology to enable a simultaneous presence, a dematerialization, an "organism." Marinetti and Masnata grasped what has since developed into a body of theory regarding mass communication as it relates to artists working in media. Their reference to the use of "interference between the stations" is in evidence today in many artists' works that point to the saturation of the airwaves and conceptual considerations of noise as information. *La Radia* predicts the shift from an industrial world to a postindustrial world, from a machine age to an electronic age, moving beyond radio into the kind of global information society that has since come to be. In that same year Marinetti wrote five short pieces for radio that he called Radio *Sintesi*, which incorporated periods of silence and various noises such as "the rrrrr of a motor."[14] These works were never aired. In the *Sintesi* entitled *Dramma di Distanze* (Drama of Distances), Marinetti most clearly elucidates his understanding of the ability of transmission to traverse the globe in a simultaneous juxtaposition of dislocated sites:

DRAMA OF DISTANCES

11 seconds of a military march in Rome
11 seconds of a tango danced in Santos
11 seconds of Japanese religious music played in Tokyo
11 seconds of a lively country dance from around Varèse
11 seconds of a boxing match in New York
11 seconds of street noises in Milan
11 seconds of a Neapolitan song sung in the Copa Cabaña Hotel in Rio de Janeiro[15]

The specific ideological and political intention of Marinetti's conceptual radio works is unclear, however, it may be useful to consider – especially in light of how the technology has developed – the premeditation that informed his enthusiasm towards transmission. It is known that at least twice during his life he maintained ties to Mussolini's Fascist Party although it appears that the Party had little interest in him. "Marinetti's most political works, *Democrazia futurista* (Futurist Democracy, 1919) and *Al di là del comunismo* (Beyond Communism, 1920)," point to a "wide gap between Futurists and Fascists. It lies in the Futurist anarchic element that rebels against all state hierarchies."[16] However, there is a thin line separating technological utopianism – the belief that there may lie in new technological developments possibilities for emancipation and cultural equality – and fascism – characterized by an elated state of mind regarding the extension of perceptual powers based on a recognition of technology's propensity for aesthetic and social control. What is clear is that by the time Marinetti had formulated his conceptual and artistic theories on the "wireless imagination," radio had firmly implanted itself into the European home and psyche in a very political way.[17]

Earlier thinkers had already recognized the impoverished implementation of radio into society and the insidious aspects of that intrusion. Among them was Bertolt Brecht who, in 1926, wrote a paper entitled "The Radio as an Apparatus of Communication." Brecht was concerned with the lack of collective participation in radio, its unidirectionality and its (even by then) apparent function as a propaganda tool for the state. He was also aware of its impact on the structure of family life stating that radio was not "an adequate means of bringing back coziness to the home and making family life bearable again."[18] Brecht elaborated on the problem that

> radio is one-sided when it should be two. It is purely an apparatus for distribution, for mere sharing out. So here is a positive suggestion: change this apparatus over from distribution to communication. The radio would be the finest possible communication apparatus in public life, a vast network of pipes. That is to say, it would be if it knew how to receive as well as to transmit, how to let the listener speak as well as hear.[19]

Although somewhat rhetorical, Brecht's desire to redesign the radio apparatus as an instrument of communication is evidence of his recognition of a crisis in cultural production and reception. Autonomy, as it relates to a diverse and democratic proliferation and exchange of forms, ideas and artistic development in general, becomes non-existent in the sender-receiver model of the authoritative radio presence. This structure is epitomized in the isolation of the individual at the cost of a diminished collective expression. As contemporary theorist Florian Rötzer suggests:

> The set up of a radio broadcast lends expression to this structure, with a voice emanating from the loudspeaker on the one hand and the many scattered individuals listening to that voice . . . linked together to form a virtual community created through the simultaneity of listening rather than a physical community created through their actual presence in one and the same place.[20]

Rötzer also points out that Brecht's notion of radio was influenced by the historical fact that radio was known to accommodate one-on-one communication, for example, in the early uses of telegraphy and wireless. He notes that "Brecht saw radio as an agora in virtual space where anyone can produce unfiltered messages and where the transmission of the message is not controlled by a censor or editor."[21] Brecht also felt that society was not ready for a technology that was capable of so much, yet was implemented on a premise of so little. He stated that "radio imitated almost all existing institutions that had anything to do with the diffusion of whatever could be spoken or sung," adding that the "result was an inescapable profusion and confusion in the tower of Babel."[22] As Stuart Hood has since pointed out, Brecht was one of the first to suggest that radio should be more than a simple transcriptional device. Hood quotes Brecht's reference to the musical compositions of Kurt Weill and Paul Hindemith, referring to the secondary ways in which they were utilized on German radio drama programs, in which Brecht states that "their work must be performed in principle and they must compose works *exclusively for radio*."[23] German historian and theorist Friedrich Kittler suggests that inherent in the history of media is the housing of one form in another, creating a kind of piggyback from one technology to the next, bypassing the exploration of any salient features present in each new development.[24] On a similar train of thought, Brecht suggested that the technological development of radio superseded the public's ability to accept and utilize it to their best advantage:

> It was not the public that waited for radio but radio that waited for the public; to define the situation of radio more accurately, raw material was not waiting for methods of production based on social needs but means of production were looking anxiously for raw material. It was suddenly possible to say everything to everybody but, thinking about it, there was nothing to say.[25]

Utopian desire, expressed through the conviction that the new technology of wireless telegraphy would serve as a catalyst to a more humane society, is evident in the formidable number of amateur wireless radio operators and inventors in the United States, whose presence was felt from 1906 and beyond. Prior to both state and military recognition of the important role that radio would play in the control, dissemination and secrecy of information, these amateurs, by 1914, were numerous enough to organize a national organization they called the American Radio Relay League, which boasted two hundred relay stations across the country. In that same year, the technical magazine *Popular Mechanics* pronounced that the invention of wireless telegraphy "has made it possible for the private citizen to communicate across great distances without the aid of either the government or a corporation," marking "the beginning of a new epoch in the interchange of information and transmission of messages."[26]

However, this model of free exchange was short lived. As the number of amateur wireless operators and technical innovators increased, so too did military and government intervention: "activities became a nuisance to wireless companies and government." It was also discovered that the ether, which previously had been considered a territory as grandiose as the universe itself, was in fact restricted: "too many people had embraced the invention and its possibilities."[27] In the end, amateurs were thwarted by corporate, governmental and military lobbyists:

> During the *Titanic* disaster of April 1912, interference from amateur stations trying to relay as well as elicit news was so great that within four months the Congress banished their transmissions to a portion of the spectrum then deemed useless: short waves. The Radio Act of 1912 also required that amateurs be licensed, and imposed fines for "malicious interference."[28]

Hence, the free play of cultural exchange via the ether was constrained at a very early stage in the development of radio technologies. Ever since artists have expressed interest in the medium, the tension between perceived possibilities and the actuality of a space controlled, regulated and creatively stifled, has sustained a frustrated and incomplete history of actual radio art practice. From Khlebnikov's notion of radio as the "central tree of our consciousness," to the *Popular Mechanics* assertion that radio would bring about a "new epoch in the interchange of information and transmission of messages," artists have come to understand that there is limited room for the proliferation and diversity of artistic works. The expressed desires and traffic of ideas that artists have applied to the apparatus of radio – as a material, a communication conduit, a vessel with which to pour out an expanding currency of autonomous cultural expression – appear to be incongruent with the technological, political and social realities of the apparatus itself. However, in spite of the perceived limitations, artists do persist. "If you should think this is utopian, then I would ask you to consider why it is utopian."[29]

A BODY INSCRIBED

the presence of my corporal
pain,
the menacing,
never tiring
presence
of my
body . . .[30]

In 1947, playwright, poet, painter and actor Antonin Artaud[31] was commissioned by French radio to create a radiophonic work for broadcast on *Radiodiffusion française* the following year. The resultant recorded work, entitled *Pour en finir avec le jugement de Dieu* (*To Have Done with the Judgment of God*),[32] was never broadcast as it was censored and, although Artaud and others attempted to have the decision overturned, they were unsuccessful. Contrary to Brecht's concern regarding the ability of the collective body politic to utilize radio as an interactive exchange system, Artaud's radio work reflects a dystopian view of the individual as he/she relates back to culture at large. *Pour en finir avec le jugement de Dieu* represents a radiophonic extension of Artaud's "Theatre of Cruelty," in which theatre, "because of its physical aspect and because it requires expression in space (the only real expression in fact), allows a magical means of art and speech to be practised organically and as a whole, like renewed exorcisms," creating a "unique language halfway between gesture and thought."[33] Although *Pour en finir avec le jugement de Dieu* contains anti-Americanisms, scatological references, sacrilegious pronouncements and excruciating screamscapes, it is more than likely that the work was censored as a result of its perceived ability to instil fear in the listener, rather than any specific content of the text. Artaud's idea of a material language, the language of a corporeal body that would utilize sounds, cries, screams, grunts, onomatopoeia, glossolalia, and so on, was well suited to the disembodied space of transmission, as it is a language that, like a gas, escapes from the entire body. The mouth in this case constitutes just one sound-emitting hole of many. This is a body without organs which, according to Allen S. Weiss, places this particular work by Artaud clearly in the realm of a radio-phantasmic space:

> The body without organs is the ultimate deboning of the voice, a recreation or disarticulation of the corporeal structure that takes on cosmic dimensions. It is thus no accident that this corporeal phantasm first arises in conjunction with a radiophonic work, radio being the site par excellence for such anatomical revisions, and ultimately for the loss of the body.[34]

Weiss goes on to comment that "it is only when our entire body becomes a mouth that we can truly speak."[35] Artaud's body was literally in pain when he recorded *Pour en finir avec le jugement de Dieu* and in fact he died shortly thereafter from rectal cancer. Theorizing about the difficulty in articulating bodily pain through speech, author Elaine Scarry has speculated that the presence of pain creates a resistance to language, actively destroying it, "bringing about an immediate reversion to a state anterior to language, to the sounds and cries a human being makes before language is acquired."[36] However, in the context of transmission, the body is prone to disappearance – the babble, the word, the scream, is never returned – for the body will not, cannot, travel with its signifier, the voice. The body poised for anatomical flight must satisfy itself with the illusion the prosthesis creates, uttering a language of severed recognition, a language of disjunction, a language without writing. The illusion of intimacy that transmission portends, through a conscious corporeal assertion, does in fact allow for diverse references of bodily signification. However, as Christof Migone has written, the temporal and spatial disjunction, accompanying a radiophonic (lack of) presence, "creates a sensual fiction, a poetic virtuality, creating a space where we can describe ourselves and still not know who we are."[37] The sterility of the voice, as heard on the majority of radio transmissions, stripped as it is of any corporeal references, trained, controlled and dead, is the child of a paranoid body, afraid to speak of and for itself. French playwright Valère Novarina, as quoted by Weiss, provides a succinct description of this "cleansing" process:

> They work night and day with immense teams and enormous financial means: a cleansing of the body in sound recording, a toilet of the voice, filtering, tapes edited and carefully purified of all laughs, farts, hiccoughs, salivations, respirations, of all the slag that marks the animal, material nature of the words that come from the human body.[38]

The lack of bodily sound on mainstream radio signifies a fear of disembodiment, a lack of will to address what is considered taboo: sub-vocal speech, scatological sounds and bodily noise in general. The conceptual frameworks that are necessary to recognize such expressions include considerations of production and reception that allow for ambiguities, a reading that oscillates towards the complex rather than a simplistic faith in the sterility of the "objective," factual, authoritative presentation methodology so often heard on mainstream radio. The phenomenon of dead air, for instance, will strike fear in the radio producer's heart, not because it may signify a deficiency in production technique or continuity, but because it allows authority to fall away. Silence has plagued the entire history of radiophonic production, as it is believed to indicate a nothingness, a space in which the listener is apt to insert his or her own idiosyncratic noise and meaning, a space in which the listener's own body may constitute a presence. As William S. Burroughs – one of the few to contemplate the phenomenon and relevance of inner speech as it relates to notions of silence – has written:

> The word may once have been a healthy neural cell. It is now a parasitic organism that invades and damages the central nervous system. Modern man [sic] has lost the option of silence. Try halting your sub-vocal speech. Try to achieve even ten seconds of inner silence. You will encounter a resisting organism that *forces you to talk.* That organism is the word.[39]

The radio is always on, or so it would seem, recalling Marinetti's "pure organism of radio sensations." For Burroughs, the word exists at the cellular level, an attachment, even, to the body's central nervous system: "what we call history is the history of the word. In the beginning of that history was the word."[40] The word is passed on genetically, as if by electrical transmission, continuing its influence over human ideas and actions – a technological parasite. Marshall McLuhan also relates the body to speech and radio, suggesting that

> radio is that extension of the central nervous system that is matched only by human speech itself. Is it not worthy of our mediation that radio should be specially attuned to that primitive extension of our central nervous system, the vernacular tongue?[41]

But to *whom* does this vernacular tongue belong, from whose *body* does it fly, from what *location* does it emanate? Peter Weibel suggests that the language of absence that accompanies the new telematic (cyber)spaces represents not so much a new form of communication – writing itself, and later the printing press, had already enabled a delocalized displacement of information – but rather, a new spatio-temporal configuration:

> Here, time dislocates space and produces a placeless space. The signs of the telematic communications revolution are more immaterial and incorporeal than the earlier ones, due to the separation of (material) messenger and (immaterial) message. As a result, the bounds of space and time are alternately reduced or expanded.[42]

In this non-locality the radiobody resides: however, even if you cannot touch it, the radiobody will not go away. Through a conscious recorporealization of the body its lack of presence may symbolically suggest its existence. The vernacular to which McLuhan alludes can be extended to include not just the tongue, but the entire environment of blood, bone, tissue and organ.

One development that opened up possibilities for including bodily and other worldly sounds in radio artworks, was phonography. By the late 1940s, Pierre Schaeffer and Pierre Henry had developed a new compositional technique referred to as *musique concrète*. By 1950 they had acquired the use of magnetic tape and were actively composing recorded works for radio broadcast. The use of concrete sounds, and the technological ability to edit and electronically alter them, led to a new form of radio that was not dependent on scripts, actors or the radio studio. In Germany (1964 to present), Neues Hörspiel – a term introduced by Klaus Schöning to describe the new developments that were influencing traditional Hörspiel radio drama – was made evident in works by Paul Pörtner, Ferdinand Kriwet, Peter Handke, Friederike Mayröker and others. Mark E. Cory, in his essay "Soundplay," documents the innovative strategies the Neues Hörspiel artists employed. They include the "testing of semantic boundaries between shaped sound and deformed language; the use of stereo, synthesizers and vocoders to manipulate acoustical material and even to generate sounds not found in nature; the flirtation with chance operations; and the substitution of musical principles of composition for traditional approaches to organizing a text."[43] Cory goes on to describe a form of Hörspiel that developed in the 1970s, called *O-Ton*, which

> differed from the features of the past by virtue of its compositional techniques. Instead of beginning with a script and then taping interviews to illustrate and give depth to the various points the author wishes to make, the O-Ton artist simply begins recording and then assembles out of the recorded original material a coherent and sometimes surprising, sound portrait . . . The O-Ton Hörspiel was the first to employ postwar technology (the tape recorder) to implement Brecht's prewar hope that radio would go beyond mere distribution (*Lieferantentum*) to organize its listeners into producers. The most productive source material for O-Ton has proved to be the voices of those otherwise disenfranchised by traditional radio art. The men in the street, prisoners, workers, apprentices – those whose distinctly nonliterary voices and nonstandard diction had seldom figured in Hörspiel – became its staple.[44]

In addition, the tape recorder introduced the ability to gather sounds from the din of a media-saturated environment created by radio, television and the media industry in general. This ability prompted artists to compose works that were critical of the new electronic landscape, turning it back upon itself. The recontextualization of the mediatized voice was the subject matter of Neues Hörspiel artists Handke and Kirwet in Germany and by, for instance, Howard Broomfield in Canada. Broomfield's *Radio on Radio: A radio program about radio* (1974) was broadcast on the national radio station, the Canadian Broadcasting Corporation. *Radio on Radio* formulated a critique regarding contemporary broadcast "flow" and illustrated the historical sounds of radio from the 1930s to the present. Broomfield, an anthropologist, utilized sound recordings as a resource for research into social and cultural habits and circumstances, paying close attention to diction, common sound environments and nonliterary aural expression. As a member of the World Soundscape Project, led by R. Murray Schafer, Broomfield believed that close attention paid to a relatively non-mediated aural signification would reap great benefits in the comprehension of cultural communication. *Radio on Radio* also reflects a criticism that Schafer levels against western broadcasting when he suggests that it "is tyrannized by an instrument we have accepted as inviolable: the clock. Radio today is the pulse of a society organized for maximum production and consumption."[45]

Another influence on Broomfield was Glenn Gould's *Solitude Trilogy* (1967–77), comprised of recordings of speech made at various locations, then treated and edited to form a collage of considerable density, blurring the distinctions between reportage and art. Challenging the myth of media objectivity Gould stated that, "one simply has to incorporate that information on its own terms – on terms which admit to no contradiction between the processes of 'art' and of 'documentation.'"[46] The tape recorder introduced a new freedom in the artist's mobility. No longer sequestered in the studio, artists could interact with the world at large, enabling them to represent the human voice in a cultural context, to deconstruct official media, to juxtapose disparate times and places, to disintegrate dominant language forms, to make evident the noise of the body, to utilize sound as a material in ways that might better elucidate the multitude of ways in which we communicate through the production and reception of sound, and, finally, to throw away the script.

CONCLUSION

> Move from that which is easily identifiable to that which is at the limit of being identifiable. Listen to them [sounds] non-knowingly but alertly. Enjoy their materiality. SUSPEND the MEANING of sounds by multiplying their naturalistic-realist role to the point where no single anchoring is possible, no message can be congealed, no analysis can be complete . . . Cutting, a sentence at different places for example, assembling it with holes, repeating it in slightly different forms and in ever-changing verbal contexts, helps to produce a constant shift and dislocation in meanings. Silences and repetitions are rejected as a failure of language when they are experienced as oblivious holes or as the utterance of the same thing twice or more. WE SHOULD NOT STAMMER, so goes the reasoning, for we only make our way successfully in life when we speak in a continuous articulate flow . . . After many years of confusions, of suppressed voice and INARTICULATE SOUNDS, holes, blanks, black-outs, jump-cuts . . . I FINALLY SAY NO: yes, sounds are sounds and should above all be released as sounds. Everything is in the releasing. There is no score to follow.[47]

Although Trinh T. Minh-ha is writing about image/sound relationships in the context of experimental film production, her words are pointedly relevant in the consideration of an art of radio. She argues for an opening up of interpretation, for a different kind of listening, one that is as dependent on the ear's work as it is on the mind's. In her critique of media manipulation, she encourages transgression of the monolithic, of the factual, of static interpretations, offering as an alternative what Frances Dyson refers to as "a speaking and listening practice which is antithetical to the voice of authority."[48] The assertion that "everything is in the releasing" points to differences between those who work *for* radio and those who wish to work *in* and *with* radio. The recognition of the historical influence of industrial models – including state, corporate and militaristic – on the relationship of artists to the radio apparatus, suggests the identification of a territory. Kim Sawchuk has written that "in establishing its spatial-temporal grid, the state creates foreign bodies within its own territory."[49] If transmission is a space in which there transpires a phantasmic loss of the body, it is also a space in which a clear boundary is drawn between the machinery of political and cultural control, and the desire to acknowledge the fluidity of cultural experience and utterance.

The history of radio art represents a struggle to overcome the enforcement of the arbitrary boundaries drawn by the paranoid hands of the state. These boundaries stifle creativity in many ways including the political, the aesthetic, the conceptual, the sensual and the multitude of creative imaginings that shape the various modes of expression and perception in a diverse cultural terrain. An autonomous and anarchistic cultural alternative that comes with the refusal to identify and participate in the control and manipulation of artistic expression, may be one of the few ways of circumventing the notion that we as artists are relegated to simply "playing" with hand-me-downs from the garbage heap of military mayhem and research. As the radio apparatus increases its range continually, through the development of new technologies such as the cellular telephone, satellite transmissions and so on, the "primitive extension of our central nervous system, the vernacular tongue," that McLuhan described remains suppressed. The development of an all too often inaudible host of vernaculars into an expanding transmission of variable and multidimensional cultural expressions will come to radio via a fluid and transgressive noise, filtered through the minds and the bodies of those eager to speak in the face of mediated taboos.

Notes

1 Douglas Kahn, "Introduction: Histories of Sound Once Removed," in *Wireless Imagination: Sound, Radio and the Avant-Garde*, ed. Douglas Kahn and Gregory Whitehead (Cambridge: MIT Press, 1992), 2.

2 Rudolph Arnheim, *Radio* (London: Faber and Faber, 1936), 236–237.

3 Ibid., 135–36.

4 Peter Weibel, "Transformation der Techno-Ästhetik," in *Digitaler Schein: Ästhetik der Elektronischen Medien*, ed. Florian Rötzer (Frankfurt: Suhrkamp Verlag, 1991). I found this translated quote in promotional material for Weibel's *Book for the Unstable Media* (Hertogenbosch: Stichting V2, 1992).

5 For an interesting discussion on the topic of "the weight of music" regarding a diminished consideration of an expanded field of sound see Douglas Kahn, "Track Organology," *October* 55 (Winter, 1990), 67–78. Kahn asserts that, "Music's dominance gained momentum from its complacent valorization as the *sine qua non* of the arts of sound. Its establishment as such has served to stifle the other arts of sound: the blinded ones, the multisensory ones, and the daily experience of aurality in general . . . Musical auto-referentiality did violence to

a system of aural signification whereby the associative characteristics of sounds, their attendant social and imaginative domains, were reduced, trivialized, or eradicated," 67.

6 See Dan Lander, "Radio Art: The Pubescent Stage," *Musicworks* "Radiophonics and Other-Phonies"53 (Summer, 1992), 20.

7 Jody Berland, "Toward a Creative Anachronism: Radio, The State and Sound Government," in this volume.

8 For more on Velimir Khlebnikov see Douglas Kahn's essay "Radio Space" in this volume.

9 *Russian Futurism Through Its Manifestoes, 1912–1928*, trans. Anna Lawton and Herbert Eagle (Ithaca: Cornell University Press, 1988), 13.

10 Velimir Khlebnikov, "The Radio of the Future," in *The King of Time*, ed. Charlotte Douglas (London and Cambridge: Harvard University Press, 1985), 155.

11 For more on Marinetti and Masnata see Heidi Grundmann's essay "The Geometry of Silence" in this volume.

12 *Russian Futurism Through Its Manifestoes, 1912–1928*, 3.

13 Filippo Tommaso Marinetti and Pino Masnata, "La Radia" in *Wireless Imagination*, trans. Stephen Sartarelli, 265–68. There are twenty separate points in the manifesto outlining what *La Radia* shall be. These excerpts were used to indicate the range of territories covered in the manifesto.

14 This excerpt is from the Radio *Sintesi* entitled *I Silenzi Parlano fra di Loro* (Silences Speak Among Themselves) published in Michael Kirby and Victoria Nes Kirby, *Futurist Performance* (New York: PAJ Publications, 1986), 293. See also Kevin Concannon, "Cut and Paste: Collage and the Art of Sound," in *Sound by Artists*, ed. Dan Lander and Micah Lexier (Toronto and Banff: Art Metropole and Walter Phillips Gallery, 1990), 163–67.

15 See Kevin Concannon, 167.

16 Pontus Hulten, *Futurismo & Futurismi* (Milan: Gruppo Editoriale Fabbri, 1986), 512: "Marinetti needs to be remembered also as a polemicist and political writer. From the beginning, politics were inherent in the movement's ideology. In fact, Marinetti and other Futurists participated in early Fascism. It was only at the second conference, held in Milan in 1920, that Marinetti, Mario Carlo and other Futurists angrily slammed the doors on Fascism because their anti-clerical, anti-monarchical proposals had not been accepted . . . Although, in 1923–24 Marinetti returned to the ranks of Fascism and in 1929 he was elected to the Academy of Italy, Marinetti and Futurism were never supported by the Fascist régime, but merely tolerated."

17 Alice Yager Kaplan, *Reproductions of Banality: Fascism, Literature, and French Intellectual Life* (Minneapolis: University of Minnesota Press, 1986), 135–37: "In the Italy of the 1930s, Mussolini organized a radio show called the 'Workers, Ten Minutes' that interrupted all activity in factories, unions and

public squares . . . In Germany, the government imposed mass production of a seventy-six-mark Volksradio, then sold 100,000 of them in one evening at a nationally organized Radio Fair. As of 1933, La Poste Parisien (a French radio station) . . . began, as part of its morning diet, a translation of the radio speeches of Hitler, the new chancellor."

18 Bertolt Brecht, "The Radio as an Apparatus of Communication," in *Video Culture: A Critical Investigation*, ed. John Hanhardt (Rochester: Visual Studies Workshop, 1986), 53.

19 Ibid.

20 Florian Rötzer, "Aesthetics of (Tele-) Communications?" *On Line: Kunst im Netz / Art in the Network* (Graz: Steirische Kulturinitiative, 1992), 51.

21 Ibid., 52.

22 Bertolt Brecht, "Radio as an Means of Communication: A Talk on the Function of Radio," trans. Stuart Hood, *Screen* 20: 3/4 (Winter 1979–80), 24.

23 Stuart Hood, 19 (my emphasis).

24 See Friedrich Kittler, "The History of Communication Media," *On Line: Kunst im Netz / Art in the Network* (Graz: Steirische Kulturinitiative, 1992), 76–77: The reference reads as follows: "The electrification of sensory input data through transducers and sensors enabled the entertainments industry to couple analog storage media firstly with one another and secondly with transmission media. The sound film combined optical and acoustic memories; radio, before the introduction of the tape-recorder, largely transmitted gramaphone records; the first television systems, prior to the development of electronic cameras, scanned feature films. Thus the content of entertainment media always remains another medium, which in this way they serve to promote."

25 Brecht, *Screen,* 24 (emphasis in original).

26 Quoted in Susan J. Douglas, "Amateur Operators and American Broadcasting: Shaping the Future of Radio," in *Imagining Tomorrow: History, Technology, and the American Future,* ed. Joseph J. Corn (Cambridge: MIT Press, 1986), 50.

27 Ibid., 51.

28 Ibid., 52. Douglas describes several reports of these so-called incidents of "malicious interference" as follows: "During what Navy operators claimed was an emergency situation, amateurs refused to clear the 'air,' some of the amateurs even arguing with the Navy men over ownership of the ether. In another instance, when a Boston amateur was told by a naval operator to 'butt out,' he reportedly made the following classic remark: 'Say, you navy people think you own the ether. Who ever heard of the navy anyway? Beat it, you, beat it.'" She goes on to make an important point regarding the programmatic and technological development of radio: "In the years after the Radio Act of 1912, the amateurs not only advanced radio technology but also anticipated broadcasting. Between 1910 and 1920, amateur stations began to broadcast

music, speech and even advertising. By 1917, amateurs were relaying messages not just regionally but from coast to coast, demonstrating the benefits of a national communications network," 51.

29 Brecht, *Screen*, 26.

30 Antonin Artaud, *Pour en finir avec le jugement de Dieu*, trans. Clayton Eshleman, in *Wireless Imagination*, 324.

31 For more on Artaud see Gregory Whitehead's essay, "Holes in the Head: Theatres of Operation for the Body in Pieces," and Douglas Kahn's "Radio Space," both in this volume.

32 A 24′ 03″ excerpt of Artaud's *Pour en finir avec le jugement de Dieu* can be heard on the five CD set entitled *Futura: Poesia Sonora*, ed. Arrigo Lora-Totino (Milan: Cramps Records, 1989).

33 "The Theatre of Cruelty (First Manifesto)," in *Antonin Artaud: Selected Writings*, ed. Susan Sontag (Berkeley and Los Angeles: University of California Press, 1988), 242. This volume also includes the complete script for Artaud's *Pour en finir avec le jugement de Dieu*, in addition to several letters pertaining to the work in question and its subsequent censorship.

34 Allen S. Weiss, "Radiophonic Art: The Voice of the Impossible Body," *Discourse* 14:2 (Spring 1992), 192. For an expanded discussion on Artaud's radio work see Allen S. Weiss, "Radio, Death, and the Devil: Artaud's *Pour en finir avec le jugement de Dieu*, in *Wireless Imagination*, 269–307.

35 Ibid., 197.

36 Elaine Scarry, *The Body in Pain: The Making and Unmaking of the World* (Oxford: Oxford University Press, 1985), 4.

37 Christof Migone, "Language is the Flower of the Mouth," *Musicworks* 53 (Summer 1992), 47.

38 Valère Novarina, "Lettre aux acteurs," *Le théâtre des paroles*, 7–26, as quoted in Weiss, "Radiophonic Art: The Voice of the Impossible Body," 187.

39 William S. Burroughs, *The Ticket That Exploded* (New York: Grove Press, 1967), 49–50 (emphasis in original).

40 Ibid., 50 (emphasis in original).

41 Marshall McLuhan, *Understanding Media: The Extensions of Man* (Toronto: McGraw-Hill, 1965), 302.

42 Peter Weibel, "New Space in the Electronic Age," *Book for the Unstable Media* (Hertogenbosch: Stichting V2, 1992), 72.

43 Mark E. Cory, "Soundplay," in *Wireless Imagination*, 363.

44 Ibid., 362.

45 R. Murray Schafer, "Radical Radio," in *Sound by Artists*, 208–209. Schafer adds: "What I am urging is a phenomenological approach to broadcasting to replace the humanistic. Let the voice of the announcer be stilled. Let situations be presented as they occur without the interruption of sponsors, clocks or editorial manipulation," 214.

46 Glenn Gould in conversation with editor Tim Page, "Radio as Music," published in *The Glenn Gould Reader* (Toronto: Lester and Orpen Dennys, 1984), 388. In 1992, Gould's *Solitude Trilogy* was republished on three compact discs (Toronto: CBC Records, PSCD 20003-3).

47 Trinh T. Minh-ha, *When the Moon Waxes Red: Representation, Gender and Cultural Politics* (New York and London: Routledge, 1991), 205–206.

48 See Frances Dyson, "The Genealogy of the Radio Voice," in this volume.

49 Kim Sawchuk, "Audio Terrorism: Low Level Flights Over Nitassinan," *Public* "Sound" 4/5 (1990), 115.

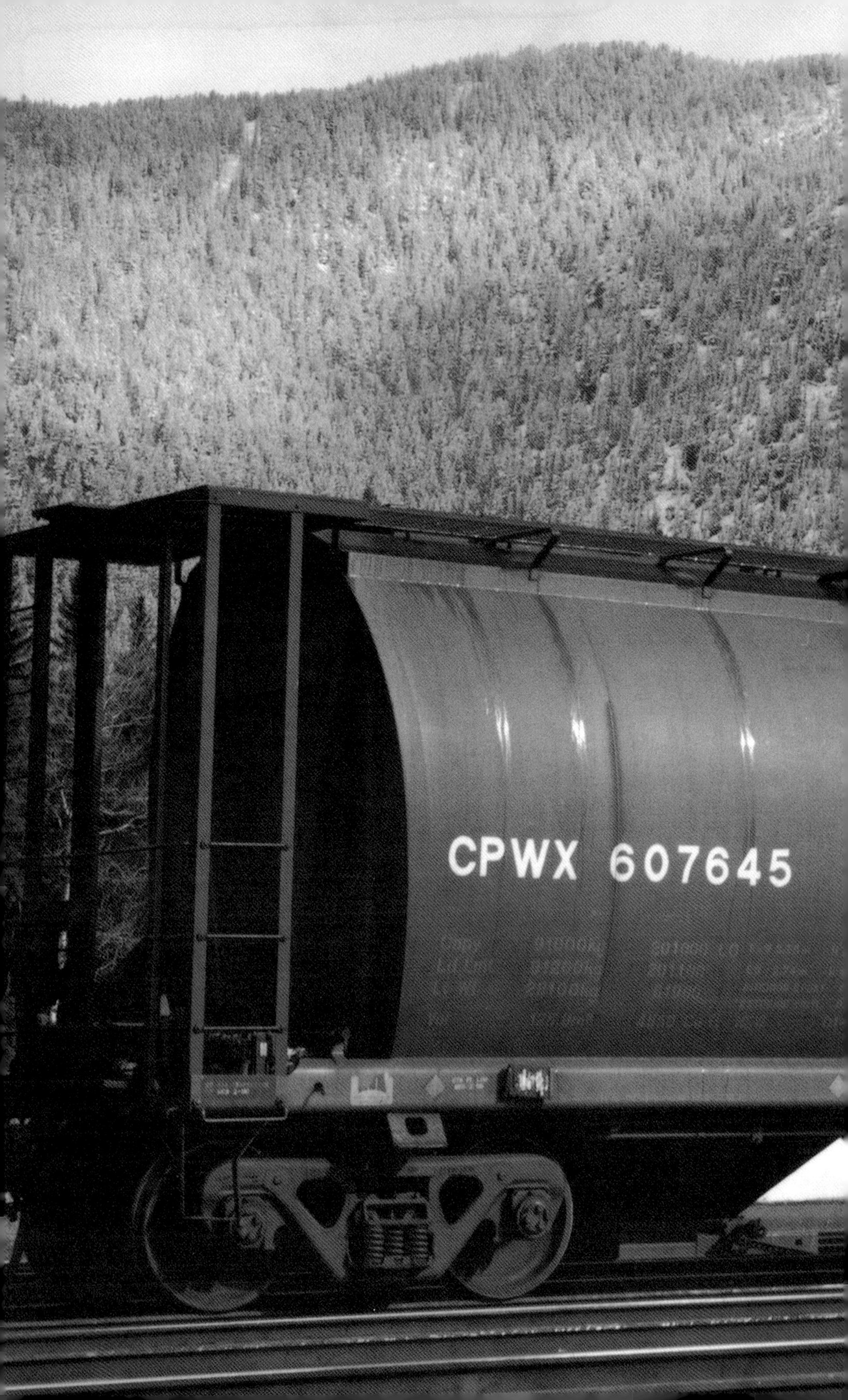
CPWX 607645

Toward a Creative Anachronism

RADIO, THE STATE AND SOUND GOVERNMENT

Jody Berland

> In a culture like ours, long accustomed to splitting and dividing all things as a means of control, it is sometimes a bit of a shock to be reminded that, in operational and practical fact, the medium is the message. This is merely to say that the personal and social consequences of any medium – that is, of any extension of ourselves – result from the new scale that is introduced into our affairs by each extension of ourselves, or by any new technology.
>
> Marshall McLuhan[1]

> I don't think we should consider the "modern state" as an entity which was developed above individuals, ignoring what they are and even their very existence, but on the contrary as a very sophisticated structure, in which individuals can be integrated, under one condition: that this individuality would be shaped in a new form, and submitted to a set of very specific patterns.
>
> Michel Foucault[2]

It has been said that music knows no boundaries; these days it is more accurate and less sentimental to say that it redefines them. Similarly, broadcasting may be said to know no boundaries (the forty-ninth parallel being notably contentious in that regard), although it is more accurate to contend that one of its major effects, particularly within the restless expansionistic reach of capitalism, is to redefine them. Like music, broadcasting is in part about the constitution of space; in establishing territoriality, there was sound long before there were fences.

Despite music's obvious temporal qualities, an analysis of its spatial

Photo Cheryl Bellows

efficacy is thus also appropriate. We surround the visual object, facing towards it as something other than ourselves; to look at something, even one's own image, is to constitute it as something separate. To listen to something is to forego that separation. Sound comes at us from behind or from the back, from any direction, and surrounds us; we are constituted as listeners within its space. "Instead of facing the sound source the listener seems immersed in it."[3] The listener is immersed in sound; the sound, entering the body, located both externally and internally, is immersed in the listener. It is as hard to describe this immersion as it is to say what music is. But in being so immersed, body and brain are brought to something or someone beyond the self, and the sound in turn is drawn inside the body and the mind, who cannot turn or close her eyes to it, making music the most intimate yet most commandingly social of all the arts.

Music participates in the constitution of social boundaries through presence, delimiting a sonic environment as a located social experience (the bar, the basement, the school yard and the symphony hall manifesting distinct versions of this) and also through absence. By drawing the listener into a special sensory space, music creates a sonic discourse that connects her to others who are not physically present but who are evoked or imagined through the music. At the same time, it distinguishes her from still other others, including perhaps those who are physically present but aurally eliminated, so to speak, with headphones for instance, or with speakers punctuating an inaudible space between them over the decibels in a larger space.

In other words, music has simultaneously the power to bind and cohere and to separate, to disperse – a dual capability that multiplies and fractures a thousand times in broadcasting, rendering both functions in the strongest, most contradictory formulation. Not by accident, these also describe the capabilities of what we call the State, which sound can variously reinforce or undermine, or accomplish both at once. It is often difficult to tell.

In that contradictory space between the identity evoked in language and constituted in sound, lies radio.

For broadcasting, listeners are both present and absent. In commercial radio, for which they are conceived as both subject and economic means, listeners are present as the target of research whose formulated identity is drawn into combinatory creation of the sound itself. For such radio each lateral division of the dial represents the sound of democracy in its most absolutist, most rationalized form; each is no more than the continuous mixing of choice and selection, identity and sound, listener and commodity. This is what has made music so important to post-television radio as an economically motivated form of mediation. It is music that draws listeners in through desire and identification, and music which makes desire and identification precisely calculable. Yet its listeners are also absent – an accidental body encountering its own measured image in temporal space, a demographic cipher finding its identity momentarily materialized in sound, an invisible figure beyond the voice who addresses her in the most familiar terms.

In public and community radio, not oriented towards the acquisition of abstractly comparable listeners as marketable commodities, radio represents a process in which sociality is to be constituted actively and variously across the same temporal space. This occurs in relation to some already-present generative activity outside of the placeless space of broadcasting: it concerns not only what the listener wants to hear, as a fraction of a sociometric calculation whose desire is both measured and reproduced by music but also – or in relation to – what she wants to do, what she wants to become. With the proliferation of stations, however, this discursive space is itself rationalized, becoming merely another station selection, a choice motivated by taste or disposition, another temporary location which can be selected or rejected in a moment.

As listening is increasingly mediated by electronic reproduction and transmission, the issue of "location" becomes very complicated indeed. Mediated by broadcasting, music and speech no longer signal any particular location or place, but rather a mediated location, a social/temporal location joining source and listener in the instant of a sound, as in, this musical interlude signals the beginning of the news, the end of *Morningside*, a weather forecast, the third song of the hour and therefore new, exciting, bound (by our mutual nomination) to be a hit. This articulation of an abstract and autoproductive location means that we are no longer concerned with the language of music – which strictly speaking no longer exists in the old sense, as something "belonging" to (or the effect of) the authorship or identity of a particular site, something previous to such transmission, though fortunately people still sometimes make it as though it could be free to be so – but rather with the language of its transmission. With the recombinatory grammar of its proliferation, music is severed from "original" physical contexts, spaces and relationships, and, with greater or less instrumentality, subsumed in a larger narrative, shaping the contours of a new sonic/electronic social space. Music is thereby contained by what it also disguises, which is the message, as McLuhan put it, of the medium itself.

Music articulates an internalized morphology of the social, its rhythm and pulse; it acts to socialize the body. So it can be said of radio, though in a different sense of the body. Through radio, music was carried into and helped to produce a whole new set of social spaces, while the new grammar of radio came to shape a larger, more mediated morphology of musical meaning. Among the products of this conjunction we might include, for instance: the permanent, unforgettable attachment of corporate symbols to individual melodies, programs and personalities; a "public" technological organ of the nation state; freeways and long daily commutes; teenagers; disc jockeys; hit parades – first regional, subsequently national and now international (the latter mainly the effect of television); the back seat of cars; dispersed communing communities (for example, Greeks or West Indians, gays or students); the many series of shops where radio helped articulate consumption more intensely and directly to the rapid currency of fashion.

Now, however, radio sounds in the shadow of newer technologies whose compliant precision delineates spaces even radio cannot reach, like Walkmans, which speak "to oneself alone, seemingly bringing the music not so much into the ears as directly into the mind."[4] Such technologies take the most instrumental radiophonic logic to its logical extreme and thereby threaten to make radiophonic territoriality (in the most general sense of the term) technologically and economically obsolete. Technically speaking, radio looks old now, iconographically cheap and naïvely social, not always manipulable for "personal" tastes, a good subject for nostalgic commercials and television shows. This is why artists – that is, producers functioning mainly in the individualized handicraft mold of the nineteenth century – are now so interested in it. We look back to radio in the way McLuhan says we look at all superseded media – as art; it appears as the "content" of newer technologies whose shapes and shapings we are not yet prepared to comprehend. That makes it a subject of innovative expression rather than a site for innovative communication. But this supposes we have fully comprehended and indeed exhausted radio. In reality we have barely begun.

Music touches and speaks to the listening body in physical and aural space; radio (carrying music and speech with it) follows and locates the body with a more abstract but no less compelling sensory and spatial logic. Radio permits us for the first time to participate in two different aural-geographical discourses simultaneously, to become one with their conjunction (or more accurately to become part of a placeless but still spatially defined third space) and to join in defining one in relation to the other. Radio locates us as both same – as when we sing along with a familiar hit, joining an imaginary community of millions celebrating the signification of our own efficacy, or as when we hear again the theme of *Morningside* – and as other: a sideways semi-flip of the dial and we are somewhere, someone else. Suddenly this tangible, powerful, intimate immersion is rendered temporary, arbitrary, disposable in a moment. That is the productive paradox, the contradictory logic by which radio, caught in the dynamics of capital, prepares the route to its own obsolescence.

If Benjamin was right to suggest that electronic reproducibility separates art from ritual and joins it to politics, the reproduction of music (which for many reasons makes that distinction dubious) has played a crucial role in reconstituting aural and semantic boundaries, so that they seemingly no longer operate in the dimension of "real space" but in the fetishizing gesture of a hand. The community, R. Murray Schafer wrote, was once defined as those who lived within the aural horizon of a church bell. Plato thought the proper size of the city was indicated by the number of people who could hear the voice of a public speaker. For McLuhan, typically enough, this measurement shows how appropriate radio is to implementing a Platonic political ideal on a world scale.[5] For us, social space is far more complex; we inhabit the intersecting production of aural space and politics, part of that constitutive power which even we Canadians can no longer clearly find in what we call the State.

* * * *

> The locality where we belong is a centre of reassurance identifiable more by the tenacity of its users than by its architecture.[6]

The first transCanada network radio broadcast opened with a rendition of "O Canada" bursting forth from parliamentary bells. The performance by the Peace Tower's carillon was carried by the Canadian National Railroad and shadow stations in 1927 in celebration of Canada's

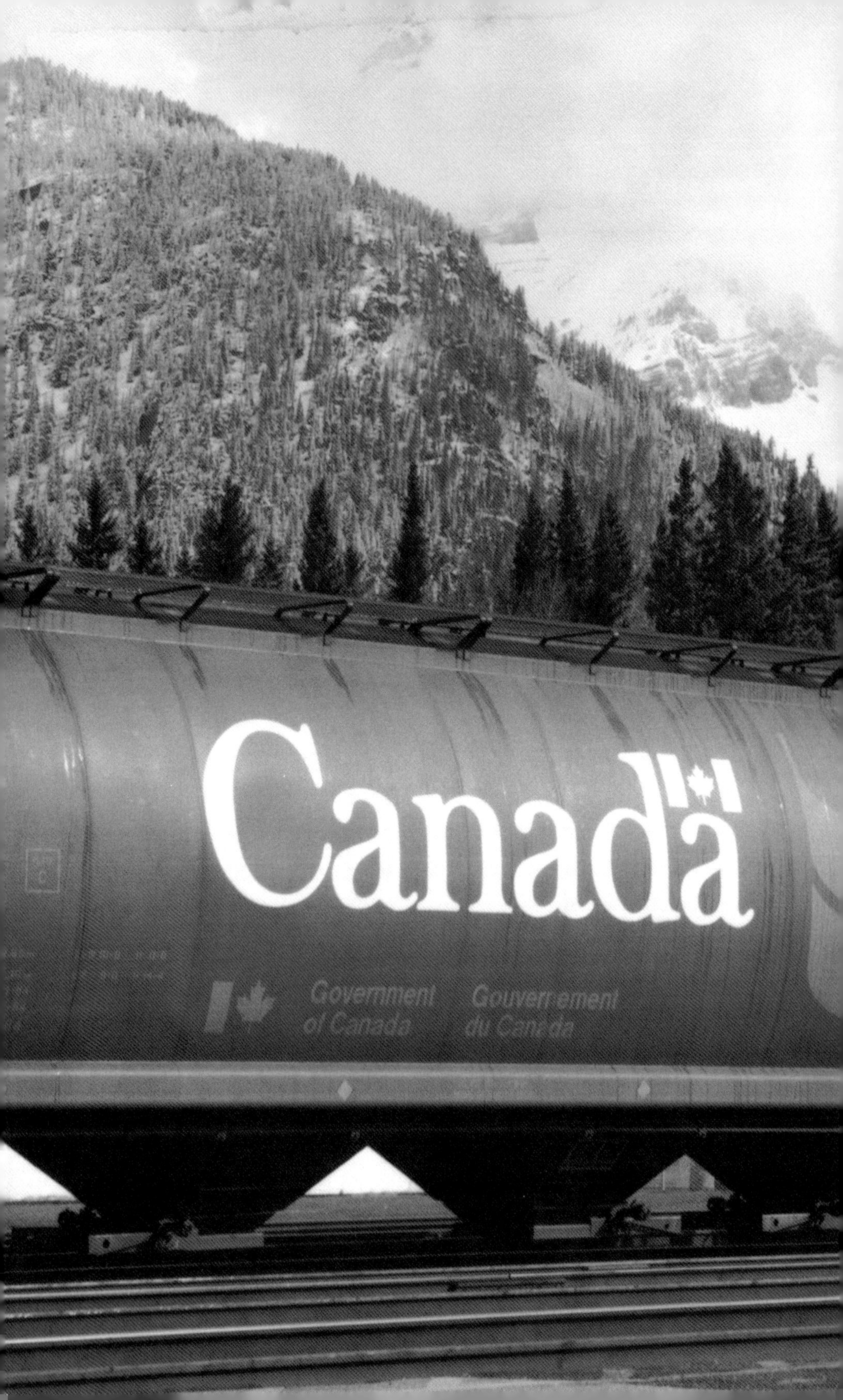
Canada
Government of Canada
Gouvernement du Canada

July 1st Diamond Jubilee. "Loyal listeners at home were thrilled by the miracle of radio almost as much as the CNR passengers hurtling across the country," writes one CBC historian.[7] For the first time the national community was the subject of common rhetorical address in shared temporal space: addressed, celebrated and circumscribed – in contemporary terms, constituted as a subject – by the resonant aural space of transcontinental bells.

The emergence of a concept of "Canada" as a nation was dependent on, and articulated through, the building of the national railway (to whose demise we are contemporary witnesses) and, subsequently, at first literally in its tracks, the national broadcasting system. The Canadian hypersensitivity to acoustics as a dimension of politics is surely based in the long-standing association of the national political process with sound, which was and probably remains its privileged carrier. We tend to think of television as American, of radio as Canadian; in the aural landscape of the Canadian Broadcasting Corporation there is still an indigenous grammar of place mainly absent from television, which depends on internationally recognizable visual conventions for signifying being at the scene. Canadian radio's formative influence and practice can be seen historically as a product of state intervention in the development of the communications infrastructure but what it represents in the present is more complicated. Indeed, it always was.

Early radio in Canada was mainly commercial, and oriented towards the production of an urban market capable of financing the development of the new medium. American radio entertainment programs, whose popularity was already by the 1920s the profitable effect of an integrated manufacturing/marketing industry, were ready to fill the airwaves of the continent. Government was forced to intervene because very quickly there would have been no Canadian radio and no space for its development. In economic terms, it was necessary to finance a technological infrastructure that would extend to the rural and northern settlements which private capital could not afford to penetrate; government initiative was the precondition to a distribution system that could span the country and enter even the most remote of living rooms. In political terms, official discourse was formed by a rhetoric of public interest whose popular acceptance was already won by the influential anti-free market polemics of cultural nationalists demonstrating conclusively that an "open" market meant American domination. Within the terms of this alliance, radio was

Photo Cheryl Bellows

conceived as an auditory means for circumscribing Canada as a nation and for providing the concept of "Canada" with a meaning that transcended (and thus of course legitimated) territoriality. Public ownership was the means to that consensual end. As long as these economic and political interests coincided, as long as public funding was necessary for the building of a technological infrastructure (or conduit for capital, we say in hindsight), official discourse on radio was a nationalist one. "Public interest" referred to the preservation of a separate (that is, not American) public sphere through national public ownership of its communication channels: the "natural" disposition of the market to neglect remote or marginal groups of citizens unable to constitute a proper market had proven the necessity to affirm and defend public control, universal access and social equity in radio broadcasting. This is all stated in political speeches, editorials and parliamentary records of the 1930s and may be found cited and reiterated in similar contexts until the early 1980s. If the original economic end has not been – and indeed cannot be – conclusively achieved (we all have three or four radios but do we all have cable and compact disc players?), the political legitimation strategy necessary for its accomplishment has changed substantially. Now government reference to "public interest" mobilizes an entirely different set of terms: choice, diversity, privatization, consumer sovereignty, capital accumulation, global competition, the "open" market.

Once the technical infrastructure of the transCanada broadcasting apparatus had been completed, triumphantly and demographically availing all citizens of radios and television sets in their homes, the national alliance between economic and political ends fractured and consolidated into the paradox we know today, in which dense government bureaucracies filter the accelerating provision of transnationally controlled communication technologies, programs and related commodities across the northern half of the continent through channels created ostensibly for quite different purposes. Broadcasting regulation has been part of a radical rhetorical shift in governmentality which now more explicitly aligns its interests with continental and global capital. Music functions in this context to displace radio from the first set of terms to the second, to displace the national "public" discourse, which helped to set the communication hardware and production apparatuses in place, in favour of an international "private" discourse of inconspicuous consumption.

* * * *

> Capitalist development has therefore to negotiate a knife-edged path between preserving the exchange values of past capital investments in the built environment and destroying the value of these investments in order to open up fresh room for accumulation. Under capitalism, there is then a perpetual struggle in which capital builds a physical landscape appropriate to its own condition at a particular moment in time, only to have to destroy it, usually in the course of crises, at a subsequent point in time. The temporal and geographical ebb and flow of investment in the built environment can be understood only in terms of such a process.[8]

Unlike in other western countries, there was no significant indigenous musical industry, profession, education or other institution in Canada prior to radio. Because of the contingent imperative for public control of radio as a national system, radio offered a real condition of possibility for music and more generally for popular knowledge and speech. Many political and artistic organizations were shaped by a succession of moves to acquire possession of this space. Public broadcasting was sought by unions, women's organizations, church federations, farmers, artists, performers, politicians, teachers – the same groups that recently joined together to oppose free trade. The nation was thus constructed, that is, its members participated in constructing – its subjects and subjectivities were individually and collectively, actively and discursively shaped in the production of – the space of and struggle for radio. These subjects and subjectivities are now the targets of the combined research/marketing practices of commercial broadcasting and newer hardware; they have been redefined as a series of already-instituted identities and actions which radio first surveys and then seeks to accompany.

The past, David Lowenthal has written, is a foreign country.[9] We visit there for purposes shaped by the present. We visit this particular past in order to repossess the public meanings and convictions that motivated the collective actions of our predecessors and which freeze into the technological legacies of the present. We re-read their histories in the wake of a government determined to function oxymoronically in relation to any previously explicable concept of a nation state. That means we are subjects of a state (and what then exactly is the state?) which, among other accomplishments dedicated to a modernized economy, is learning to govern through the eradication or cynical conversion of all collective memory, whether from yesterday or from the more distant past.

For us, radio represents one of our history's most continuous and living voices. It is not a relic, in other words. It is a connection.

This is exemplified by students and community groups involved with community and campus radio. And who then is us? That there is no longer (and was there ever?) a unified subject, a coherent "we," comprising the national identity has become a commonplace assertion. For some postmodern intellectuals there is the added difficulty in conceding any positivity to terms such as "public interest" or "national sovereignty," to see struggles over public space and political autonomy as anything other than complicity with one set of governmental mechanisms over another, all of them dissimulated technologies of domination to begin with. It is as though new corporate space might be nicer, as though the state ceases to regulate with its ascendancy.[10]

What is being disappeared in that foreign country which is our history is not only a large familiar construction of a large familiar state. It is also a not-yet-realized (and once again radically endangered) possibility: a collective sound creation of/in public space. "Us" is no more than what can happen in that space, that discourse, among people for whom broadcasting has always been a controversial, actively defended part of public life. In that sense every new technological space has been at one and the same time a new horizon and a closure, an intoxicating possibility and a dangerous suppression of something just beginning to happen.

CBC Radio provided a model for radical, alternative and community broadcasting practices in many parts of the world. Even today the CBC can evoke the "magic" of its origins while remaining a site of debate, difference, critique and gossip. Where else could there be a Gzowski[11] or a Banbury doing what they do here, everyday, at/in the possession of the diverse spaces(s) they occupy, though no one writes about this but Gzowski himself. Yet from a bureaucratic and economistic point of view the CBC is mainly obsolete; its existence can no longer be justified in terms of its old political mandate (this change can be found in the new Broadcasting Act) as something belonging to the singular authorship of an identifiably unified site, something nominated as "Canada," something previous to such transmission yet broadly unified by it. That it is now the government's foremost sacrificial lamb is well known, and easily justified economically as well, since aside from representational problems arising in terms of legislation, mandate and identity, commercial radio is more popular.

One defence mounted for the CBC is that people actually listen to it. This is no longer necessarily expected of radio, which emulates its competitors in trying to circumnavigate the ears, aiming to provide an appropriate aural backdrop to the well-surveyed, well-disciplined topography of daily life.[12] Judging by current transformations of radio and related listening technologies, both the listening body and the state are being refunctionalized to accommodate new global corporate-political structures and (by the way) to better facilitate the market for new transnational technologies such as digital audio and satellites. Though commercial radio on the whole is thriving, it is no accident, as historical speculators like to say, that Canadian teenagers now listen less to radio of any kind than ever before; nor is this only because teens are shrinking in demographic terms and therefore cannot find what pleases them. Having been pragmatically reduced to a post-television mobile or "secondary" music soundtrack, radio's functions can now be performed just as well by television, cassettes, Walkmans and compact discs, which combined can do everything radio does, but without the disc jockeys and commercials – the last gasp, last vestige of the local.[13]

Radio's successes remain to evoke what is lost. Each magic moment poses the question as to what prevents the radiophonic "subject" from coming into possession of the space that constituted it. Who knows how such a subject would have spoken, or would sound now, in the context of an emancipated radiophonic discourse?

Thanks to Lyndon Way for scouting for information

Notes

1 Marshall McLuhan, *Understanding Media* (New York: Signet Books, 1964), 23.
2 Michel Foucault, "The Subject and Power," *Ideology and Consciousness* (1979), 6.
3 R. Murray Schafer, *Tuning of the World* (Toronto: McClelland and Stewart, 1977), 116.
4 "Personal Listening Enters a Golden Age," *High Fidelity* (February 1986), 55.

5 Schafer, 54. McLuhan, 268: "Even the printed book, let alone radio, tenders the political assumptions of Plato quite irrelevant for practical purposes. Yet radio, because of its ease of decentralized intimate relation with both private and small communities [sic], could easily implement the Platonic dream on a world scale."

6 David Lowenthal, *The Past is a Foreign Country* (New York: Cambridge University Press, 1985), 38.

7 Sandy Stewart, *From Coast to Coast: A Pictorial History of Radio in Canada* (Toronto: CBC, 1985), 39.

8 David Harvey, "The Urban Process under Capitalism," 1978, cited in Edward Soya, *Postmodern Geographies* (London: Verso, 1989), 102.

9 Lowenthal.

10 See Herbert Schiller's recent *Culture Inc.: The Corporate Takeover of Public Expression* (New York: Oxford University Press, 1989) for a discussion of this issue.

11 A popular Canadian Broadcasting Corporation radio host.

12 The issue of music format and spatial production in radio as a "secondary medium" is addressed in Jody Berland, "Radio Space and Industrial Time: The Case of Music Formats," in *Rock and Popular Music: Politics, Policies and Institutions*, ed. Tony Bennett, Simon Frith, John Shepherd (London: Routledge, 1993), also *Popular Music* 9:2 (summer 1990). The theme of cultural technologies and its relevance to the Canada-U.S. Free Trade Agreement is addressed in Jody Berland, "Angels Dancing: Cultural Technologies and the Production of Space," in *Cultural Studies Now and in the Future*, ed. Lawrence Grossberg, Cary Nelson and Paula Treichler (New York: Routledge, 1991).

13 "Radio attracting fewer teens," *Mediascene* 7:1 (January 1988). Bureau of Broadcast Measurement surveys show that teens are listening to radio less, in a decline that began in 1985. BBM officials attribute the drop to increased competition from cassettes and music videos, and of course to changing demographics whereby radio tends to target the 25- to 54-year olds. At the same time radios are also being displaced in cars, where "high-line audio systems are a new weapon in automakers' marketing arsenals," according to *Automotive News* (23 October 1989); and on subways and streets, as any literature on or observation of Walkmans reveals.

Photo Cheryl Bellows

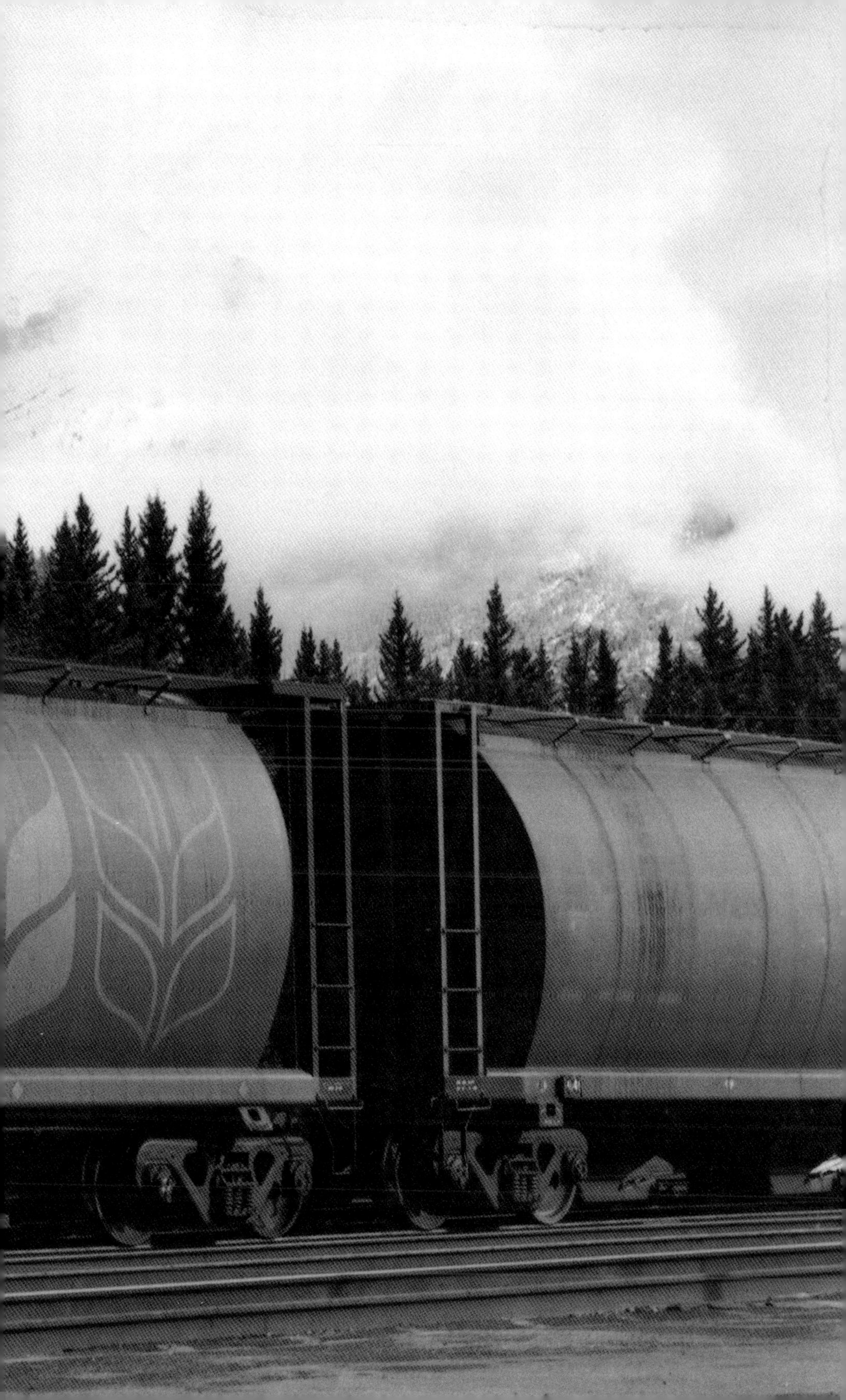

The Story of *The HP Show*

Hank Bull and Patrick Ready

Hank Bull and I decided to do a radio show on Vancouver Co-operative Radio in 1975. *The HP Show* (later called *The HP Dinner Show*) was the fruition of a relationship that began in 1967 in Peterborough, Ontario, and was maintained via cassette tape letters and occasional visits until we found ourselves collaborating on art projects in Vancouver.[1]

At that time the art community in Vancouver was quite lively and in the spirit of this milieu, Sheila Kincaid, director of the Burnaby Art Gallery (BAG) hosted an art fête called *Video Bag*.[2, 3] *Video Bag* included a number of performances. One of these, curated by Gerry Gilbert, was a collaboratively written radio play by members of the New Era Social Club,

---

1 HANK: The acronym HP was invented when we were corresponding, me in Vancouver and Patrick in the Rocky Mountains. We needed a name. We decided to invade the mind of the HP Sauce corporation. We redesigned labels and stuck them onto bottles in supermarkets. We communicated in cryptic shorthand and tape-recorded our meetings. Like parasites "we moved in on history and occupied images, emptying them of meaning." (General Idea, "Glamour," *File* 3:1)

2 PATRICK: Acronyms for other galleries around here are even more unfortunate – VAG (Vancouver), SAG (Surrey), CAG (Contemporary).

3 PATRICK: *Video Bag* started with Taki Bluesinger running the whole distance from Vancouver City Hall to the BAG, changing his beautifully silkscreened t-shirts for each of the fifteen kilometres he was running. For one of those kilometres he was carried in a sedan chair

the Western Front and others. It was about beavers in the sewers of Ottawa.[4] This play was significant in two ways that deserve to be addressed here. It was HP's first experience with radio, though it was not recorded in any way. The concept of taping did not really exist in what for us was a pretechnical age. This was a performance, but done in the style of a radio play.[5] Secondly, it entirely bypassed individual creators. The piece had come out of everybody yelling and scribbling and stringing together ideas. This separation of the creative act from a particular individual's effort allowed concepts to emerge that could not have come from one person alone. Nor could one person take credit for the piece. Nor did it even matter whether or not one was an artist.[6] This became an important

---

that looked like a large, upright, black HP Sauce bottle and was in fact called the *HP Sedan Bottle*. A periscope stuck out of the top allowing the passenger to peruse without being perused. A single hair hung against a wedge-shaped graph, past which wind was allowed to blow via two tubes, permitting the passenger to ascertain approximate horizontal velocity. The *HP Sedan Bottle* was eventually blown up with dynamite as part of a palindromic movie.

4 HANK: The play was called *The Barge to Banality*, a name dreamt up by Michael Morris. It featured the introduction of the Soni Twin, played by Kate Craig (a.k.a. Lady Brute) and Glenn Lewis (a.k.a. Flakey Rosehips). The Soni Twin spoke its lines in unison and the listener was supposed to imagine a two-headed Siamese private detective.

5 HANK: It was visual art, actually, which is something we have always felt about radio. The listener closes his or her eyes and pictures some tremendous visual experience, like two old salts, drifting across the Pacific on the carcass of a burned out man-o-war. Radio is actually a form of sculpture, considering all the space involved.

6 PATRICK: We had just heard about, and were inspired by, Cornelius Cardew, who had started the Scratch Orchestra in the north of England in 1969. They played all sorts of music with whatever was handy, in a collaborative spirit, and eventually acquired a house in Berlin. When the members realized how many homeless there were in Berlin they turned the house over to the homeless. That was the end of the Scratch Orchestra. Shortly after this, Cardew came to Vancouver

tool in everything HP later became involved in.[7, 8]

After that people banded together in the large performance room at the Western Front, called the Grande Luxe,[9] and did Lux Radio plays (later called Luxe Radio plays when Victor Coleman reminded us of the earlier Lux Radio) off and on until about 1982.[10] The more regular members of the group were Kate Craig, Helen Tuele, Mary Beth and

---

playing songs of the IRA.

[Footnote to footnote 6] HANK: What inspired us was the thought that we were at the end of the era of the masterpiece, the avant-garde and the individual creative genius. What mattered now was to be part of a network (Filliou's Eternal Network) that would have its effect through a kind of spontaneous combustion of the social imagination.

7 PATRICK: There is nothing original about collaborative art. It is traditional in dance and music, the making of canoes and the making of cathedrals. However, it is definitely not part of the contemporary art market where products attached to an artist's name are what is sold. Of course exceptions do come to mind.

8 HANK: A close investigation of the nature of collaboration became one of HP's main obsessions. We developed a theory called the Third Man, whereby it was not one or the other of us who came up with an idea but a mysterious being who inhabited the ether between us. The Third Man had HP build a special conveyance for him, the *HP Sedan Bottle* referred to above.

9 HANK: The name comes from William Burroughs, *The Wild Boys*.

10 HANK: Radio Luxe could have a whole article to itself. It was an essential element of the Western Front's early years. Each play would be conceived and brainstormed at uproarious group meetings. People would come back to the next meetings with bits of script already composed. The final script would usually be edited by Patrick. After a couple of rehearsals the play would be performed as a live event, with lots of sound effects using rice, glass, cardboard, rocks and so on, and recorded at the same time. We recorded over a dozen plays between 1975 and 1978. They had names like *The Clear Cut Case, A Bite Tonight* (the world's longest radio play), *Soni's Boner, The Raw and the Plucked, Yalp, 87-EMPTY* (the world's shortest radio play, done for Byron Black's answering machine). Radio fever even caught on in

Warren Knechtel, Glenn Lewis, Bob Amussen, Donna Balma, Gretchen "Greenbean" Perk, Suzanne Ksinan, Eric Metcalfe, Muriel Coleman, Bill Little, Jane Ellison, Byron Black, Henry Greenhow, Lin Bennett, Peter Fraser, Robert Amos, Josephine Rigg, Opal L. Nations and Andy Graffiti. Most of the visiting artists to the Western Front would get involved in these plays as well. They were always performed in front of audiences, usually in costume. Some members only did sound effects. The potter, Charmain Johnson, only did breaking glass, for example. Eric Metcalfe was a specialist in horse whinnies and ricocheting gunshots. There were usually songs backed by live music for which some of us learned to play musical instruments. Sometimes the instruments themselves were invented. The plays were performed at the Western Front, in several art galleries and on CBC.

It was as members of The Luxe Radio Players that HP first learned such radio fundamentals as how reel-to-reel tape recorders worked, some ways of avoiding sixty-hertz hum and how to type script. It was only with this knowledge that we ventured to the newly formed CFRO-FM, Vancouver Co-operative Radio, to start our own radio show.

Liora Salter, who had worked hard for years getting Co-op Radio licensed and on the air, and another member of the station, Hildegard Westerkamp, interviewed us to ascertain the suitability of ourselves as hosts and our proposed program as they both related to the station's mandate. I had broken my glasses before the interview and had to squint to see any details and Liora asked if scowling at her was necessary. It was explained I was squinting and we agreed it was a good thing the Co-op was not a television station.

Hildegard asked if we were going to do bourgeois art radio. It was a question I was entirely unprepared for. In the previous five years I had

---

Toronto. After the production of *Murder in the Fog* at A Space in September, 1975, the Hummer Sisters got together with Victor Coleman and John Bentley Mays to produce *Audiothon*, a three-hour extravaganza with appearances by Raoul Duguay, the Four Horsemen and William Burroughs. The edited tapes of these plays would later be aired on the fledgling Vancouver Co-operative Radio, and I think that's how we were eventually invited to do a regular show.

Courtesy HP Archives. Photo Byron Black

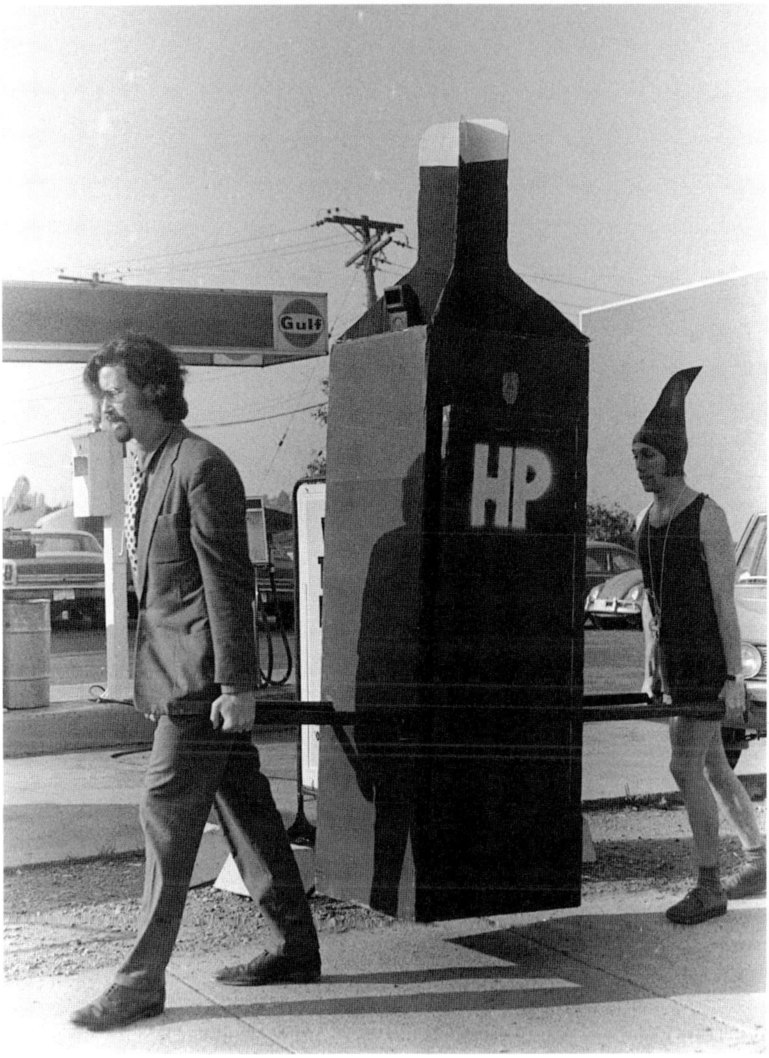

Patrick Ready and Hank Bull in 1975 with the *HP Sedan Bottle* in Vancouver

worked on the green chain, been a crane operator, logged, cooked, fought forest fires, been a book reviewer, roughnecked, been a deck-hand on a tugboat, lined track on the railroad, been a gravel-crusher operator, drove a cab, worked in a steel mill and installed awnings among other things and was quickly trying to think about the myriad of workers I had known and that some liked country and western music and some did not. Four or five people sat outside, under the window of the room we were in, sharing a bottle of Similkameen Superior and I was wondering what they think about somebody else deciding what would be appropriate for them to listen to, when Hank responded by asking, "What art isn't bourgeois?"[11]

Abbie Hoffman chanting to elevate and rotate the Pentagon was not bourgeois art. Or was it? Where was his funding coming from? Images of the Louvre being liberated after the French Revolution, Russian Constructivists playing factory steam whistles and Karl Marx wagging his finger from the Watts Towers at Alfred Jarry seriously confused and diverted my attention until I was surprised to hear we were being assigned a half hour on a weekday afternoon.

Friends told us that the first program was not exactly bad, but that we spoke too quickly to be understood and that the overall sound was unpleasant. As a result, on the next program we left deliberate spaces between our words which slowed everything down to a crawl.

We showed up one day with an unclaimed collection of The Columbia School of Broadcasting records that had been left in the trunk of a rented car. We played them on the air sometimes as a means of using radio to poke fun at itself and gradually, unconsciously, whether we liked it or not, our radio voices changed because of this exposure.

After a few weeks the station changed our time slot to Saturday evenings and the length of the show went from a half hour to an hour and a half. In fact, because it was the last show in the evening it was open ended; bands, poets or visiting artists would drop by and we would open the phone lines. Content varied a lot but as in any art form the medium

---

11 HANK: It was you, Patrick, who said after we'd got out of there, "I thought all art was bourgeois."
(Footnote to footnote 11) PATRICK: I think you're mistaken there, Hank. Otherwise where did all those thoughts come from?

itself provided much of material to work with. The play back of pre-recorded tapes involved an interesting time factor. Hank did a religious bit,[12] for example, where he said "I am now going to split my voice into two. This is a miracle! This is a miracle!" into a cassette tape recorder. Then he rewound it and played it back while saying live into the mike, "This is a miracle. My voice is now split in two." It was effective on the air.

Another thing with time was that you could turn it around by playing tapes backwards. "Say" is "Yes" and "No" is "One" when played back backwards. I can still count backwards from ten to one so that when the tape is played back from the end to the beginning it comes out sounding "one, two, three . . ." Hank became expert in playing music, especially sea shanties that, when played back backwards, sounded like Norwegian songs of felicitude. His traditional instrument, the piano, sounded like a truncated accordion playing when it was played back backwards because of the reversal of the attack. Afterwards several attempts were made to make the accordion sound like a piano with little success, which was a pity because the accordion was much more portable. We have sustained a strong interest in palindromes ("Sit on a potato pan, Otis")[13] and palindromic things ever since. Byron Black wrote from Jakarta to remind us it was the nineteenth day of the ninth month of 1991.

Then there was the spatial element of being in multiple places simultaneously. This used to get quite complicated conceptually when you listened at home as Hank and Réal Carrier (who at that time spoke no English) climbed down the fire escape at the end of an extremely long microphone cable and continued across the alley and onto the dance floor

---

12 HANK: "Religious bit" he calls it! We're not talkin' about a "bit." We are talking about *Religion Canada*, in the name of the Beaver, the Moose and the Holy Goose, of which Hank is the Great Homunculus. As well as performing miracles, ReliCan made regular pitches for money, not only on *The HP Show* but on television, as part of John Anderson's "Gina Show." (Come to think of it, there were a lot of artists broadcasting in Vancouver at this time).

13 HANK: Otis Spann was a great influence on my piano playing. Otis Spann was the piano player in the Muddy Waters band and one of the all time great bluesmen.

of the Rainier Pub[14] where they interviewed customers until getting kicked out by a rude bouncer, while I was in the studio commenting on the venture with someone somewhere else on the telephone.

William Burroughs and Brion Gysin had developed a writing form called "cut up" which involved writing a page or pages, then cutting it up and rearranging the pieces and rewriting it to make linear, but not overall, sense. As Burroughs said, "When you break open the sentence, the future leaks out." Applying this idea to audiotape means cutting it with a razor and taping it together in a new order, laborious but very effective. Amazing sounds and statements can be made by "cut up." It is another way of using spatial collage concepts to work with language and sound, normally thought of as time-based.[15]

An important element of the program was the dynamic tension between our two ways of seeing the world and doing things.[16] Hank had

---

14 HANK: I think we could make a claim for the world's longest microphone cable with that one. We strung together all the cables in the radio station, which was on the third floor. I also remember that there was a fire down the street, which gave us the convenient chance to interview a fireman.

15 PATRICK: In 1983, Hank was in Paris visiting Brion Gysin while I was working on a fundraiser for Co-op Radio. Gysin and Burroughs had invented a device called the Dream Machine consisting of a tall cardboard tube with cathedral window-shaped holes in the side and a light bulb suspended in the middle. The tube was put on a turntable so that the light emerging through the holes flickered over one's closed eyes as the tube turned. After a while this will induce an awake dream state with brilliant hallucinations. I made up one and brought it down to the station and promised to use it and describe the dream if people would call in and pledge money or get a membership. It raised about forty or fifty dollars (one person promised a pledge conditional to my promising that the Dream Machine would only be used for peaceful purposes). Afterwards I told Hank about it who reported it to Gysin who became upset about this because it was the first time any money had been made with the Dream Machine and he hadn't made it.

16 HANK: Now somewhere in here it should be mentioned that the

been raised as the son of an Anglican priest, master at extemporaneous homiletics. Hank had played music professionally with several successful bands (The Bonnevilles, Downchild Blues Band and others), and studied painting. For Hank the energy generated in performance was as important as anything and if the energy was flowing well, the audience would pick up on it. I learned a bit about how to use this energy from him – when we were "on" we could do no wrong and you could almost feel the proverbial golden thread. But for Hank it was the art. This energy at the edge, the act itself of creating, was the art. He once painted a picture while playing the piano as a performance at Pumps.

I, on the other hand, was always concerned with product. What will the listener think, understand, enjoy? I could never logically accept Hank's aesthetic stance, though I realized that it did work when it worked. I would spend worrisome hours in script preparation and got to be quite fast writing dialogue for us. At any rate our differences tended to complement each other in useful ways and radio became the predominant element in our lives.

In some cases where we had established formats for regular pieces like *Tales from the Days of Sail* (salty stories about two sea dogs and an albatross), *The Cave Men* (an excellent section devised by Hank that necessitated nonverbal, preverbal communication and kept you on your toes). In our longest running serial, *Captain Bonnard and Captain Lafarge and Carolyne in Space*, we were often better without scripts, just rough outlines. *BL&C in Space* had the added characteristic that it required each of us to take turns doing each of the three voices as the next voice came up.

---

show's time slot was moved again, this time to Sunday evening at seven. This was when the we changed the name to *The HP Dinner Show*. The show would open with me on accordion hitting dramatic building chords while Patrick intoned, "Uh . . . uh . . . uh . . . uh. Don't Touch that Dial! Whether it's raining in the east or snowing in the west, it's time now for the fields of gloom to be plowed under as we begin another mouth-watering episode of *The HP Dinner Show*, scientifically designed to help you prepare, eat and digest your dinner. And now, here they are, live at the mikes, HHHHH PPPPP!" The effect of this was always electrifying.

Courtesy HP Archives. Photo Rodney Werden

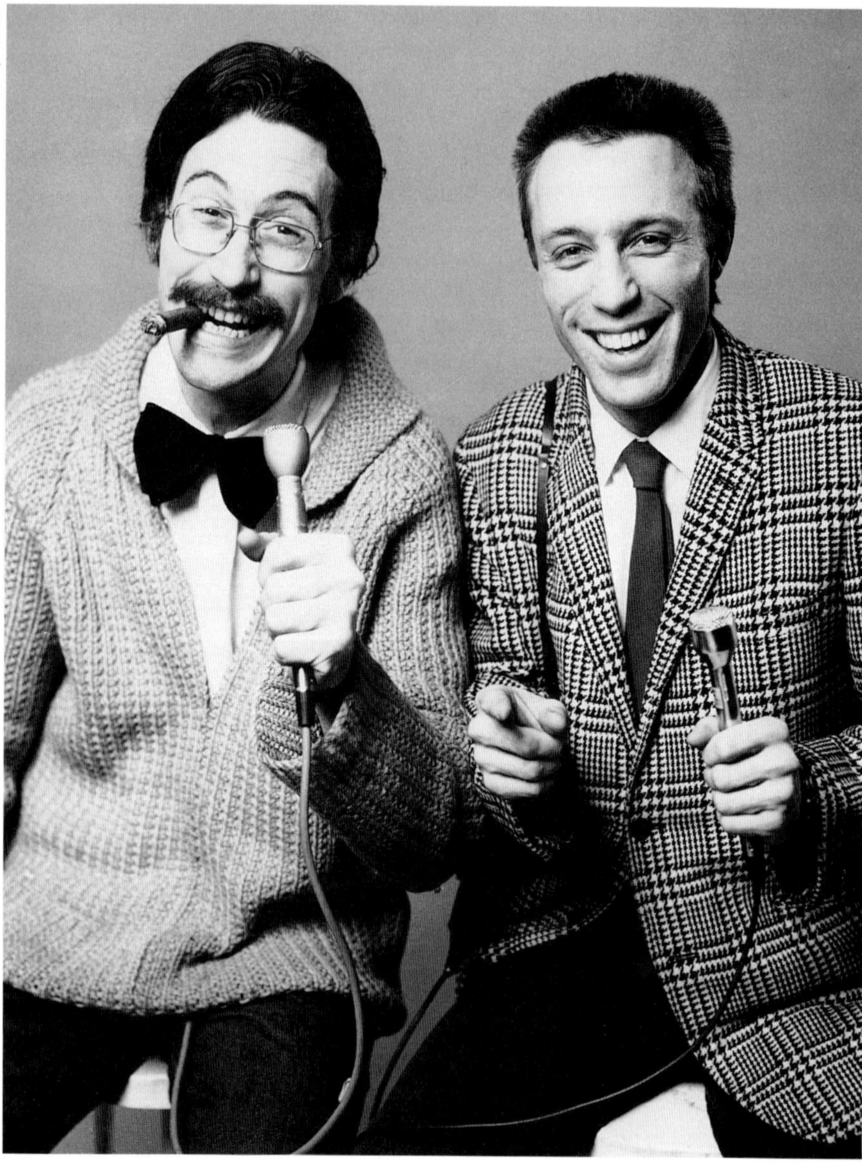

Hosts of *The HP Show* Patrick Ready (left) and Hank Bull in the early days

Most of this early work was done while we lived in a condemned house on Seymour Street that we rented from an old character named Joe Philliponi. It had a large space ideally suited to group rehearsals. At one end was a piano, a stand-up bass and other instruments. The walls were lined with various sound effects devices – bird calls, bags full of balloons which you'd blow up with beans inside and bang against your head for thunder claps, small strawberry boxes used for the sound of splintering wood during shipwrecks, the rain-making machine which was basically a record turntable we'd put rice onto so that it fell off onto different surfaces. We had something we called "the rhythm machine." It was the analogue precurser to the cheap little beater box every solo bar musician uses today and consisted of a large cranked wooden drum with pegs sticking out of it that hit the ends of long wooden pivoted arms when the drum was cranked. These arms rattled cans full of bird shot, rang bells and one struck a bass drum. The pegs could be repositioned to change the rhythm pattern.[17]

Eventually we moved out of the house on Seymour and into another ramshackle place at 422 Alexander Street in Japantown.[18] The most memorable radio show we did there (memorable at least in the doing) was The HP Underwater Special, *The World's First Completely Underwater Radio Show*. Everything we did was necessarily low-budget and the only

17 HANK: I believe we managed to get it to do a reasonable facsimile of the slow *agbekor* rhythm of the Ewe people of Ghana.

18 HANK: The house was squeezed between a noodle factory and a fortune cookie factory. It still had fruit trees in the backyard. We hung an old Coke sign painted gold on the garden wall as a gong and kept a sixteen-foot length of drain pipe on hand as an echo chamber. Bicycles hung from the ceiling. There was an endless stream of visitors but one in particular deserves mention. Jed Van had been mistaken as an eccentric when he appeared at the radio station with a box of tapes to give away, so naturally he was referred to HP. He turned out to be a seasoned road man and raconteur who had hung out with the Berbers during the Spanish civil war and worked as a boiler maker in Zaïre during the sixties. The nightclubs of Lubumbashi were full of a new kind of music at that time combining electric guitar and traditional drums. Jed had taped hundreds of hours of this music. It was a gold mine.

person we knew with a boat was an old watchman who lived in a barge at the foot of Main Street. He took us out into the Burrard Inlet in his dinghy and we gave him a pint of rum. The rum and the condoms were our expenses for this program. The condoms were for putting over microphones under the water.

We took a white plastic bucket and keel-hauled it upside down to form an airlock. Then, donning appropriate bathing costumes, we jumped over the side with the microphone covered with two condoms and came up inside the bucket. The sounds in the harbour were distant metallic clinking, throaty motors purring, water slapping our boat's hull. Then, from inside the bucket came a suppressed scream as the microphone joined our shocked heads in the airlock. We did this about eight times which exhausted about everything you could say about being inside a white plastic bucket. I was able to stay in the bucket about thirty seconds before all the air was exhausted. Hank breathed less and stayed longer. All sound for the show was guaranteed to have been recorded under, or passed through, water before it was broadcast.[19]

So that's a brief chronology of the first two years of HP on radio, perhaps the most interesting period, as we worked with pliable beginners' minds. Our interests changed and developed as the show grew. When we began, Hank was most concerned with the effect radio would have on us as we experienced the energy of live performance. As the show progressed, this emphasis expanded to where his primary attentions are now focused; on global networking, involving radio as part of a larger field of communication which also involves computer mail, faxes, telecommunications.

I had begun by being primarily concerned with the families and car drivers at the other end of our speakers, but now expend as much or more attention on the physical nature of the elements which make up the medium – from hardware to sound and electromagnetic waves.

A large point of contrast existed between our worldviews that we

19 PATRICK: Just after the program my parents paid a rare visit from Hamilton, Ontario. My father gave me an icy look when he went to pick up the telephone receiver. As a strict Catholic with six children, this may well have been the first time he actually confronted a condom and he was obviously trying not to imagine what one was doing over his weird son's telephone receiver.

learned to work with as well. Hank's approach to the way things are was based on how he perceived things to be. "Perceive" here is an active verb in the sense that one can consciously look for what is interesting and beautiful in a situation. On the other hand, my basis for approaching things is that there is a way things are, which lends itself to a more cautious and scientific approach.[20] The result for us both was an appreciation of people who transcend the borders between art and science and technology. Artists such as Alfred Jarry, Raymond Roussel, Marcel Duchamp, Alvin Lucier were viewed with no less respect than Paracelsus, Tesla, Volta and C.V. Boys. We had a particular fascination for the many wonderful Victorian inventions that ended up as cul-de-sacs.[21]

Altogether *The HP Show* lasted eight and a half years, with a few breaks and sometimes one or the other of us transmitting from afar. Throughout this entire period I do not ever recall discussing any actual rules or systems we should use to work together, other than to casually talk about one day writing the definitive text on collaboration.[22] The regular and constant live improvisations on air necessitated such an enveloping understanding of each others' minds, abilities, weaknesses and strengths that our everyday relationship became virtually just a slower version of what we did on radio.

---

20 HANK: I think Patrick has always seen himself more as an experimenter or inventor than as an artist in the conventional sense.

21 HANK: Patrick's *Water Powered Radio Receiver* (1989) is inspired directly by this tradition.

22 HANK: Ray Johnson once remarked that "the thing about collaboration is that it doesn't work," a good motto for collaborators, including the audience. What appeals to me about radio is its ephemeral quality. It exists out there, somewhere between the broadcaster and the listener, who is, like the Third Man, fugitive. Radio is the broadcaster's collaboration with this invisible phantom.

Photo Monte Greenshields

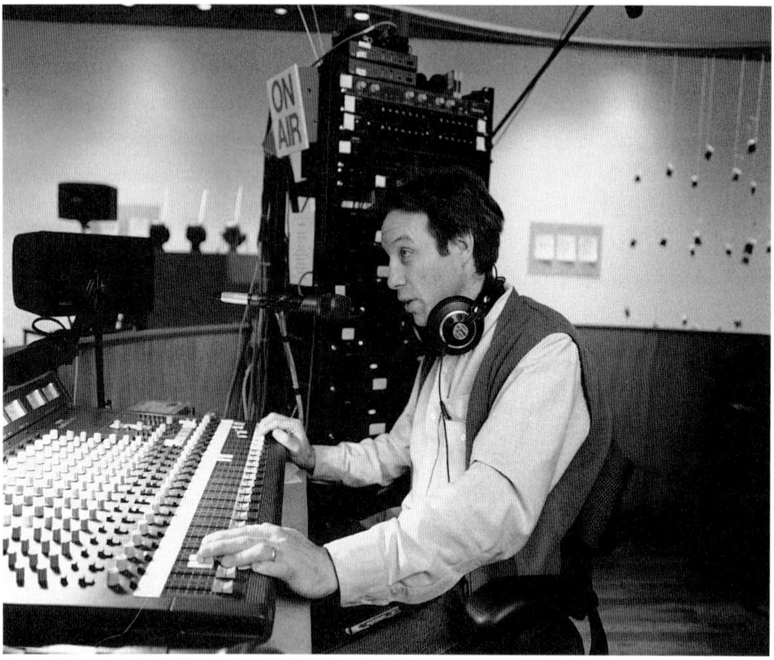

Hank Bull in the *Radio Rethink* booth in the Walter Phillips Gallery (1992)

Radio Letter

Hank Bull

Dear Listener,

This transmission is coming to you from the silence of a late night in Banff. It is a silent broadcast, tuned into your reading ear. The night is quiet here, radio flashing like a beacon into the starry sky, drifting over vast stretches of empty FM band – it is just us, the weather report and some rock 'n roll.

Banff is the perfect place for radio. The Rocky Mountains prevent most radio signals from entering the valley, guarding the air for their own impassive conversations. Our little station – Voice of the Rock, we call it – bounces like a train whistle off the cliffs and up the valley.

The listeners? Mainly the elk and wolves, but there is a small cluster of humans, most of whom live within a two minute walk of the studio. We may not have our own radio shows, but we probably know someone who does, and it is only a matter of time before we each will get dragged onto the air. Watch what you say. You are about to meet the listener face to face.

Here for one brief utopian moment, the Brechtian dream of a truly interactive radio comes to life. This is not the coin-in-a-slot-freedom to choose this or that pop, this or that politician, this or that channel, but the real, experiential involvement in a conversation.

For me the experience has been a dance, like running some radio rapids. Here are some of the highlights.

Setting Out

The first week was spent sorting tapes and scripts, printing photographs and working on the chronology of radio art in Canada. I had brought to Banff several boxes of tapes and scripts that had been stored in basements and attics since the 1970s, and was able to reconstruct certain key programs.

Friday January 17th – Inaugural Broadcast and Celebration of Art's Birthday

Art's Birthday was first proposed by Robert Filliou as a celebration to mark the birth of art one million years ago (which apparently happened when someone dropped a dry sponge into a bucket of water). Taken up by various network artists, Art's Birthday is now celebrated internationally every year. *Radio Rethink* chose the occasion to launch its ten-watt transmitter, making connections to other network nodes with fax, voice and videophone. The day started with a live interview with Radio Canada, Vancouver, and continued with videophone connections to InterAccess in Toronto, the Western Front in Vancouver and Metropophobia in Phoenix. In the afternoon a proper birthday party took place with balloons, cake and champagne. The sound of two commentators on the floor was mixed with incoming phone calls, party sounds and a number of children in the booth. At one point the kids took control of the mixing board. We continued live for seven hours without using any pre-recorded material.

Saturday January 18 – The Radio Painting

The Radio Painting is a live interactive piece intended to demonstrate that radio is a visual art. The time frame can be set in advance; in this case it was four hours. The space frame is defined by listeners calling in to identify their locations, which are then marked on a map. This broadcast piece was particularly useful because it offered the first opportunity to test the range of the transmitter for the *Radio Rethink* project. It was seen to handsomely cover the town of Banff, a radius of over ten kilometres. It also resulted in calls from a couple of listeners-at-large, which was surprising considering that we hit the airwaves with no advance warning. After one call, the listener actually came to the gallery in person and joined me in the booth. Very visual.

Friday January 24 – The HP Radio Show

Patrick Ready suggested Elk Stories as a theme: "Everybody has an elk story." He was right. Banff is virtually infested with elk, who rightly have a claim to the place. They have recently begun to defend this claim in an aggressive fashion and some of the stories were quite sobering. My favourite, however, was told by Iris, who runs the mail room:

> One day a couple returned home from shopping with a large bag of rice, which they inadvertantly left on the back porch. An elk appeared in the night and consumed the whole thing. Realizing too late what he had done, it was three days before he was able to leave the yard.

Tuesday January 28 – Radio RUT Part 1

This afternoon's tabloid, like several others I hosted, began with live classical music performed by artists resident in the Banff music program. This hearkened back to the early days of radio when live music was the norm. (I am one of those who have mystical feelings about transmitting live; I believe it requires faith on the part of the listener to believe that the show is indeed live and, on the part of the broadcaster, that there actually is somebody out there listening.) Another feature of these afternoon shows was an open microphone in the gallery. Visitors to the exhibition could see the broadcasters in the booth and were encouraged to join the show.

Coinciding with *Radio Rethink* was a visual artists' residency on the theme of Technology, Rhetoric and Utopia. It was fitting that some of the ongoing discussions should take place on the radio. I proposed and hosted this first one, choosing as a springboard the idea of Dream, and referring to a number of analogies: George Brecht's conceptual proposal for *Dream Economics*, the Burroughs-Gysin Dream Machine, Martin Luther King's "I have a dream" and *The Impossible Dream*, a book on the development of the Banff Centre by its founder, Donald Cameron. Taking place as it did amid layoffs and budget cuts, this discussion on the dream of utopia found a parallel in real life.

Friday March 31 – Radio for Wolves

Expanding the animal stories of the previous week to create a model of interspecies communications, *Radio for Wolves* was born in the discovery that wolves in Banff National Park are outfitted with tiny radio transmitters.

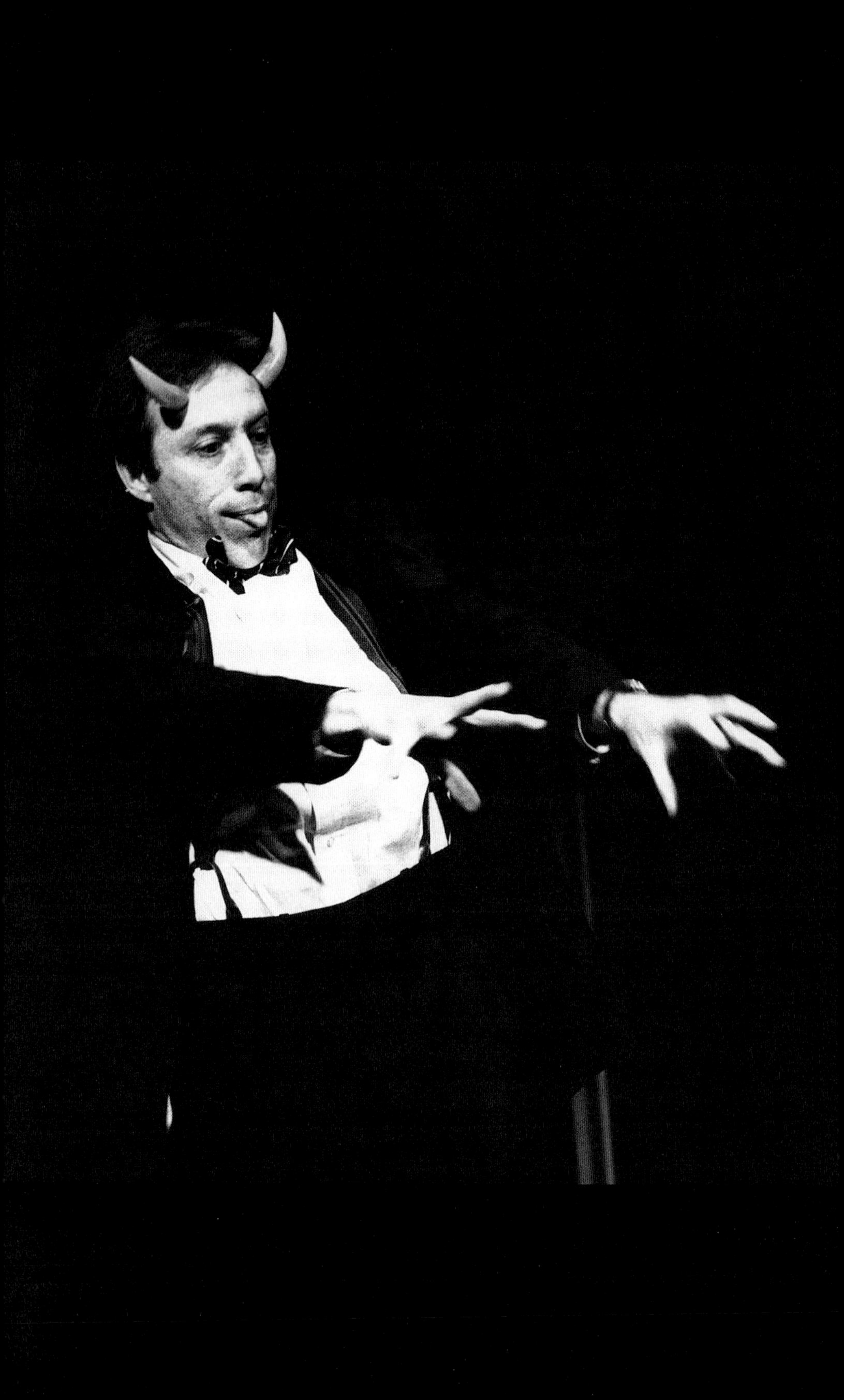

By bringing a scientist into the studio and triangulating with an agent in the field, it would be possible to pinpoint the location of the wolves and transmit their own animal broadcast to our human listeners. It was also proposed to complete the loop by asking listeners to place their radios in their windows while we played recordings of wolf howls. The show was advertised as "radio by wolves, for wolves." A missed rendezvous prevented the scientists from coming to the radio station, but the sounds of wolves, combined with music by the Howlin' Wolf, created a haunting tribute to these noble creatures and their tragic predicament.

Tuesday February 4 – Radio RUT Part 2

As a way of overcoming the authority of the microphone, this second discussion adopted the formal device of the "talking feather." A feather is passed to each person in turn around the circle. In this way each person is given a voice, making it easier for even the most reticent to participate. Substituting microphone for feather resulted in a stimulating debate between those who considered utopian ideals to be hopelessly Eurocentric and outmoded in a world where we already know too much about the future and others who still cherished some hope for the human race.

Wednesday February 12 – Faust in India

Faust in India was a live performance piece, transmitted simultaneously over the RADIA airwaves. I had hoped to remaster audio cassettes recorded in South India in 1981. The quality was surprisingly good, and access to SoundTools software suddenly made the precise editing of these tapes quite easy. I chose fifteen sounds, more or less in the order in which they had been recorded, carefully removed any of my own journalistic voice-overs and let the sounds speak for themselves. Kids singing on a beach, a symphony of Madras traffic, a recording studio, a temple, a parade. The only voices heard are Tamil, Telugu and Malayalam. (Malayalam, Patrick points out, is the longest palindromic name for a language.) These belong to the pre-Sanskrit, Dravidian language group. Tamil is called the oldest living language in the world; from it comes the root for the word rice. But to most of us, these languages are incomprehensible.

Photo Monte Greenshields

Hank Bull performing *Faust in India* (1992) to a live audience at the Banff Centre

As this piece was played on the radio, a formal theatrical performance took place before a live audience in which I enacted a mimed version of the Faust story (this time Faust and not Margaretha dies in the end). My intention was to give the audience two conflicting mental pictures – one conjured up by sounds from south India, the other by the movement on stage. At times the two would come together, but often they would move far apart, creating two divergent narratives. The listener/viewer intervenes to finish telling the story.

Signing Off

Rather than present a single piece or production, I have followed the flow of debate – about the nature of radio, the precarious future of its arts and institutions, the end and/or beginning of the world – and in that dance with the rapids, I have come up afloat and looking back at a tumbling cascade of activities, interruptions, cross rhythms and white noise.

Radio and Beans

AN INSTALLATION BY PATRICK READY

Dan Lander

> There is increasing interest in the possible effects of exposure to power frequency electric and magnetic fields. Public interest about these fields first emerged in the late 1960s when power companies began constructing more high voltage power lines to meet the increasing demand for electricity. Present knowledge of the biological effects of exposure to these fields is inconclusive . . . The first evidence to show that power frequency fields may have an effect on human health came in 1972. Soviet investigators reported that workers in high voltage switchyards suffered from a number of ailments. Since then, much scientific research has been done. Some results show that electric and magnetic power frequency fields can cause effects in living organisms, including people. Other studies show no effects.[1]

Wherever there is electric power, there are electric and magnetic fields. It has long been suspected that these fields – produced by electric power systems, transmission sources and electric appliances – may pose a potential threat to public health. These phenomenon are often referred to as electromagnetic fields (EMF), electric fields arising from any given electronic charge and magnetic fields from the motion of that charge. EMF also arise from many natural sources, appearing throughout nature and in all living things. The forces of EMF are responsible for holding atoms together in molecules and regulating chemical compounds, including those of bodily functions. Modern devices such as television, radio and microwave ovens all depend on electric and magnetic fields for their operation.[2]

During the course of an ordinary day we are exposed to the presence of pulsating EMF in many contexts and situations. Our exposure to these forces and the impact they may have on our health is determined by both the strength of the electric current or magnetic field, and our proximity to it. In addition, the amount of time that one is exposed to EMF has a significant bearing on measurable symptoms. An early experiment by American scientist John Ott was conducted and published in 1973. He was specifically interested in a study undertaken by the United States Air Force which concluded that watching television is not necessarily bad in and of itself, however, prolonged exposure to it may bring about nervousness, continuous fatigue, headaches, loss of sleep and vomiting. The lack of consideration of possible radiation exposure in this study lead Ott to devise and conduct the following experiment:

> In order to determine if there might be any basic physiological responses in plants or laboratory animals to some sort of radiation or other form of energy being emitted from TV sets, we set up an experiment using a large-screen colour TV. One-half of the picture tube was covered with one-sixteenth inch solid lead, customarily used to shield x-rays, and the other half was covered with ordinary black photographic paper that would stop all visible light but allow other radiation to penetrate. Six pots, each containing three bean seeds, were placed directly in front of the portion covered with the black photographic paper, six more were placed directly in front of the portion covered with the lead shielding, and another six pots were placed outdoors at a distance of fifty feet from the greenhouse where the TV set was located.
>
> At the end of three weeks, all the young bean plants in the six pots outdoors and the six pots in front of the lead shielding showed approximately six inches normal appearing growth. All the bean plants in the six pots shielded only with the black photographic paper showed an excessive vine-type growth ranging from up to thirty-one and one-half inches. Furthermore, the leaves were all approximately two and one-half to three times the size of the outdoor plants and those protected with the lead shielding.[3]

Like the vast majority of scientific investigations into the effects of exposure to EMF and radiation, Ott's research was only able to conclude that there is a correlation between exposure to EMF and, in this case, deviation in the growth pattern of bean plants. Although this relationship has sometimes proven to be a very strong one, like many other environmental symptoms of sickness and degradation, actual proof of causal effect is difficult to verify. In most research instances only one aspect of EMF is measured and evaluated, leaving other effects undetected. In addition, the bulk of funding money for research into the electromagnetic spectrum in general is granted to the same organizations that have a vested interest in its propagation. This would include electronics manufacturers and hydroelectric power companies. Some scientists and cultural critics, however, have suggested that there is a conspiracy to silence information on the effects of EMF by state, military and corporate interests.[4]

One thing is for certain: in a world with an ever-increasing dependency on information generation and exchange, it would be advantageous to gain a more concise understanding of how biological systems are effected by EMF. We are a long way from that understanding. In a 1988 publication by the Canadian Centre for Occupational Health and Safety, it is noted that "this topic is very controversial" and that although, for instance, "there have been reports of high rates of birth defects or miscarriages among clusters of pregnant video display terminal operators, there is *no conclusive scientific evidence* linking work with VDTs to adverse pregnancy outcome of VDT operators."[5] Perhaps through alternative avenues of investigation, the effects of the bombardment and penetration of EMF can be more clearly elucidated.

Patrick Ready's installation *Radio and Beans* represents such an alternative. Ready was aware of Ott's experiment and its inconclusive results. In fact, Ready's interest in the intermingling of art and science has been the definitive thrust of many of his works, dating back to his collaborations with Hank Bull on *The HP Show* beginning in 1976. His approach to artmaking is informed by a keen technical understanding of how things work, a healthy skepticism of sanctioned scientific norms and methodologies, and a belief that it is through art that an understanding of complex relationships may best be explored, observed, exposed and discussed.

There were two components to *Radio and Beans*. The first consisted of a variety of familiar electrical devices including a television set, computer monitor, space heater, iron and a portable radio/tape player.

Photo Monte Geenshields and Cheryl Bellows

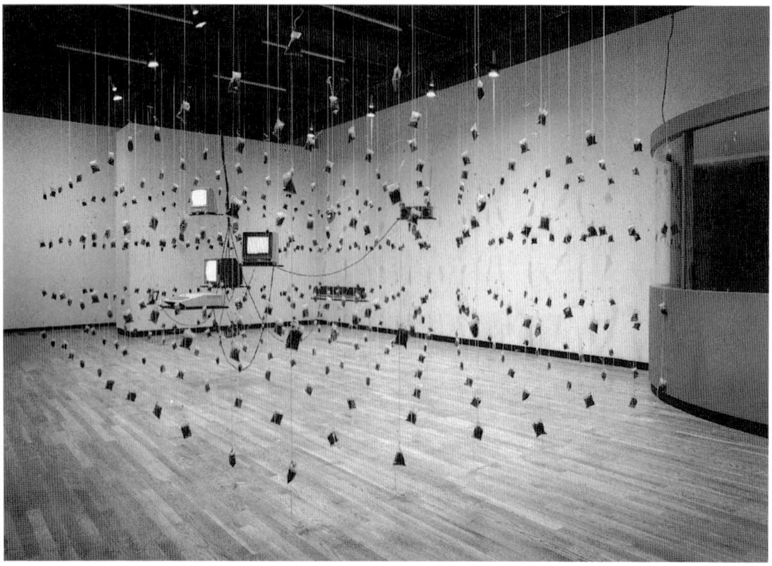

Patrick Ready's *Radio and Beans* (1992) installation at the Walter Phillips Gallery

These appliances were placed on wooden shelves which were suspended from the ceiling. All of them were in working order and turned on, consuming varying amounts of current and emitting various types and strengths of radiation. Since the installation came into contact with the *Radio Rethink* booth, the electronic devices used during transmission and production also contributed to the presence of EMF, including the ten-watt FM transmitter used for the project.

The second component involved mung beans, chosen for their well-deserved reputation for being fast sprouting. Under normal daylight circumstances they grow an average of six to seven inches in three weeks. The beans used in the installation were "certified organic" in order to reduce the chance of chemical contamination. After being soaked in water for twenty-four hours previous to planting, they were placed two at a time in small paper packets and filled with topsoil. These packages were stapled to strings suspended from the ceiling at equal distances from each other in three dimensions, then watered three times a day. The beans were later transferred to small plastic bags, as the gallery air was extremely dry and the paper packets did not retain enough water. It was hoped that over the duration of the exhibition the beans would respond to the concentrated electrical fields, demonstrating deviated growth patterns much like the patterns catalogued in Ott's research.

The phenomenological basis for *Radio and Beans* is the acknowledgment that radio is more than what we hear when we tune into a station on the radio dial. The entire spectrum of electromagnetic pulsation – which, as noted above are produced both naturally and through human-made devices – constitutes Ready's subject matter. In this regard, Ready is a radio biologist, investigating the interaction of biological systems and radiant energy. However, unlike a true scientific experiment, there were no control factors in *Radio and Beans* with which to compare the results. Nor could this "experiment" be repeated, as is required by the scientific method. Although Ready felt that the growth pattern of the beans would "contain a message," it is clear that he was not concerned with devising an experiment that would enable a quantifiable outcome. Ready's inspiration is derived from a position of quasi-scientific thought, an attitude that can be traced to Alfred Jarry, and in particular his writing, *The Exploits and Opinions of Dr. Faustroll, Pataphysician.*[6] The artist as inventor has been a predominant theme in Ready's art practice for a number of years, enabling him to construct a hybrid form of artistic expression, one in which assumed ideas concerning "progress" and scientific methodologies can be challenged.

> If I had approached the same phenomenon . . . as a scientist, I would have worked much more straightforwardly; I would have tried to keep the work as primitive, as fundamental, as possible. But my idea was to work as a Victorian scientist, to add embellishments that are sometimes more suggestive than purely functional.[7]

Radio and Beans is an ironic comment on the prevailing methodologies of science and industry. As an electronic garden, the installation provides a site of contemplation for those of us who would place our house plants close enough to the stereo loudspeaker to perceive an effect on the plant's growth. Here, science and folklore combine, creating an environment of technological "fact" on the one hand, and artistic expression and discovery on the other. The social space suggested by *Radio and Beans* created a community among those responsible for watering the plants three times a day, which necessitated organizing groups of people to gather together in order to insure the plants' survival. The bean – one of the world's basic foods – is a metaphor for all life sustained in nature, compelling us to nurture the garden. Even in the midst of the various electronic buzzes, the sound of the television set and the drone of the portable radio, these plants remind us of the utopian desire to develop ways in which to harmonize relationships within the earth's ecosystems.

If in fact science is unable to provide us with definitive proof about the environment we have created, a metaphorical juxtaposition such as *Radio and Beans* may offer a healthy alternative. Like global warming, electromagnetic fields now encompass the entire earth, as part of communication, industrial, military, medical and domestic activities. With an ever-increasing dependency on an ever-expanding radio apparatus, the chaos[8] suggested by Ready's installation points to a vision of the world as a series of interrelated phenomenon, offering an alternative to scientific "truth." Ultimately, *Radio and Beans* is about nourishment in both the biological and artistic sense of the word.

Notes

1 *Power Frequency Electric and Magnetic Fields: Questions and Answers* (Hamilton: Canadian Centre for Occupational Health and Safety, 1990), n.p.: "Some studies report an increase in the incidence of leukemia in children and adults who live close to distribution lines which produce strong power frequency magnetic fields . . . A more recent study found that children whose mothers used electric blankets during pregnancy had higher risks of brain tumors and leukemia. Other studies link exposure to power frequency fields to depression and suicide."
Other studies have indicated that exposure to EMF can effect the central nervous system, stunt growth, induce sleep and mood disorders, and affect a variety of cellular functions. It should be noted that none of this evidence is conclusive. To date, there are no governmental health standards in Canada regarding exposure to power frequency fields. See also, *Health Aspects of Radio Frequency and Microwave Radiation Exposure* (Ottawa: Department of National Health and Welfare, 1977), n.p.

2 Indira Nair, *Biological Effects of Power Frequency Electric and Magnetic Fields* (Pittsburgh: Carnegie Mellon University, 1989), n.p.

3 John N. Ott, "The TV Radiation Story," *Health and Light: The Effects of Natural and Artificial Light on Man and Other Living Things* (Old Greenwich: The Devin-Adair Company, 1973), 119–120.

4 Paul Brodeur, *Currents of Death* (New York: Simon and Schuster, 1989).

Detail of Patrick Ready's *Radio and Beans* (1992) installation at the Walter Phillips Gallery

Photo Monte Greenshields and Cheryl Bellows

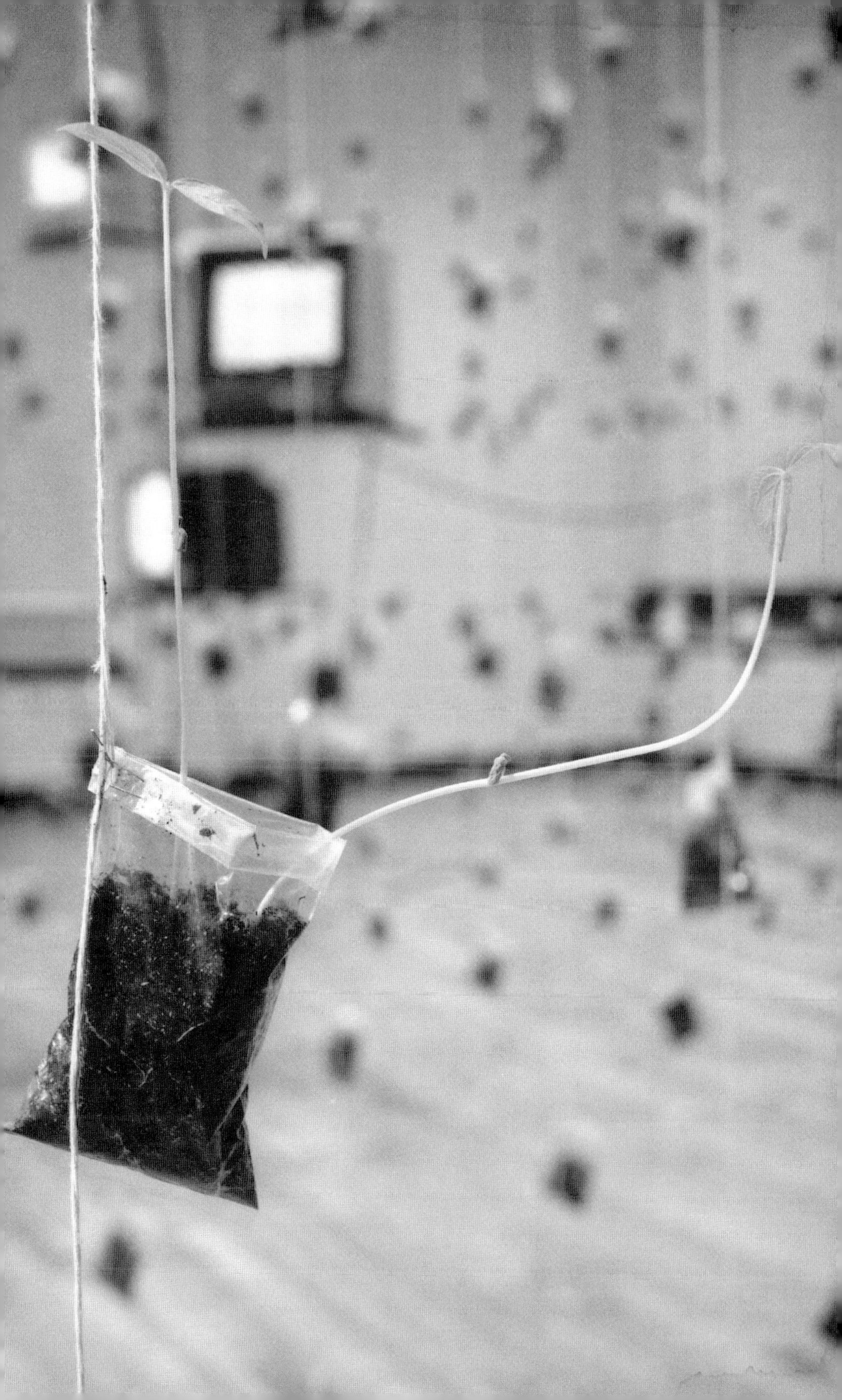

5 *Health Hazards of Radiation from Video Display Terminals: Questions and Answers* (Hamilton: Canadian Centre for Occupational Health and Safety, 1988), n.p.: "Most completed epidemiological studies have dismissed the possibility of a link between VDT work and birth defects or miscarriages. But a recent epidemiological study found an increased risk of miscarriage for women who work with VDTs. While this study does not prove an association between VDT work and miscarriages, it is the first study to show a statistically significant increase. Yet, none of the studies thus far have measured actual operator exposure to EMF. This omission weakens the validity of results from studies intended to determine if there is an association between radiation emissions from VDTs and health effects. Exposure of laboratory animals to magnetic fields similar to those emitted by VDTs has produced controversial results. It is not yet clear whether exposure to EMF is hazardous."

6 Richard Huelsenbeck, *Memoirs of a Dada Drummer* (New York: Viking Press, 1974), xxvii. Quote from the introduction by Hans J. Kleinschmidt: "[Alfred Jarry] was the "inventor" of "Pataphysics," the ironic "science of imaginary solutions," in which Dr. Faustroll explains that the world consists of nothing but exceptions, and that the rule is precisely an exception to the exception. The philistines' blind faith in progress through technology, their pride in material gain had provoked his devastating gibes. As early as 1902 he [Jarry] satirized the influence of the machine in contemporary life."

7 Patrick Ready, "Jets of Water and Sound," *Musicworks* 23 (1983), 16.

8 See James Gleick, *Chaos* (New York: Penguin Books, 1987), 5: "The first chaos theorists, the scientists who set the discipline in motion, shared certain sensibilities. They had an eye for pattern, especially pattern that appeared on different scales at the same time. They had a taste for randomness and complexity, for jagged edges and sudden leaps. Believers in chaos – and they sometimes call themselves believers, or converts, or evangelists – speculate about determinism and free will, about evolution, about the nature of conscious intelligence. They feel that they are turning back a trend in science toward reductionism, the analysis of systems in terms of their constituent parts: quarks, chromosomes, or neurons. They believe that they are looking for the whole."

Observations on Public Reception

Friedrich Kittler

Radio runs as easily as water from a tap. And the same state that, since 1870 systematically imposed upon its populations the obligation to wash,[1] brought radio to the Europeans. These days the fact that radio receivers come with station finders seems to be obvious only while driving: at home however – according to the households surveyed – it has sunk into complete oblivion. While the crisis of television has at least produced a new popular sport called zapping, the radio station, once selected, remains on permanent reception that is only interrupted by on and off.

ONE

Media that have reached their levels of saturation are hard to write about. They disappear at the juncture of high technology and triviality. They reach your ear from neighbouring yards as only the nightingale once did and, in the best-case scenario, just like the bird of all poetry, they spark Gottfried Benn's poems.[2] The normal scenario however (to quote the engineers) is that transmission is constant although, or just because, it is wireless. Due especially to being the first electronic medium to program day and night, radio has become a Platonic substantiality that causes it to vanish irresistibly as a technological medium.

Yet the vanishing on the receiving side only corresponds to that on the transmitting side. What finally reaches the listener in the constant though wireless transmission has nothing to do with the technology of the medium. Here low frequency, there high frequency, here acoustic vibrations, there electromagnetic ones. It was with good reason that Shannon's information theory, with which all modern media comply in practice, categorically distinguishes between the receiver and the recipient of the information, that is, the radio sets and listeners – because he wanted to be able to leave the recipient out of the mathematical theory altogether.[3] There is thus a dividing line, inaudible in itself, between what is heard and what is broadcast. Even the technical premise of all radio transmission draws this line: the high frequency carrier waves, which are modulated by the low frequency speech or music signal, only start radiating from the transmitting antenna into space at frequencies higher than the threshold for human ears. Therefore transmission begins where any possibility of reception has ended.

In addition to the technical borderline there is a military-industrial one, which is a continuation of the origin of all radio connections in World War I. All the civilian frequency bands on long, medium, short and ultrashort wave, no matter how far they travel beyond the recipient human ears, will disappear as tiny windows in a spectrum that includes everything from the gigahertz range of spy satellites to the extremely long-wave radio of submarine rocket carrier systems. The fact that here, on the civilian side of the military-industrial borderline, there is normally only a single wireless transmission, corresponds all too well with the distribution of frequency bands. However, in the electronic no man's land, "where the non-existing empires rule"[4] Shannon's sender-receiver theory applies absolutely. First, there have been laws and decrees in effect since the beginning of civilian radio systems that have basically sealed civilian radio sets (including their human recipients) against receiving military-industrial information.[5] Second, the imperial systems can by now completely dispense with information recipients: with the National Security Agency, the world's largest radio monitoring secret service in the United States at Fort Meade, the evaluation of intercepted signals has been carried out automatically since 1957 through decoding computers.[6] Thus the end of radio as an entertainment medium corresponds exactly to a self-closing of information technologies on the part of the sender, the side disassociated from people. What the receiving antenna picks up, consequently, is not just perception between two invisible borderlines, for example, between infra-red and ultraviolet in the case of light, as defined by Herschel and Ritter and described in Goethe's books; it is an imperceptible but still permitted special case in the large arsenal of the *arcani imperii.* Whenever or only when there is another *coup d'état* is it suddenly a known fact to everyone. Then the armoured personnel carrier units appear in front of the broadcasting buildings, whether in Vienna, Moscow or Baghdad, in order to create a singular short-circuit between empires and people. Sadam Hussein is supposed to have said once that the alleged social revolution that brought him to power was of course a simple radio putsch, but the last one in Iraq's history. Since he has held that power all broadcasting stations in Iraq have been moved to the heart of the putsch itself: into the heavily guarded inner courtyards of tank division barracks.[7]

TWO

To begin with, however, in the intervals between states of emergency, there are standards between empires and people in most cases. These standards ensure that the inaudible becomes sound in the loudspeaker, that the invisible becomes an image on the screen, and that this happens in a certain way. Since entertainment media will only run if they dodge all measures of perception for time and space, standards are necessary as controls to select what is appropriate for the ear or eye from a salad of waves. Whether what is appropriate corresponds to the physiological bandwidth of the senses or, as in the classic case of medium wave, is only a compromise between available frequency bands and interested broadcasting stations, is irrelevant as long as there is not yet any new standard that in retrospect exposes an established one. For the very reason that the selection always separates the possible from impossible phantasmagorias at the media exit, the selection process in itself can only remain hidden. That is the entire difference between media standards and art styles.

In the era of the universal arts, culture consumers were in principle allowed to see or hear whatever was aesthetically the case. Excluded were only the secrets of the workshop and possibly, since the age of Goethe had elevated a phantom called author into legal and aesthetic life, the secrets of an artist's life. The style, however, whether or not already identical with this person alias artist, simply had to become a phenomenon so that from the individual work of art it was possible "to tell what it owes to other works of art and what it means for further, new works of art."[8]

In the media era, although there is so much more to see and to hear, there have developed many new secrets far behind the workshops and the artists' souls. Before a television image is broadcast or a radio program is on the air, to say nothing of style, there must be infrastructures in place whose technology defies almost any description. What is determined beforehand on data sheets or in standardization committees has power over eyes and ears for the very reason that it in itself can be neither seen nor heard. Before any interpretation by the ultimate recipients, but also before any artistic intentions on the part of the directors or program designers, there are technical standards and electronic basic circuits that pre-program our so-called media aesthetics much more strictly than any historical or individual style.

THREE

When all of this was new, people got frightened. The doppelgänger effect in early silent films, that is, before World War I, invoked only the fear of the movie camera itself, of how it could transform bodies into their doppelgänger. The mines and trench shelters in early radio plays after World War I invoked only the fear of radio itself, of how it could carry off bodies into invisible worlds of listening. Behind such melodramatic panic, which in the *Studenten von Prag* or the *Comedy of Danger* could carry entire movie or radio play plots, there was however the impossible realization of belonging to an era where the conditions of existence were and are characterized by applied mathematics. Differential equations, and only these, describe what the case is with electric waves; values of Boolean algebra, and only these, describe what is the case with digital circuits. This resulted in the complete horror of lawyers around 1900 at having to add properties to the legal system that no longer belonged to the realm of the mind, which was as untraceable as it was vague to the realm of Maxwell's fields. In all areas, from copyright to martial law, immaterial property had first to be invented.

The phantom called author, as it had been enthroned through the copyright of Goethe's time,[9] was given numerous technical doppelgängers or competitors in film and radio. But after the first shock had passed, the doppelgänger suppliers wanted their rights and even more so "the most annihilating significant there is with regard to signification: their money."[10] One German radio network, which in its first three years of operation had quite casually ignored copyright in the case of actors and their speeches as well as authors and their works, had to be sued in a test case by the stage union in order to experience not just competition but also profit in the market of technical media. The theatre people were finally given their rights and their money, however, settlement was not based on a title of property to the radiophonic simulacrum of human voices but only a compensation for impairment that the personality as such suffered, according to the lawyers of 1925, due to the radio broadcast of his or her voice.[11]

Things developed not much differently on the battlefields. A blockade, as a time-honoured law of war had defined it, simply did not allow for the idea that, since the 1905 Russian-Japanese War, modern blockade-runners were operating with immaterial radiowaves. An emptiness beyond people has undermined even the old trade of war, and in the Second Gulf War gained an early victory as electronic warfare on all sorts of radio frequencies eleven hours before the first bomber pilots violated Iraqi airspace.

It is not surprising then that the conceptions of the unreal lagged behind its reality for so long. Professor Adolf Slaby, to whom by imperial order the honour had fallen of treating Wilhelm II and his navy (long before any kind of radio entertainment) to wireless telephony, called his non-fiction book *Voyages of Discovery into the Electric Ocean.* And Lee de Forest, who, at least according to American interpretation, made radio possible as a mass-produced article due to his invention of the triode and its feedback circuit, boasted autobiographically of having "discovered an Invisible Empire of the Air, intangible yet solid as granite, . . . imponderable yet most substantial, both mundane and empyreal."[12]

FOUR

By now, due to a multimedia system which imputes to each medium the next one as content, until radio and television, press and music industry become merged in a single feedback loop, there is no more room for such amazement. The fear of the immaterial and the awe of the empyrean have given way to a triviality that proves, as much as hides, the general acceptance of media technologies. For that reason alone, the great temptation of all media science, namely to use the approach of media history, is only an attempt. Certainly the dramatization of pioneer heroes, on the wide trail of their autobiographies, can show us the amazement of the early radio amateurs, television technicians or film directors. But first of all it has been a long time since their patents, especially the American ones, fell to the more legally astute electrical companies. Second, there is the danger that media technologies, which perhaps mark the end of history in the traditional sense, for example, history as writing, will be unquestioningly reintegrated into that history.

Under such circumstances there may be only two ways of thinking about the absent presence of media technologies without paying homage to a new historicism: the path of mathematization or that of a turn-around. Lacan, when the students of 1968 besieged him with a certain Red Book, chose the first path and made fun of revolutionaries who, for all their old-fashioned textbook knowledge, were forgetting the state of technology:

> Without us suspecting it in the least, the world that used to be considered ours is nowadays inhabited, in exactly the space that we take up ourselves, by a considerable number of so-called waves. This is not to be neglected as a manifestation, presence or reality of science and really makes it necessary to not just speak of atmosphere, stratosphere etc. when dealing with the surroundings of our earth. Nowadays, one would have to consider something that reaches a lot farther . . . [13]

The expansion of science – which oddly enough also proves to be very effective in determining what *is* – has surrounded the earth with its fabrications, with nothing other than the effects of a formalized reality. We are dealing with a space that is really and truly taken up by electric and other waves. No phenomenology of perception would have ever given us the least idea of them, it would certainly never have led us to such waves.[14]

Media as extensions of science are obviously not, as McLuhan states, extensions of the human being. On the contrary, the ironic allusion to Merleau-Ponty's phenomenology of perceptions makes it sufficiently clear that technologies are withdrawn from any insight or introspection. As "effects of a formalized reality" they solely refer to chains of signs of a large paper machine called mathematics. All the more open remains the question of how these waves, once more de Forest's "Invisible Empires of the Air," are supposed to be able to rule the everyday life of the people, whom after all Lacan called "subjects" of the media.[15]

FIVE

The one-and-only Heidegger possibly succeeded, at whatever price, to grasp, as such, the circuitry between equipment and people. For

Heidegger, technology always meant the event in the history of being that does not allow us to think in terms of any ontological separation between person and being anymore but rather, no matter how terrible the implications, provides the first ever evidence of the fact that they have always been part of one another. The very same thing, according to Heidegger's interpretation, was meant by Hölderlin's saying about the danger and the saviour.

For the same reason it was Heidegger who received the call of radio not only in the well-known and often described temptations of politics but also in his very thinking. What he called his turn-around, that is, the attempt to describe the event of being and man no longer in phenomenological terms starting from the equipment of a living being, arose simply from the untenability of a philosophy that tried to explain media as extensions of man and thus attempted to humanize them. In 1927, in *Being and Time,* he had still said:

> In the Dasein lies an inherent tendency towards nearness. All types of the increase of speed that today we are more or less compelled to take part in push towards the overcoming of distance. With the "wireless," the Dasein is now performing a not yet calculable removal of the "world" by means of a widening of the everyday environment.[16]

Radio, at the time not yet five years old in Europe, had already reached the rank of a philosophical category. For the purpose of basing ontology no longer on the usual objects but on relationships that are real and nevertheless immaterial, so that in the "real tendency towards nearness" they don't need to move a single foot or stone, there could not have been a better model than *Rundfunk,* the Germanized term for radio officially enforced by the Reichspost. And yet this postal service disappeared again immediately behind a "we" that only endured the engineering progress of Central Europe, although or because it, as an "existence," and thus as a being of man, very much "carried out" this singular extension not of itself (as stated by Freud or McLuhan), but nevertheless of the everyday environment.

In 1938, in the time of the world image or pan-Germanic radio, there was a sudden end of such ambiguities. At exactly the point where the existence had on the one hand proceeded to an engineering-type self-extension, only to, on the other hand, suffer in its own being as a radio consumer or Black Forest inhabitant, the "modern age" itself progressed to a stage of fulfillment of being, towards which "it is racing at a speed unknown to the participants":

> One sign of this process is that everywhere and in the most varied disguises gigantic things appear. At the same time this gigantism also materializes in the direction of getting smaller and smaller. We need only think of the figures in nuclear physics. The gigantic aspect pushes to the forefront in a form that seemingly makes it disappear: in the annihilation of large distances by the airplane, in the random presentation, produced by a flick of the wrist, of strange and remote worlds as an everyday occurance in radio.[17]

Eleven years after *Being and Time* all the premises have thus been reversed: first the worldwide everyday occurrence of short-wave transmissions replaced the environmental, that is, German everyday occurrence of Reichspost and medium-wave broadcasting. Second, radio enters into a syntactic interconnection with the airplane which, since Lindbergh's and Balbo's transatlantic flights, can only confirm its media technical interconnection and the fact that space annihilation would not have been possible without radio connections. Third, no existence removes its environments or worlds anymore, but rather modern age technology itself is racing at a speed that can only be that of electric waves towards the fulfillment of its being. The radio, in other words, forced Heidegger's turn-around. Its call compelled his thinking, for no other reason than to comprehend the modern age, to do without its first and last leading idea: any talk of the subject (even in its conceptual liquidation as an "existence") would again present a falsified image of man, whom technology subjugates as much as it needs him, as the master of technology.

SIX

However, it is one thing to perform this turnaround and another to work with it. On the other side of the moon, as the discourse (ever since Schiller[18]) has always paraphrased the media, things and differences also run without becoming events (in the everyday sense) or being events (in Heidegger's sense of the word). Only in an interval period, when analogue media like radio came into power but (according to a remark by the radio inventor Marconi) unlike newspapers disappeared again immediately,[19] did the media have no time for themselves, no memory and therefore no strategy. The media systems only formed switch networks whose output variables were clearly determined by the input variables, but not yet control mechanisms where "the output variables additionally depend on the particular condition of the system and thus on the previous history."[20]

By contrast, in today's multimedia systems, the privilege of having dynamic memory or history has long been taken away from humans. Subsystems which store their own previous histories can form entire populations and operate with one another on a strategic level. Therefore there stands before the ultimate consumers, those masses of buyers and recipients, an inserted mass of actual system elements. Ultrashort-wave networks can only be so efficient in reaching populations in even the remotest mountain valley because their antenna towers follow the principle of concentration reception, so that due to interception, intermediate amplification and re-beaming, they themselves constitute a population. Computer operating systems, at least if they do not date back to the stone-age partnership of IBM and Microsoft, provide so many and in part such hidden programs that the demon named UNIX is gradually turning into the refutation of all concepts of society, that is, into truth.

Heidegger's event, at the human-technology interface, therefore collapses into diversities of which it is unknown whether – like the programming languages that have meanwhile reached the fifth generation – mediated societies still have any history themselves. What is certain is that all these populations have strategic abilities at their disposal, and one might speculate that they are strategies pure and simple.

Among these strategies, however, radio is still of crucial importance. As radio is becoming more and more trivial as a secondary medium of entire populations, as its glamour shifts to television pictures (that are still radio), or to glass fibre cables (that no longer are), it will likely become as remote to human beings as it is physically. Marconi already speculated whether the background noise that so much afflicted the first transatlantic experiments in wireless telephony was no malfunction at all but rather radio communications from far-away stars.[21] And when Kurt Mondaugen, the engineer in all the Pynchon novels, intercepted this background noise at his listening post in the Kalahari, the finally deciphered radio message said:
"THEWORLDISEVERYTHINGTHATISTHECASE."[22]

There is thus a point of intersection where radio as a "fabrication of science" coincides with radio as cosmic electronics. Public reception, just in case, remains connected to it.

Translated from German by Anna Lausch

Notes

1 See *Meyers Grosses Konversations - Lexikon (Meyer's Encyclopedia)*, 6th edition (Leipzig and Vienna, 1902–8). Article on water pipes: "Since it has been recognized how important it is for health and standard of living to provide the cities with an ample supply of good water, many cities have been supplied with water. At the same time, arrangements have been made that aim at increasing water consumption in all classes of the population(!)."

2 See Friedrich Kittler, "Benns Gedichte, 'Schlager von Klasse,' ein Lyriker unter medientechnischen Bedingunge," *Manuskripte: Zeitschrift für Literatur* 106 (1989), 56–62.

3 See Claude E. Shannon and Warren Weaver, *Mathematische Grundlagen der Informationstheorie* (Munich: Oldenbourg, 1976), 43–45.

4 Bernhard Siegert, "Der Untergang des roemischen Reiches," in *Paradoxien, Dissonanzen, Zusammenbrüche: Situationen offener Epistemologie*, ed. Hans Ulrich Gumbrecht and K. Ludwig Pfeiffer (Frankfurt: Suhrkamp, 1991), 511.

5 See Heinz Pohle, "Der Rundfunk als Instrument der Politik," *Zur Geschichte des deutschen Rundfunks 1923/38* (Hamburg) (1955), 45–47.

6 See James Bamford, *NSA – Amerikas geheimster Nachrichtendienst* (Zurich: Wiesbaden, 1986), 133–137 and 308f. First published as *The Puzzle Palace: A Report on America's Most Secret Agency* (Boston: Houghton Mifflin, 1982).

7 See Zuhdi Al-Dahoodi, "Moscheen als Rundfunkzentralen: Das (v)ideologische Patchwork Sadam Husseins," in *Medien/Revolution*, ed. Wolfgang Ernst and Friedrich Kittler (Leipzig, 1992).

8 Niklas Luhmann, "Das Kunstwerk und die Selbstreproduktion der Kunst," in *Stil, Geschichte und Funktionen eines kulturwissenschaftlichen Diskurselements*, ed. Hans Ulrich Gumbrecht and K. Ludwig Pfeiffer (Frankfurt: Suhrkamp, 1986), 632.

9 See Heinrich Bosse, *Autorschaft ist Werkherrschaft: Über die Entstehung des Urheberrechts aus dem Geist der Goethezeit* (Munich: Schoningh, 1981).

10 Jacques Lacan, "Das Seminar über E.A. Poes der entwendete Brief," in *Schriften (Ecrits) I (1973–1980)*, ed. Norbert Haas (Weinheim: Quadriga, 1991), 37.

11 See August Soppe, "Der Streit um das Hörspiel 1924–25," *Entstehungsbedingungen eines neuen Genres* (Berlin 1978), 68–73.

12 Lee de Forest, *Father of Radio: the Autobiography of Lee de Forest* (Chicago: Wilcox and Follett, 1950), 4.

13 Jacques Lacan, "Le seminaire, livre XVII," in *L'envers de la psychanalyse*, ed. Jacques-Alain Miller (Paris: Editions de Seuil, 1991), 174.

14 Ibid., 185, 187.

15 See Jacques Lacan, "Le seminaire, livre XX" in *Encore* (Paris: Editions de Seuil, 1975), 76. "(Le discours scientifique) à engendre toutes sortes d'instruments qu'il nous faut, du point de vue dont il s'agit ici, qualifier de gadgets. Vous êtes desormais, infiniment plus loin que vous ne le pensez, les sujets des instruments qui, du microscope jusqu'à la radio-television, deviennent des elements de votre existence."

16 Martin Heidegger, *Sein und Zeit* (1931; reprint, Tubingen: M. Niemeyer, 1967), 105.

17 Martin Heidegger, "Die Zeit des Weltbildes," in *Holzwege*, 4th edition (Frankfurt: Klosterman M., 1963), 87.

18 See Friedrich Schiller, "Was heisst und zu welchem Ende studiert man Universalgeschichte? Eine akademisache Antrittsrede," *Saemtliche Werke: Saekularausgabe* XIII, ed. Eduard von der Hellen (1855; reprint, Stuttgart: Cotta, 1905), 17.

19 See Orrin E. Dunlap Jr., *Marconi: The Man and His Wireless* (1937; reprint, London: Macmillan, 1971), 266: "A reporter inquired if (Marconi) agreed with the theory that broadcasting would harm newspapers. The idea seemed to amuse him. "Radio can never take the place of the newspapers," he exclaimed. "Rather do I believe broadcasting encourages newspaper reading. For instance, I listen to some interesting news. I call my wife to share it and discover I cannot find her. She has gone out. If she wants the same news later she must get it from the newspaper and not from the loudspeaker. The newspaper has a distinct advantage; it is a record. When a man speaks over the radio he can deny he ever made such a statement, unless a recording is made of the speech. It is not so with the newspaper. The matter is there in black and white. Newspaper clippings can be preserved in a scrapbook. You cannot do that with broadcasting."

20 Ulrich Tietze and Christian Schenk, *Halbleiter-Schaltungstechnik*, 5th edition (Berlin: Springer-Verlag, 1980), 454.

21 Dunlap, 267f.

22 Thomas Pynchon, *V* (New York: Bantam, 1981), 258.

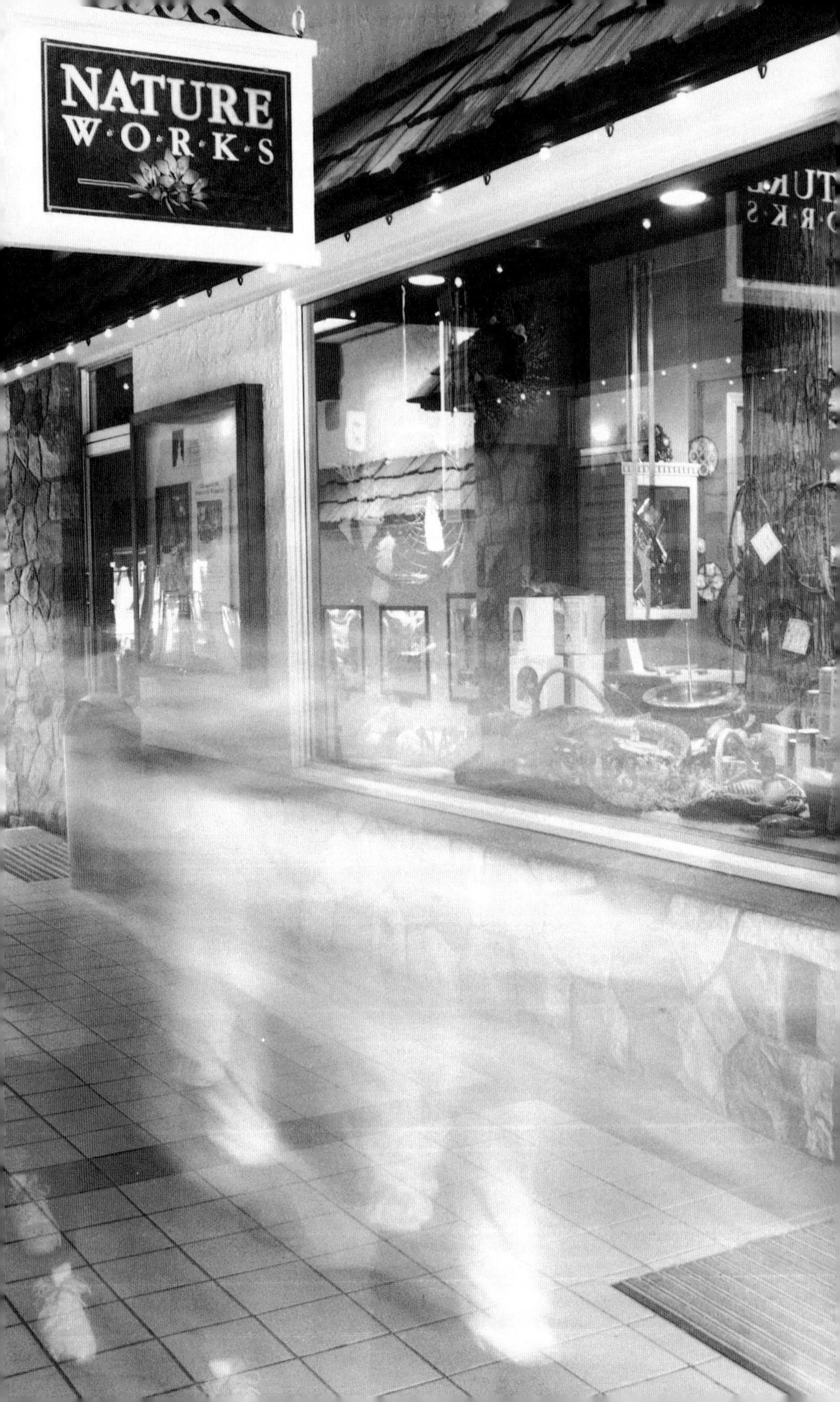
NATURE
W·O·R·K·S

The Soundscape on Radio

Hildegard Westerkamp

In the mid-1970s, two events coincided that have changed the way I think about sound: the World Soundscape Project and the founding of Vancouver Co-operative Radio. The first opened my ears to sounds beyond the classical music I had studied for many years and enhanced my understanding of the soundscape; the other provided the opportunity to organize and broadcast these sounds and thus to "speak back" to the community with the sounds of its own making. Both made me think about sound design, composition, acoustic ecology and how we hear and listen.

The World Soundscape Project (WSP), founded by R. Murray Schafer in the late 1960s, was one of the first attempts to study the acoustic environment and the impact of technology on it. Through systematic and critical study, the project coordinated and researched the scientific, aesthetic, philosophical, architectural and sociological aspects of soundscape ecology. When Schafer left Simon Fraser University in 1975, the project wound down and completed the publications of its work through the imprint of a Vancouver publisher. I was one of six members of the original research team that dissolved when Schafer left, but along with Barry Truax I have worked to maintain and expand the archives of over three hundred audiotapes we had collected, and have continued to disseminate and develop the project's legacy through publications, recordings and lectures. My involvement with this project changed the way I thought about listening and soundmaking, as I came to appreciate them in a delicately balanced relationship with each other. With these new ways of thinking about sound in mind, I became involved in the founding of Vancouver Co-operative Radio.

Photo Don Lee

At first, members of the newly formed Co-operative Radio were challenged by the vast silence of the airwaves that accompanied the license to broadcast. We knew how fragile silence was and that it could be enhanced or destroyed by sound. In some ways, making radio is like composing music. The same care for form and content has to be taken in creating radio as in creating a piece of music. The same questions arise: when to have sound and when to have silence; what sense of time to create; what sounds to select; what to say and how to say it; how to retain the dimensions of silence under a stream of sound; how to attract and keep a listenership. The Co-op Radio airwaves may have been silent at first but the social environment and soundscape into which we were to broadcast our radio programming was already crowded with sounds. The challenge was to make ourselves heard.

Most of Vancouver Co-operative Radio's founding members desired closer interaction between radiomakers and listeners. We wanted to do something that no other station was doing at that time – to involve the community in the making of radio so that radio sound would embody the voice of the community. Any listener could also be a radiomaker, who might then become an increasingly active listener because of his or her immediate involvement with the station.

My own involvement with Co-op Radio gave me the opportunity to consider radio as an artistically expressive medium and to address issues of environment and acoustic ecology. I was attempting to make radio a place of environmental listening by broadcasting the soundscapes that listeners experienced in their daily lives. With that I had hoped to create a state of resonance within listeners so that when they encountered sounds in the actual environment, recollections of the radio broadcast would alert them to the soundscape in which they lived – creating participating listeners, that is, listeners of the broadcast who could then also be receptive to the soundscape as a whole.

Most of us have been conditioned, especially if we have lived in the city for awhile, to ignore the soundscape, including radio. The result is that we often do not even know what our ears put up with every day, how our whole being might be affected by an overload of sound input, and that we might unconsciously assist in the proliferation of increasingly noisy soundscapes. A question, then, is raised: how do we, as audio artists/composers, create the desire to listen in a world where the tendency is predominantly not to listen – to radio or the soundscape?

RADIO THAT LISTENS

Imagine radio that, instead of numbing us to sounds, strengthens our imagination and creativity; instead of manipulating us into faster work and more purchasing, it inspires us to invent; instead of overloading us with irrelevant information and fatiguing us, it refreshes our acoustic sensitivity; instead of moving us to ignore thoughts and surroundings, it stimulates listening; instead of broadcasting the same things over and over again, it does not repeat; instead of silencing us, it encourages us to sing or to speak, to make radio ourselves; instead of merely broadcasting at us, we listen through it.

Ideally, when we listen to radio we are listening to a listening medium. Radio listens through its microphones to the world, to human voices, to the environment. However, the microphone does not make choices. In itself it is without culture: the way it listens to the world is entirely determined by the recordist behind the microphone. Radio that listens then is about the recordist's position and perspective, the physical, psychological, political and cultural stance shaping the choices when recording. My choices are influenced by an understanding of the sonic environment as an intimate reflection of the social, technological and natural conditions of the area. I attempt to maintain an acoustic balance in the environment and to consider how its quality may be improved. To some extent, my recording choices are shaped by a desire to educate, to raise awareness of the present state of the soundscape. By encouraging listening and questioning, I hope also to make people aware of their roles as soundmakers and their responsibility toward the soundscape. My own first attempt to create radio that listens was called *Soundwalking*, a weekly one-hour radio program that took a very specific approach to the medium as a conveyor of environmental sounds.

Produced in 1978 and 1979, *Soundwalking* took Co-op Radio listeners into the soundscape of Vancouver and surroundings. With tape recorder and microphone I ventured into environments such as the quiet winter landscape of the nearby mountains where my footsteps, my voice and the snow falling from trees were the loudest sounds. I went to a shopping mall, park, zoo, factory, residential area located under a flight-path and the streets of Vancouver. It was my first attempt to create a program that listened to the communities of Greater Vancouver without attempting to report about them. It brought community soundscapes into listeners' homes and simultaneously extended listeners' ears into the soundscape of the community.

It is still relatively unusual to hear environmental sounds or soundscapes on the radio. This type of radiomaking presents the familiar as though artificial, through a loudspeaker, second hand, framed in space and time, and therefore highlighted. Daily life is thus presented from a new acoustic angle. Such radio can assist us in listening to our everyday lives, to who we are as individuals and as a society.

In some soundwalks I speak "live" from the location of the recording directly to the listener. My voice forms the link to the listener who is not physically present. I speak about the sounds or soundscapes that are audible but also about aspects extraneous to the recording such as the weather, time of day or night, the feel of the place, the architecture, how the environment looks. The voice transmits information about a place that would otherwise not be apparent from raw environmental recordings and assists in transporting the listener into each specific soundscape that is broadcast. It is also a constant reminder of the recordist's presence in the environment and of the fact that this presence creates a specific acoustic perspective for the listener – that this particular microphone, this particular recording presents only one truth about the environment. By doing so, it is intended to create an awareness or curiosity in each individual listener of a unique acoustic perspective.

Another way to create radio that listens is with a stationary microphone, where its "perspective" remains constant during a given recording process. Through this approach the microphone listens by recording whatever occurs in the soundscape during a specified duration. There is no voice-link to the radio listener and the recordist remains still or may be absent while the microphone records. Because the recordist is removed from the situation, unusual sounds may be recorded – such rareties as a bird singing very close to the

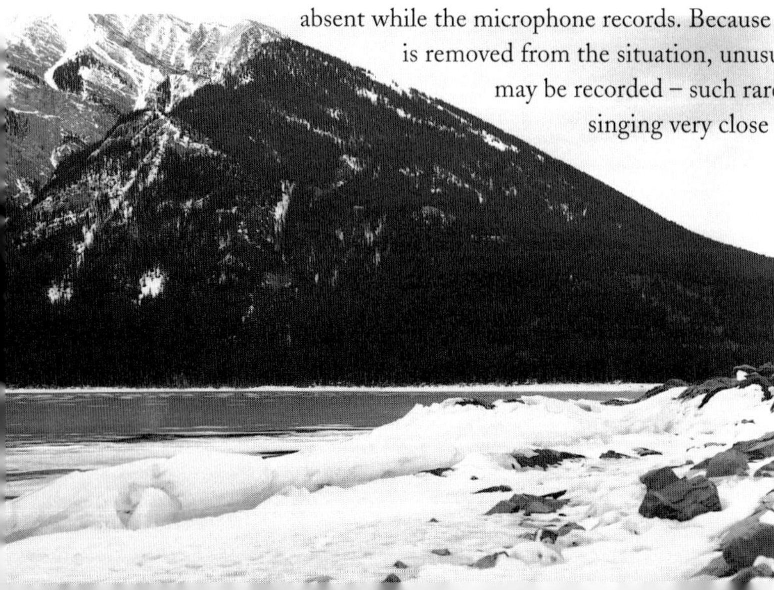

Photo Cheryl Bellows

microphone just when a street saxaphonist finishes a piece (and in harmony!), or a neon sign flashing in the same rhythm as the nearby idling bus.

The "musical theme" that signalled the start of each *Soundwalking* program was created by such a stationary microphone. The microphone was hung out of the studio window and picked up the voices of the people who sat on the benches in Pigeon Park, the little square below. Their voices were often masked by the traffic sounds, whose rhythms were determined by the pace of the traffic lights. Seagulls, pigeons and boat horns from the nearby harbour punctuated this soundscape with their calls. Every week radio listeners were earwitnesses to the changing acoustic events in this neighbourhood park.

In addition, there is the searching microphone. I did not really discover this more active approach until I started recording in quieter, more natural environments. In the city many sounds present themselves to the microphone; the recordist can remain quite passive and end up with a lot of sound on tape. Not so in quiet environments. There the recordist often needs to take a more active role with the microphone in order to record any sound at all. It is a wonderful opportunity to search for the microscopic sounds in such sonic environments. By recording them at close range, an entirely new world of acoustic complexity can be discovered, all with a relatively silent backdrop. Working with such a recording engenders respect for the source of the sound. If we can hear the small, quiet sounds of nature amplified on radio or in any electroacoustic context we may understand that even these less perceptible sounds have an important place in the environment as a whole and warrant respect and protection. The small, quiet sounds in the natural environment are symbolic of nature's fragility, of those parts that are easily overlooked and trampled, whose significance in the ecological cycle is not fully understood.

The technique of close-miking existing sounds and creating new sounds by touching the material of the environment reveals sonic resonances, timbres and textures of a place. In Banff, for example, I became a soundmaker by touching the materials of the place, exploring and recording this process from very close range. Because it was winter, I found small winter sounds, cold sounds, sounds of ice. I spent time on a side channel of the Bow River where the water was frozen in horizontal sheets layered on top of each other. By rubbing or knocking small chips of ice on the contours of the large sheets of ice, a very glassy resonance was recorded, ever-changing in its timbre as it encountered different hollow spaces underneath. The sounds had an almost unbearable crispness to them if amplified too much. Because of its incredible clarity the surrounding silence seemed emphasized.

Silence does not actually exist on the airwaves. It cannot be broadcast, produced or reproduced. An atmosphere of silence can be created with certain types of sound but it is only a simulation. These ice sounds had all the characteristics around which the contours of silence could be brought out: clarity, crispness, acoustic phrasing, changing timbres like the close-up intimate whispers of a human voice. To broadcast these sounds effectively, utmost attention must be paid to the nature of the original recording. For example, focus on foreground sound gives the recording a very specific acoustic perspective. In any case, the selection process involved is a reminder of the subjectivity of the recordist who is making these choices.

ONE VISITOR'S PORTRAIT OF BANFF

One Visitor's Portrait of Banff is the radio program I produced for *Radio Rethink*. It listens into the community of Banff and its surrounding soundscape, consisting of differing formats: soundwalks, collages, earwitness accounts, sound object studies and short compositions. Unlike *Soundwalking*, it is not about the community in which I live; rather, it is about a place I have visited and to which I am a stranger. I, the recordist, am the visitor to Banff. The visitor's acoustic perspective is audible through the perspective of the microphone broadcast on radio. It is the perspective of an outsider. A visitor brings fresh ears to a place and may be alert to sounds that local inhabitants have become accustomed to. Knowing little about the place, the visitor needs to decode the meanings of sounds in an unfamiliar environment and tends to approach a new place with a searching and curious ear.

The visitor with the microphone may also be interested in understanding the relationship that exists and evolves between individuals and their environments. My relationship to Banff, for example, is shaped by connections through my family history. In 1911 my grandparents came to Banff by train, moving on a few days later to Glacier National Park to go mountain hiking and stay in a grand hotel. In 1959, after my grandfather's

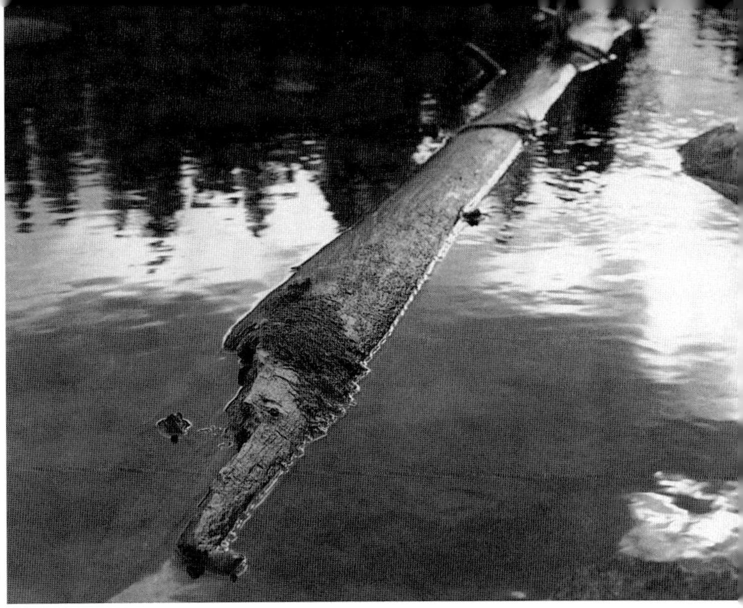

Photo Cheryl Bellows

death, my grandmother invited my two older sisters and our cousin to retrace that memorable trip. Only thirteen years old, I was left behind. From Banff they sent me souvenirs, including a postcard of Mount Rundle. They went on to find the grand hotel but it had long gone and they ended up finding another place where my oldest sister met her future husband, which led to her subsequent emigration to Canada. In 1962, when I was sixteen, my parents took me on a trip to Canada to visit my sister. We travelled, again, by train. When we got to Banff I recognized Mount Rundle and made a drawing of it from my roomette on the train. On that trip I met my future husband; six years later I emigrated to Canada. Banff has been part of some life-changing journeys for my family.

I now have an audio portrait of Banff shaped in part by these memories. I used to think of a portrait as something definitive, framed, static, a face from a certain angle, something that captures a person in totality. This audio portrait tries to consider many aspects of Banff with open ears. At the same time, it allows listeners to construct their own portrait of the place.

RADIO, SOUNDSCAPE AND ECOLOGY – AN EPILOGUE

Ecology implies balance. Acoustic ecology implies balance between sound and silence, between listening and soundmaking. In Canada the potential for such balance lies in community radio stations offering airwaves that can be designed with an ecological consciousness; we also have vast stretches of land that are not yet dominated by noise. Compared to many other countries, we have room to move, physically and psychologically.

We are also a country of immigrants who have brought and continue to bring their experiences from other countries. What happens when we come into a new place, speaking before listening, as does most radio on

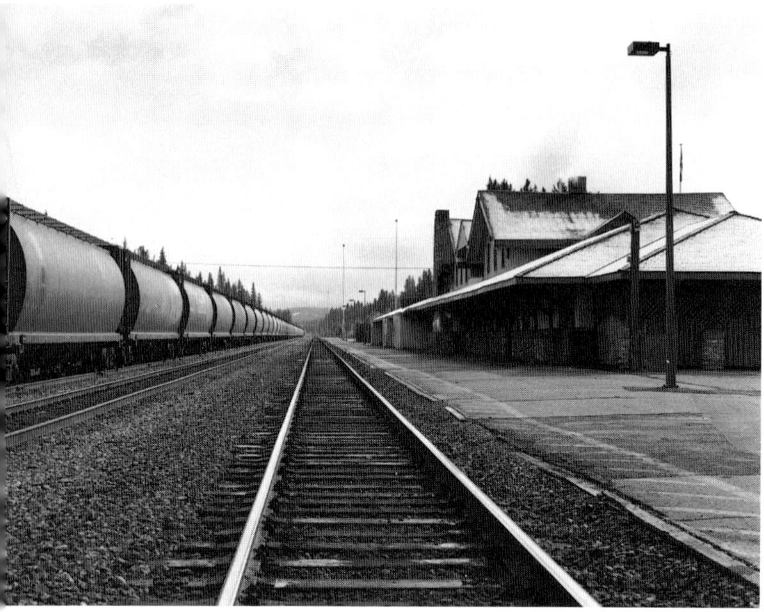

Photo Cheryl Bellows

this continent? What happens when immigrants and tourists enter a new place and speak before listening? What happens when on a daily basis we enter rooms and start to speak before we listen? Most radio engages in relentless broadcasting, a unidirectional flow of information and energy, which contradicts the notion of ecology. What would happen if we could turn that around and make radio listen before imposing its voice like an alien into a new environment? What if radio was non-intrusive, a source for listeners and for listening? Can radio be such a place of acceptance, a listening presence, a place of listening? Is it possible to create radio that listens, that in turn encourages us to listen to, and hear, ourselves?

Radio Space

Douglas Kahn

Certain things have become evident while researching radio in the western avant-garde. First, most artists responded to radio only rhetorically, at a distance from the thing that trafficked in distances, because access to the technology was limited, even when it existed. The situation is comparable to the recent fascination with virtual reality technology as a sign of artistic possibility while access to the equipment by artists remains extremely limited: the interest in radio during the avant-garde too rode on the trope of its perceived inevitability. Second, radio then is not necessarily radio now; it could include microphony, sound that was recorded or amplified in an auditorium or studio, the transmission of visual images and was not necessarily broadcast from a single source to a mass of listeners. Frequently, radio was interchangeable with wireless telegraphy, wireless telephony, wirelessness, and was often fused with other auditive or quasi-auditive phenomena; it could easily be called upon to signal a modernist reconfiguration of political economy, technology, thought, language, communication and spectation. Third, radio was routinely considered, especially when generalized to wirelessness, in relation to space: psychological and psychic space, the intimate space of love, the international political realm and the far reaches of the cosmos. Often these characteristics of space did not remain spatial but were quickly deflated to ciphers,[1] a code, a technology, a body, or collapsed at once to define the designs of language or furniture, leaving an empty space in the history of the arts. Although radio has been used and imagined as a space of possibility in avant-garde literature, music and the visual arts, it has received little treatment within historical writing. This has distanced not only present-day radio and audio artists from their ancestry, but media artists in general. Furthermore, it is important to rethink all the arts from the understanding that the phonographic, telephonic, telegraphic, wireless telegraphic, microphonic, radiophonic and other communications media have transformed the conduct of life since the late nineteenth century. Current thought about contemporary art has inherited too much from mechanics and an allegiance toward isolated objects and, more recently, toward bodies; the reason to pursue radio space is to create a theoretical electrolocality where objects and bodies interact more in a social world and less in a solipsistic one of artistic romance or marketing.

The following material is but an introductory listing of spaces related to wirelessness in the early avant-garde, starting with love and ending with an apocalypse, moving in the general direction of the Soviet Union to Italy to France. These spaces are a glut on the one I have here, leaving no room for certain curious continuities among them with respect to militarism, water, global cataclysm, starlight, looking back upon the present, and discrete voices of conscience. Nor have I included the more familiar entries in the historical annals of radio art: Walter Ruttmann and Weimar Hörspiel, the *La Radia* manifesto and Radio *Sintesi* by F.T. Marinetti and Pino Masnata, Antonin Artaud's *To Have Done With The Judgement of God*, the proliferation of works by John Cage, Fluxus, Das Neues Hörspiel and others in the 1960s and after. Instead, I have concentrated on the more rarefied realm of wirelesness manifest in ideas or literature or in works never realized. Although projects such as this may seem to bear little relevance to "practical" work, often the best art resides in idea alone, unencumbered by inhibiting pressures bound to time and place. This is especially so when these ideas are about radio, which is by its nature at least two places at once.

ONE

On his visit to the United States in 1925, Vladimir Mayakovsky sent numerous telegrams to Lily Brik, "I kiss you. I love you," and, "I kiss you from Chicago. Lonely. I love you," and, "Give me address in Italy. Lonely and bored. I love you kiss you." Although the lines may have been personal, this relationship was very public, as attested by one of Alexandr Rodchenko's photomontages for Mayakovsky's book *About This*; in this photowork Lily Brik's phone number follows a line across the New York skyline while Vladimir and a dinosaur listen intently to a telephone, but Lily is not home, just the housekeeper.[2]

Mayakovsky had long celebrated new technologies and yet he too, like many people since, discovered the inadequacies of technology for long distance love. The Russian Ego-Futurist Vasilisk Gnedov wrote in 1913 that indeed "even now the human membrane is capable of calling and answering sounds from unknown shores"[3] but this could provide little solace for the membrane that was only partially sensate. The Polish Futurist Stanislaw Mlodzeniec conducted an affair over the airwaves through his poem *radioromance*:

> Oh how is it – how?!! – Oh – Hello-lo ——— Oh – mia "lumba"
> – you told me a distant "yes" and disappeared in Chinese flowers

– all the while keeping a wary ear out: "Weep softly – my wife is coming – sensitive as a radiowave – Oh hello-lo – Oh – how is it? – how?" The Martiniquen poet Aimé Césaire, writing in his Surrealist book, *The Miraculous Weapons*, also has a wireless love problem. In the poem "The Automatic Crystal" he attempts to make contact with his love – "hullo hullo" – tries to transplant distant lands – "there are cicadas which deafen both their life and their death there also is the green water of lagoons even drowned I will never be that colour"[4] – and in attempting to establish intimate space he begins to confuse her with the technology:

> hullo hullo I would like to be on the clear other side of the earth the tips of your breasts have the color and the taste of that earth hullo hullo one more night there is rain and its gravedigger fingers there is rain putting its foot in its mouth on the roofs the rain ate the sun with chopsticks hullo hullo the enlargement of the crystal that's you . . .[5]

Elsewhere, in a poem called "The Thoroughbreds," Césaire sees a melding of radio into an entire species unfettered, having evolved from the air travel of our primal past:

> Radiolarians we drift across your sacrifice
> with a wavelike doddling I leap
> ancestral to the branches of my vegetation[6]

The Russian avant-garde painter and poet David Burliuk melded himself with the machine: upon arriving in New York in 1927 via Japan (1920–1922) he announced that he was a radio artist, radio Futurist, part of the Universal Camp of Radio-Modernists, founder of the radio movement, the person who says that "Radio-epoch and radio-style is our present." In short, he claimed that "the Radio-Era is here!" because David Burliuk is in New York City.[7] For typographer Jan Tschichold there was also a link between radiocity and New York: ". . . the works of today, untainted by the past, primary shapes which identify the aspect of our time: Car, Aeroplane, Telephone, Radio, Neon, New York!"[8] Mayakovsky too hung his hopes on airwaves, having once imagined a radio station for poets alone[9] – much like Rilke and Apollinaire had argued for the use of phonography for poetry and, much later, Nam June Paik for the inevitability of Mozart-only and Cage-only radio stations.[10] Yet Mayakovsky held no loyalty to the United States; he found Manhattan, the glitzy fast lane of modernity, to be an urban blight shrouded with a haze of petty moralizing. In fact, he had great difficulty reconciling this bitter island with the very existence of radio:

> It is dull here, while in our parts it is gay. Here everything smells of decay, is dying, rotting, while our life is boiling over, the future is ours. We are walking now through one of the richest streets in the world [Fifth Avenue] – skyscrapers, palaces, hotels, shops, and crowds. But I have a feeling I am walking among ruins, and I am depressed. You don't have . . . aspirations; you have only dirty little "moralizing," sentimental sniveling, as if one suddenly found oneself in the deepest provinces, in the Middle Ages. How can this kind of "moralizing" coexist with the highest technical achievement – I mean radio?[11]

Mayakovsky continued his examination of New York City in the 1925 poem "Brooklyn Bridge." In it he imagined the United States after global cataclysm where "over the rock of extermination . . . a future geologist of ages . . . will recreate our world . . . " He will say:

> – This here
> steel paw
> prairies and seas
> had joined,

from here
        Europe
                crawled to the West,
having set,
                with the wind,
                                Indian feathers on fire
Electric yarn
                had supplanted steam –
from it I see
                what at that time they could do:
send a winged machine
                        up to the skies,
in a big voice
                to each other
                                roar on the radio.[12]

The class injustice of United States society was not lost on Mayakovksy who noted "some carefree led their lives, others howled from hunger,"[13] the fruit of a "futurism of naked technology."[14] However, it was almost lost on him. In an earlier version of "Brooklyn Bridge" he sang the praises of technology, how its girders uplifted other accoutrements of modernism. Upon reciting the poem to a working class audience in New York, an audience member yelled out from the balcony, "Don't forget, Comrade Mayakovsky, that unemployed men often jump off of that bridge into the water."[15] Upon returning to the Soviet Union, Mayakovsky stated that the organizational task of LEF should be

> not to extol technology but to curb it in the name of humanity's interests; not to look for aesthetic delight in iron fire-escapes of skyscrapers but to arrange living quarters . . . Not to extol noise but to put up sound absorbers we poets must talk in the cars. Flight without an engine, wireless telegraph, radio, buses which push streetcars out of the way, the subway which drives underground everything that could be seen above. Perhaps the technology of tomorrow, multiplying man's strength a millionfold, will find a way to abolish scaffoldings, booms, and other technological surfaces.[16]

Dziga Vertov had an intense interest in the development of radio in the Soviet Union and he too counterposed it to the decay of capitalism:

> The "Radio-Eye" should be seen as the most powerful instrument in the hands of the proletariat, as an opportunity for the workers of the world to hear, see and understand one another in an organised fashion, as an opportunity, unlimited by space, for agitation and propaganda with facts, as an opportunity to contrast the radio-cine-documents of our socialist construction with the documents of oppression and exploitation, the radio-cine-documents of the capitalist world.[17]

His usage of the term *radio-eye* refers to film although at times it could refer to television because the visual image is "transmitted by radio."[18] The "radio-ear," on the other hand, is the microphone used in remote recording for sound film.[19] Vertov strongly criticized Walter Ruttmann's use of studio-generated sounds as pure deception in the cross-cut film, *World Melody*, which he contrasted with his own progress in getting outside the studio to the distant Donbasin region where he was making his film *Enthusiasm,* or *Symphony of the Donbas.*[20] Vertov was not testing the technology but felt it was politically important that the workers were recorded speaking for themselves and heard making their own sounds. The progressively remote recording developed something like this:

1. open the window at the Radio Centre and record the outside
2. transmit sound back to the studio using microphone wires
3. use mobile sound unit nearby
4. use mobile unit at greater distance to film a Party Congress
5. use mobile unit far away in many situations in the Donbas region[21]
6. ultimately, transmit the audio-visual sound film back to the studio via radio[22]

Velimir Khlebnikov, the Russian avant-garde poet, enlisted the ciphering function of starlight, with its scientific and secular illumination, to bring Pythagorean cosmological space down to the earthly abode of historical chronology in a much more poetic practice. His self-defined job description as the King of Time can be best read in his "Tables of Destiny," a set of calculations mathematically extrapolating the temporal relationships of past events in order to prophesize about the future. In his key theoretical essay of 1919, "Our Fundamentals," he beseeches the nations of the future to pay heed to this prophecy-turned-science, hoping they will seek stability in the arrangement of the stars and find harmony in the strings that had structured earlier models of the universe. The music of the spheres, in other words, was forwarded as the model for international politics: "the harmony of strings can replace the disharmony of nations." According to Khlebnikov, starlight concentrated millions of miles and light years into a foreshortened pinpoint, a sign, a *signal* containing life, history and wisdom: "Let us suppose that a wave of light is inhabited by intelligent beings who possess their own government, their own laws, even their own prophets."[23] He then takes the trajectory of starlight as it traverses across the heavens to earth as a wireless signal that better situates nations in accord with each other than their current terrestrial suspension which carries them puppet-like from the strings of the older, wired telegraphy and telephony:

> And is not the purpose of division to dismantle the wires of states and governments that intervene between the eternal stars and the ears of mankind? Let the power of the stars be wireless.[24]

In another essay, "The Radio of the Future," Khlebnikov finds other strings standing at the top of a radio antenna like tousled hair. "More obedient than strings beneath the violinist's hand, the metallic apparatus of Radio will talk and sing, obeying every marked pulse of the song," he observes. The radio he imagines is not broadcast but sends its signal to speaker walls set in a prominent city and village locations across the Soviet Union (following the agit-prop practices of ROSTA, the Russian Telegraph Agency), perhaps to one of the "radio orator" or "radio tribune" agitation stands designed by Gustav Klutsis in the early 1920s or the kiosks equipped with radio loudspeakers by other Soviet artists.[25] The broadcast itself may have originated from the room revolving once a day atop Vladimir Tatlin's *Monument to the Third International*, its cylindrical shape housing media-related functions, including a telegraph office, equipment for large screen projections and a radio station. Khlebnikov's entire essay is quite remarkable, exemplified by this excerpt on a radiophonic anthem of production:

> It is a known fact that certain notes like "la" and "ti" are able to increase muscular capacity, sometimes as much as sixty-four times, since they thicken the muscle for a certain length of time. During periods of intense hard work like summer harvests or during the construction of great buildings, these sounds can be broadcast by Radio over the entire country, increasing its collective strength enormously.[26]

In 1928 Stalin had another type of national health mission in mind when he said that radio and cinema would cure alcoholism and displace vodka, "the ulcer of society."[27]

TWO

Khlebnikov's radiophonic muscle intoner was somewhat similar to Marinetti's "Nourishment by Radio." Marinetti continually invoked new technologies to sanction his ideas as he did by bringing communications technology to the writing of a cookbook. He quotes Luigi Colombo, one of his compatriots in a later generation of Italian Futurists:

> NOURISHMENT BY RADIO
> The Futurists by declaring themselves against pasta and indicating new developments in Italian cooking, are not only assisting the important goal of national savings, but intend to change the tastes and eating habits of the Italians. Therefore it is not just a question of replacing pasta with rice, or of preferring one dish to another, but of inventing new foods. Many mechanical and scientific changes have come into effect in the practical life of mankind that it is also possible to achieve culinary perfection and to organize various tastes, smells and functions, something which until yesterday would have seemed absurd because the general conditions of existence were also different. We must, by continually varying types of food and their

> combinations, kill off the old, deeply-rooted habits of the palate; and prepare men for future chemical foodstuffs; we may even prepare mankind for the not too distant possibility of broadcasting nourishing waves over the radio.

Marinetti then adds:

> The really miraculous idea, which may even have escaped Marconi, is the possibility of broadcasting nutritious radio waves. After all, the notion is not so extraordinary. Since the radio can diffuse asphyxiating and sleep-inducing waves (lectures, jazz, poetry readings, to-conclude-ladies-and-gentlemen, etc.) it surely should be able to diffuse some extracts from the best dinners and luncheons. Then what abundance there would be![28]

And just in case a radio delectation is needed to follow one of these meals:

> CANDIED ATMOSPHERIC ELECTRICITIES
> These dear and unforgettable "electricities" looked like little brightly coloured bars of marbled soap, containing a sweetish cream made from ingredients that only an exhaustive chemical analysis would be able to define.[29]

F.T. Marinetti was the creator almost two decades earlier of the term *wireless imagination*. For him, wirelessness implied the collapse of syntax and analogy and the radical modulation of orthography; the result was his *parole in libertà*, words-in-freedom. All conventions of relationality, traditionally confined to local and manageable structures and comparisons, would break down once bombarded by a global infinitude of possible relations, all arriving at once with an unprecedented speed having "no connecting wires."[30] His contributions to avant-garde poetactics gained quite a bit from the military, evident for example in the aerial foreshortening of combat formations and military field maps,[31] the onomatopoetic recording of battle sounds heralding the sound poetry that was to follow in the avant-garde. In his graphic poem, "Captive Turkish Balloon," he documented a scene from the battle at Adrianopolis. In this work, a surveillance balloon signaled its sightings back to the ground like any surveillance balloon using TSF, the abbreviation for wireless telegraphy.

The mere fact of radio was also used in Italian Futurism as a soft hedonistic underbelly to its militarism and fascism. Just as "Candied Amospheric Electricities" related radio to cuisine, so too did Italian Futurists relate radio to interior design. Ivo Pannaggi's design for the "Radio-Listening Room" (1925–26) found rationale in how radio eliminates "location and space...: one travels thousands of kilometres and changes countries at will. It is therefore reasonable to create a fantastic setting using the freest inventions of plastic architecture."[32] The freest inventions also happened to be quite opulent:

> A shiny black truncated cone, amidst the red, black and grey masses of the furniture and walls, surmounted by a disk of folded parchment circled with nickel, [which] expresses the ideal axis of the construction. This is the loudspeaker, whose base projects it from the equipment bank toward the centre of the room. The equipment in view is present as a plastic assemblage of the most savoury materials: valves made of mirrors, porcelain insulators, spools swathed in celluloid, ebanite, brass, nickel finishings. Solid full-relief letters connect typographical taste with the mechanical precision of elementary geometry in dynamic interpenetration, indicating the call letters of the principal stations and the names of the inventors: Herz, Righi, Marconi, Popoff.[33]

THREE

Guillaume Apollinaire, in his most ambitious graphic poem, "Ocean Letter," was directly inspired by Marinetti's "Captive Turkish Balloon"; the same TSF that tied the balloon to the ground connected Apollinaire with his brother across the Atlantic. In this poem Apollinaire also phonographically denotes sounds that, with their implied acoustic spatiality, have the effect of raising the surface of the poem off the paper: an avant-garde pop-up poem.

The Ukrainian Futurist Mykhailo Semenko constructed a similar poem, "Cablepoem Abroad" (1920–21),[34] in which the global reach of the wireless was also intended to encompass possibilities for worldwide revolution; the signal would carry a new universal language, naturalized by what fell under the signal's arche and by a common politics:

listen!
I pressed the button
50 parallel 50
Moscow-Himalaya-Kyoto
Our language –
Cities and mountains and seas and a field of snow
Words will be forgotten
It is constricting to think in details!
We will return to a collective thought
....
Learn the language of the Future![35]

Once unleashed the signal would not just revolve around the world:

To the technicians
An imperative decree:
1925
! RADIO – tram !
Earth – – –
– – – MARS.[36]

In his 1916 story "The Moon King," Apollinaire uses radio to sample sounds occurring across the span of oceans and continents. A traveller seeking shelter is drawn into the subterranean passages of a mountain, where he hears sounds from a remote room. He finds there an elderly man he recognizes as King Ludwig II of Bavaria, thought to be drowned, sitting at an unusual keyboard instrument. When a key is pressed, Japan at dawn was heard:

> The flawless microphones of the king's device were set so as to bring in to this underground the most distant sounds of terrestrial life. Each key activated a microphone set for such-and-such a distance. Now we were hearing a Japanese country side. The wind soughed in the trees – a village was probably there, because I heard servants' laughter, a carpenter's plane, and the spray of an icy waterfall. Then another key pressed down, we were taken straight into morning, the king greeting the socialist labor of New Zealand, and I heard geysers spewing hot water. Then this wonderful morning continued in sweet

> Tahiti. Here we are at the market in Papeete, with the lascivious wahinees of New Cytheria wandering through it – you could hear their lovely guttural language, very much like ancient Greek. You could also hear the Chinese selling tea, coffee, butter, and cakes. The sound of accordions and Jew's harps . . . [37]

It carried on to a train in the United States, urban noises of Chicago, vessels along the Hudson, prayers for Christ in Mexico, a carnival in Rio, a teacup in Paris, a chorus in Bonn, hand games in Naples, and finally ten o'clock in Tripoli. Then the "king's fingers ran over the keys at random, simultaneously raising all the sounds of this world which we, standing still, had just toured aurally."[38]

André Breton also takes up wirelessness in "The Introduction to the Discourse on the Paucity of Reality" where he begins with a brief discussion of the expression *wireless* which "has too recently found its place in our vocabulary, has had too rapid a career, for much of the dream of our epoch not to go along with it; for it not to afford me one of those very rare and specifically new orientations of the mind."[39] The fashionably modern quality of the term provided an occasion for him to rethink the present while the intrinsic uprootedness of wirelessness allowed him to unfetter his thoughts. Before he proceeds too far in the essay Breton mentions what is excluded, what technology does not evoke – the sands of the shore, spiders, a willow tree, the sky – each with its own ability to evoke responses, after all, "the sky . . . is only an antenna with a wide range."[40] That given, he decides to rethink the present by choosing a different past. He imagines himself "in the vestibule of the chateau, lantern in hand, (throwing) the light on one after another of the gleaming suits of armour." The suits of this armour transmit a "great mute colloquy" once they are donned, as though they are but death masks cast from other people's bodies. However, the masks do not speak and the suits' ornate etchings are not phonographic inscriptions; the armour instead tunes in to the past: "Listen. Don't you still hear the galloping of horses through the country? The sun of the dead shines in vain, even for them, the living running always at full speed in aid of the unaidable. They make it an affair of state." Breton hears the past through these suits; he hears a voice, a woman's voice, another woman's voice and finally he puts on his own armour and speaks through it into the present tense of the text itself where he continues to discourse on the paucity of reality.[41]

In the fields of transmission the unknown expanses of the psyche were as intriguing and explorable as those on the earth's surface. The two were brought together in the psycho-technics of Surrealist automatism. Inscriptive, stenographic practices took down the "magical *dictation*" from the "mouth of darkness" (Breton), the noisy gate to the unconscious,[42] but the action of the unconscious itself, its "voice," was delivered to the Surrealist by narrowcast. Even the literary ear privy to having overheard the unconscious could be described along these lines. In his 1928 *Treatise on Style*, Louis Aragon describes the physiognomy of being unable to hear such a voice as having "your ear trimmed with a festoon of broderie anglaise, your ear the color of calves' feet, your tender ear of rubber, your ear, ever as waxy and buzzing as a hive, your little dirty cartilage that looks more like a poorly puffed fritter than a phonograph horn . . . "[43] For Aragon, the ear that can hear is equipped with a sensitivity that, much like Apollinaire's keyboard, radiophonically spans the oceans and becomes "more and more able to grasp in the grassy hollow of sentences the clear tinkling of a clinked glass that causes a man to die at sea each time, and the same ceremony takes place, the sailors line up at the flag at half-mast, plop! the bag in the waves carries the sleeper away."[44] Similarly, the oracular voice of the unconscious was inverted into a vast subterranean region that could be heard residing on the other side of the earth's surface. In the course of discussing the "timbre" of Lautréamont's style, Aragon describes the work of the intellect as an acoustic mining.

> When the worker who was digging into the bowels of the earth – whether in knotty Asia or near the Italian sea, where the dust is lightest because it is made with the powder of statues – when this worker suddenly hears the steel of his pickax ring strangely, he bends over, questions the distant depth, and thinks he hears a dirge. To the bottom of the pit he glues an ear that is used to romances. What is this perpetual rumbling? A monstrous parade, an enormous troop which nothing wearies. Profuse resonance of subterranean carriages. The ebb and flow of hidden waters, where everything merges.[45]

Aragon's mining strikes an aqueous metaphor which continued to flow in his description of the automatic speech of the poet Robert Desnos during the Surrealist "period of sleeps": "He spoke like no one speaks. The great common sea suddenly found itself in the room, which was any old room with its surprised utensils."[46] Here, the subterranean waters "where everything merges" are themselves transmitted into the room through the buccal spigot of a "sleep talking" Desnos, as though he were but a puncture on the surface of the earth and of consciousness, a breach through which can be heard, "the echo of what we are tempted to consider as universal conscience."[47] Desnos was such an avid "sleeper" that he eventually pressed the patience of his listeners too far, as evidenced by the episode when an intolerant Paul Eluard, to awaken Desnos, emptied a jug of water onto his chest, fighting water with water. In 1932, several years after leaving the Surrealist ranks, Desnos replaced the transmission technology of his own body for that of radio broadcasting proper to create what he thought of as either an extension of poetry or a return to radio advertising: "I threw myself passionately into the almost mathematical, yet intuitive, work of adapting words to music, of fabricating sentences, proverbs and mottoes for advertising, the primary exigency of this work being a return to the people's taste in the way of rhyme."[48] As his wife Youki Desnos recounts, "Robert's ambition – and how many times he repeated it to me – was outside of his pure poetic work, to create songs which could sweep through the streets, to be whistled by a boy pedalling a carrier tricycle, for example, or murmured from ear to ear by lovers."[49] In other words, Desnos abandoned the "universal consciousness" that populated the unconscious for the crowded unconscious of "the People." Goods and services lodged in the bodies of jingles and songs were recorded into the minds of thousands of French people with the hope they would be irrepressibly repeated. Desnos thereby socialized himself by radiophonically transmitting an entirely denatured "period of sleeps" and extending the transmitter from the psycho-technical device of his own body to the crowd.

Edgar Varèse's most ambitious unrealized projects happened to be radiophonic in character and very much above ground. Beginning in Paris in 1928 and lasting for over a decade, he pursued the series of related symphonies named *Space*, *The Red Symphony*, *Symphony of the Revolution* and *The Astronomer*, collaborating at different times with Robert Desnos and Alejo Carpentier, André Malraux[50] and with Antonin Artaud. The idea for radiophonic link-ups was formed between 1937 and 1939 in an argument sketched out in 1941:

> Voices in the sky, as though magic, invisible hands were turning on and off the knobs of fantastic radios, filling all space, criss-crossing,

overlapping, penetrating each other, splitting up, superimposing, repulsing each other, colliding, crashing. Phrases, slogans, utterances, chants, proclamations. China, Russia, Spain, the Fascist states and the opposing Democracies all breaking their paralysing crusts.

. . . I suggest using, here and there, snatches of phrases of American, French, Russia, Chinese, Spanish, German revolutions like shooting stars, also recurring words poundingly repeated like hammer blows or throbbing in an underground ostenato, stubborn and ritualistic.[51]

Varèse's biographer described his plans in more detail:

Varèse had imagined a performance of the work being broadcast simultaneously in and from all the capitals of the world. The choirs, each singing in its own language, would have made their entries with mathematical precision. The work would have been divided up into seconds, with the greatest exactitude, so that the chorus in Paris – or Madrid, or Moscow, or Peking, or Mexico City, or New York – would have come onto the air at exactly the right moment.[52]

In 1932 Varèse asked Antonin Artaud to supply a scenario about the earth's collision in 2000 AD with the star Sirius for *The Astronomer*. In response Artaud wrote "There is No More Firmament" but the text remained unused and the fifth and last section was uncompleted. Artaud adopted ideas about sound directly from some of Varèse's figurative formulations, specifically, the idea that sound could attain some type of mass, an object-like palpability. This can be found in Artaud's stage instructions for "There is No More Firmament" where he has music –

falling as if from a vertiginous height. Chords are struck in the sky; they dissipate, going from one extreme to the other. Sounds fall as if from a great height, stop short and spread out in arcs, forming vaults and parasols. Tiered sounds.[53]

In a 1936 interview about his *Space Symphony*, Varèse talked about sound in the same way:

> I seemed to feel the music [during a performance of Beethoven's Seventh in Paris] detaching itself and projecting itself in space. I became conscious of a third dimension in the music. I call this phenomenon "sound projection," or the feeling given us by certain blocks of sound. Probably I should call them beams of sound, since the feeling is akin to that aroused by beams of light sent forth by a powerful searchlight. For the ear – just as for the eye – it gives a sense of prolongation, a journey into space.[54]

This practical projection into space was thought of by both Varèse and Artaud primarily in terms of loudspeakers, and with his space symphonies Varèse unleashed this concept in this formulation of radio. For Dane Rudhyar, the very sound of Varèse's music immediately provoked scientistic/spiritual notions catapulting into outer space and the cosmos. "Every tone is a molecule of music, and as such can be dissociated into component sonal atoms and electrons, which ultimately may be shown to be waves of the all-pervading *sonal energy* irradiating throughout the universe, like the recently discovered cosmic rays which Dr. Millikan calls interestingly enough 'the *birth-cries* of the simple elements: helium, oxygen, silicon, iron.'"[55]

In the script for Artaud's "There is No More Firmament," the telegraph appears at the point of imminent annihilation to salve the earthlings' fears with the promise of a truly universal language. Over public loudspeakers comes the news:

> STUPENDOUS DISCOVERY. SKY PHYSICALLY ABOLISHED. EARTH. ONLY A MINUTE AWAY FROM SIRIUS. NO MORE FIRMAMENT. TELEGRAPHY BORN. INTERPLANETARY LANGUAGE ESTABLISHED.

Amidst the clamour of the crowds scientists are heard worrying that space might be "done away with." At one point in the script a scientist shouts in a deaf colleague's ear, saying he has done away with space and gravity.[56] Apparently the scientist has discovered a device for "instantaneous radiation" even though it "means the end of the universe." This instantaneous radiation is communicative; it is apparently the "CELESTIAL TELEGRAPHY" mentioned earlier. Despite the danger, the scientist says, "I have already begun signaling." At this point the curtain falls and behind it

> the rumble of air savagely thrust back begins to swell up. Sounds rush forward, made up of the blast of several sirens at their highest point. Violent percussions intermingled.
> Cold light reigns everywhere.
> Everything stops.[57]

Perhaps this is why Artaud never completed the fifth and final section of the script.

FOUR

This brief summary requires elaboration, not just with additional material but with explanations of the many similarities occurring within a relatively small and otherwise divergent set of examples. In order to translate the understanding of radiophonic space or, rather, spaces into present day artistic practice it is important to remember that during the early twentieth century it was common to think of wirelessness in terms of *communication* because it existed prior to the redundancies of contemporary mass media. To counteract the present day regulation of possibilities, I suggest we open up the myriad spaces not travelled and reorder the spaces trampled. Thus, considerations of space would not try to distinguish any *natural* features of say, inside or outside the studio, but would attempt to distinguish the plethora of spaces existing both inside and outside the studio, both real and imaginary, the multiple ways people and other creatures communicate across and within them, tracking and constituting them to where they exist in cipher, code and other figures. The density that comes with the collapse of spaces into ciphers could then be accelerated, if so chosen, because since the mid-1950s it has been possible in media-saturated societies to apprehend highly codified sounds at a qualitatively accelerated pace. This pace, when compared to earlier quotational practices within music which required the organization of material such as a melodic fragment, exists now at the atomistic site of the material itself. Thus, spaces also no longer need room to be heard. It seems to me also that the movement of and within spaces created by radio, transforming into other spaces or ciphers, and vice versa, presents a figure inconsistent with the obedience to genre which is still widespread within the arts. The mobility among genres that phonography implies through its equalization of all audible phenomena is elaborated by radiophony through the traversing of space. Finally, because space is the place in new audio technologies, there is no reason not to nest one space in another, or move one through several, in both a sustained or immediately disappearing way and then bring the whole conglomeration into a cipher which finds itself nested or moving somewhere. Then there are the considerations of sound and space in relation to visual, tactile and other sensual space, and to psychic, discursive, institutional, international, cosmological . . .

Notes

1 By cipher I refer to an elemental material entity that is imbued with space in one form or another while otherwise preceding or exceeding most other meanings. Two examples of ciphers in the examples that follow are found in the instantaneous influence of global distance upon the breakup of syntax, orthography and phonetics in Italian Futurist *parole en libertà* and the concentration of space and historical experience into the line and point of starlight in Khlebnikov's cosmology.

2 Christina Lodder, *Russian Constructivism* (New Haven: Yale University Press, 1983), 199–200.

3 Cited in I.B. Ignatyev, "Ego-Futurizm," *St. Petersburg Herald* (St. Petersburg, Russia), 1913. Reprinted as "Ego-Futurism" in *Russian Futurism Through Its Manifestoes, 1912–1928*, trans. Anna Lawton and Herbert Eagle (Ithaca: Cornell University Press, 1988), 127.

4 Aimé Césaire, *The Miraculous Weapons*, trans. Clayton Eshleman and Annette Smith (Berkeley and Los Angeles: University of California Press, 1983), 123.

5 Ibid., 123.

6 Ibid., 99.

7 David Burliuk, *Radio-Style Manifestoe*s (New York: private publication, 1926–27), n.p.

8 "These objects designed without reference to the aesthetics of the past, have been created by a new kind of man: the ENGINEER!," Ruari McLean in *Jan Tschichold: Typographer* (Boston: David R. Godine, 1975), 36.

9 Viktor Shklovsky, *Mayakovsky and His Circle*, trans. Lily Feiler (London: Pluto Press, 1974), 177.

10 *Nam June Paik*, ed. John G. Hanhardt (New York: Whitney Museum, 1982), 34.

11 Wiktor Woroszylski, *The Life of Mayakovsky*, trans. Boleslaw Taborski (New York: The Orion Press, 1970), 375 (paraphrased by Michael Gold, then editor of the *New Masses*).

12 Ibid., 376–77. Similar to Charles Babbage's *The Ninth Bridgewater Treatise*, in which he imagines a state of global extermination over which the undissipated voice of the Negro cries out from the pains of slavery.

13 Ibid., 377.
14 Ibid., 380.
15 Edward J. Brown, *Mayakovsky: A Poet in the Revolution* (Princeton: Princeton University Press, 1973), 282.
16 Woroszylski, 380.
17 Dziga Vertov, "The Radio-Eye's March" (1930) [as in month of March] in *The Film Factory: Russian and Soviet Cinema in Documents, 1896–1939*, ed. Richard Taylor and Ian Christie (Cambridge: Harvard University Press, 1988), 301.
18 Ibid., 301.
19 "Speech to the First All-Union Conference on Sound Cinema," ibid., 301. "The manoeuvring Radio-Ear – the microphone."
20 Ibid., 301–5.
21 Ibid., 301–5.
22 Ibid., 305. "But it is not adequate if we are talking about location shooting in the broad sense of the word, on the level of the 'Radio-Eye's' general prospects, and we shall have to orientate ourselves beyond the mobile film unit to the sound-recording and sound-reproducing radio station."
23 Velimir Khlebnikov, "Our Fundamentals," *Collected Works, Vol 1: Letters and Theoretical Writing*, trans. Paul Schmidt (Cambridge: Harvard University Press, 1987), 387. This bears an uncanny resemblance to the relationship of light and sound in Raymond Roussel's early novels and writing method. However, whereas Khlebnikov comes to the transition from vibration, and thus is more easily transferable to the spatialities of transmission, Roussel sits definitively on the side of inscription.
24 Ibid., 390.
25 Lodder, 163–69.
26 Velimir Khlebnikov, "The Radio of the Future," 395.
27 Anatoli Lunacharsky, "Speech to Film Workers" (1928) in *The Film Factory*, 196 and 215.
28 F.T. Marinetti, *Futurist Cookbook*, trans. Suzanne Brill (San Francisco: Bedford Arts, 1989), 67.
29 Ibid., 92.
30 Marinetti, *Stung by Salt and War*, trans. Richard Pioli (New York: Peter Lang, 1987), 48.
31 See Linda Landis, "Futurists at War" in *The Futurist Imagination*, ed. Anne Coffin Hanson (New Haven: Yale University Art Gallery, 1983).
32 "Furniture" entry by Giancarlo Ferro in the "Dictionary of Futurism," *Futurism/Futurisms*, ed. Pontus Hulten (Milan: Bompiani, 1986), 481. Ivo Pannaggi was the painter/architect whose 1922 "Futurist Mechanical Dance" with Vincino Pladini was accompanied by the noise of two motorcycles, much in the manner that Luigi Russolo had tuned the airplane exhaust manifolds for a performance by the "aviopoet" Fedele Azari.

33 Ibid., 481.
34 Myroslava M. Mudrak, *The New Generation and Artistic Modernism in the Ukraine* (Ann Arbor: UMI Research Press, 1986), 162–70.
35 Ibid., 169.
36 Ibid., 170.
37 Guillaume Apollinaire, "The Moon King" in *The Poet Assassinated*, trans. Ron Padgett (San Francisco: North Point Press, 1984), 80.
38 Ibid., 81.
39 André Breton, *What is Surrealism?* (New York: Pathfinder Press, 1978), 17.
40 Ibid., 17.
41 This type of return to the present also existed in Mayakovsky's "Brooklyn Bridge" when the geologist who reconstructs the remains of New York City unearths the fact that Mayakovsky himself wrote the very lines "syllable by syllable."
42 André Breton, "Entrée des médiums" (1922), excerpted and translated in *The Autobiography of Surrealism*, ed. Marcel Jean (New York: The Viking Press, 1980), 101.
43 Louis Aragon, *Treatise on Style* (1928), trans. Alyson Waters (Lincoln: University of Nebraska Press, 1991), 106.
44 Ibid., 106.
45 Ibid., 103–4.
46 Ibid., 104.
47 Breton, "Entrée des médiums," 101.
48 Quoted from Robert Desnos, *État de veille* (*Walking State*), in Mary Ann Caws, *The Surrealist Voice of Robert Desnos* (Amherst: University of Massachusetts Press, 1977), 9.
49 Youki Desnos, "Desnos poète populaire," quoted in Steven Kovács, *From Enchantment to Rage* (Rutherford: Fairleigh Dickinson University Press, 1980), 52.
50 Fernand Ouellette, *Edgar Varèse* (London: Calder and Boyars, 1973), 133.
51 Dorothy Norman, "Edgar Varèse: Ionization-Espace," *Twice a Year* 7 (Fall-Winter 1941), 259–60.
52 Ouellette, 132.
53 Antonin Artaud, "There is No More Firmament," *Collected Works 2*, trans. Victor Corti (London: Calder and Boyars, 1971), 79. Artaud's script was based on ideas that Varèse had begun to work on in 1928. See Ouellette, 115–19.
54 "Varèse Envisions 'Space' Symphony," *New York Times*, 6 December 1936, Section 2–7.
55 Cited in Henry Miller, "With Edgar Varèse in the Gobi Desert," *The Air-Conditioned Nightmare* (New York: New Directions, 1945), 170–1.
56 Ibid., 91.
57 Ibid., 92.

The Technology of Entrapment
Open Your Mouth and Let the Air Out

Christof Migone

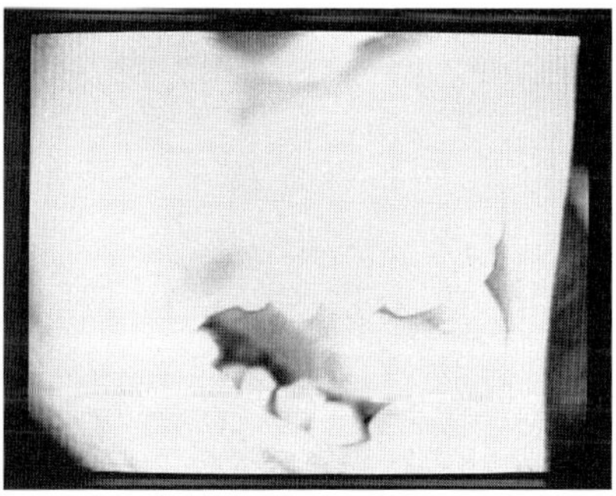

Photo Bruce Gottlieb

A RADIO-IMAGINARY CONVERSATION

JOHN CAGE
Sometimes when I speak, I give the impression that I am against feelings. But what I am against is the imposition of feelings.[1]

DANIEL CHARLES
So in your ideal society, people would be near each other, but not communicating.[2]

JOHN CAGE
They would not communicate, but they would talk, they would carry on dialogues, I much prefer this notion of dialogue, of conversation to the notion of communication. Communication presupposes that one has something, an object, to be communicated. Communication is always imposing something: a discourse on objects, a truth, a feeling. While in conversation nothing imposes itself.[3]

RAYMONDE
You play mute, I don't know if you play deaf too.[4]

ERIK SATIE
We must bring a music which is like furniture – a music, that is, which will be part of the noises of the environment, will take [it] into consideration. I think of it as melodious, softening the noises of the knives and forks, not dominating them, not imposing itself. It would fill up those heavy silences that sometimes

fall between friends dining together. It would spare them the trouble of paying attention to their own banal remarks.[5]

BERTOLT BRECHT It was suddenly possible to say everything to everybody but, thinking about it, there was nothing to say. Radio should be capable of not only transmitting but of receiving, of making the listener not only hear but also speak, not of isolating him [sic] but of connecting him [sic].[6]

DIANA BURGOYNE By placing the viewer in a position of control, it takes them out of a passive role and places them in a very active one . . . setting up relationships which raise broader questions about human co-existence with technology.[7]

SOL YURICK Now, it is said, all can be linked: electrical grid systems, voice conversations, on-line-in-real-time accounting systems, financial markets, telemedical diagnostic and treatment-delivery networks . . . All change the notion of time and timing. The movement of humans, matched up to the movement of the records of humans and their endeavours change the notion of time, timing and human behaviour.[8]

MARSHALL MCLUHAN Radio is that extension of the central nervous system that is matched only by human speech itself. Is it not worthy of our meditation that radio should be specially attuned to that primitive extension of our central nervous system, the vernacular tongue?[9]

JEAN BAUDRILLARD The non-directed interview, speech, listeners who telephone in, participation at all levels, blackmail through speech – all say: "It's your concern, you are the event, etc." More and more information is invaded by this sort of phantom content, this homeopathic graft. It is a circular set-up in which the desire of the audience is put on stage, an anti-theatre of communication.[10]

ELIAS CANETTI All questioning is a forcible intrusion. When used as an instrument of power it is like a knife cutting into the flesh of the victim. The questioner knows what there is to find, but he wants to touch it and bring it to light. He sets to work on the internal organs with the sureness of a surgeon. But he is a special kind of surgeon, one who keeps his victim alive in order to find out more about him, and, instead of anaesthetizing, deliberately stimulates pain in certain organs in order to find out what he wants to know about the rest of the body.[11]

MILAN KUNDERA

The only person who had ever really interrogated her was her husband, and that was because love is a constant interrogation. In fact, I don't know a better definition of love. Which means that no one loves us better than the police, . . . and I wouldn't be surprised if lonely people secretly yearn to be taken in for cross-examination from time to time to give them somebody to talk to about their lives.[12]

EMILE BENVENISTE

From the utterance stems the establishment of the category of the present, and from the category of the present is born the category of time. The present is precisely the source of time. It is that presence in the world that only the speech act makes possible, since (if we reflect on this) man has no other way of living "now" at his disposition besides the possibility to realize it through the insertion of discourse in the world.[13]

DAVID WOJNAROWICZ

I'm a xerox of my former self. I am a stranger to others and to myself. I am shouting my invisible words. I am vibrating in isolation among you. I am signaling that the volume of all this is too high. I am waving. I am waving my hands. I am disappearing. I am disappearing but not fast enough.[14]

Photo Bruce Gottlieb

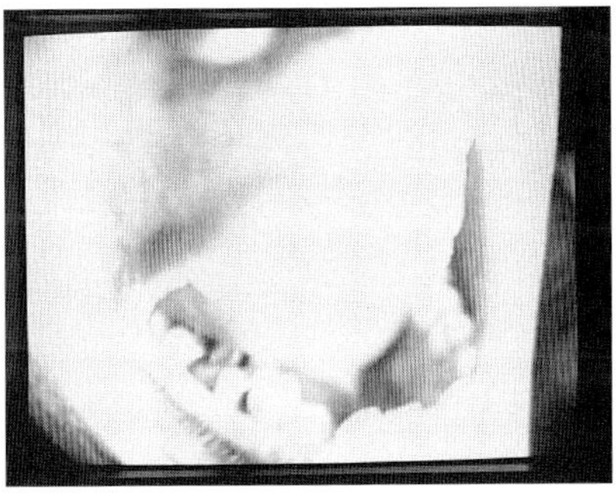

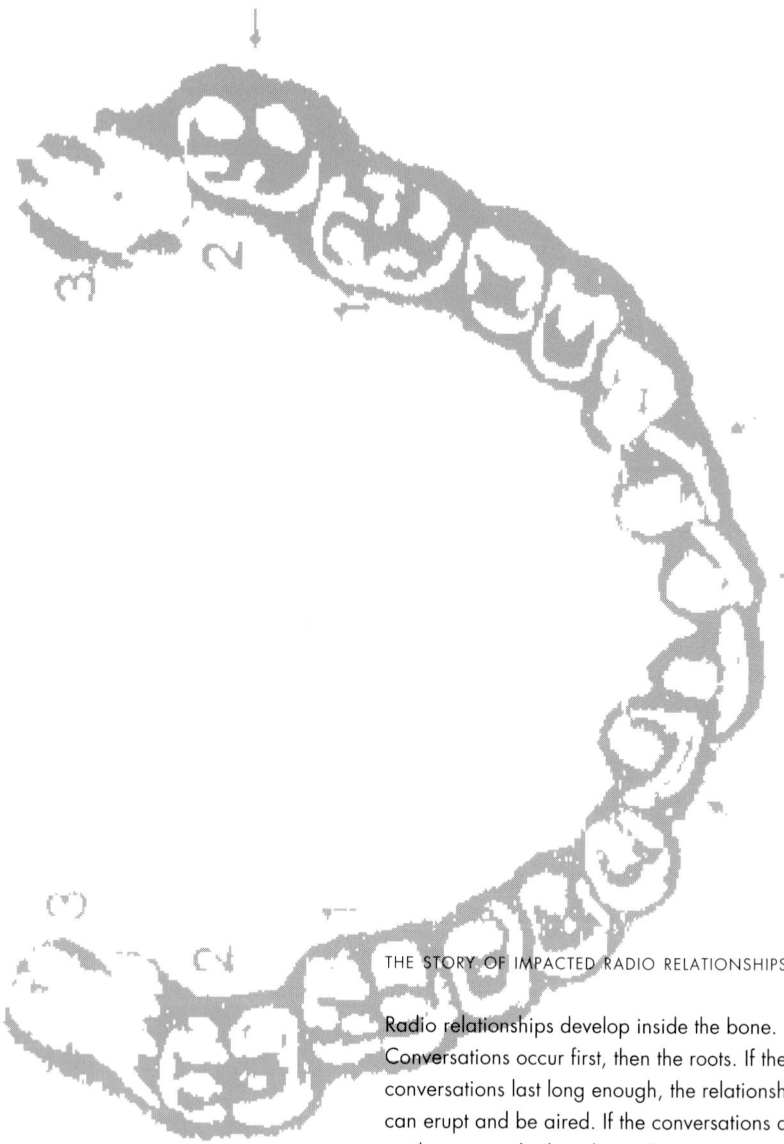

THE STORY OF IMPACTED RADIO RELATIONSHIPS

Radio relationships develop inside the bone. Conversations occur first, then the roots. If the conversations last long enough, the relationship can erupt and be aired. If the conversations are not long enough, the relationship stays impacted inside the bone. Impacted relationships can cause: *A.* Infection of the air over and above the two involved: *B.* Destruction of the next caller: *C.* Destruction of the bone by the formation of a sound: *D.* Other relationships pushed out onto the airwaves.

THE TECHNOLOGY OF ENTRAPMENT

For all of radio's broad and long-range casts, the radio booth rather resembles an implosion – a foreboding cubicle at the point of production in antithesis to an expansive space of diffusion. Wired, convoluted and cramped, the radio booth resembles an inanimate brain rather than a great communicator. Radio is constrained not only by commercial interests and governmental regulations but also by itself. The obfuscation of its apparatus is endemic.

Radio naked, stripped of its hardware, becomes radiophony, becomes metaphor. Radiophonic sites are numerous and refer not to radio's technology but to its character. The confessional is one such radio phony, a radio without transmitter. As with radio the confessional's claustral architecture exists in paradox of its far-reaching impact.

In the installation for *Radio Rethink* entitled *Open Your Mouth and Let the Air Out*, the radio booth – cranium cockpit – was transformed into a computerized and personalized confessional. A call-in radio program becomes a call-within program; a site where obsessions, absurdities, non-sequitors and frustrations find a home. Radio does not knock at your door, it lets itself in. Once in, it hunts you down with game calls, calling to air your confession.

Bound tightly in the radio confessional we – a call-in guest and me, the host – amalgamate via mimicry. Roles confuse themselves: I find myself ousted from my radio booth chair by my desire to wander in the rough terrain of conversation, controlling not even mouth and feet. Trapped into a confession, we can unravel ourselves by stumbling noisily into thousands of ears. Naked, radio becomes the in-between separating one from another. In the case of the confessional, the partition traditionally transmits sins and absolutions.

The airwaves are the ideal playground for two strangers to have an intimate conversation. You can perform a *pas de deux*, you can step on each other's toes in the imaginary confines of the radio confessional. The conversation does not have to go anywhere, like a dance, it can twirl and twine. I bored her, *You bore me*! she said. I said: *I think your voice became mine as soon as you called.*

Trapped into a radio, we sink our teeth into its electricity and find our speech running away without us.

NOTE: *The first of the following confessions is the original conversation between myself and a caller on CKUT-FM, Montréal, in the fall of 1990. Confessions two and three are composites of the responses from people who interacted with the computer in the confessional booth of the* Open Your Mouth and Let The Air Out *installation at the Walter Phillips Gallery in Banff.*

CONFESSION 1

Hello
Hello
Is that my voice? Talk! Talk!
It sounds like mine. I think your voice became mine as soon as you called.
How could that be?
Oh, some kind of relationship that began.
And does it end?
It ends as soon as you hang up.
Are you trying to tell me something?
I think so.
Should I be insulted?
You should be happy, angry, insulted.
Does that make sense what you just said? I don't think so.
What is sense?
What is what? Are you nervous?
No, but I was earlier.
I still think you're nervous, I think I know that you're nervous.
Yeah. I think you know everything about me.
Only if I want to.
Do you want to?
Not really. You don't intrigue me. Does this thing ever end?

Describe yourself.
I have knobby knees and a rib cage.
And a tattoo. I know all about it.
You do? Describe it then.
We won't get personal now.

Christof Migone's installation *Open Your Mouth and Let the Air Out* (1992) at the Walter Phillips Gallery

Photo Monte Greenshields and Cheryl Bellows

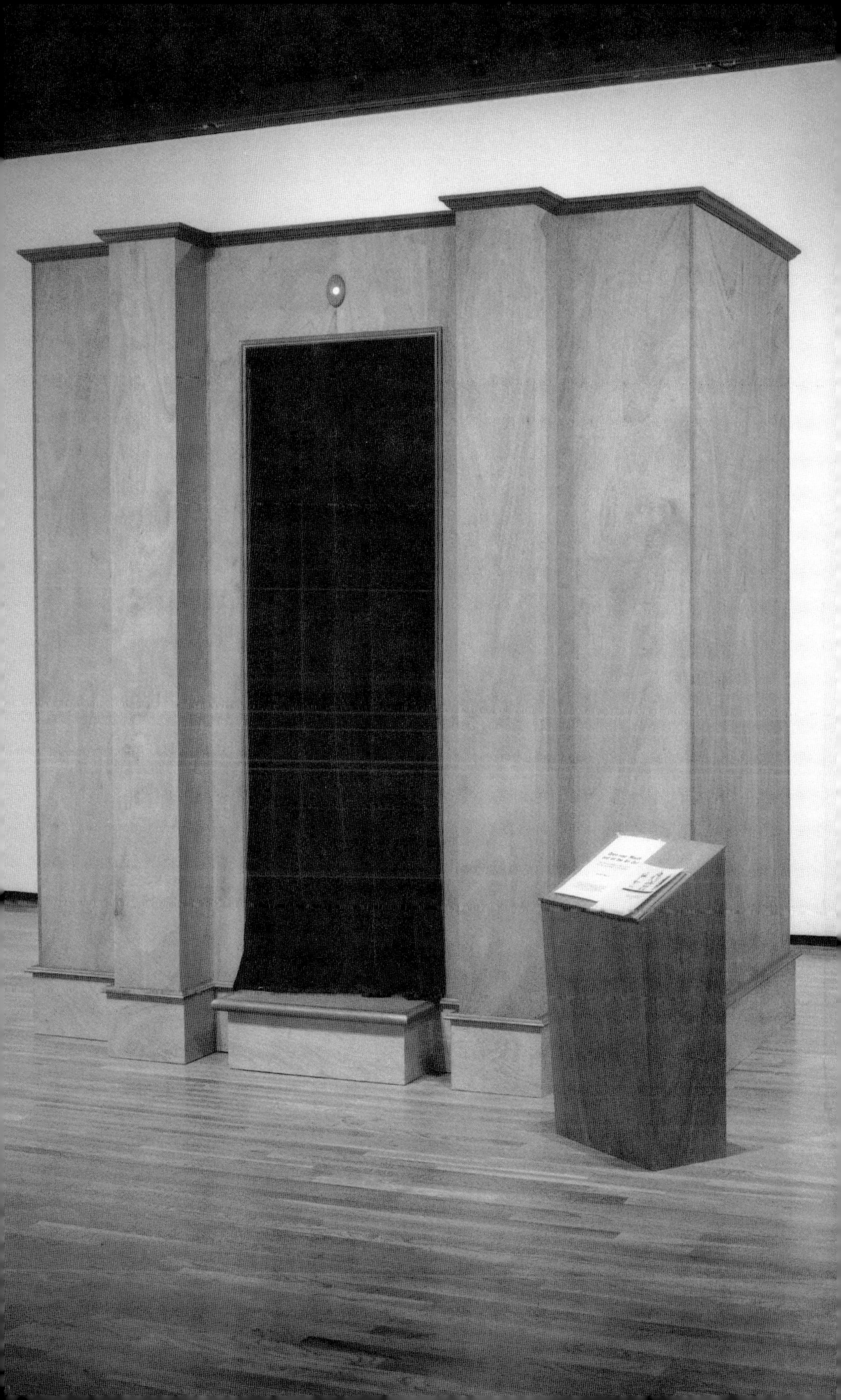

Why not?
I don't think it's the time or the place.
This is not a time nor a place.
So what is it then, if it's not a time nor a place, what exactly is it?
It's in between.
In between what? Can you be a little bit more specific? Is that where you are?
That's where I try to be, so that only few people can find me.
Who are you waiting for?
Somebody who can find a place and a time.

Who are you?
Who am I? Just another nameless, faceless being in this planet.
And . . .
There's lots to say that hasn't already been said.
That's true. It's becoming kind of empty.
Does this ever end?
It's just you and me.
Strange. It feels like I've had this conversation before. Are you still you?
No. I think I've changed.
Grown within the past minutes have you?
No. I haven't progressed or regressed, just changed.
You bore me.
Sometimes I bore myself too.
This conversation is going nowhere.
I agree. Goodnight.

CONFESSION 2

Testing one, two, three . . .
Is that my voice? Talk! Talk!
It's been three years since my last confession.
How could that be?
I suppose I should have gone to church, but I didn't.
And does it end?
Anxiety, money, anxiety.
Are you trying to tell me something?
Totally abstract you.

Should I be insulted?
I spread the Ritz Cracker with peanut butter.
Does that make sense what you just said? I don't think so.
Oh, sorry.
What is what? Are you nervous?
No, but I was earlier.
I still think you're nervous, I think I know that you're nervous.
What about you?
Only if I want to.
Do you want to?
Not really. You don't intrigue me. Does this thing ever end?

Describe yourself.
What do you want to know about me?
And a tattoo. I know all about it.
Can you hear me?
We won't get personal now.
Why not?
I don't think it's the time or the place.
I don't know what to do about that.
So what is it then, if it's not a time nor a place, what exactly is it?
Revisit the spots I once knew.
Can you be a little bit more specific? Is that where you are?
This is off the topic, but I saw *My Private Idaho*, which is really bizarre.
Who are you waiting for?
The idea as it dissipates.

What about you?
Who am I? Just another nameless, faceless being in this planet.
I wonder if there's somebody in there doing this.
There's lots to say that hasn't already been said.
You won't listen, it's your fault.
Does this ever end?
The idea as it dissipates.
Strange. It feels like I've had this conversation before. Are you still you?
We're all us.
Grown within the past minutes have you?

I'm just a generic type fellow.
You bore me.
Who's the artist who put this together?
This conversation is going nowhere.
Aren't you going to tell us a story?

CONFESSION 3

I don't hear anyone . . . oh, I see a light now.
Is that my voice? Talk! Talk!
Show me the on button.
How could that be?
What does that mean?
And does it end?
You're talking to me or am I hearing your confession?
Are you trying to tell me something?
Totally abstract you.
Should I be insulted?
No, you should not be insulted.
Does that make sense what you just said? I don't think so.
There is somebody in there isn't there?
Are you nervous?
No, but I was earlier.
I still think you're nervous, I think I know that you're nervous.
Can you describe yourself?
Only if I want to.
Are you nervous, really?
Not really. You don't intrigue me. Does this thing ever end?

Describe yourself.
I feel like a comedian or something.
And a tattoo. I know all about it.
No way.
We won't get personal now.
Why not?
I don't think it's the time or the place.
I don't know what to do about that.
So what is it then, if it's not a time nor a place, what exactly is it?

Looks like a confessional.
Can you be a little bit more specific? Is that where you are?
It's very interesting here.
Who are you waiting for?
Is this a dialogue with a computer or is this a dialogue with other people?

Um . . . yeah, um so how are you doing today? Yeah, this is wild.
Who am I? Just another nameless, faceless being in this planet.
Weird, some chick just said who am I?
There's lots to say that hasn't already been said.
It's becoming rather metaphysical.
Does this ever end?
Did you say something?
Strange. It feels like I've had this conversation before. Are you still you?
No way.
Grown within the past minutes have you?
We all need contact, we all need communication.
You bore me.
Oh, sorry.
This conversation is going nowhere.
See ya later.

I would like to thank Henry See for the HyperCard script, Bruce Gottlieb for the video, Pierre LeFebre for the kneeler, and Mimmo Maiolo for the construction

Notes

1 John Cage, *For the Birds* (London: Marion Boyars Publishers, 1981), 148.
2 Ibid.
3 Ibid.
4 Raymonde, transcribed from audio material used in *Open Your Mouth and Let the Air Out* installation.
5 Erik Satie in *The Recording Angel*, ed. Evan Eisenberg (New York: Viking Penguin, 1987), 75.
6 Bertolt Brecht, "Radio as a Means of Communication: A Talk of the Function of Radio," *Screen* 20:3/4 (Winter 1979–80), 24–25.
7 Diana Burgoyne quoted in *Siting Technology* (Banff, Alberta: Walter Phillips Gallery, 1988), 37.
8 Sol Yurick, *Metatron* (New York: Semiotext(e) Foreign Agents, 1985), 156.

9 Marshall McLuhan, *Understanding Media: The Extensions of Man* (Toronto: McGraw-Hill, 1965), 302.

10 Jean Baudrillard, "Implosion of Meaning in the Media," *In the Shadow of the Silent Majorities* (New York: Semiotext(e) Foreign Agents, 1983), 98.

11 Elias Canetti in Jean-Jacques Lecercle, *The Violence of Language* (New York: Routledge, 1990), 46.

12 Milan Kundera, *Book of Laughter and Forgetting* (New York: Penguin, 1981), 163.

13 Emile Benveniste in Giorgio Agomben, *Language and Death* (Minneapolis: University of Minnesota Press, 1991), 36.

14 David Wojnarowicz, "Spiral," *Artforum* (March 1992), 100.

Anita Rocamora inside the confessional booth of Christof Migone's *Open Your Mouth and Let the Air Out* (1992) at the Walter Phillips Gallery

Photo Monte Greenshields and Cheryl Bellows

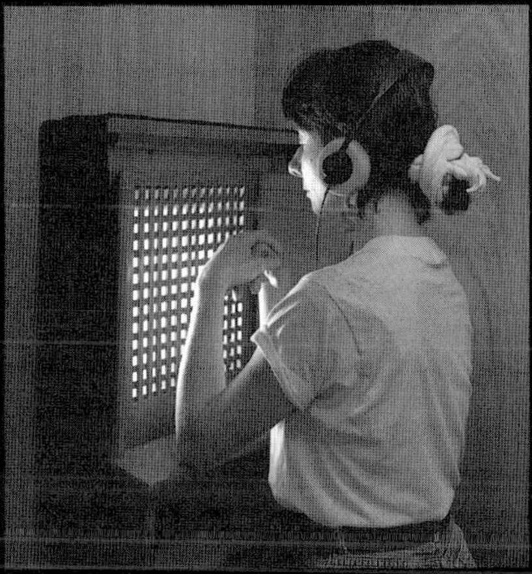

The Geometry of Silence

Heidi Grundmann

As I write this (expanded) English version of a text originally written for a symposium in Vienna[1] *there is silence on the radio:* Folie/Culture (1989–91), *a piece by Jocelyn Robert*[2] *aired on RADIA 89.9 in Banff as part of* Radio Rethink, *contains soundless elements – silences – that force each listener, wherever he or she may be, to become conscious of the sounds in the immediate surroundings.*

It is certainly not by chance that the *Radio Rethink* station-identification is announced as RADIA 89.9.[3] *La Radia* is the title of a Futurist manifesto published by Filippo Tommaso Marinetti and Pino Masnata in October 1933 in *La Gazetta del Popolo.*[4] According to one analysis, this significant article

> emphasized the new sensibility that Marinetti felt was inherent in modern experience. Sound waves, creatively used, could offer a "universal cosmic human art." This was a world without "time, space, yesterday and tomorrow." Futurist radio art would utilize the characteristics of the medium. Interference, static and the "geometry of silence" could play a part in the general Futurist overturning of conventional values.[5]

Seen today, *La Radia* – and other Futurist manifestoes – possess an iconic force: they are statements about the contemporary world, images of the industrial age, that have changed the world entirely. Inside the Futurist manifestoes we find ideas very close to those sought today by philosophers and media theorists to describe the state of a society which is characterized by the rapid development of electronic technology. The

Futurists were able to "see" the image of a worldwide network of distributed electricity just as well as they "saw" the image of the crisis of time-space in today's telecommunications. Moreover, informed by utopian enthusiasms about predicted technologies which, in their opinion, required a rethinking of all cultural attitudes, the Futurists were able to develop in their writings such as *La Radia* the image and concept of an art that they themselves could not put into practice. Even now – when the predicted technologies are all around us – anything resembling the concept of art formulated in the Marinetti/Masnata manifesto has been, at best, only partially realized and, if so, only by that small group of people who still (sometimes reluctantly) call themselves artists, for the lack of a better word. The activities of these people – who come not only from the visual arts but from music, literature and even technology – have often very little in common with the notions of art propagated by the traditional art institutions and their constituting and legitimizing forces. The traditional meaning of concepts such as the author, the piece/work of art, the original, the object, the medium, and so on, are constantly and consciously challenged by the practices of those artists, who confront the conditions of postindustrial society and situate their work in the immaterial space of new communications technologies. Radio, as one of the ever-changing media that collect, store, manipulate and radiate data, serves some of these artists as one possible site and/or object for activity.

Marinetti, together with fellow Futurist Fortunato Depero, made a first radio broadcast in Milan in 1933.[6] There is no recording of this broadcast, which was devoted to phonetic poetry, or other broadcasts: we know Marinetti's voice only from the records he made. In 1934 Depero published *Liriche Radiofoniche*, poetry especially created for the new medium: Marinetti himself left the scores for a few pieces of his radio art which were reconstructed in the 1970s.[7] These *Cinque Sintesi dal Teatro Radiofonico* demonstrate an understanding of the medium that goes much further than its definition as a distribution medium for phonetic poetry or compositions, including noise. This is indicated in the titles of the *Sintesi*, which were not realized by Marinetti simply because the necessary radio technology had not yet been developed: *Un Paesaggio Udito* (A Soundscape), *I Silenzi Parlano Tra Loro* (The Silences Talk to Each Other), *Battaglia di Ritmi* (Battle of Rhythms), *La Costruzione di un Silenzio* (The Construction of a Silence) and, lastly, *Dramma di Distanze* (Drama of Distances). The scores for the *Sintesi* read (approximately): "ten seconds of dishwashing, one second of rustling, eight seconds of dishwashing" or "forty seconds of pure silence, 'do' by a trumpet, crying of a doll, eleven seconds of pure silence; ooooo! surprise of an eleven-year old girl." In scores like this, Marinetti underlines the character of sounds and/or recorded information as material, a strategy that continues – even after all these years – to play an important role in media art, especially now with the advent of digital equipment such as the sampler. In addition, if, as in *The Construction of a Silence*, he constructs a terrace open on two sides using recorded sounds, he displays a very sculptural concern with sound and radio. It is this sculptural concern that makes it possible for artists today to conceive of their work with new technologies as art in the electronic or digital space. In his *Drama of Distances* Marinetti anticipates a worldwide net of live radio lines (eleven seconds of a military march played in Rome, eleven seconds of tango danced in Santos, eleven seconds of Japanese religious music performed in Tokyo and so on). In other words, Marinetti works with the specific characteristics of the radio medium, its lines and channels, its mix of live and recorded material, its ability to be in many places simultaneously. By using network-like images and concepts, as in *Drama of Distances*, Marinetti can be seen from today's standpoint as referring to newer communication technologies such as electronic mail and conferencing systems. Friedemann Malsch has pointed out that the manifesto *La Radia* would be too narrowly interpreted if only related to the medium of radio, which in Italian is also called "radio" and not "radia." "The wordplay in the title of the manifesto relates much more to the way radio functions – by transmitting radiating waves – than to the institution *radio*."[8] If *La Radia* anticipates television, this anticipation is very relevant today because, as Malsch shows, television in the context of this Futurist manifesto is one of several metaphors for an electronic culture, as it has been described much later by Marshall McLuhan. In this culture of *La Radia* we now discern a dissolving of the media, as this press release for the meeting of the heads of several international computer manufacturers in Vienna, 1991, suggests:

> Newspapers, magazines, books, radio, TV will just be different contents. They will have one common node: the personal computer, which via powerful dataline networks will plug us into global gathering points of information.[9]

It is again the manifestoes of the Futurists that contributed formulations of "the socially already existent and aesthetically intended *'confusion des differences entre les disciplines de l'image, de l'écrit et du son'* of many artists of the avantgarde,"[10] long before this "confusion" was contained in (computer) technology itself.

Contemporary radio art defines itself within issues raised by the Futurist manifestoes. The development of a sound language, of new narratives, does continue but such approaches reside in a tradition established before the digital revolution. This was the special brand of European Public Radio that supported the development of artists in Neues Hörspiel, electroacoustic music and the radio program *Ars Acustica*, all of which contributed to notions of the avant-garde at the beginning of the century – albeit mostly within the traditional framework of the "original work" by an "author," with a copyright and, most significantly, within the conventional definition of radio as a specific medium in its own right. Self-referentiality was more or less a problem of acoustic art or audio art – art for the ear – and did not necessarily carry any wider notions about communications technology or cultural change in general.

However, there is another form of radio art that is only incidentally related to the ear. This art deals with the public space of radio as one among many that, together, constitute an electronic space. Rapidly becoming a digital space, this construction envelops the world and reaches out into orbit. Artists working in this realm, in which radio is just one point of reference, are not so much concerned with the recording and representation of sound or music as with the delineation, by using its lines and channels, of electronic/digital space itself. For these artists, radio art cannot be reduced to program slots devoted to *Ars Acustica* nor to the many different forms assumed by the institutions of radio under the different national broadcasting laws and even pirate radio. Radio art, in the tradition of *La Radia*, is less concerned with sound than with transmission, the radiation of data – ham radio, CB radio, surveillance transmitters, electronic warfare, television, picturephone, taxi radios and many others.

In *Radio/Zeit* (Radio/Time), a performance for the Styrian Autumn Festival and ÖRF *KunstRadio/RadioKunst* in Graz in 1988, Richard Kriesche underlined this contemporary definition of radio art by bringing the line signals of a weather satellite into his studio in Graz. The signals triggered a keyboard to play Mozart's *Eine Kleine Nachtmusik*; at the same time the signals were represented as a weather map projected onto the wall. In the darkened studio the artist sat by a lamp in the mixed light of this projection, reading a text on radio art that was completely unintelligible for the audience. With unassisted human ears, the audience could not differentiate between the voice of the artist, the white transmission noise and the music from the keyboard. An image developed that underlined the fact that "the digital representation of form loses its identity as form and . . . digital recording media do not give up their content without appropriate decoding technology."[11] A mix of excerpts from Kriesche's text and recordings of *Eine Kleine Nachtmusik* was broadcast later, but the real piece of radio art was the performance itself. It was a striking image of our situation – immersed in and surrounded by the white noise of transmitted data.

In autumn 1991, Richard Kriesche developed his *Radio/Zeit* project even further and organized *ARTSAT*, another project that delineated the electronic/digital space of communications technology as the site of a contemporary non-object-oriented art in the public space. Kriesche managed to get an art project accepted for inclusion with the projects and experiments to be carried out by the first Austrian cosmonauts to travel in space aboard the Soviet MIR space station. This was an artwork using radio as a technique and strategy to connect and control populations of electronic systems in the mostly militarily defined extraterrestrial space. To make and keep his project visible amidst the patriotic drumbeating of the media, Kriesche appropriated social and artistic clichés, for example, transmitting a live message from the Austrian cosmonaut, as his orbit carried him over eastern Central Europe in the MIR space station, to a television studio in Graz.

This message, sent via a ham radio device, triggered a synthesizer to play the Blue Danube waltz, directed an industrial robot to weld a pattern onto a huge steel disc and was also recorded on audio tape. The tape was mailed to ten Austrian composers who turned the data of the message into short compositions that were aired first on *KunstRadio* and then published as a compact disc. The compact disc is an audio (and visual) counterpart to the huge welded disc that has in the meantime become a public monument. The project had many layers, the most important of which was perhaps that Kriesche succeeded in getting, at very short notice, a live national television program on a Sunday morning that lasted exactly as long as the full MIR orbit – one hour and thirteen minutes. The project also made clear that a profound change had taken place in recent years in art, especially an art positioned in public (electronic) space. For instance, Christina Weiss could write in 1984: "the artist . . . used sign material, communications material with the aim of sharpening the 'critical' glance of the reader . . . and by that to make the manipulative behaviour of everyday information media more transparent."[12] After the Gulf War and media events such as the "revolution" in Romania, everyone knows about the manipulative behaviour of the everyday information media. Attempts by artists to critically "make visible" the mechanisms of the media often end up in the involuntary affirmation of media structures and contents. In this situation many artists have consciously adopted affirmative strategies; their art is concerned with the balance between its own visibility and disappearance. Well-defined roles may be appropriated, disguises adopted, fictions created, just to balance barely perceptible forms of appearance and the sensation of drowning in the white noise of data.

The hollowness of concepts such as author, work, object, original, (knowing) sender and (learning) receiver, the dissolution of disciplines and media have been proclaimed again and again by individual artists and art movements. However, artists' work has constantly been defused and undermined by the art market, art history and art museums – and even now, when these concepts have been irrevocably built into the technological fabric of our society, we witness, in catalogues, exhibitions, art magazines and art fairs, a series of rescue operations for the traditional concepts of an object-oriented art.

"Everything I decide to record belongs to me and I can do with it whatever I please," says Australian radio artist Rick Rue whose strategies are "appropriation and piracy."[13] The Austrian/Swiss group Radio SubCom calls a very similar working method the "recycling of clichés." Everything that can be recorded and stored becomes material or fragments of material that can immediately be changed into something quite unrecognizable. Altered and manipulated fragments can be merged with fragments recorded and stored at other times and other places into ever-changing mosaics, which in turn can be transmitted to become material of a new and completely different form. "If we create a digital analogy or representation of something, this representation is subject to the logic of the host system and no longer belongs to the logic of the former context."[14] Material, cut off from any original context, is stored in the databank of culture, floating in a permanent value-free present or non-time and non-space. If there is an appropriate decoding technology (including electricity), the stored data can be called upon everywhere and be put into any historical, political or art context. The data can become "an art that passes down phone lines, that proliferates as invisible electromagnetic waves that can be broadcast."[15] Such an art demands a different model of communication than the hierarchical one of an artist creator on one side and a (passive) recipient on the other who must be in an "adequate attitude" or receiving mode. As Roy Ascott suggests,

> In telematic art, meaning/content is no longer something which is created by the artist, then distributed through the network and received by the recipient. Meaning is rather the result of an interaction between the observer/participant and the system, the content of which is in a state of flux, of endless change and transformation. In this state of uncertainty and instability the content becomes . . . embodied in data which themselves are immaterial – pure difference – until it is reconstituted at the interface as image, text or sound.[16]

There are artists who, especially if they work for a mass medium like radio, renounce their copyright and do not care whether their name is mentioned or not. Some of them produce works with variable beginnings and endings (or no beginnings and endings at all) so that the pieces fold into the flow of radio, sometimes surfacing to catch the attention of a listener only to dissolve again into the background of other radio sounds. Work of this kind is not usually comfortable in the increasing number of gallery-like programs (such as *KunstRadio*) that public radio stations in Europe dedicate to radio art. This type of work tends to seek a place in the public space of everyday radio broadcasting – popular music, regional and local programs. Of course, as with works in physical urban space, the users of that space will exercise their rights to comment on, debate and eventually make decisions about the sculpture, artwork or radio art in their territory. Artists who want to position their work in the public space of the mass media must employ similar strategies, patience, strength of concept as in any other public space.

The following examples of an art in the public space of the broadcasting medium radio indicate, together with the other projects described above, the range of possibilities this space offers to artists. In 1989, during the Ars Electronica Festival in Linz, Chris Mann, Australian performance and radio artist, philosopher and writer, had the listeners of the regional radio tell dog stories interspersed with the usual daily programs. The dog stories could be sent by cassette or phoned in and they were broadcast in their original form without commentary.

One of the radio art projects that was most successful in infiltrating the public space of radio was Bill Fontana's *Landscape Soundings* a co-production between *KunstRadio* in 1990 – representing the ÖRF (Austrian Broadcasting Corporation) – and the Vienna Festival. Fontana used both analogue and digital technology to have sounds transmitted into the centre of Vienna from microphones carefully positioned about thirty kilometres away in the Danube marshes. This was a politically sensitive site (the *Stopfenreiter Au)* because it was the scene of mass protests and sit-ins which, several years earlier, had saved the marshes from destruction by a hydroelectric project. The ÖPT (Austrian Post and Telecommunications – the state communications monopoly) installed sixteen lines from the marshes to a nearby village, reactivated sixteen old disused telephone lines and connected them to the new ÖRF digital microwave transmission equipment (newly purchased for remote television sports reports) which had been mounted on a farm for line-of-sight transmission to Vienna. The sounds from the microphones in the marshes were converted to video signals for digital transmission to the ÖPT Kahlenberg relay station, a high point in the Vienna Woods, and from there to the roof of the Kunsthistorische Museum in Vienna and, finally, down to an improvised studio in the museum. The digital signals were then changed back into analogue and distributed live to seventy loudspeakers installed in shrubbery and topiary of the Maria Theresia Platz, a formal garden (with a statue of Maria Theresia) and on the façades of the Kunsthistorische Museum and Naturhistorische Museum which flank the park. A spectacular live sound sculpture unfolded (twenty-four hours per day without interruption) for two weeks. The work had another dimension: the signals from the sixteen lines went into a stereo mixer and at the same time were transmitted in stereo to the radio station. Bill Fontana controlled the live mix both in the park and for the radio, at all times – either personally or by means of a "score" based on his intimate knowledge of what sounds would arrive when and on which lines.

Originally Fontana was to do two forty-five minute live mixes for the *KunstRadio* program on Thursday evening during the event and produce short live mixes on the same days for other programs on *Österreich 1*, the

ÖRF cultural program, as a kind of introduction to the longer *KunstRadio* mixes. But very soon, program makers at all three channels of the ÖRF started to tune into the live line, which was open twenty-four hours a day, and to incorporate the real-time sounds of frogs, birds, water, thunderstorms, and rain into their broadcasts. By the end of the fortnight, the piece became so popular that the radio director decided to have the last five minutes of the sculpture transmitted live on all three channels of Austrian Radio.

An increasing number of artists, like Fontana, consider their radio work as sculpture, not in the sense of transmitting sound sculptures but rather as a delineation of sculpture itself. Austrian sculptor and conceptual artist Gottfried Bechtold makes it very clear that his radio sculptures exist for the duration of the transmission, the sound travelling from the transmitter to all the places where a listener is located and thereby defining a sculpture. It ought to be mentioned here, as Robert Adrian X has pointed out,[17] that it was conceptual art which made it possible to conceive of an electronic space at all. Artists like Lawrence Weiner and, in Austria, Gottfried Bechtold have made it possible to consider the radio (broadcast) space as a public sculptural space in which music, sound and language are the material of sculptures. In the same way that Jocelyn Robert sends out silences that make listeners aware of the environment, Bill Fontana sees his radio work as developing into individual sculptures for each listener as the broadcast sounds mix with the environment of each listener wherever she or he may be. With such works it becomes very obvious that the author has no means of knowing the actual shape of the piece. The artist knows only that, at the moment of transmission, the sounds will be perceived by a dispersed audience simultaneously. There is no way of knowing in what spaces the transmitted sounds are mingled with other material or whether the listener is paying any attention at all. This element of dispersal becomes even more obvious in artistic events that make use of e-mail networks or conferencing systems. Since his first involvement with network projects in the late 1970s, Roy Ascott has used the term "distributed/dispersed authorship" for events of this kind. Software such as HyperCard or HyperText facilitates the development of non-linear and, in their sequence, unrepeatable narrative forms, in which again the relationship between author and user is changed to such a degree that the user becomes an active co-author. Under such conditions a work of art cannot be experienced as a closed or neatly repeatable original by either the author/participant nor the user/co-author/participant. The piece grows in many different places simultaneously and is kept in a state of flux by the cooperation of many unknown people, who comprise anything but a traditional "audience."

An art of this kind, which demands the cooperation of experts in a variety of disciplines, is difficult to grasp for theoretical analysis and classification in the traditional sense. On the other hand the artists themselves must be knowledgeable about theory in order to position their work in electronic space. In order to approach an understanding of this type of work, new forms of documentation, theory and criticism will have to be developed that not only pay attention to the last stage of the work but observe the entire process of the development of a project as well as the role that the artist plays in this development. The critic and theoretician may have to become a user, an active participant in such a piece of art and, like the artist/initiator and all the other participants, will have to work from the memory of his or her personal experience when evaluating a piece that cannot be reproduced, reconstructed or repeated.

Notes

1 Heidi Grundmann, "Die Geometrie des Schweigens," paper presented at the symposium, The Geometry of Silence, November 1991, at Museum moderner Kunst Stiftung Ludwig Wien in Vienna.

2 Published on compact disc by RéR MEGACOR in London, England, 1991.

3 The name was given to the transmission frequency when it was first used in 1987.

4 An English translation can be found in *Wireless Imagination: Sound, Radio and the Avant-Garde*, ed. Douglas Kahn and Gregory Whitehead (Boston: MIT Press, 1992), 265.

5 Caroline Tisdall and Angelo Bozzolla, *Futurism* (London: Thames and Hudson, 1977).

6 In 1927 "Sonate in Urlauten" by Schwitters was broadcast by Süddeutscher Rundfunk, Germany.

7 Gianni Gitti and Odersa Rubini in *Harpos Bazaar*, Bologna.

8 Friedemann Malsch, in *Vom Verschwinden der Ferne: Telekommunikation und Kunst*, ed. Edith Decker and Peter Weibel (Köln: DuMont Buchverlag, 1990).

9 Press release issued for meeting of heads of international electronic corporations, Vienna, 1991.

10 Gianni Gitti and Odersa Rubini.

11 Simon Penny, *Simulation, Digitization, Interaction: Implications of Computing in the Arts* (Sydney, 1986), n.p.
12 Christina Weiss, "Seh-Texte," (Zirndorf: Verlag für moderne Kunst, 1984).
13 Rick Rue interview by Heidi Grundmann for *KunstRadio*, ÖRF, Vienna, 1989.
14 Simon Penny.
15 Ibid.
16 Roy Ascott, "Beyond Time-Based Art – ESP, PDP & PU," in *ZEIT*, special issue of the magazine *Sterz* (Graz 1990).
17 Robert Adrian X, "Im Netz der Systeme," *Kunstforum* 103 (September/October 1989).

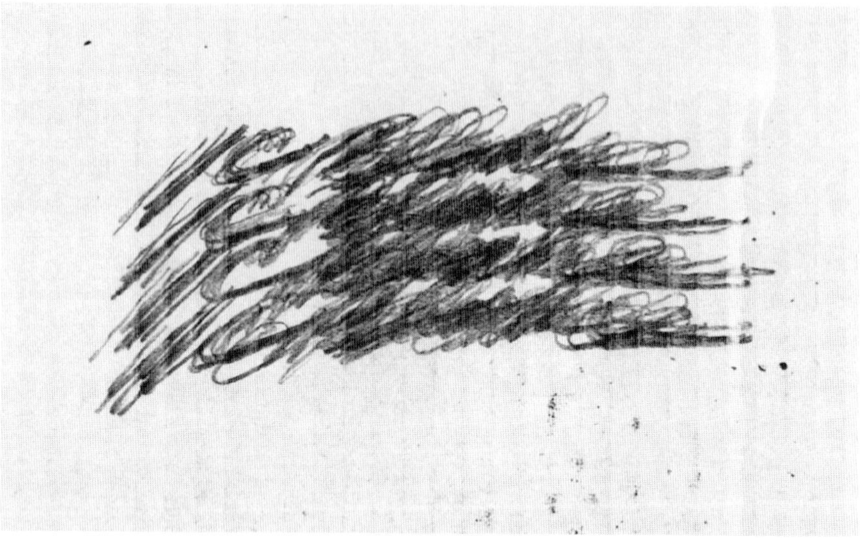

Sound Signatures

Rober Racine

Handwriting possesses a rhythm, a cadence, a sound all its own. When writing, each individual creates a unique music. Writing on paper, slate or heavy cardboard with felt pen, graphite pencil, chalk or charcoal stick creates new tones that resonate with acoustical precision.

The visible side of writing conceals its invisible side: sound.

Writing is an intimate and private activity. We are reluctant to show others our handwritten manuscripts; in this, modesty seems to have the upper hand. It is even more rare for us to draw attention to handwriting's aural images. This is what prompted me to compose *Sound Signatures*.

In 1992, twenty-two people filed into the Banff Centre's Electroacoustic Recording Studio (EARS) to record their signatures. During the recordings, each of which lasted approximately two minutes, participants were provided with a variety of pencils and papers.

The result was a peculiar work. Something organic and animal-like began to take shape. One could have been listening to the scratching of some unknown insect.

It is particularly gripping to hear the piece over a sound system, to witness the acoustic expansion of a secret, intimate and barely audible world. The writing lives and breathes, moves about inside the space. It, not us, leads the way. The air becomes charged with a multitude of textures and rhythms. A new facet of the signatory's personality emerges. Some people sign their names quite rapidly, while others take more time. The signature of some is smooth, calm and serene; that of others is aggressive. At times one almost detects a frenetic race against time.

Much is due to the choice of writing instrument. Charcoal offers a polyphony of voices that is at the same time high and solemn, and incredibly rich. Graphite is essentially monotone. Felt pen is also polyphonic, yet it emits harsh tones punctuated by squeaks. Heavy paper or cardboard generates muffled vibrations in contrast to thin, delicate papers that resound in a sharp, clear register.

Add to all this a wide variety of rhythms and tempos. The word *contrapuntal,* for example, does not have the same rhythm as the word *sound.* Thus, writing the word *contrapuntal* with graphite pencil, felt pen, charcoal stick, chalk or fountain pen on different papers will result in as many sound images. It is as if one could play the same melody on the piano, horn, bassoon and violin.

It is, therefore, possible to orchestrate handwriting for specific instruments. One could compose a quartet or a piece for thirty or forty different pens and pencils.

One can talk of *sonography* just as one talks of choreography. The possibilities are endless.

When broadcast on radio, however, the work takes on another dimension. It resembles a faint whispering, a gentle presence that reconnects with the original intimacy of the handwriting. Doubtless because the medium of radio is itself solitary and secretive.

Radio is not, of course, suited to the world of orchestras and symphonies. It is first and foremost the incarnation of a privileged listening experience, a sort of confidant. Sound writing and radio may be seen to converge in that both draw upon each other's intimacy for the expression of a mild polyphony.

Photos on pages 140 and 143 to 148 Monte Greenshields

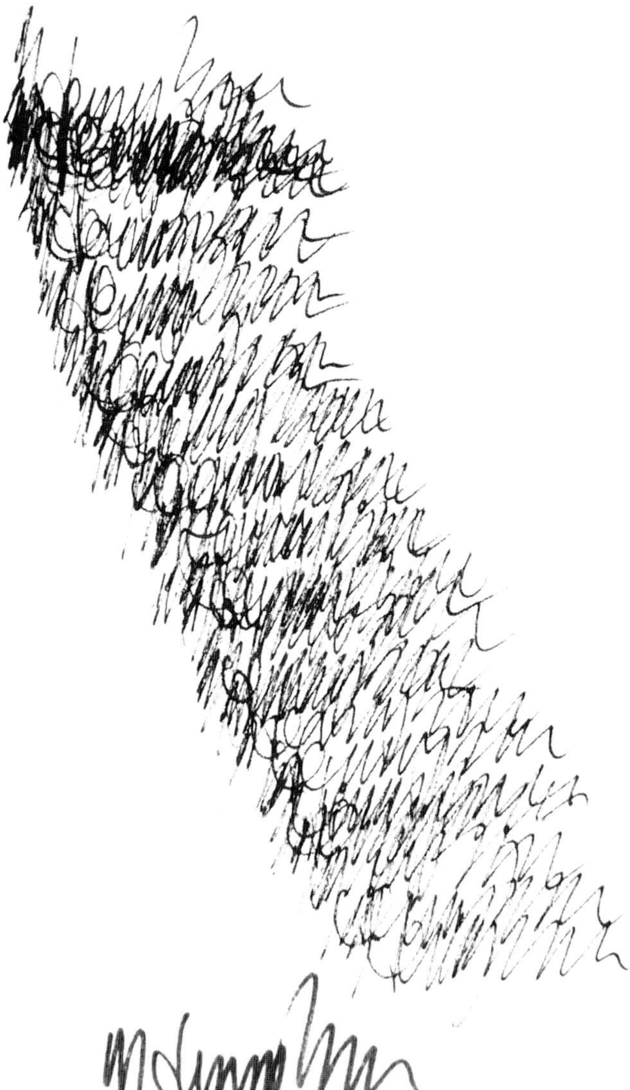

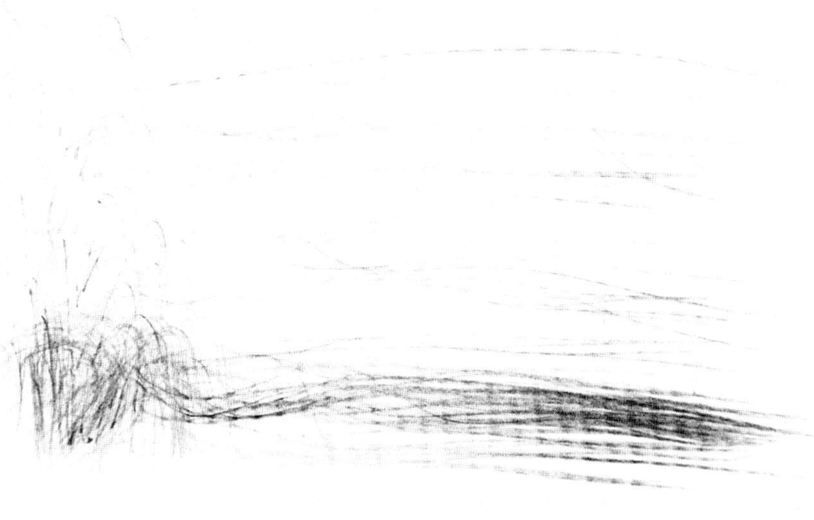

LUCE LUCE
LUCE LUCY LUCY
LUCY LUCY
LUCY LUCY LUCY
LUCY LUCY LUCY

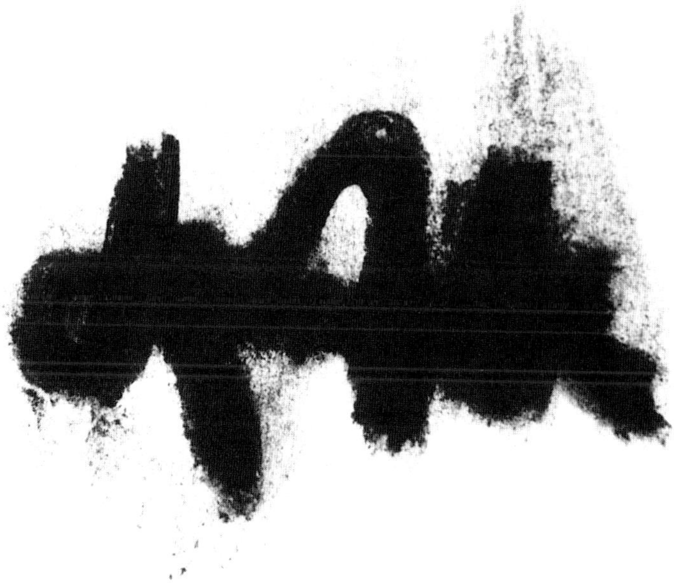

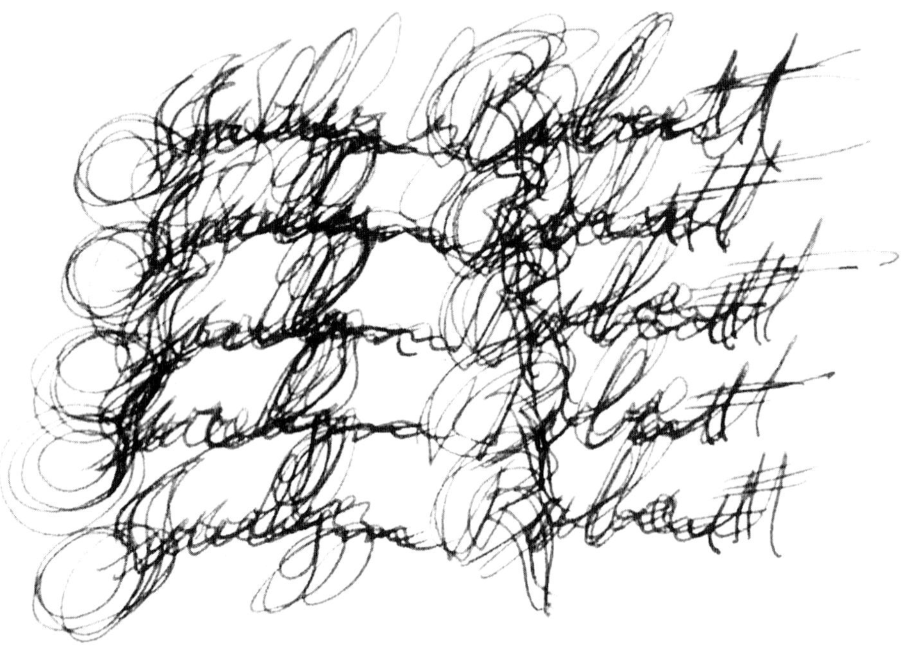

Holes in the Head

THEATRES OF OPERATION FOR THE BODY IN PIECES

Gregory Whitehead

Since my earliest radio experience listening to a small transistor throb beneath my pillow in the dead of night, I have been struck by radio's profoundly split identity. Into one ear plays the happy folk band of Radio Utopia, brainwaves and radiowaves mixed into a grand electromagnetic community: *I dream of a time when everybody on the planet lives, breathes and touches each other on air*. Whilst into the other ear, a different band marches on, the trigger-finger crash band of Radio Thanatos, with its twisted carnage of countless broadcast aircraft rattling with great gusto, straight into oblivion.

In time, I have come to realize that the two bands are as inseparable as a pair of ears stuck on a single head, with radio's dreamland promise forever haunted by lethal ghostland interference. Incorporating the promise of universal communication bound together with the more immediate prospect of irreversible decay, the radiobody is a strange and unruly composite of opposites: speaking to everyone abstractly but no one in particular; ubiquitous, but fading without a trace; forever crossing boundaries but with uncertain destination; capable of intimate communion but charged with enough power to trigger sudden destruction. It comes as no surprise, then, that some of the more notorious early proposals for radio should be populated by so many zombies and aliens, limbo dancing, inside out: Khlebnikov's lightning birds, Marinetti and his pure organism of radiophonic sensation, Welles and his bellicose Martians, Artaud's body without organs.

If radio is to retain any cultural identity at all in the infomediate age of fibre optics and data highways, radio makers must find ways to exceed and disrupt the restrictive conceptual boundaries of "sound art." For while radio *happens* in sound, sound is no longer what matters about radio. What does matter is the endlessly intricate play of position, a play that unfolds among far-flung beings, for the most part unknown to each other: bodies and antibodies, living and dead, the scratched and the remembered, floating mouth and severed ear, screams and incantations, songs and parasites, all on parade, destination unknown.

What I propose, then, is a passage from the "theatre of sounds" to the "theatre of operations": a theatre for the body in pieces, for *organs without bodies* in search of a place to settle, a theatre born from (and for) *holes in the head*, an outcast theatre of crossed circuits and hot wires, offering both a sanctuary and a colloquium for our most committed schizophonics, the assorted monsters and marvels of the digital age.

LEAKS

Successive generations of technology do not so much displace as *digest* each other. Marinetti understood this very well, and urged his Futurist comrades to cook the books so as to facilitate digestion. Churning through several generations of media, such digestion is never complete: dissect a radio and you will find the remains of a book; dissect the book and you will find the remains of a larynx; dissect the larynx and you will find the skeletal trace of a twitching finger lighting a match and sending a telegram; take the prints from the finger and there you will rediscover the origins of radio.

All the above stages of digestion do produce one thing in common – gas leaks, from one hole or another. What we usually classify as "interference" is in fact the direct acoustic representation of leaking gas, the potentially explosive product of radiophonic digestion. This gas, a natural product of the radiobody digesting itself (time decay through weak signal processing), is a key material for radio art, and is best stored in glass bottles with cork stoppers.

Example: In 1984, I conducted an interview with a retired businessman named Steven V. N. Powelson for inclusion within my radio docufiction *Dead Letters*. Powelson's ambition for the remaining years of his life was to become the first individual ever to recite by memory the entire *Iliad* in the original Greek. A curious ambition, given the status of the *Iliad* as a consensual transcription of group performance most probably enacted over several nights; now it would be recited by one individual in a dead language learned through a book, in a single rapid-fire endurance monologue. The idea only makes sense if you read backwards in time. Even more curious was his motive, "to achieve immortality by attaching myself to a poem that is itself immortal."

By having the whole text written into his own body at once, Powelson believed (and I suppose still believes) that he could essentially become one with the body of the text. But since there is no "original" recording of the *Iliad*, Powelson would memorize by listening to his own book-on-tape. Because the text is full of difficult tongue-twisters, he had to mouth the text as he read, training lips and tongue. In effect, Powelson was lipping (and digesting) *himself*, a novel form of auto-erotic behaviour. Sometimes, the procedure gave him a serious headache. After all, the *Iliad* is one of the bloodiest war stories in the history of western literature and Steven V. N. Powelson was an avowed pacifist.

Memorization is a form of self-inscription; drop stylus to perform oral recitation. Taking such a vast quantity of bloody text into a retired body already beginning to peter out does raise serious questions of phonographic technique. Powelson described the procedures of his private memory theatre by way of analogy: picture a row of leaky buckets, with each bucket representing a book of the *Iliad*. As each successive bucket was filled (perhaps with his own brain fluid), water in the other buckets would gradually leak out, and Powelson would then go back and fill them up again. As each new book added a new book/bucket, each step towards immortality put another hole in Powelson's head. By airing his strange *Iliad* odyssey on radio, I could at least help bring the intermedia cycle full circle. War stories, holes in the head and the leakage of partially digested dead language – in this vocabulary, radio is perfectly capable of speaking for itself.

NEEDLES

Sometimes when you try to talk about radio art in public, you get needled. At a (rare) conference on sound and art a few years ago, I presented a brief series of remarks about how radio is actually at its most lively when most dead. Since the living cast themselves out through the articulated corpses of advanced telecommunications equipment, the whole idea of "live" radio is nothing more than a sensory illusion. Electrical currents express dead labour before they give voice to anybody else. The more dead the transmission, the more "alive" the acoustic sensation; the more alive the sensation, the more "dead" the source body has become.

When I finished, a hand started waving at the back of the auditorium, though through the stage lights I was unable to see the face of its owner. Somewhat urgently, The Disfigured Hand called out, "*Hey Whitehead, you gotta believe . . . you gotta believe that it's better to talk to livin' people than to talk to dead people*! "

The real problem, of course, is how to tell the difference, a problem that was very much in evidence during my own "live" broadcasting debut. The program/performance centred around staging a fake New Age call-in show designed to allow listeners a live consultation with the renowned Dr. Vicekopf, chief language analyst at the Paul Broca Memorial Institute For Schizophonic Behaviour. Listeners were invited to call in and offer their most peculiar linguistic behaviours for deep brain analysis. Our expectation was that everyone would realize right away that this was just a language game, and that we would end up mixing telephonic glossolalias into the World's Largest Take-out *WortSalat*.

Instead, we were confronted with a number of listeners who desired serious consultation; some, of course, just *heard* other voices ("They've been telling me I'm a schizophrenic – but after listening to you, I think I may be a schizophonic") but others described various forms of uncontrollable voices that would erupt from their throats at the most embarrassing times. Several were acutely aware that their language had become infected by the electronic media, that their language was in fact no longer their own, and often found themselves talking like cartoon characters or American presidents.

Any committed schizophonic will tell you that those born into the dense saturation of the electronic media have no choice but to swallow an overwhelming quantity of pre-packaged lingual emissions, from down and dirty drive-time jingles to spotless digital recordings of Handel's *Messiah*. Sitcom patter becomes fused in the memory with the speeches of candidates and the numbing rhythms of traffic reports and weather forecasts. Needles are an inescapable fact of life for the schizophonic, and still amply animate the radiobody even if laser beams have made it possible to get off without them. As the possibility of public discourse collapses into communal lip-sync extravaganzas, perhaps the most direct form of radio art (and certainly the cheapest) is to simply get wired, stick a needle in the brain and *spin those tunes baby, cause you're a tightly twisted, roller derby brand a' wild thing*!

SHAKE, RATTLE N' ROLL

Every now and again, the quaint idea of radio as a kind of Talking Drum for the Global Village comes around for one more spin. In this romantic scenario, radio art is cast as an electronic echo of oral culture, harking back to ancient storytellers spinning yarns in front of village fires. The idea has a seductive ring to it, and can be embellished in all kinds of ways, making room for everything from *Finnegan's Wake* to Street Rap: Radio as Universal Language, Electronic Community, Planetary Boombox, Here Comes Everybody, *like let's just hang out and tell stories and maybe dance.*

Radio Talking Drum – a utopian transposition that loves to forget. Most forgotten are the lethal wires that still heat up from inside out, wires that connect radio with warfare, brain damage, rattles from necropolis. When I turn my radio on, I hear a whole chorus of death rattles: from stone cold, hard fact larynxes frozen in every stage of physical decomposition; from talk-show golden throats cut with a scalpel, transected, then taped back together and beamed out across the airwaves; from voices that have been severed from the body for so long that no one can remember who they belong to, or whether they belong to anybody at all; from pop monster gigglebodies guaranteed to shake your booty; from artificial folds sneak-stitched into still living throats through computer synthesis and digital processing; from mechanical chatter boxes dead to begin with; from cyberphonic antibodies taking flight and crashing to pieces on air.

During November 1988, I had an infrequent opportunity to become abruptly and eternally united with my own metaphors. While en route to Australia, my flight, a Boeing 747 stuffed with tour groups, came very close to crashing on take-off from Honolulu. With stabilizing flaps damaged by metal bars that had broken away from the landing gear, the plane barely lifted off the ground before it began to rattle violently. In the wake of each fresh plane crash, I confess to reading survivor accounts with intense curiosity, and keep voluminous files. Such accounts almost invariably refer to "violent rattles" moments before disaster, so as the luggage compartments sprang open above our heads, I felt certain that we were seconds away from rattling right into a burn unit. But the Qantas pilot immediately lightened our load by dumping thousands of litres of fuel into the Pacific Ocean, and we lumbered back to Honolulu airport for a surprisingly uneventful emergency landing.

Several hours later, in a typically incongruous late twentieth-century change of scene, I sat watching the surfers ride the waves at Waikiki, a

Qantas complimentary cocktail in hand. I thought about other waves, *air*waves, the risks of mechanical vibration. I thought about all the radio art transmissions that dump their fuel and make premature landings, about the countless audio aircraft that never arrive at their true destinations, or that shake, rattle n' roll violently without coming to the climax. And after three or four more complimentary cocktails, I thought about the crash/rattled post-Rodez body of Antonin Artaud, thereafter resurrected as Artaud Le Mômo.

When Artaud was finally released from his psychiatric internment at Rodez, his body had been thoroughly wasted by the nervous explosions of his mental illness, externally administered electroshock treatment, frequent insulin injections and a terminal case of (undiagnosed) rectal cancer. Convulsed by electricity, and with disease spreading inward from the anus, Artaud returned to Paris in 1946. From this time on, his vision of a "body without organs," with its promise of pure redemption, takes centre stage.

Artaud's desired new body, stripped bare, scraped clean and turned inside out, quickly assumed a pseudonym. Le Mômo: the pure energy of direct brainwave transmission, born from an occult synthesis of needles, electricity and a cacophony of irrefutable inner voices. Le Mômo: giving voice to the prosthetic language of the disembody, the antibody, the radiobody. Le Mômo: full of vocal flatulence, noisy jolts, black magic and bloody nothings.

In 1947, Artaud Le Mômo gave voice to his final public pronouncement, *Pour en finir avec le jugement de Dieu (To Have Done With the Judgement of God)*, a lacerating, scatophonic performance scheduled for national broadcast on February 2, 1948, but cancelled at the last minute by the Director of French Radio, one Wladimir Porché. The official explanation rounded up all the usual suspects – obscenity, sacrilege, anti-Americanism. But after listening to a recording of the work, one suspects the presence of a deeper fear, the fear that Artaud Le Mômo might yet reverse the voltage and wire countless brains to the shock treatment of his unearthly howls, jolting a million ears into the next world. As Le Mômo himself writes, "The magic of electric shock drains a death rattle, it plunges the shocked one into that death rattle with which one leaves life."

PRESSURES OF THE UNSPEAKABLE

I returned to Sydney in 1991 with a proposal for the Australian Broadcasting Corporation's *Listening Room* program: to install a related form of public electroshock circuitry, a human screamscape, assembled from "donated" screams recorded on an answering machine housed within a fictive Institute for Screamscape Studies. Everything that happened in, across or through the circuits of the Institute would become part of a citywide nervous flow, culminating in a national screamcast. In addition to framing the nervous system, the telephone-microphone-tape recorder-radio circuitry would also provide the key index for the acoustic demarcation of *pressure in the system*: distortion, the disruption of digital codes, pure unmanageable noise. The scream as seismic eruption, well in excess of prescribed circuitries capable of blowing communications technologies not designed for such extreme unspeakables.

As the research samples came in, lubricated by the jelly of discourse and publicity, the scream trickle soon became a flood, and the producer ganglia at the Institute began to feel the first effects of THE PRESSURE on our own increasingly jangled nervous systems. Strange things began to happen as we listened again and again to hundreds of blown and distorted screams. As needles pinned wildly inside the studio, bones rattled inside the body, and the brain began to play curious tricks on the rest of us, our dreamlands turned into deep screamlands.

At last, the narrative authority of Dr. Scream himself simply dissembled into pieces and he left the Institute to start a rhythm and blues band in Louisiana. Without him, however, the Institute then delivered a national broadcast montage of the assembled "report," which immediately triggered hundreds of additional post-broadcast screamline calls: objections, responses, counterscreams, reflections, wrong numbers, confessions and bold polemics. Finally, following a moment of absolute silence, the screamline was unplugged and the circuit of unspeakables was put to rest.

In a last "memo," the Institute circulated a quote from one of the more remarkable nervous systems of the twentieth century:

> When you are philosophizing
> you must descend into primeval chaos
> and feel at home there.
>
> Ludwig Wittgenstein

The clinic of the production studio felt at times like a Room 101 of my own design, the psychoacoustic descent into screamland chaos resounding through the rattle of my bones. Yet the variably magnificent, affirmative, ecstatic, violent, explosive, wounded and irrepressible nature of the materials, restored me, if not to my "home," at least to my real place. Beyond all forlorn attempts at reconciliation, Radio Utopia and Radio Thanatos had danced a mad jig together. Amidst the ensuing din, there resounded at least the rumour of a future for a medium on the fade.

Thanks to Jacki Apple, Martim Avillez, Regine Beyer, Herb Blau, Roz Cheney, Martin Harrison, Douglas Kahn, Dan Lander, Bonnie Marranca, Christof Migone, Ios Smolders, Susan Stone, Helen Thorington and Allen Weiss. Without the benefit of their discursive friction, generated over many years, the thoughts summarized in this essay would literally have no place.

Rita McKeough's *My Teeth are in Slivers*

A CALLING FROM THE OTHER SIDE OF TRAUMA

Paula Levine

> *To call is not originally to name, but the other way around: naming is a kind of calling . . .*[1]

Sharp rhythm of breath, in and out, perforates, punctuates space.

Women's voices, high and loud, wailing, wailing, wailing
bump into each other without apology.

Voices link and stretch, forming chords of dissonance
that remind of the distance remaining –
  to reach the comfort and safety of harmony,
  or merge into an almost immutable synchronicity.

Vocalizing the traumas which spawned them,

five notes – three up/two down – and vowels held for a beat of five

ooooh
ooooh

ahhhh

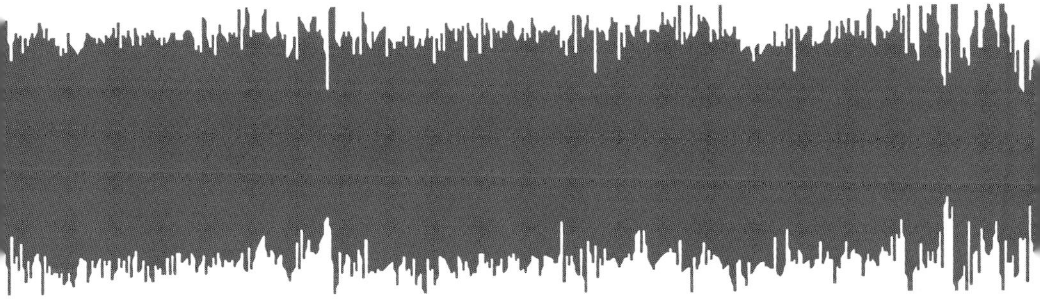

slide into each other while breath ripples space.

These voices are back from the battlegrounds,

I have pulled a fist from my mouth, severed hands lie beside me . . .
struggling to reconstitute

Slowly air returns to my aching lungs . . .

after the battle.

Slowly air returns to my aching lungs . . .
Slowly air returns to my aching lungs . . .
Slowly air returns to my aching lungs . . .[2]

* * *

My Teeth are in Slivers takes place just the other side of trauma. For twenty-four minutes, three female voices, orchestrated in a twelve-part score, are layered one upon the other – breathing, singing, speaking in punctuated rhythms carried by long, sustained vowels that ebb and swell and slide from dissonance into momentary strained/strange harmony, and then out again.

Held together by threads of affect and detail, words describe the observing body in its moments of insight as it moves away from pain and anger after the impact of violence.

Commissioned for radio broadcast as part of the *Radio Rethink: Art, Sound and Transmission* exhibition and symposium, the work is the first sound piece made by Rita McKeough to exist outside an installation context.

Imagine a carcass, a body composed of pleasures and pains, bone and flesh. Imagine its smell and the quality of light. It is as though one comes upon one's memory.

Pull the guts of the memory out through the voice and rummage through its remains.
Gnaw at the residue,
scrape the flesh from the bone,
make use of the past but do not preserve the unbearable.

The flesh drops away from the bone.

Walk around it, view it and leave it.[3]

In translation of mind to matter, memory is a carcass lying in state – unembalmed, deteriorating, decomposing, unceremoniously exhibited with no attempts made to detain it in time.

We are called upon to listen . . .

I listened and talked to women who have been silenced by violence and women who worked in shelters and supported friends who have been through it – spent years of looking and thinking and searching this issue. In my work through the sound tapes, my desire was to reconstruct a fictive history using what I had learned. I tried to use the layering of the audio in the sound tracks as a way to grab language and kind of shake it and strangle it, in a sense to force it . . . in a way to communicate the complexity of the experience of having been a victim of violence, specifically, domestic violence.

to the voices . . .

The sound tracks . . . layer the information, . . . the language, . . . the sounds of the body . . .

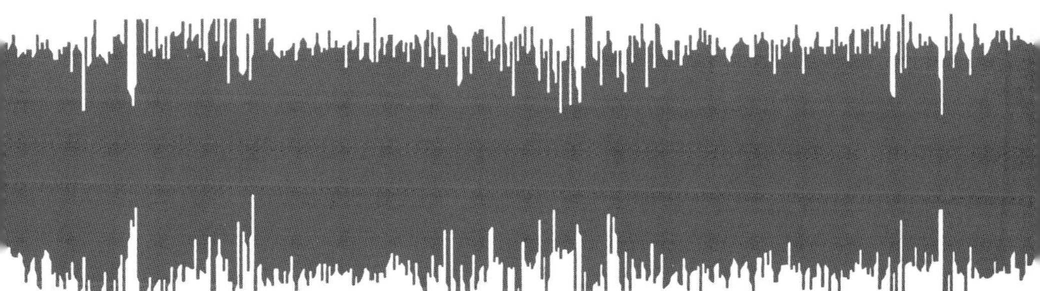

. . . as they reconstitute the affective network of the body, recanting sensations of states along the way, moving from what is deeply embodied, outward – resisting, remembering, recalling, retelling, recovering.

. . . and communicate in a very specific way the emotional and physical effects and consequences on the body and the individual because of that silencing.

Silencing does not erase memory. Instead, it drives it deep "within the fastness of the individual so as to create more fear and uncertainty in which dream and reality comingle."[4] The memories return and when they do they transform space, taking up residency in places they do not belong[5] and changing those places as the result of their presence. Memory changes what is known to be foreign to seem familiar, causing a sense of "disquiet because of its absolute proximity . . . [deforming] space by this experience."[6]

Expressing the memory of pain makes demands. Expressing physical pain, says Elaine Scarry, eventually opens into the wider frame of invention, for pain (and pleasure) throw the body into unstable states, states which lie outside the order of language. Physical pain "does not simply resist language but actively destroys it, bringing about an immediate reversion to a state anterior to language, to the sounds and cries of a human being before language is learned."[7]

The body in pain involves the "making and unmaking of the world"[8] and speaking (the pain) is the making and unmaking of oneself.[9]

I do not scream with the desire to frighten you away . . .
but to use my voice to cut a thin slice off of you
an unredeemable, irreplaceable slice
unforgettable . . .

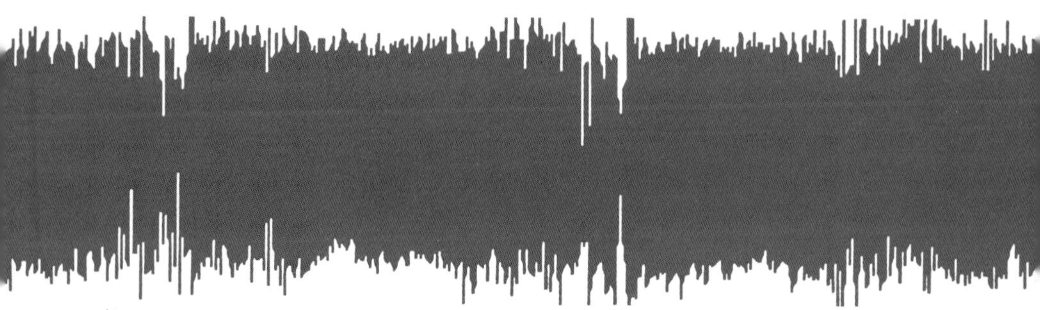

THE BODY AS ARCHITECTURE . . .

Since 1981, Rita McKeough has reinvested a presence into matters rendered invisible. Her installations have addressed issues of pollution, public housing and homelessness.[10] Earlier work on the politics of urban housing involved the anthropomorphizing of structures, giving voices to construction sites and building materials to speak their historical pasts or call for help in the face of being demolished.[11]

Since 1983, McKeough has worked with the female body, domestic violence and the politics of "home."[12] Her installations, often suggesting domestic spaces within gallery settings, have been designed to "move [violence] into the architecture as a way to . . . make it visible."[13] Walls, standing in for skin, bear the marks of scars and bruises from the violence.[14] Rooms covered with broken furniture bear testimony to the inversion – safety to threat, furnishings to weapons, refuge to prison.[15] This work suggests a kind of empathetic architecture where environments are both filled with and shaped by the affect and senses of those living within.

Sound further transforms these architectural sites into articulating sites. McKeough uses her collections of stories and interviews of women who have come through abuse and violence to create audio texts that act "like a rented apartment . . . [transforming] another person's [experience] into a space borrowed for a moment by a transient."[16] Audiotaped voices of women speak of what was once silenced and buried within the privacy of domesticity, transforming the unforgettable into words and changing the space through language.

No longer private, these sites open up for shared occupancy as viewers walk through the spaces – listening.

> *But calling is something else than merely making a sound . . .*
> *In reality, the calling stems from the place to which the call goes out.*
> *Calling offers an abode.*[17]

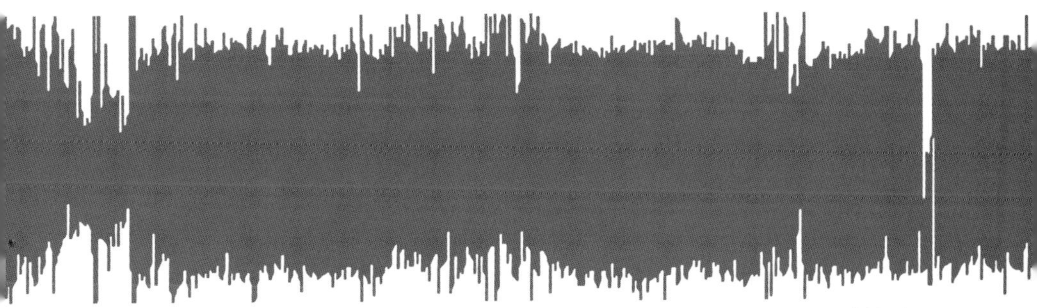

ARCHITECTURE AS THE FEMALE BODY . . .

In McKeough's operatic performance/installation, *In bocca al lupo (In the Mouth of the Wolf)*[18] space itself is corporealized and interior forces are made visible. The gallery becomes body as nine personifications of angers, frustrations and fears take on a visible face. In sound, dress and gesture, each anger is shaped by the ties that bind – religion, academia, social law and conventions; all that haunts, hurts, holds back, forces down and in until the labyrinthian mappings of the body's internal states become a complex network of twists and turns which can no longer be followed, accounted for or understood.

Viewers sit in the seats of privilege. As if possessing x-ray vision, they see inside the body itself, bearing witness to the Gulliver-like play of forces within.[19] The forces call out and cry and gyrate, gesticulate, run into the walls of the body/gallery or up to the faces of the viewers who sit on piles of old books/old knowledge that slip and slide under weight.

And the forces within the body speak – in a language full of rhythm and repetition located somewhere at the intersection between politics and poetry –

I have waited   waited
for this moment   Shake it
to throw my head back   Throw it . . .
To throw my head
from side to side . . .
My voice burns   Shake it . . .
. . . it wasn't being heard
Behind the flesh walls   Shake it
A mirror in Disarray   Throw it[20]

What is it that calls on us to think?
Where does the calling come from?
How can it make its claim on us?
How does the calling reach us?[21]

MAKING WAVES, SO TO SPEAK . . .

"Bodiless voices are carried by radio waves to the receiving ears of the listeners: from body to body, private to public to private again. Voices, once buried in the domestic architecture, now return to reinhabit private domains."[22]

As in her previous work on domestic violence, the language of *My Teeth are in Slivers* is in the language of the body's interior – private recollections and descriptions of the struggles away from trauma and pain made audible to public ears as a way to make the experience habitable by others.

It is "narrativity in its most delinquent form," this "implantation of memory"[23] for true to the character of sound, its ability to merge with whatever is standing in its way, it simulates an intimacy usually reserved for . . . intimates, creating a bond that no theoretical construction can so easily forge.

This is what sound does best – invade.

Sound is as deep as empathy, invading the body, creating a mimetic presence where there was once none. It penetrates the body, seeps into it, compelling it to resonate, to the extent it is able, in response to the vibrations which enter.

This is what McKeough is working with – the spatial conflations of body to body which takes place through connections of sounds as well as the transformation of space where the unspoken is spoken and the naming takes place.

Michael Taussig speaks of "talking terror" in the face of oppression in South America. The Dirty War, he says, is a war of silencing. There is no officially declared war. No prisoners. No torture. Just silence consuming terror's talk for the main part, scaring people into saying nothing in public that could be construed as critical of the Armed Forces.

> It is this presence of the unsaid which makes the simplest of public-space talk arresting . . . the naming by the Mothers of the Disappeared in public spaces of the names of disappeared, together with their photographs, in collective acts acquiring the form of ritual in which what is important is not so much the facts, since they are in their way well known, but the shift in social location in which those facts are placed, filling the public void with private memory.[24]

> *What is given words or named is a kind of calling and what is called appears as what is present.*[25]

Listen to what has happened, is happening, as I/you take note of the configurations shaped by the aftershocks. In the aftermath of abuse and repression, a forbidden space is created, a detested space, for in it are the voices of resistance.

The strange face, the all too familiar face . . .
I reconstruct the features, disconnected, disintegrating
powerless
This is how I forget.

Memory is a reconnaissance operation.[26] Name the changes in the body as recollection takes place, as memory gathers all that has transpired.

Having felt unbearable weariness
The weariness of pain.
Now I pump my blood hard
It scrubs my bones
rinses my mouth
caresses
This is how I remember.

My sincere thanks to those whose ideas, writings and actions influenced the shape and content of this article. In particular, my thanks to Rita McKeough for the valuable discussions about words, rhythms, metaphor and the body; to Mary Anne Moser for her editorial contributions and for making the rendering of the voice graphs possible; and to the Canada Council for their "B" grant support in 1992, which gave me the opportunity to begin researching, writing and pondering many of the ideas on space and the gallery site which appear in this article.

Notes

1 Martin Heidegger, *What is Called Thinking?* trans. J. Glenn Gray (New York: Harper & Row, Inc., 1954), 123. All text in this typeface is quoted from Heidegger.

2 All text in this typeface is from Rita McKeough's *My Teeth are in Slivers* (1992), unless otherwise indicated.

3 From a telephone conversation with Rita McKeough on *My Teeth are in Slivers.*

4 Michael Taussig, *The Nervous System* (New York: Routledge, Chapman and Hall, 1992), 27.

5 Michel de Certeau, *The Practice of Everyday Life,* trans. Steven Rendall (Los Angeles and Berkeley: University of California Press, 1984), 86.

6 Psychoanalyst Mahmoud Sami-Ali as quoted by Anthony Vidler, *The Architectural Uncanny: Essays in the Modern Unhomely* (Cambridge, Massachusetts: MIT Press, 1992), 222.

7 Elaine Scarry, *The Body in Pain: The Making and Unmaking of the World* (Oxford: Oxford University Press, 1985), 4.

8 Ibid.

9 Julia Kristeva speaks of language "as the signifying system in which the speaking subject *makes* and *unmakes* himself," *Language The Unknown: An Initiation into Linguistics*, trans. Anne M. Menke (New York: Columbia University Press, 1989), 265.

10 McKeough's installation work is too voluminous to describe in detail. For the purpose of this article, a few are mentioned along with their primary concerns: *Afterland Plaza*, Mendel Art Gallery, Saskatoon, 1985 (pollution); *The Embrace,*

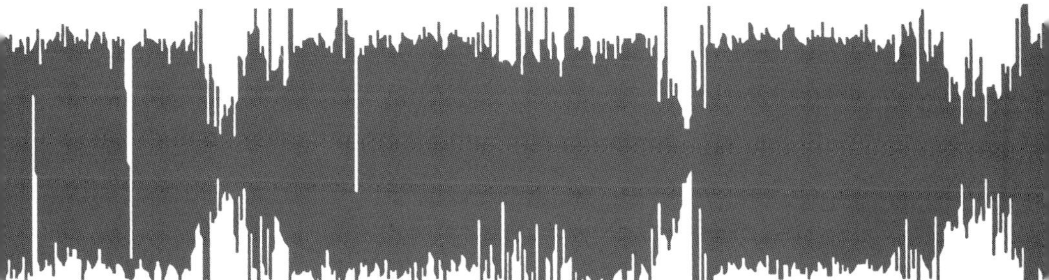

Art Gallery of Windsor, Ontario, 1990 (pollution); *Defunct*, Calgary, 1981, (public housing); *Retrieval*, Plug-In Gallery, Winnipeg, 1985 (homelessness).

11 *Skeletal Development*, Walter Phillips Gallery, 1983: A skeleton structure of an apartment block was built using the refuse from homes demolished for urban development. *Destruct*, University of Lethbridge Art Gallery, 1983: Viewers watched as a single-family dwelling, built to one-third scale in the gallery, is chased by a backhoe, also built to scale.

12 Some examples are: *Retaining Wall*, 1986: the domestic home as prison and the relationship between the architectural structure of the home and family dynamics; *Mimicry*, 1988: two adjacent apartments with a broken wall between the audiotaped voices of a woman in one room speaking of her attempt to leave the relationship while in the other, the voice of a man promising to find her; *Tremor*, 1989: constructed rooms where women's voices spoke of the struggle to integrate the trauma of violence and abuse into their lives.

13 From notes by Rita McKeough.

14 *Blind Spot*, 1987, Eye Level Gallery, Halifax, Nova Scotia.

15 *Tremor*, 1989, Dunlop Art Gallery, Regina, Saskatchewan. See also Elaine Scarry's discussion in "The Structure of Torture" in *The Body in Pain*, 38–45.

16 de Certeau, xxi.

17 Heidegger, 124–5.

18 *In bocca al lupo (In the Mouth of the Wolf)*, was a ninety-minute operatic production performed in Halifax, Toronto and Vancouver, in 1991 and 1992, written and directed by Rita McKeough.

19 *The Gallery as a State of Mind and the Work of Rita McKeough*, by Paula Levine. Unpublished videopaper presented at the Glenbow Museum, January, 1993, as part of *An Excavation*, installation and performance by Rita McKeough, January – April, 1993.

20 From *In bocca al lupo* "My Heart Beats Too Fast."

21 Heidegger, 124.

22 In conversation with Dan Lander on *My Teeth are in Slivers*.

23 de Certeau, 86.

24 Taussig, 38.

25 Heidegger, 120–123.

26 Gail Scott, *Spaces Like Stairs* (Toronto: The Women's Press, 1989), 24.

The Genealogy of the Radio Voice

Frances Dyson

The radio voice seems to come to us as something established, something we take for granted, having characteristics which are easy to recognize. Generally, the dominant radio voice talks – its speech is clear, articulate, sometimes eloquent. Most of what it says is perceived by the listener as factual and informative, newsworthy, or at least dedicated to the betterment of life. It does not mumble or stutter, it pronounces full and meaningful sentences, it says something. As a voice, it is traditionally male, having a certain timbre and intonation that suggests a belief in what it is saying and a degree of authority in saying it. Critics of the dominant radio voice have dubbed it "the voice of authority." Yet, although this voice appeared with the advent of radio and seems therefore to have sprung from the twentieth century, it in fact has been a long time in formation and has accumulated a host of characteristics that connect it to the deepest symbolic and epistemological structures governing thought, speech and media in western culture. The origins of the contemporary production and reception of the voice can be traced to the remote past of western culture, where the guidelines for "proper speech" – speech which is authoritative, meaningful, gendered as masculine and representative of a particular worldview – were first set in stone.

In this paper I want to return to those origins in order to understand the radio voice's inheritance from its pre-broadcast past. I want to understand why it is that the radio voice is paradigmatically masculine and why it is perceived as both the voice of authority and the voice of truth. If, as radio artists, we are committed to presenting other voices speaking other ideas in languages not sanctioned by the institutions of broadcasting, then we must ask: where does the prerogative of the radio voice come from, what voices and voicings does it exclude, and why, against all odds, is it so convincing? As a way of dealing with these questions I will focus on two ideas which point to an era of philosophy and an area of cultural production where the voice of authority is neither heard nor heeded: the idea of flux and the idea of rumour. *Flux* reintroduces the phenomenality of sound, its impermanence and unboundedness, into the concept of the voice, while *rumour* designates both noise and the circulating speech of the other, the *silent*, or rather silenced, multitude. Neither true nor false, entirely present nor entirely absent, both rumour and flux gesture towards a speaking and listening practice which is antithetical to the voice of authority. Returning the voice to sound, and speech to the forbidden arena of rumour, gossip, hear/say – a simultaneous speaking and listening – is, I believe, one way to counter the weighty silence with which the voice of authority smothers us daily.

BETWEEN BEING AND BECOMING

At the beginning of Judeo-Christian civilization, the Word had great import. Indeed, in the beginning was the Word, and the Word *was* God – origin and explanation of all things. In Christian theology the Word is made flesh, becoming the Logos, second person of the Holy Trinity and deliverer of God's law. The Logos in both pre- and post-Christian usage, is the precursor of the modern concept of logic as reason, order and law, all characteristics of meaningful speech, all found in abundance in the voice of authority, yet all abstract concepts existing independently of vocal utterance. Nowhere is it mentioned that the Word/God was or must have been spoken. However, the Word was not always so devoid of voice – in fact, the evacuation of the voice from the concept of Logos as logic can be traced to around 400 BC, when existence, 'being,' was made dependent upon visualist, object-centered criteria. For something to be said to exist, it had to display endurance, self-identity, stability and permanence, all characteristics of material objects rather than aural events. As a result, sound was regarded not as a thing in itself but as an attribute or quality of objects. More importantly, sound and the speaking voice were lost to the quest for stability and order because, being qualities rather than objects, they represented impermanence, instability, change and becoming – in short *flux*, and for a philosophical discourse bent on arriving at certainty, determined to grasp, measure, define, explain and ultimately control the world, the idea of an ever-changing flux was abhorrent.

During this period (500–300 BC) the broad cosmology which had structured pre-Socratic thought is replaced by what might be called the mechanics of existence. 'Being' is delineated, its qualities are named as infinite and enduring and it functions as the necessary cause and origin of all things. With an increasing distrust of the senses, and anything subject to change or 'becoming,' there is a greater onus on Mind to substantiate its knowledge of the universe. As a result the concept of Mind becomes associated with the *urstoff* (the primary element or matter) and the idea of a single universal cause. In doing so it has access to both the spiritual truths of the cosmos and what will later be thought of as the scientific truths of reason. Indeed, Mind or *Nous* becomes the defining characteristic, the supreme achievement of human existence, and the unfortunate matter that houses this achievement, the body, is subject to a purification process whereby its corporeality is abstracted, its substance etherealized. Later, with the development of Atomism, the *urstoff* is conceived as both a thing and a cosmic force; the goal of ascension becomes dominant, as does air, the invisible, thought, *Nous*, and with this dominance the world becomes divisible and mechanical. The body, ever conceived as a machine, now presents a problematic knowledge – a knowledge which cannot be articulated because it consists of qualitative speculations rather than quantitative facts. Within this mechanistic system, the body is mute.

HERACLITIAN FLUX

What is forgotten in these beginnings of western thought is their proximity to a truly radical worldview, one which could accommodate not only sound, but all phenomena which lie beyond the scientific, mechanistic yardstick. In the doctrines of the pre-Socratic philosopher Heraclitus, knowledge is based not on the quantification and objectification of phenomena, but on "listening to the Logos" – the Word referring to both the *saying* and *what is said*. For Heraclitus there is becoming, but nothing which becomes, there is the One, but it is made of change, there is a unity existing in the form of First Cause or Logos, but it is constituted by the diverse, paradoxical and multiple manifold in a perpetual state of tension, there is no 'being' – all is 'becoming.'[1] The One, 'becoming,' is represented by fire, a perfect symbol since fire is always either kindling or diminishing and, being both seen and felt (in the same way that sound is both heard and felt), it has impact both outwardly and inwardly at once – destroying the illusion of difference between exterior and interior, perceiver and perceived.[2]

Heraclitus, dubbed "the obscure," was criticized for being ambiguous in his writings. However, the ontological import of such ambiguity and paradox is profound for it allows the 'being' of a thing to be as yet unfixed; a thing is constituted by its qualities which, like the fire, are always changing. And this mutability prevents the 'thing' from being objectified. Not yet distinct from the mind that beholds it, the Heraclitian 'thing' short circuits the speculative philosophical formula whereby the assumed objectivity of the object ensures the subjectivity of the subject. Knowledge is not based on an epistemology which privileges order and stability, rather, both object and subject are impermanent and unstable:

> Everything flows and nothing abides; everything gives way and nothing stays fixed.[3]

However, later philosophers, notably Aristotle, needed the concept of the substratum or 'thing,' an object which could reconcile opposites and accommodate difference within a unity, in order to proceed with their dualistic epistemology. Thinghood came to represent both the cause, the explanation and the unity of existence, indeed, it represented 'being' itself. With 'being' defined according to object criteria, all things which share those attributes (of stability, permanence) share also in 'being.' This formulation had two consequences: first, it guaranteed that a name could be associated with a thing, meaning could be established (not just the meaning of words, but ultimately the meaning of man) and the Logos – the fundamental principle or law – could be uttered. Second, it favoured the representation of beings, things, in terms of an enduring presence – both the temporal present and the presencing of a thing to the senses. Because that which is most obviously present is the visible, tangible object, meaning, knowledge and spirituality began to be conceived in visualist metaphors ('to be': etymologically associated with 'to know' and 'to see'). In this context the words of Heraclitus are uncanny. When he says,

> listening not to me but to the Logos, it is wise to acknowledge that all things are one,[4]

he does not speak of an absolute Being in terms of visible presence, but of the Word – Logos with its connotations of both *saying* and *what is said*.[5] Listening is a vehicle for understanding the unity of the universe, however, this unity is not theistic, rather, it is paradoxical, a unity in difference – flux. Listening to the Logos is not merely paying attention to the meaning of the words or measuring their 'truth content,' for the very ability to listen depends upon a prior attunement with the Logos:

> The hidden attunement of the Universe is better than the open.[6]

Attunement here suggests a sonorous resonance with the Word: a becoming part of the Word as one listens to it. Elsewhere, Heraclitus invokes aural metaphors to suggest an aspect of listening which has been forgotten. Listening is not simply hearing, he says, for one must be able to understand the Logos, be able to sense within its workings the subtle law by which the universe kindles itself before one can hear it properly. *Listening* to the Logos, being Word and being voiced, is at the same time a sensual and intellectual experience, involving an appreciation of structure, language and law while demanding also that one *become* the Logos by entering the flux which it both is and reveals.[7]

The position of humans within this flux and paradox is ambiguous. For instance, Heraclitus writes that, "Into the same rivers we step and we do not step."[8] But what kind of subject does it take to both step and not step into the same river? And is a river ever the same? One could suggest that the Heraclitian subject is a listening subject, immersed in yet separate from, sound – no longer a subject confronting an object, while the object, like a river, is itself constantly changing and can never be called the same. Like the river also, the Heraclitian flux provides an originary movement which is neither up nor down and therefore cannot be interpreted in terms of the telos of spiritual ascension characterizing Christian and later Idealist thought. This is an important difference because later western philosophy and especially the contemporary idea of progress, privileges the theistic notion of ascension over the downward "return" to the body, matter and the earth. Furthermore, the notion of ascension is identified both with knowledge and with masculinity. Plato, in *Cratylus*, notes that, like wisdom,

> the words . . . (male) and . . . (man) also contain a similar allusion to the same principle of the upward flux.[9]

Further, one of "man's" senses, sight, is credited with indicating the upward movement or telos of "his" soul, while at the same time distinguishing "him" from animals:

> the word "man" implies that other animals never examine, or consider, or look up at what they see, but that man not only sees but considers and looks up at that which he sees, and hence he alone of all animals is rightly called man.[10]

The imperative to ascend, to rise above matter has repercussions for the concept of the Logos as *spoken* Word, for it demands that either the voice be eliminated from the Logos, or that the voice itself – partner to the Word, be evacuated of any earthly element whatsoever.

VOICE, SOUND AND LANGUAGE

It is very difficult to conceive of the voice in such an abstract way, since it has an actual association with the body. In the development of western metaphysics this difficulty is overcome to some extent by splitting the voice. There is a voice of the body and a voice of the mind; the voice of the body has its origins in the passions, it does not speak so much as babble, its fluidic nature continually escapes the grid of the symbolic, of meaning – it mutters, but it is in a sense, mute. The voice of the mind on the other hand produces symbols, language, meaning. It names the phenomena of the world, and in naming is united with the 'truth' of nature and the world. Plato for instance, describes the voice as an instrument for evoking the essences of things through naming – a name being "a vocal imitation of a thing":

> names ought to be given according to a natural process, and with a proper instrument, and not at our pleasure.[11]

Essences, as forms, are permanent and abiding and not subject to change, and names recall and re-present their enduring form through a sonorous resonance between the sound of the voice naming and the nature of the thing named. The permanence of essences is necessary for Plato, not only to provide order in the universe, but to ensure the certainty of language and speech. He says:

> if [Beauty – a supreme form] is continually escaping from our grasp, how can we properly apply to it the predicates *that* or *of such a kind*? Must it not rather become different, and retire, and no longer be thus while the word is in our mouths?[12]. . . But if that which knows and that which is known exists . . . ever then I do not think that they can resemble a process or flux, [for if they did] . . . no man of sense will like to put himself or the education of his mind in the power of names: neither will he so far trust names or the givers of names as to be confident in any knowledge which condemns himself and other existences to an unhealthy state of unreality; he will not believe that all things leak like a pot or that the whole external world is afflicted with rheum and catarrh.[13]

The voice, in naming, evokes the essences which make language possible and, in doing so, demonstrates the stability of the universe and the certainty of the subject. In naming, the voice confirms that words correspond to referents, not through mere imitation but through a sonorous reconnection.[14] The voice therefore occludes the fact of representation, hiding the absence which language is, behind the sonorous presence of the voice naming the object.

Within this schema the voice is indeed a very good instrument. On one level it unites 'man,' 'truth' and the cosmos; on another, it provides a pivot between the senses and the mind, allowing the mind to know and represent (speak) the world with complete certainty. This is a very delicate position for the voice to occupy, for even as instrument, its non-representational imitation given through sound draws it downwards, towards matter, while its function of naming the world aligns it with the telos of man; the ascent towards knowledge and truth (man, in Greek, also meaning upward flux). Although for Heraclitus this tension was not a problem, indeed it constituted the Logos, the spoken Word itself, it presented later philosophers with an impasse. One direction had to be chosen and, in representing the voice as the voice of reason, those favouring ascension also encouraged the voice's dematerialization. Aristotle, for instance, declared that the voice is:

> a significant sound; not the sound (merely) of air respired, as coughing is;[15] . . . a striking by the soul . . . upon air inhaled through the windpipe is voice.[16]

While the voice is "the sound of a living thing"[17] it must be differentiated from "animal sound . . . For not every animal sound is voice, . . . there is clicking the tongue, and the noise made by coughing. There is needed a living being to utter the sound, and some accompanying phantasm."[18] St. Thomas Aquinas (circa 1260 AD) interprets "phantasm" as "image" and concludes that:

> He [Aristotle] observes . . . [that] for voice to be produced it is required that what strikes the air should be something alive, or with a soul, and also, accompanying this, that an image be present which is meant to signify something. For voice must be a significant sound, – significant either by nature or conventionally. Hence the statement that vocal impact proceeds from the soul; for operations proceeding from imagination can be said to be from the soul . . . Not air, then, is the principal factor in the formation of voice, but the soul, which uses air as its *instrument*.[19]

What now characterizes the voice is first, that it is caused by the soul and, second, that it is a "significant sound." Voice proper is the voice speaking language; a significant sound and, of course, language is limited to human rather than animal vocal production. Proper voice is devoid of unintentional sound – the cough or the clicking of the tongue and, as such, it bears no traces of the body, representing or voicing, only the signifying image.

For Plato the naming voice is an "instrument" of cosmic synthesis; for Aristotle the breath required for vocal production is interpreted by Aquinas as an "instrument" of the soul. Such definitions are important in determining the true voice as a voice of the mind, instrumental in the achievement of a higher good, distanced from the alarming presence of the body. Even the breath, the most spiritual aspect of all human corporeality, is eradicated in this system. Not surprisingly, because the breath moves inward and outward, it is both present and absent in the act of breathing.

So when Aristotle declares that

> we cannot produce voice while inhaling air nor while exhaling it, but only while retaining it,[20]

he is not just stating a physiological assumption. "Proper" voice can only be produced by barring the entry of the breath. And the breath must be held, despite its deathly effects on the body, because the rhythm of the breath – moving through the body, setting up a flow which must continue for the body to survive – is a constant reminder of the fragility of life and, on a deeper level, the flux of existence, 'being,' itself. Because the breath is also the first and generally the last sign of human animation, its coming and going represents the coming and going of life – the passing into and out of existence which Heraclitus would consider part of the universal flux, but which later philosophers, obsessed with stability and permanence (read immortality), considered far too threatening. Flux eradicates the notion of the stable subject, the subject who *should* endure through the intransigence of the breath, who *should* be more than the perishable matter of his or her body. The coming and going of life which the breath represents brings the inevitable mortality of the body too close to the voice – that "instrument" set in motion by the soul. It interferes with the smooth functioning of the voice of the mind – that bodiless instrument which continues to speculate and reflect uninterrupted in the mind's I/eye for all eternity. It allows death, absence, to touch the light of reason and the vision of the soul. Without breath the voice becomes silent and death is displaced.[21] As instrument of the soul, the inner voice knows no termination – indeed it no longer makes sense to speak of its mortality since neither machines nor souls will die.

THE PRESENCE OF THE VOICE

Thus the voice of the mind, the "proper" voice that is, becomes anaerobic and static. But still, flux, with all its attendant connotations – lack of certainty, lack of meaning, etcetera – is at one with the rhythm, or coming and going of *sound*, and sound is an integral part of the voice. Aristotle's solution is to eradicate sound from the voice. Mere sound such as the cough, is not considered voice proper. Like the breath, sound cannot be held. It cannot, in the pre-recording era, be collected, stored and exchanged. And metaphorically it cannot, in its invisibility and temporality, its essential flux, be grasped by a mind already committed to an ontology of stability and presence. So the anaerobic voice also becomes anechoic. The sounds of the body are eliminated, and the inner voice comes to replace the spoken word as the paradigmatic "sound" of reason. That aspect of the Logos, the dialogical *saying* of the Word, is dismantled, leaving only the processes of the silent Word, the interior Law, functioning within the concept. With *saying* gone, so is the listener or, rather, the listener existing outside and independently of the speaker. The inner voice, (a misnomer), becomes a metaphor for intellection or reflection. The mind now listens to itself – the voice of the Logos is solipsistic.

Solipsism, however, is a philosophical strategy with few returns. A connection with the exterior world must, for many reasons, be maintained and this is made possible, in part, through a very subtle conflation of the presence of the voice with the (temporal) present. For the voice, being sonorous, necessarily speaks in the present, is accompanied by the actual bodily presence of the speaker, and is heard (perceived) at the moment of its production. The presence of the voice means that it can emerge from the subject while only being barely externalized, and this makes it the perfect tool for ensuring the dominance of the mind. By apparently integrating subject and object, reducing the distance between the inside and the outside, the voice gives the speaker, in hearing him- or herself speak, proprioceptive access to the world without the necessity of actually inhabiting the exterior – coded as foreign and other.[22] At the same time, because the voice speaks language, giving sound *and* meaning to the images of the mind, it closes the gap between the intellect and the contents of its reflections – nature, coded as mute and unknowable. The circuit is narrowed even further by Descartes, for whom one only has to think, with the voice of the mind, rather than say (and perhaps stutter or cough) "I think therefore I am." This silent soliloquy, providing existential certainty for the one who utters it, draws its potency from the idea that the images which the voice vocalizes can be grasped in the I/eye of the speaker and held or repeated indefinitely. Thus the threat of uncertainty is displaced by the potentially eternal presence of the dictum *cogito ergo sum*, uttered to oneself in the presence of the infinitely presentable images of the mind's I/eye, themselves formed from the intentions of the eternal soul. In short, the inner voice need never be absent. Unlike speech, it does not come and go with the flows of sound or the rhythms of the breath but persists as a perpetual phantasm: an image, an object, a metaphor of the mind.

THE RADIO VOICE

The characteristics of inner speech – that it is silent, atopic, self-directed and timeless – enable it to establish a philosophical system where the mind can be conscious of itself without reference to the world, and without interruption or interference from the uncertainty of life. Yet being abstract (there is no real voice) it is also able to assume, as metaphor, all the sensuous characteristics of voiced speech. This is where the notion of presence develops an additional meaning – we often associate personal presence, sincerity, integrity, depth of character and truth, with the fullness and depth of the voice. This is related, first, to sound's ability to indicate the interior of an object in a way that is prohibited to sight (for instance, the fullness or emptiness of the vessel) and, second, to the resonant aspect of sound – such that we say a person's words resonate with us.[23] Interiority, presented through aurality, stands *for* presence and truth: the veracity of the here-and-now and *against* absence, simulation and re-presentation. But while in cultural production, and particularly in mass media, the model for presence is the speaking subject, the real significance of presence is caught up in the notion of inner speech. For 'truth,' we know, can be spoken only through the technology of language. Despite the simulation of interiority by the media, the voice comes full circle – back to language, and back to its silence in the anaerobic, anechoic chambers of the mind.

It is within this topology that the radio voice can be heard operating in unison with the voice's philosophical heritage. Indeed, through the presence of the transmitted and amplified voice, the voice of authority, and the immense power of radio institutions, one glimpses the catastrophic shift from a philosophy of 'becoming' to one of 'being.' In the contemporary counterpart to this shift we find the grinding out of sound as flux, the imposition of identity, certainty and sameness, and the smothering of noise, rumour, the voices of many – anything that might threaten the myth of presence, the guarantor of immortality – structuring the forms and flows of radio. Thinking about the voice of the mind already outlined, and the voice of authority that we hear regularly on the radio, certain similarities emerge. First, both voices strive towards *disembodiment.* While the voice of the mind reflects on truth in solipsistic certitude, the ideal radio voice represents the world for the listener from the anechoic space of the studio – a space which acoustically is, in the jargon of sound technicians, "dead." Coming from a dead space, it speaks without a body, accomplishing through technology what the voice of the mind was unable to accomplish through metaphysics – the final severance of corporeality. Disembodiment is a necessary goal for both radio and metaphysics because the body represent *noise*, that is, an interference in the transmission of 'truth.' 'Truth' of course is the belief system which those in positions of power want others to accept, and the noise which might interfere with its transmission or acceptance also interferes with achieving another goal – that of speaking a perfect, self-present language through a perfect medium. That is why the voice of authority rarely stumbles on air, that is why its coughs or sneezes are edited out, because a stumbling, stuttering, coughing and wheezing voice brings "sound" to mind, tarnishing it. Lacking the veneer of authority, this voice fails to speak language, fails to transmit the images of the mind purely, fails to connect the mind of the speaker with that of the listener. Listeners have been trained to associate the stumbling voice with a poor command of the language and the inappropriate presence of the body. It is as if, in stuttering, the speaker is subject to the irrationality and hysteria of the flesh, in the same way that the "loose tongue" is guided by the irrationality and hysteria of rumour. There is no law, no master, nor mastery, behind that voice. Such a voice represents the body and the many – that uncontainable mass, formed from multiplicity and difference – rather than the singular, stable, unified, identifiable and ultimately God-like One.

Of course the dominant radio voice is a purely technological construct, crafted from language and electronics, having undergone extensive shaping by elocution and electrocution.[24] The radio voice, with the loudspeaker and the telephone, is entirely dependent upon technologies of amplification, which in turn are designed to reflect the characteristics the radio voice is supposed to have. The ideal of sound reproduction is, in the words of Harry F. Olson, the famous pioneer in sound recording and reproduction,

> the elimination of distortion and the reproduction at the listeners ears of sound waves *identical in structure* with those given out at the source.[25]

Reproduced sound must be 'true' – without distortion and as ontologically identical as possible to the original. Later, sound theorists and artists will argue that the reproduced sound, even when recorded on magnetic tape, *is* the original sound. This reflects a desire to technically and rhetorically close the gap between real and reproduced sound and, like the inner voice, it follows a logic based on the need for presence. Since a reproduced voice, having presence, seems less a representation than a *re*-presentation, it appears closer to the mind, the soul and the truth.[26] Distortion and interference, on the other hand, suggest a reduction of presence through contact with the external world, by aurally evoking another place and time, the illusion that the voice is "present" with the listener. Sound technology echoes these beliefs. In fact, the success of microphone design is measured in terms of the credibility of the presence it simulates, indicated by the clarity, the central stereophonic perspective, the volume, crispness and articulation of the voice it amplifies.

After amplification the radio voice is often mechanically edited, producing an unlikely speech: faster, clearer, more audible, more in line with the ideal that voice-communications media have established, beginning with the voices of European high culture.[27] Yet despite its unlikeliness, and the fact that most listeners are aware of its mechanical and electronic mediation, the radio voice is convincing. Its credibility has to do with the listener's desire to believe, to engage in the mechanisms of belief which culture constructs and media tap into, and to be seduced by the intimacy which the well-trained and well-microphoned voice can convey. This sense of intimacy, of being personally addressed by the speaker, and of hearing her or his voice close up – almost as if the speaker were whispering in one's ear – is, again, constructed from the desire for presence. Yet one of the ironies of the radio voice is that the distance it annihilates and the aura of liveness it projects is due less to its live, real time transmission, than the entirely constructed aliveness which technology bestows.

Like the inner voice of western metaphysics, the radio voice has to be denuded of its body, its spatio-temporal existence, in order for it to be abstracted, idealized and evacuated so that it, too, can become the pure instrument of the Law – be it of God or of the state. Once refined through the technologies of language, speech modification, recording and editing processes, the bare bones of the voice are then given life through the addition of the simulated spatiality offered by *reverb*. This has two effects: first, it gives the voice a depth, associated with depth of character, sincerity and truth, but also evoking a kind of transparency or hollowness – as if the insides of body have been evacuated leaving nothing but a shell or temple for the soul. Second, it places the voice in an abstract and idealized space, a space which sounds spacious and therefore sounds as if it should be somewhere, but because it lacks noise it cannot be placed in any particular there. This atopia, projected by reverb onto the voice, can connote the heavens, the electronic ether and the omnipresent mind simultaneously, but it is particularly powerful given our familiarity with the reverberant space of the cathedral, since we associate it with the voice of the preacher and are at once reminded of both the unquestionable Law and authority of God, and our place as passive listeners. Interestingly, the reverberant space is not suitable for hearing the articulate response of the multitude – the masses – since reverberation would return its murmuring voices as a subdued babble.

In both senses then, the reverberant voice suggests that there is no body to interrupt its vocal missive – corporeality has been dematerialized and language flows unimpeded. But also, the body politic has been silenced. It is considered heresy to answer back, either in the cathedral or in one's home listening to the radio. Answering back belongs to the social arena, to face-to-face conversation, to the multitude, here and now engaged in hearing and saying – the Heraclitian Logos, circulating speech, flux and rumour. In western culture, hearing and saying has been reduced to hearsay. It is discounted as gossip, babble, noise. Being neither refined nor electronic, it is censored. In this way conversation is stopped, the broadcast becomes a monologue; dissidence, like dissonance, is contained within an enforced social harmony. Even in so-called democratic radio institutions like talk-back, the technology ensures that the voice of authority prevails. Listen to the presence of the host's voice compared to that of the callers as their voices (particularly those of women) crackle and cackle over the phone lines. Listen to their respective eloquence, and remember that there is always the seven-second delay and the dump button to silence any unwanted opinions. The same imperative for callers to be brief (a pressure which often makes them stumble and pause) structures the listener's response to the direct address of the radio voice. Because the speech of this voice is always short and condensed, moving from one topic or news item to the next, segueing between information and advertising, there is simply no time for response. The radio voice is so *in the present* and its presence is so overwhelming that response is always deferred – the listener waits for a pause but there is none. The speaking never stops.[28]

It is not difficult to locate the voices excluded from radio. Look to any race, gender or cultural group which poses a threat and listen to their voices on radio. The most consistently excluded or derided voice is feminine. Not only has radio's mode of direct address developed from oratory, a traditionally masculine pursuit, but radio's fundamental technology, the microphone, was originally designed for the male vocal range. In fact the radio voice, characterized as masculine, has become so idealized in contemporary culture that feminine voices of authority like Mrs. Thatcher, have had to train their voice to speak in a lower pitch and develop microphone technique in order to be accepted as authoritative by the listening public.[29] Higher pitch is associated with nervousness and a lack of confidence, suggesting that the speaker neither believes in themself nor what they are saying. A rising pitch often produces a shrill voice, and is associated with hysteria and irrationality. These characteristics, among many others, are designated feminine in western culture, and heard as signs of women's essential lack – both of presence and of truth. On radio they are particularly relevant, since it is a medium in which the subject is represented by voice alone. Thus to be listened to or even heard on radio, women have to adopt the persona (from the Greek, meaning through sound) of the ideal male voice.

Apart from being paradigmatically masculine, the radio voice is also singular. There is only room for one speech at a time; other voices are reduced to background noise or ambiance, and the voice in a crowd is either singled out (the cult of the individual) or rendered meaningless. For instance, the dissident, interviewed on the street, in front of a screaming crowd, some distance from the microphone, has to shout in order to be heard. Perhaps some words get lost in the general din, perhaps the shrillness of the voice marks it as hysterical – in either case its potential for influencing the listener has been destroyed. The voices of the crowd, of the many, are literally hard to hear on radio. Like the feminine voice, they air as noise: babble, rumour, noise, gossip, hearsay.[30] The voice of the crowd, like the voice of the ill, the aged, the disturbed, signals the presence of a different and multiple body – the body politic – which, being potentially disruptive and eruptive, has to be kept at a distance at the same time that distance is annihilated. The voices of the many, spreading rumour, telling tales, speaking in the vernacular without regard for 'truth' or scientific proof, are designated "rabble rousing" and broadcast as unorganized sound, another term for noise. It is no coincidence that information theory uses noise to refer to the phenomenon of *interference* in the message. The noise – sound and rumour – speech of the crowd signals the possibility of vagrant information randomly distributed in a context of genuine dialogue and participation and, for this reason, is also considered disruptive. Yet despite the threat of noisy masses and uncontrolled rumours, the body – be it social or individual, sonorous or symbolic – must, however, be incorporated while it is being contained. This is perhaps the most potent function of the radio voice in contemporary western culture – like other media, its aim is to simulate democracy in order to subdue it, with the voice of authority supposedly representing the people, speaking for the people, being the voice of the people – who in turn will cast their votes (vote: voice) silently, through the ballot box, once every four years.

CONCLUSION: THE ROLE OF RADIO ART

To summarize so far, the words of Walter Ong are particularly apt:

> Sound . . . bound to the present time advertises presentness. Even the voice of the dead, played from a recording, envelops us with *his* presence.[31]

The inner voice of western metaphysics and the radio voice of western technology both share the same imperative: to envelope us with *his* presence. However, with the increasing power of media institutions and sophistication of audio technologies (for instance, virtual audio – placing the listener 'there'), such envelopment threatens to suffocate. As radio artists, many of us want to return the breath to the voice, and the voice to the multitude, where it is engaged in hearing and saying. But the question is how?

Critiques of the voice of authority found in both contemporary theory and audio art have focused on returning the body to the voice. However, often we discover that the body inserted through writing (*écriture*) or bodily sound, is still masculine. After listening to a recording of his favorite opera singer, Roland Barthes, for instance, wrote about the voice with body, or "grain," as a voice which, in his words, has a certain "physique," it is "raised," it is "a voice which gets an erection."[32] So we have a masculine grain, emerging from a technological apparatus, and possibly only apparent through the recording. Barthes' "grain," his voice with body added, comes out of the absence that technology engenders, which is precisely the absence of the body. But even if devoid of gender specification, the notion of the grain of the voice, what some have called the underside of language, is bankrupt, for the voice has been subject to such control by the technology of language that it is now impossible to locate its body in speech. When is a cough a cough? When is it a sign? Trying to find the body in the voice and isolating it in some utopian pleasure or *jouissance* could be another way of repeating the same dichotomy between sound and voice, voicing and language, 'becoming' and 'being,' which has so preoccupied western metaphysics.

My proposal here is to focus not on the body of language, the grain of the voice, but on the sound, to concentrate not so much on the reinvigoration of absence – the forgotten half of the presence/absence dichotomy – but on its origin in the shift from a philosophy of 'becoming' to one of 'being.' That means, for both philosophy and radio art, a return to the thinking of Heraclitus, to the concept of the Logos, the Word, as the saying and the said in the state of flux. The *saying* is the presence of many voices, conversational rather than informational radio, the presentation of rumour rather than fact. *Rumour* represents the voices of many, amplified through numerous exchanges, but it is also noise, "unorganized sound," the rabble, recovered perhaps by moving out of the studio (real and metaphoric) into the world. *Noise is interference*: it allows the outside in – talk-back, participation radio, pirate radio, the interference of the airwaves, in other words, meta-radio. *Flux* represents the serendipity of the production process – occurring when one improvises in the studio or collaborates with friends: it embraces rather than excludes. Flux is also ubiquitous – not restricted to any style or subject matter, indefinable, emerging in all fields and concerns. The *Logos* prompts a certain kind of listening – a perceptual/cognitive shift created by radio which mixes voice and sound without discrimination, and in which sound rather than language attracts the listener. *Listening* to the flux of sound provides an opening through which other voices can enter and the listener can escape the one voice (preacher), one experience (logocentrism), one view (western), and one history, which dominant radio insists upon.

Notes

1 Frederick Copleston, *A History of Philosophy*, vol. 1 (Westminister: Newman Bookshop, 1946), 20.

2 Thus, the image of fire is, for Heraclitus "neither strictly physical nor strictly metaphysical; [it is both]; for it is the feeding flame, perceptible both to outward sight and as inward exuberance, and at the same time it is the universal fact of perpetual change." From Philip Wheelwright, *Heraclitus* (New York: Atheneum, 1964), 93. That a physical element of undecided materiality such as fire, which like sound, passes into and out of existence, could also function symbolically, representing what modern philosophy would consider an "in-between," ontologically ambiguous concept, is understandable given that there was no antithesis between spirit and matter, or object and subject, in early Greek philosophy. The resulting ambiguity might be interpreted as a lack of discursive sophistication – philosophical thinking having not yet developed to the point where such distinctions could be made. However, there is reason to believe that Heraclitus' ambiguity was intentional, and that the philosophical discourse of the time, far from being unsophisticated, was capable of dealing with contradiction and paradox to an extent the modern mind finds intolerable.

3 Wheelwright, fragment 20.

4 Wheelwright, fragment 118.

5 Wheelwright suggests that "the connoted idea of speaking is largely metaphorical and transcendental; much as when nowadays, with somewhat less conviction, we employ the phrase "the voice of truth." In Heraclitus' day the sage or lover of wisdom was still the man who found himself called by the voice of a presence greater than he, to speak forth the truth as it might be revealed to him." [Ibid., 23] However, in the same way that Heraclitus used fire as both metaphor and actuality, might not he also have used the voice?

6 Frederick Copleston, 42. "Open" – referring to what is seen; the Word as fixed and static Law.

7 According to Wheelwright, "there is [the] suggestion that we come to know reality not by merely knowing *about* it (fragment 6) but by becoming of its nature one can hear the divine Word only be becoming an expression of It through voice and deed," ibid., 25.

8 Wheelwright, fragment 110.

9 Plato, "Cratylus" in *The Dialogues of Plato*, vol. 3, trans. B. Jowett (Oxford: Claredon Press, 1953), para. 414.

10 Ibid., para 399/c.

11 Ibid., para 387/c.

12 Ibid., para. 440.

13 Ibid., para. 440.

14 "[A name is] not a musical imitation, although that is also vocal; nor, again, an

imitation of what music imitates . . . All objects have sound and figure, and many have color . . . But the art of naming appears not to be concerned with imitations of this kind; the arts which have to do with them are music and drawing," ibid., 423/b.

15 *Aristotle's DE ANIMA, in the version of William of Moerbeke and the Commentary of Thomas Aquinas*, book 2, trans. Kenelm Foster and Silvester Humphries (New Haven: Yale University Press, 1954), para. 477.

16 Ibid., para. 476.

17 Ibid., para. 466–9.

18 Ibid., para. 477.

19 Ibid., (my emphasis).

20 Ibid., para. 478.

21 As David Applebaum notes, "Voice is a proto-technological triumph of human signification over a vital intelligence . . . which explains why inner monologue is a final solution to the unreliable bodily-based voice. No such check [on the breath] is needed. The breath is dispelled from the mind's voice altogether. The mind does not perish like the breath. Therefore mental voice is immortal," in *Voice* (Albany: State University of New York Press, 1990), 31. Perhaps this is why the obscene phone call is characterized by heavy breathing. The obscenity lies in the return of breath to the site of its elimination, the return of archaic breath, the breath of the body, to the clean and infinite topos of electricity.

22 For an extended analysis see Jacques Derrida, *Speech and Phenomena* (Evanston: Northwestern University Press, 1973).

23 See Walter Ong, *The Presence of the Word* (Minneapolis: University of Minnesota Press, 1981).

24 As Applebaum remarks, "Technology applied to voice leads to the amplification of the symbolizing 'act of imagination' which Aristotle has stipulated . . . Technology marks the final stage of conquest by the word, the unit of cognitive meaning, and its engine, the phoneme, the unit of sound discrimination. In the erasure, technology installs itself as nature. Voice without technology becomes inarticulate, ill–framed, 'natural' babble [words as signs, plus technology, redeems voice and nonsense from the 'tower of Babel' the curse of mute individuality]. Without phonemics and grammar, the fundaments of technology, history would be meaningless balderdash," 8.

25 Cited in Rick Altman, "The Technology of the Voice," *Iris* 3:1, 11 (my emphasis).

26 As Rick Altman notes, "The technology of sound contributes to the overall effect of dissimulating its very existence." The basis for this dissimulation, he suggests, is "the fundamental rhetoric on which all ideology is based: presenting the cultural as the natural," ibid., 13, 15.

27 But even prior to any overt machinery, certain communication codes operate – the speech is self-edited, cleaned up even while sounding informal or off-the-cuff.

28 See Max Atkinson, *Our Masters Voice* (New York: Methuen, 1984).

29 Ibid., 112–13.

30 Hence the denigration of "women's talk" as "rumour," itself characterized as feminine. From one of the canons of western literature we find the following:

> At the world's centre lies a place between
> The lands and seas and regions of the sky,
> The limits of the threefold universe,
> Whence all things everywhere, however far,
> Are scanned and watched, and every voice and word
> Reaches its listening ears. Here Rumour dwells,
> Her chosen home set on the highest peak,
> Constructed with a thousand apertures
> And countless entrances and never a door
> Here is Credulity, here reckless Error,
> Groundless Delight, Whispers of unknown source,
> Sudden Sedition, overwhelming fears
> Rumour observes and scours the whole wide world.

Ovid: Metamorphoses, trans. A.D. Melville (New York: Oxford University Press, 1986), 275–76.

31 Walter Ong, 101 (my emphasis).

32 Roland Barthes, "Music, Voice, Language," *The Responsibility of Forms* (New York: Hill and Wang, 1985). Other contemporary writers on the subject, such as Deleuze and Guattari, have admitted sound into their analysis but only in terms of music (especially rhythm). Music, it should be remembered, is a technology and a semiotic system, itself tending towards the eradication of "unorganized sound" and flux.

Looking out from the *Radio Rethink* booth in the Walter Phillips Gallery

Photo Cheryl Bellows

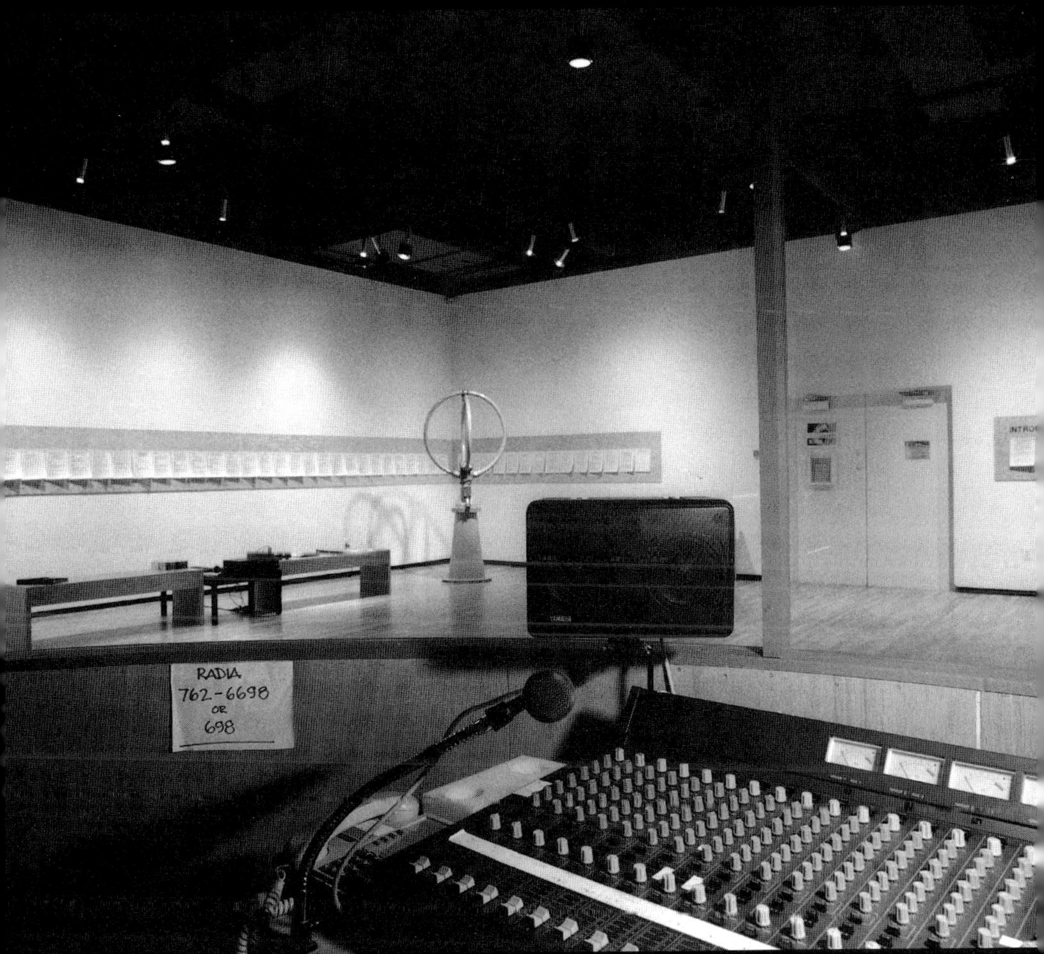
RADIA
762-6698
OR
698

Photo Monte Greenshields

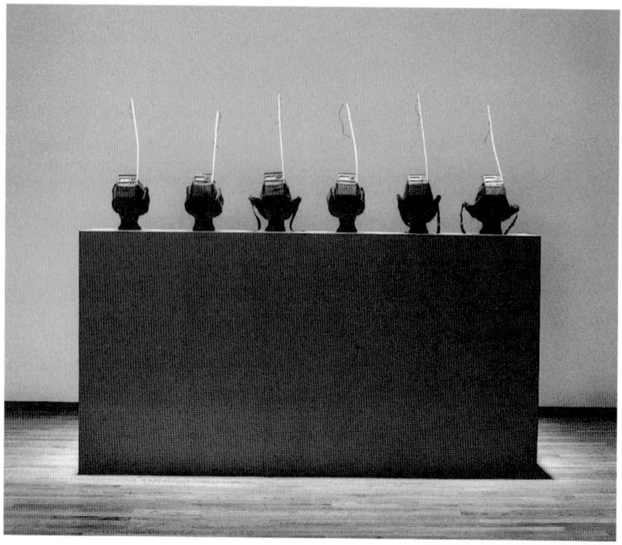

Colette Urban's *It's On Your Head, It's In Your Head* (1992) installation component in the Walter Phillips Gallery

Urban Radio

Tim Westbury

Technology has contributed to the development of a strong visual bias in the western (Eurocentric) cultural milieu, according to Marshall McLuhan, whose media theories to a large extent examine cultural change as oral/aural societies become more literate and visual. While this might indeed be the case in general, subjective experience provides most of us with constant reminders that even if sight is predominant now, it does not occlude hearing – our ears remain a vital component in the experiential environment mapped out for us by the senses.

This fluid and mutually dependent relationship between seeing and hearing also defines a possible context for the work of Colette Urban. Consider *Blind Spot*, a performance work of the late 1980s. Blindfolded, bound by bungee cords and facing into a darkened corner of the gallery, the artist's physical presence prompted questions about sight. Tango music and the disembodied voices of children defined the performance area aurally – while every twenty seconds, the flash from a camera momentarily illuminated the visual space. For the audience this piece relied centrally on sound; the single visual aspect, the performer herself, vainly struggling against the tension of black elastic, seemed increasingly reduced to a trope with each sporadic appearance. The artist herself, of course, was effectively isolated from the visual component of the piece, except for the series of *post facto* documentary photographic images. In its use of several different media, this work confronted the spectator with the awareness that sensory experience is often mediated, so that eyes and ears are forced to negotiate new ways of interaction. Aural/oral relationships, as McLuhan pointed out, are considerably influenced by changing technologies.

More than thirty years have now elapsed since the early days of broadcast television, when McLuhan was producing his most widely read texts. The intervening period has seen the development of cultural phenomena which he probably never could have conceived of from his own historical vantage point – among them the rapid development of the music video (via cable television) and the introduction of the Walkman, both in the decade following his death in 1980. These two technologies question, though in almost opposing ways, McLuhan's hypothesis that the "magic world of the ear" has yielded to the "neutral world of the eye."[1]

In the case of music video, the sensory experiences of hearing and seeing are forced together – rendered equivalent to each other so as to almost eradicate any differentiation between the two very separate streams of information. A rapid succession of video images, whether or not they are narrative, can now become as vital a part of the experience of music as the traditional audio component.

The Walkman, on the other hand, effectively severs the aural experience from the other senses, isolating it in a singular, almost virtual "space" that is delineated by the hearing mechanism of the person wearing the headphones (unless, as is all too often the case, they have it turned up too loud). Self-contained personal audio devices temporarily privilege sound in the hierarchy of the senses – you can carry your own environment with you, in your head and on your head.

Wearing a Walkman, you can easily forget how unusual that technology can make you appear to others who are not in the same aural environment, despite their physical proximity. While you may occupy the same physical space, Walkmans disrupt the previously seamless aural continuity of a shared environment.

Several recent performance works by Colette Urban may be read as experiments that publicly elucidate the subjective phenomenon of shifting sense ratios. The same pataphysically inspired logic evident in *Blind Spot* surfaced later in her 1992 performance in Banff, *It's On Your Head, It's In Your Head.* This week-long performance, both for and with radio, involved seven collaborators. Every day, a different, predetermined member of the group remained behind in the *Radio Rethink* broadcast booth at the Walter Phillips Gallery. The others met in the gallery exhibition space and each performer would don one of six special radio hats that the artist had constructed for the piece.

The performers' hats were ordinary-looking Canadian winter headgear: dark, navy blue, wool caps with a black fun-fur flap that folds down to cover the ears. However, sewn on to the front flap was a nylon mesh pocket designed to hold a small AM/FM receiver equipped with a built-in LCD digital clock and timer. Each radio was pre-tuned to Radia 89.9 FM, the *Radio Rethink* transmission frequency. Topping it off, the antenna wire dangled haphazardly down to the wearer's shoulder like a long, unruly lock of jet black hair.

Outfitted with hats, the group travelled to one of seven public locations in the Banff townsite which had been designated as performance sites for the piece. As each clock reached noon, the radios would turn on automatically and the piece for that day would begin.

The oral/aural component of the work was cumulative. On the first day, the member of the group who remained in the booth at the Walter Phillips Gallery transmitted anything of choice for exactly one minute. On day two, another member of the group would broadcast for two minutes and, after one minute, the recorded version of the previous day was "mixed in" at the soundboard by Dan Lander, sound engineer for this project. By Sunday, the end of the performance, the seven-minute broadcast was composed of individual audio segments from each of the seven days layered upon each other.

Although Colette Urban conceived the piece and decided on the seven locations, it was important to her that she did not dictate other aspects of the performance to the rest of the group. By drawing numbers from one of the radio hats, each performer selected a turn in the booth; what would be broadcast was unknown to the roaming members until it was emitting from their own hats – and soon after, at always slightly different times, heard from the hats on the heads of the five other performers nearby.

It's On Your Head, It's In Your Head began on a Monday morning with Neil MacInnis in the radio booth. The other six performers arrived at the first broadcast reception site, the local Alberta Liquor Control Board store, a little before noon. We browsed the aisles as normal shoppers while, after a few seconds of radio static, Neil's disembodied voice occasionally emanated from our hats – reading from Dylan Thomas about a drunken couple getting into a bath with their clothes on. This one minute, which ended with the strains of Kurt Weill from Brecht's *Three Penny Opera*, seemed to pass very quickly. After several more seconds of static, the radios fell silent. By the time anyone within earshot realized the hats were emitting sound, it was all over.

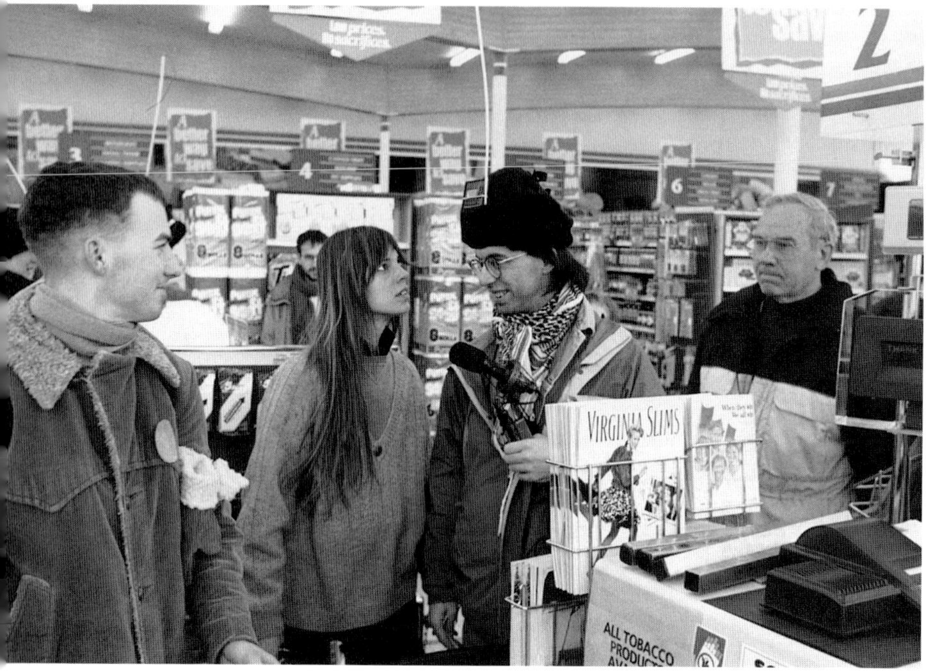

Photo Monte Greenshields

In the Banff Safeway store on day four of Colette Urban's *It's On Your Head, It's In Your Head* (1992)

Photo Monte Greenshields

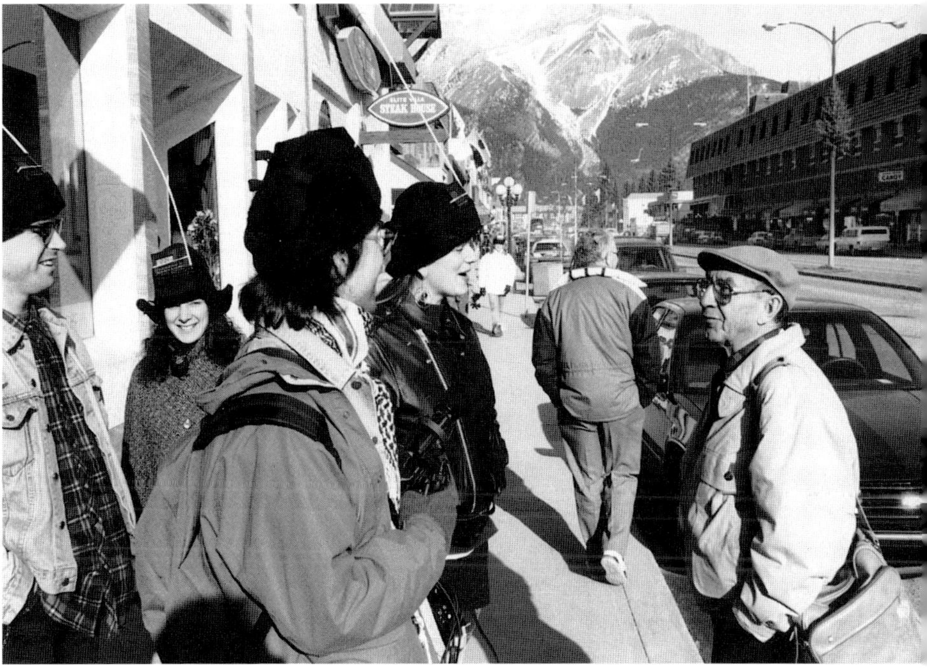

On the main street of Banff on day five of Colette Urban's *It's On Your Head, It's In Your Head* (1992)

While wandering around inside the liquor store we quickly discovered that the radio receivers picked up the signal better in some spots than others and that clarity varied dramatically, depending on the direction you were facing. Urban felt that perhaps the flexible antennae were partially to blame and, overnight, modified the radio hats so that for the rest of the week, each antenna was held erect, the wire running through a thin white plastic tube about two feet long, so that just a short tail hung out the top. The hats were all the more conspicuous when I took my own turn in the radio booth the following day.

Day two constituted the "blind spot" for me as performer. While I knew that everyone else would be sitting in a different kind of booth at the Rundle Restaurant at noon, my knowledge of what happened to the rest of the group during the two-minute broadcast would necessarily forever be indirect, mediated: I was both absent and present at the same time. Ironically, I read the opening paragraphs of the 1967 Time/Life Science Library edition, *Sound and Hearing*.

Allison Cameron was on the radio on Wednesday, while the rest of us went down to the Banff Post Office. This day's performance was high profile because we were accompanied by a CBC (Canadian Broadcasting Corporation) television news crew – the presence of television cameras an easily visible signifier that an "event" was occurring. The spectacle was neatly détourned, however, by Cameron's last minute decision to replace her prepared text with the sounds of children's farm animal noisemakers. When her transmission began, the six of us lining up in a queue to buy stamps spoke eloquently through our hats.

The performance on the fourth day took place in the large Safeway grocery store downtown. A tongue in cheek response to the site – as a place typically providing sustenance to suburbanites – Sheilagh O'Leary read a text adapted from the diary of a midwife, repeated several times in the course of her four-minute broadcast. Here the radio hats caused their first little bit of trouble as well. After passing through the check-out with our purchases, the group was approached by the store manager. He had watched this episode from behind the one-way glass window in his office overlooking the produce aisles. Urban described to him the intent of the piece as an artwork that functions outside gallery walls – intended to stimulate awareness of the environment for viewers by presenting the unexpected. In addition, she explained, as a former resident of Banff, she was interested in bridging the distance between the art world of the Banff Centre and aspects of downtown life in Banff.

Colette Urban herself was on the air on day five. The weather was unseasonably warm so the rest of us were very content with the performance location that day: the sunny side of Banff Avenue. Emphasizing the small-town intimacy that characterizes even this most overtly commercial part of Banff, Colette's voice greeted tourists and locals alike with a friendly "Hi! Hello! How are you? Oh, hi there . . . " Because we were outside and the transmission signal was unimpeded, the reception was exceptionally clear – consequently, many people turned around to see who was recognizing them in the street; but while the words may have momentarily suggested identification, the speaker remained invisible. Like a character in a Beckett play, craving basic human contact but encountering only the silence of a void, Urban's component essentially formalized the temporarily disembodied voice, which characterized the piece as a whole.

Punctuating the stereotypical differentiation between working week and leisure-filled weekend, Saturday's performance occurred at the mini-golf course in the Banff Springs Hotel convention centre. Loosely based on the world-renowned, full-size course run by the hotel during the summer, artificial turf and stones provided an idyllic setting for Jocelyn Robert's turn in the booth. His text, read from an advanced geometry textbook, was abstract mathematical theory that underscored the architectural precision of the golf course, pointing to the politics of getting the ball in the hole.

It's On Your Head, It's In Your Head culminated, outside once again, in the Upper Hot Springs bathing pool. Rita McKeough was pleased to be the person in the booth on the final day – she really did not care much for bathing in the sulphurous hot pool. For the rest of us, a week of getting used to the radio hats seemed not long enough when our only other item of clothing was to be a National Parks-issue bathing suit. As we gradually entered the pool from the changing rooms, we drew a few sidelong glances. Several other bathers were soon intrigued enough to approach us and ask what the hats were for. We were in the midst of trying to explain the artist's intentions for the piece when the clocks reached noon.

Initially, McKeough simply pretended that she was in the pool with the rest of the group: "Oh, it's so hot . . . I'm burning up . . . " Then, without warning, "I'm up to my neck in spit, piss and pubic hair . . . I'm

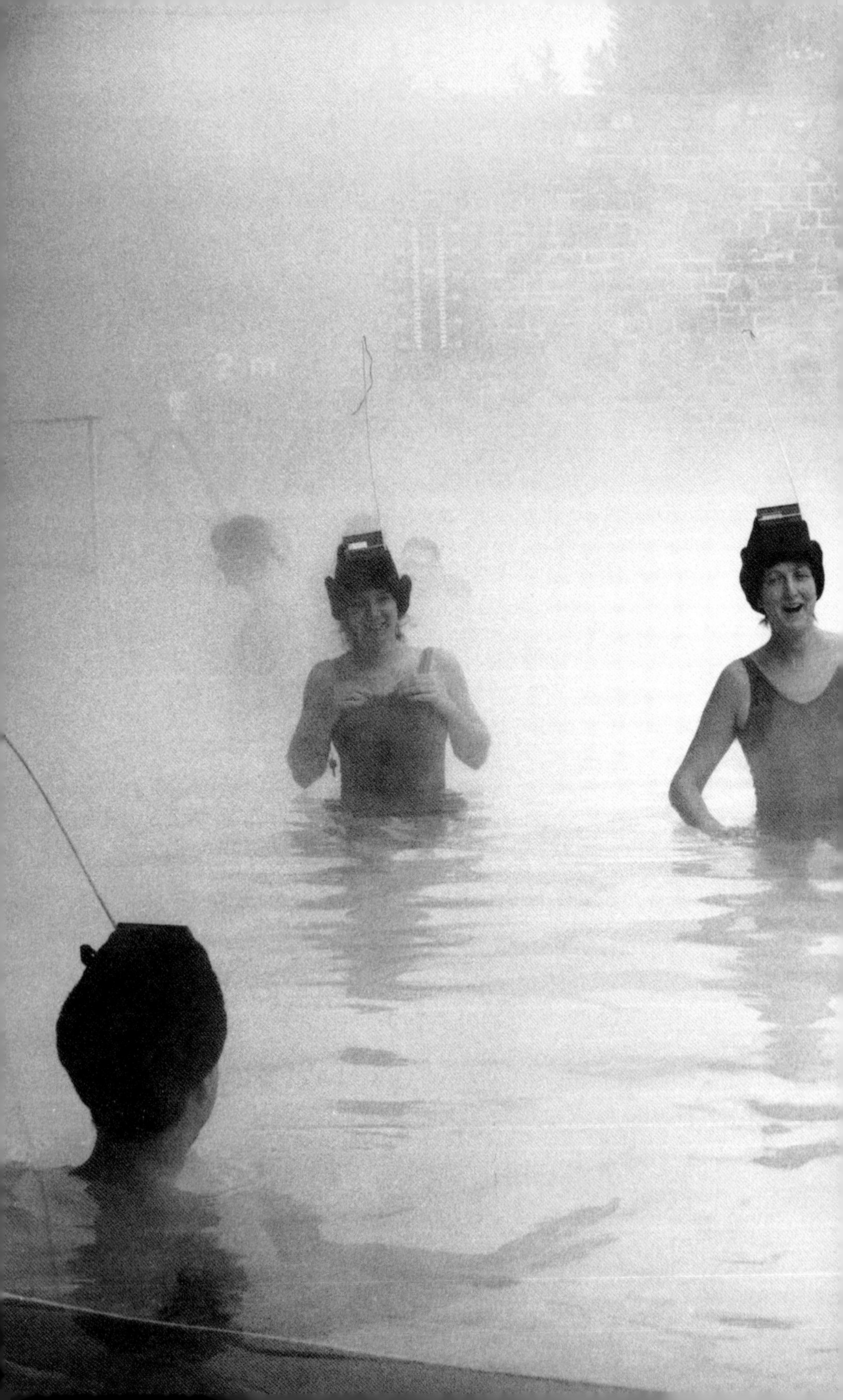

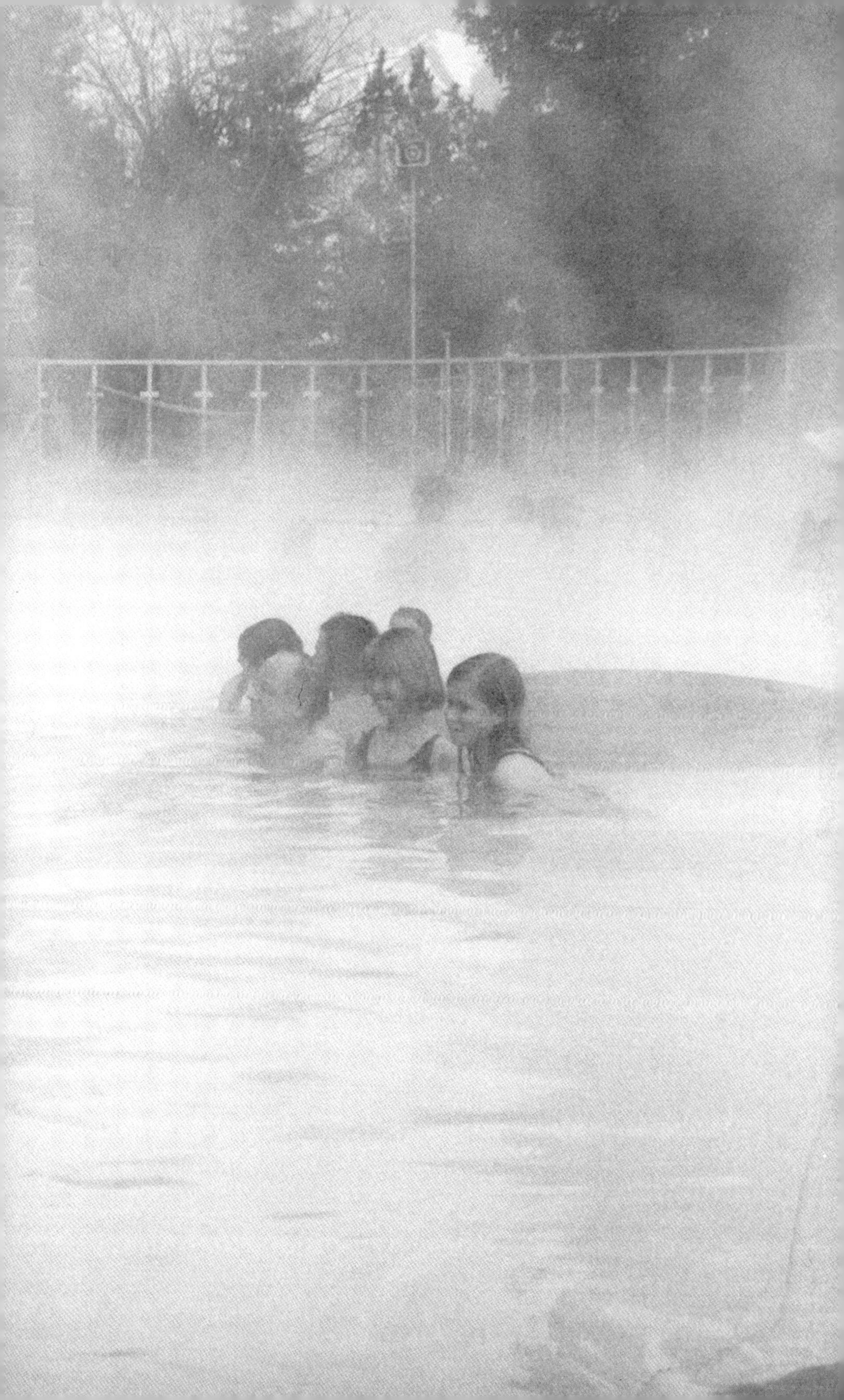

up to my neck in hot water *now*, aren't I, Colette?" As one might expect, these words emanating from our hats very suddenly took the performance out of the realm of the whimsical for a few members of the audience, including a woman I was speaking with. After telling me that what we were doing was clearly illegal, she approached the lifeguard, urging him to have all of us immediately removed from the pool. McKeough's voice, its speaker invisible, had evidently encroached upon a blindspot. I tried my best to explain the work to her, knowing that whatever was said would increasingly become submerged in the mix. After almost three minutes had passed, she had had enough. Pausing only long enough to collect her children, she headed back to the changing room. As the radios returned first to static and then dead air, our group left the pool.

Although her art has often attempted to work outside the framework of the gallery, Urban was drawn to use radio for this piece because broadcasting literally carried it into public space. Having worked in downtown Banff years earlier, and knowing firsthand of the distant relationship that existed with the Banff Centre, Urban was interested in addressing a lack of communication between two communities from the outset. She conceived the whole performance as a catalyst to jolt people out of their normal routine: "By throwing something at them in this way, it may help them question what it is that they are doing, possibly stimulating a different relationship to the environment that they are in." The several episodes where artistic intervention was perceived as confrontation served to crystallize areas of dissolution, to identify points where communication begins, and where it begins to break down.

It's On Your Head, It's In Your Head relies on radio as a tool to both expose and attempt a renegotiation of these complex social relationships. Aural/oral technologies rely on the existence of a "public." In Urban's piece, the performers, as radio (re)transmitters themselves, address a storyteller-size public from the much larger one made possible through broadcast technologies. The structure of the piece defers accountability by distributing it evenly amongst the seven performers, but those seen wearing the hats assume the ultimate responsibility. The artist's and performers' interactions in this case emphasize the responsibility that lies with broadcasting to a public.

Previous page: In the Banff Upper Hot Springs on the seventh and final day of Colette Urban's *It's On Your Head, It's In Your Head* (1992)

Photo Monte Greenshields

Humour, a thread which seems to run through much of Colette Urban's work, functions here both to diffuse the act of intervention and make way for people to engage with each other – she acknowledges the performance as existing at "that edge where, at any moment, things could turn in the other direction," concurring with McLuhan's suggestion that

> Environments are not passive wrappings, but are, rather, active processes which are invisible. The groundrules, pervasive structure, and over-all patterns of environments elude easy perception. Anti-environments, or countersituations made by artists, provide means of direct attention and enable us to see and understand more clearly. The interplay between the old and the new environments creates many problems and confusions. The main obstacle to a clear understanding of the effects of the new media is our deeply embedded habit of regarding all phenomena from a fixed point of view.[2]

Through the use of voices and sounds, *It's On Your Head, It's In Your Head*, effectively attempts to disrupt that artificial rigidity demanded in a visual universe defined by the laws of Renaissance perspective. It serves as well to remind us that the relationship between the aural and visual senses has not likely ever been a static one. Just as each new technology seems to require the invention of new relationships between the senses, negotiating new methods of interaction seems to be necessary for continued communication in mediated environments.

Notes

1 Marshall McLuhan and Quentin Fiore, *The Medium is the Massage – An Inventory of Effects* (New York: Bantam Books, 1967), 44.

2 Ibid., 68.

Pirate Writing

RADIOPHONIC STRATEGIES FOR FEMINIST TECHNO-PERVERTS

Kim Sawchuk

CHARACTERS

storyteller
operator
alter ego

SETTING

Outside the doors to the gallery rests a photocopied geological map of the world. On the map an arrow points to a large red dot where Banff is reputed to be located. *You are here* is scrawled beside the arrow. Inside the gallery, balalaika music can be heard. Large *X*s have been marked on the floor with black tape. They are highlighted by spotlights, and surrounded by chairs. The word *Here* is marked beside each *X*, including the *X* under the table where the storyteller sits.

operator
Begin with "Moyi Yaseny" (The Ash Tree), a cut from Dreams of the Ukraine: Popular Dancing Songs *(Long Island: Apon). Fade to sounds of the ocean. The storyteller will continue to read over the sounds of the water. Fade out ocean after "You are hear," then wind the tape forward and cue it to "postulating identity" section.*

storyteller (whisper)
You are here
You are here
You . . . are . . . **hear**

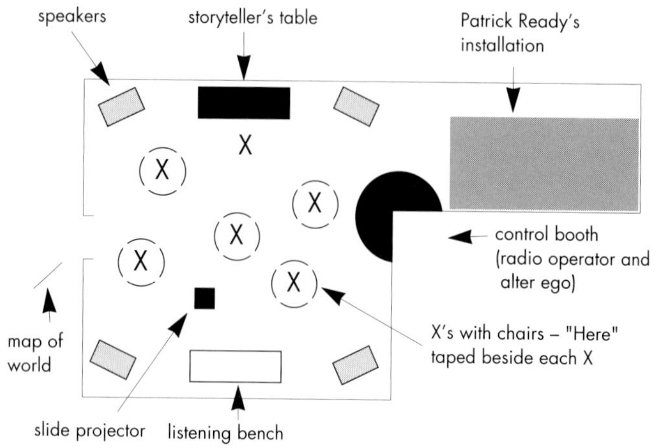

alter ego

Pictures of me . . .

storyteller

I would like to begin with a picture of me. It is June, 1962. I am just about two years old and I am sitting on a couch with my paternal grandfather who looks distinctly uncomfortable. I am in drag – pirate drag. I sport a big black moustache, a fearsome hat with skull and crossbones and I hold a bottle of beer in my hand.

A second picture. I am two. Again. Only this time, I wear a little girl costume. Eggbeater in hand, I pretend to bake a cake. A bird perches on my shoulder, one of many budgies in my family, all named Perky.

A third picture. I pose for a picture with my maternal grandmother, great-grandmother and my mother. I am five years old amongst these three very dignified Ukrainian women. Apparently someone has asked me to smile, say "cheese." I grit my teeth, my hands are clenched, my face is twisted in an evil grin. It looks like I am about to bolt from the picture or attack the photographer. Maybe it's the dress.

storyteller with alter ego (whisper)

IDENTITY IS NOT A FACT, IT'S AN ACT
IDENTITY IS NOT A FACT, IT'S AN ACT
IDENTITY IS NOT A FACT, IT'S A PRACTICE . . .

storyteller

. . . determined by repeat performances.

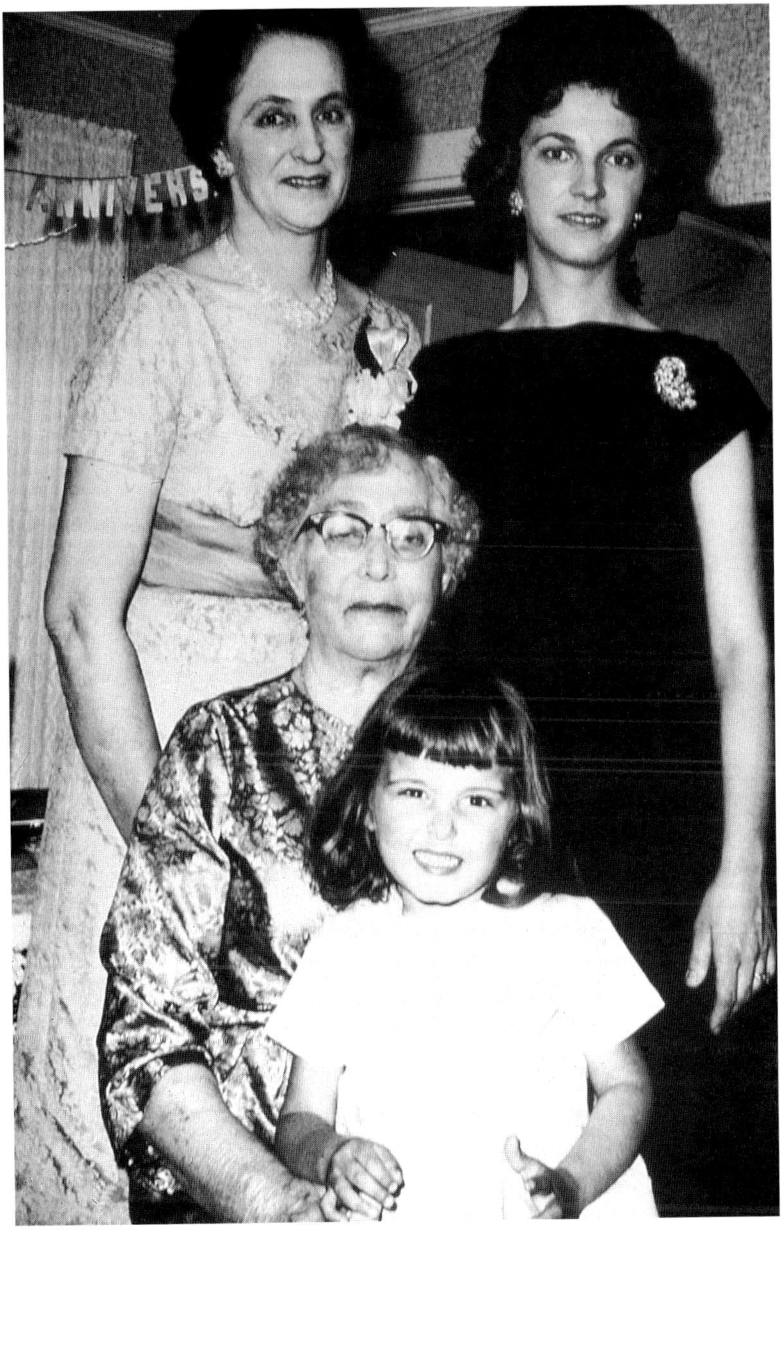

Photo courtesy the author

Identification is a performative in-corp-oration of discursive possibilities, an interactive writing of bodies in motion. In the twentieth century, these bodies are located within a variety of technological circuits.[1]

When I was asked to write on "questions of authority" for this radio conference and the term pirate was mentioned, a persona began to surface, a memory that had sunk into the deep recesses of my consciousness, a memory that I have subsequently recovered and rewritten through the presentation of these photographs – my life as a pirate.

Pirates live on the high seas foregoing the stability of land, territory, and national laws for other forms of community. Pirate subjectivity provides a potential metaphor for understanding my feminist appropriation of language and radio technology. Like women who often work with technology but rarely own or control it, we must search for ways to explain our ambiguous relationship to its seductions; we are both excluded and complicit.[2] Perhaps the pirate is such a conceptual tool and provisional identity. Like women in relationship to phallocentric cultures, pirates are border creatures crossing languages, power, money, genders, dependent upon tools, such as compasses to navigate our way through these territories, but at the same time susceptible to the vagaries of the natural elements.

I want to explore my relationship to radio technology through the persona of the pirate.

I would like to connect performance with identity with history with the body with autobiography with technology, specifically radio. I remind you that this is an experiment, and not a fixed theoretical positon.

alter ego

A cautionary note is necessary.

storyteller

This will be a meandering tale, a traveller's tale of work, love, theory, family, play and politics cross-stitched into a textured vocal weave.

operator

Play the voice on pre-recorded tape. It is the storyteller's voice, but she speaks slowly, solemnly, pompously. The voice has been manipulated with a slight effect so it has a tinny timbre and sounds like it is located in a large hollow room. The repetition of the word identity is stressed in the reading.

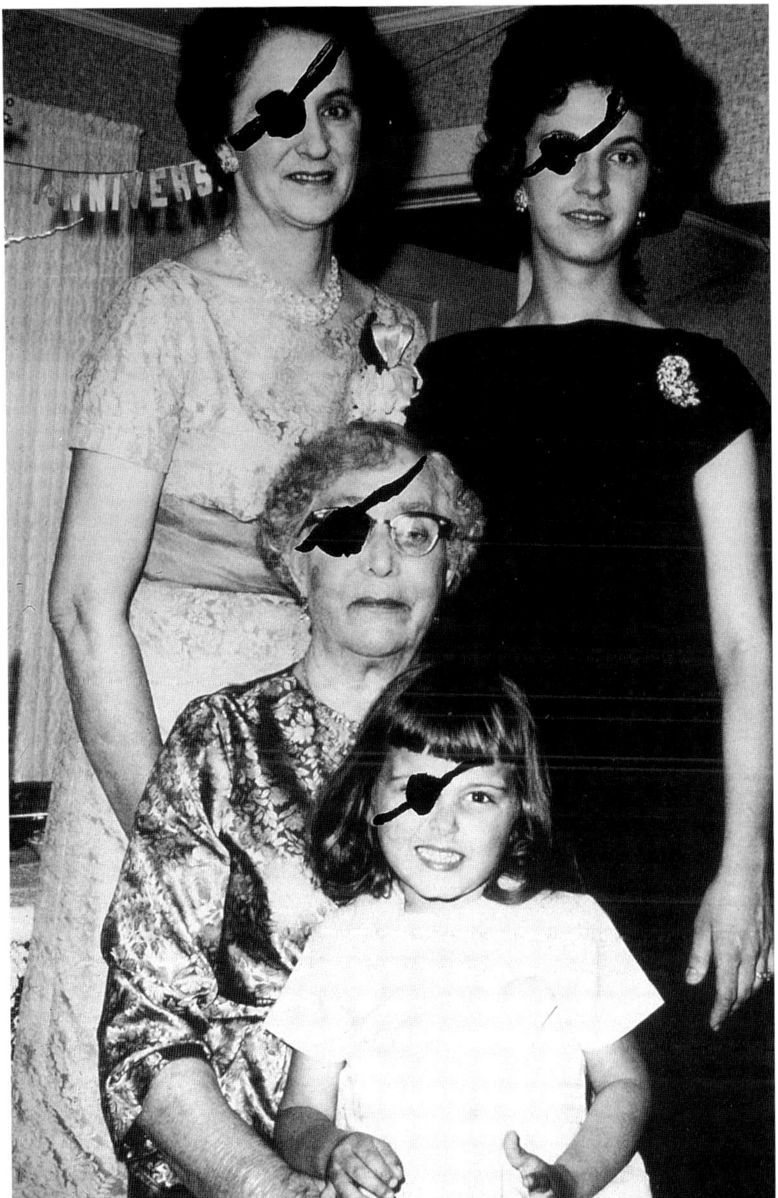

Photo courtesy the author

> *Postulating identity as performance isn't the same as promoting a voluntaristic performative identity. The latter fits into the logic of consumer capitalism where everything is absolutely equivalent. Everything is the same and can be infinitely recombined. Go to the store and buy your identity. It can always be exchanged, it is only a simulation, after all. However, not everyone has the same amount of capital, either cultural or monetary, in this supermarket of transmutation.*
>
> *The former, identity as performance, attempts to understand identity as a social discourse based on public interactions; it is not an object to be bought or sold, but a becoming, limited by a finitude which for lack of a better term I would call the real.*

storyteller

As subjects we do not always choose how we will be identified. It is not clear to me when I look at this picture whether *I* put on this costume or whether it was placed on me by my parents. As first born I was to have been a boy. In this case, the costume projects their patrilineal desires.[3]

Let me continue on the same hand but in a different vein.

To use an evocative metaphor from the sea I found in an interview with Donna Haraway, the history of the self and the self in relationship to history and politics can be understood as the accumulation of barnacles.

alter ego

"[Y]ou come into the historical world encrusted with barnacles. Metaphorically speaking, I imagine a historical person as being somehow like a hermit crab that's encrusted with barnacles. And I see myself and everybody else as sort of switching shells as we grow . . . But every shell we pick up has its histories, and you certainly don't choose these histories."[4]

storyteller

We become accountable to each other by remembering which barnacles we carry.

My pirate history is a story that I did not so much uncover, as fiction that I have written back into my life. Pirate writing is an act of thievery where I reconstitute my self on the basis of seizing the tools to mark the world that has marked me, a world at every turn mediated, affecting my self-perceptions and perceptions of others. I want to pilfer this image of the electronic pirate, currently lodged in popular culture as a white macho, individualistic masculinist challenge to "society." This myth fallaciously bifurcates individual and community.

In doing so, I want to rearrange these monolithic structures to promote alternative technological and social interactions, just as I have rearranged these chairs.

alter ego

MULTIPLE PERSONAS

storyteller

In the past five or so years, I have been creating personalities for myself. In my theoretical personas I have donned the voice of a telephone solicitor and a garbage picker. Sometimes these voices have been accompanied by visual accoutrements. As an advertisement cop I have performed with a box of Cat Chow on my head. I also have been a preacher in polyesters, an accordion player and a Mountie – to name only a few.

Each of these personas and performances has been written and repeated in various sites – radio, performance space, lecture hall, conference room, classroom. They have been "live" – and in many layered permutations of liveness. Some of them are recorded on video and on cassette. Many are not.

alter ego

Another cautionary note.

storyteller

I don't think of this use of the voice and multiple personas as schizophrenic. The adoption of multiple *personas* to explore my multiple *positionality* is not the same as feigning multiple *personalities*. Multiple personalities implies a series of discrete, atomistic characters, each vying for control of the subject's ego. My ego is not unified; the personas have a fluidity, the stories overlap, interconnect. They seem to be housed in the same body.

alter ego

Or are they? What are the boundaries between interior and exterior? How does such a rigid demarcation explain, for example, the exchange of stories?

storyteller

Embracing these internal contradictions is not simply a performative strategy but a pedagogical strategy to recover the joy of group work: one position does not have to prevail, although all positions are bound together by virtue of a chosen, common topic or body. Think of the chairs arranged in this room as diagrammatic of this concept.

To return to my story . . .

operator

Play tape of Ukrainian words. These are the only words that the storyteller can remember. They are the whispered fragments of a lost memory. The majority are words that refer to comfort and food. They have been given a slight echo.

> *peruhe, holupchi, keilbasa, moloka, hribe, yichi, dwako yu, zibulya, yak tum, gido, baba, borscht, keeshke, kolomeka, macaron, zupa, dimenyi chum, hroschi, yenesniyu, figusmaku, klopitz, deutchene, die boja, bo prevechne, peruschke, studenettes, vereneke.*

storyteller

Writing the voice through radio provides a way to navigate and chart where I have been and who I have become through my involvement (not always voluntary) in different networks of the cultural and economic apparatus. Most of them come from my experience as a woman working within a high-tech, information-based capitalist system. To survive in this system, I have learned to be "flexible" with my skills. In some of these jobs, I have in fact, used my voice to play roles.

Amplified, exaggerated, embroidered together from tattered remains, these personas reconstruct the life of a Ukrainian prairie exile who migrated to Toronto then Montréal, caught within an increasingly globally connected integrated circuit. My position in this circuit is not singular, not even double, but like my identity, multiple and irreconcilably contradictory.

Fictionalizing my situation expunges the nausea I have felt after long periods in jobs I dislike intensely. Creating autobiographical fictions functions as a tool to develop a particular theoretical point at a particular moment, and a map to overcome a cultural condition of psychasthenia, which Celeste Olalquiaga characterizes as a disturbance in the relation between self and surrounding territory. Psychasthenia is . . .

alter ego

"a state in which the space defined by the coordinates of the organism's own body is confused with represented space. Incapable of demarcating the limits of its own body, lost in the immense area that circumscribes it, the psychasthenic organism proceeds to abandon its own identity to embrace the space beyond. It does so by camouflaging itself into the milieu. This simulation effects a double usurption: while the organism successfully reproduces those elements it could not otherwise apprehend, in the process it is swallowed by them, vanishing as a differentiated entity."[5]

storyteller

Consumer capital seems to be aware of this problem. In the United States the supermarket chain Pathmark has put video terminals on shopping carts. As you wend your way through the aisles, your movements are detected by sensors on the ceiling – losing oneself is a real possibility. In these miles of aisles you know where you are at all times.

operator

Play Song of the Volga Boatman from Balalaika Favourites *by the Osipov State Russian Folk Orchestra (Polygram/Philips Classics Production 1992) hummed by the storyteller and a low-voiced friend. This is very short.*

storyteller

Although there seems to be an intensification of its present logic, this displacement is not simply a 1990s condition. I understand this voyage of psychic, social and economic displacement as a continuation of my grandparent's journey from the Ukraine at the turn of the century. My contemporary nomadic tale continues this saga of movement across countries and continents. It is quintessentially North American. I am the daughter of assimilated Ukrainians and the granddaughter of a gravedigger-trapper, a factory worker, a farmer and the great-granddaughter of a matriarchal homesteader – deterritorialized persons who travelled on ships to a place called North America supposedly empty and devoid of human habitation. Examining this legacy makes me question categories of identity and privilege based on ahistorical ontological divisions. It forces a recognition of the active role of historical contingency in structuring the limits of my identity.[6]

To survive this condition of psychasthenia, I don't want to consolidate exclusive boundaries. I want to play within the leakiness of borders between the shores of past, present, future, the sentient world, the technological world and the human world. I acknowledge the danger of this game, but the risk of ignoring these collisions and collusions seems greater than the risk of learning to live within this instability.

alter ego

TECHNO-IDENTITY

storyteller

Why, when thinking of performance and identity, should the body be thought to end at the skin?

Sound artist Christina Kubisch maintains "the fear of electronics ignores the fact that each note is an electrically converted vibration and that live sound material can be produced 'naturally' by current, in the same way as traditional instruments."[7]

I experience an embodied ecstasy in the technological interface of the radiophonic performance.

operator

Play this pre-recorded section for two minutes. The tape is read very fast, with a sense of urgency. The storyteller improvises along with this pre-recorded section.

The Control Room is an Instrument.

Radio trepidation. The terror you feel as you walk into the control room alone. The first time. You have your songs, your tapes organized. You know there is a connection between the buttons on the control panel in front of you and the machines that surround you. Will you be able to make them work? Will you be able to move your body in and around the studio with the practised ease of the regular controls?

Channels on – off.

Not all of the lights work.

You load up the machines with your materials. You push the appropriate buttons to connect monitors to machines.

You are on the air.

Dead air.

You fumble for the buttons and the mike. Instead of cassette one, you've pushed two. Panic. You read from one of the typed public service announcements, one of the many items programmed into your time. Panic, as you try to read and decide what to play next. Panic. Even if you could see the monitor, which you can't because you can't talk into the mike, read, and look at the board all at the same time, you can't remember what you've put where.

It's all gotta be automatic. Your fingers must be familiar with it. Through repeated performance, perhaps it will. Just like playing the piano, you think.

Only . . .

The monitor is part of a larger instrument, the control booth. It differs from other instruments you've played because of the sense of immersion you have inside of it. It engulfs you. It is around you. It surrounds you. Instead of you being outside of it, you are in it. Completely. As I sit here speaking into this mike looking at the equipment on the other side of a glass wall, I realize at this moment that the gallery is an extension of the radio booth. The glass wall simulates an artificial barrier because we are all miked and transmitting.

We are on air.

You realize that the best way to guard against dead air is to load everything up. Every piece of equipment in the control room. That way if you hit a button, something is bound to happen, though it may not be what you intended. This could be interesting.

You apologize to your listeners for your clumsiness, for the gaps and missed cues, the silences. In radio there can be no silence. Silence equals death – a sign of your ineptness with technology. Just like a girl they will think.

By the end of your first hour you are more familiar with the space, with the buttons, the procedures. You are making transitions. You fade in and out. You compose and improvise on the radio, although you can't yet speak. It's not simply a technology to transmit sound. You must play the space.

(storyteller hums along with the tape in this section to indicate her pleasure)

What a feeling of pleasure to drive this studio, to handle the mike, the switches, the buttons, to know that you are transmitting yourself into the ears of unseen listeners. You want to reach them. You want to dazzle them with your witty repartee, but you're too busy trying to make it flow smoothly. It's a pleasure not seeing who they are, and enjoying the anonymity of your radio personality.

storyteller

Donna Haraway's feminist readings of technology, cybernetics and nature continue an ambiguous intellectual legacy. Cybernetic theory questioned the body's boundaries and promoted a philosophic-scientific worldview that could be applied to animal, human or machine.

In cybernetics, the central nervous system no longer appears as a self-contained organ "receiving inputs from the senses and discharging them into the muscles." As Norbert Wiener, often attributed with the lofty title of the founding father of cybernetic theory, explains, "on the contrary some of its most characteristic activities are explicable only as a circular process, emerging from the nervous system through the sense organs, whether they be proprioceptors or organs of special senses."[8]

According to cybernetics, our neurophysiological makeup is part of a whole integrated circuit of continual reception and transmission of information. Wiener dreamed that one sensory organ could be re-wired to pick up signals for another impaired sensory organ. If our vision became damaged we could hook up our sight with our ears.

This new field of inquiry, which had no name in 1947, thinks of the self as an information system.[9] Wiener described the advent of cybernetics as a coming together of a group of scientists who "had already become aware of the essential unity of the set of problems centering on communication, control and statistical mechanics, whether in the machine or in living tissue."[10] From this perspective our bodies are complex feedback mechanisms that automatically adjust to the flow of information and affect its flow through our adjustments.

The twentieth-century feminist pirate, as both the product of information and language, is located in this techno-identity.

alter ego

RADIO GIRLS/PIRATE LANGUAGE

storyteller

But wait! In most contemporary versions this cybernetic discourse masculinizes technology. Happy Harry Hard-On in the 1990 film *Pump up the Volume* is a typical representation of the techno-pirate in popular culture. The mike illegally broadcasts the voice of teenage discontent and male sexuality engendering this pirate transmission as the prerogative of phallocentric culture. How limited. The mike not only broadcasts, it records and therefore listens. As a technological device it has no inherent gender identity or function: it all depends on what articulations to what hardware you make.

We need to rescue this cybernetic vision from gurus like Timothy Leary who reinterpret the notion of the governor in cybernetics as a heroic male pilot.[11]

Remember that pirates were members of communities. Recall that in cybernetics a governor was not one who governed, but a ship's steering mechanism to take in information from the outside, to adjust the pattern of movement in harmonious accordance with its environmental conditions.[12]

But what does this all mean for women, technology, radio, language and the voice, let alone my personal story?

Women need opportunities to acquire technical literacy. It is a question of survival.

The pirate, like Haraway's feminist cyborg, emerges as one of the illegitimate offspring of a culture of information, communications, not to mention capital: a culture where information *is* capital.[13]

But pirating is also a euphemism for a political radio strategy. I must admit that I have stolen voices intended only for private use and played them for public consumption.

alter ego

In *The Pirate's Fiancée* Meaghan Morris tells the tale of a "very curious girl" who lives on the edge of a village with her goat and her tape recorder. She makes money from the men and from cleaning. In the village the townspeople spurn her and fear her because of her sharp insolent tongue and her sullied reputation. But in her house the village men confide in her at the same time as they allow increasingly vicious public attacks on her establishment. But she has saved their money, and with her tape recorder, their words. She leaves town, and as she heads down the road, she leaves behind a village listening in horror not to her voice but to their own – their most intimate secrets and confessions playing loudly in public for all to hear.

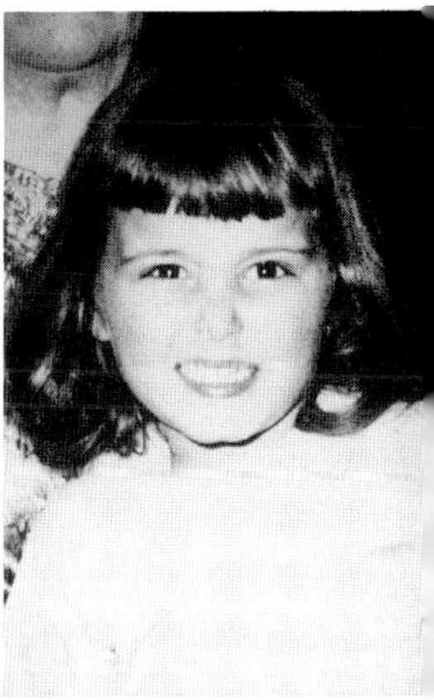

Photo courtesy the author

storyteller

For Morris, the village is undone by the broadcast of its own presuppositions; it is destroyed by an intensification of its own exploitative logic.

The Pirate's Fiancée allegorizes women's relationship to language and suggests one form of feminist radio practice – restless thieves of language and technology.[14]

The myth of Prometheus, man stealing fire from the gods, has been used as a metaphor to understand man's acquisition of technology. But, in Lizzie Borden's 1983 film *Born in Flames*, women operate the technology in the feminist revolution.

operator

Play CD *of Bulgarian women singers. Play "Chansons Chopes de la région de Sophia" from* Le Chant de Femme Bulgares *by* Choeur des femmes de Sophia *(Arevidas, 1988). Fade "radio girl" text, which is on tape one into the music at the end.*

In this pre-recorded section, the pitch was changed throughout the text. This created a doubling effect on the storyteller's voice on tape. Added to this confusion, the storyteller reads along, trying to keep apace with the lightening speed of the taped text.

Radio girls are pirates. We speak in a multiplicity of tongues, fracture the notion of a coherent internal space from which to uncover our own voices.

We deploy its accidents and excesses to communicate multiple desires. Radio girls refuse to clean up the noise. Beneath the scrubbing there is always sound: the squeaking sound of a hand rubbing a table or, better still, the sloshing of water on the deck of a ship.[15]

Radio girls pervert speech.Their talk verges on the dirty, vulgar, obscene carnivalesque. Parrots on their shoulders, they prefer dialects and regional vernacular. Parrots are magical birds. They share our language and communicate between the animal and human worlds.

Pirates sing songs, drink rum, dress in drag. A number of women, including Anne Bonney and Mary Read, have been pirates. A heavily coded iconic body, pirates parody the official costume of the sailor. Masculine figures with feminine features? Feminine creatures with masculine features? Long hair, jewelry, a single gold earring, gold teeth, a striped shirt, a black patch. Mary Read declared "that the profession of pirate was not for everyone, and that to engage in it with dignity one had, like her, to be a man of courage." It was definitely an ideal persona for a two-year-old girl living in patrilineal culture.[16]

storyteller

Radio girls have participated in the re-creation of Montréal's oral culture as hosts, producers, technicians in several community radio stations – most notably CIBL and CKUT. In addition, countless women have broken the boundaries of academic taste by modifying their texts for radio and participating on the PoMoCoMo radio show between 1988 and 1991.[17]

alter ego

PIRATE PROBLEMS

storyteller

Pirates are not all fun, however.

operator

Play "Pirate Jenny" clip from Three Penny Opera *by Bertolt Brecht and Kurt Weill (CBS, 1976). This is cued to the exact spot where you hear a loud thunderous beat in the musical text. Play it until you hear her sing "and we'll croak him," then the sound of the triangle.*

storyteller

Ulrike Ottinger's Madame X, a sadistic cruel mistress, promises the liberation of women from daily drudgery and routine. At the same time she roams the world for women to augment her pleasure. In the 1977 film, *Madame X*, she dresses in silver glitter. She is white while her crew are ironic stereotypes of women from around the world.

The Widow Ching, a ferocious female pirate who ruled the waters of the Shi-kiang in the seventeenth century decreed, "The punishment of the pirate who abandons his post without permission will be the perforation of the ears in the presence of the whole fleet; repeating the same he will suffer death."[18]

Madame Ching challenged the state authorities but also plundered fishing villages along the banks of the Shi-kiang.

alter ego

Even this is not so simple. How do we know? All we have are official histories.

storyteller

Piracy is an act of thievery but, like the issue of appropriation, its ethics depends on who you are stealing from. In 1992, I question who were the real thieves five hundred years ago.

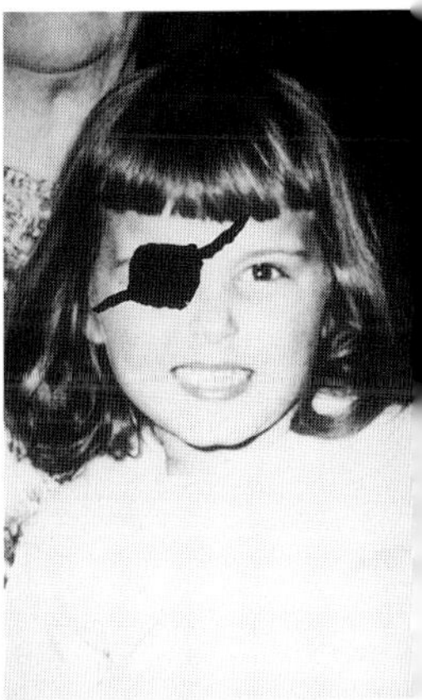
Photo courtesy the author

One of the compelling reasons for adopting such a persona is precisely its ambivalent nature. The pirate image is not a clearly utopian identity that can place me on the morally superior side of a polarized dialectic of oppressed and oppressor. It highlights the multiple positions of relational powerlessness and empowerment that we now occupy as social subjects. It can be used as a compass to explore these relations. Ambivalence is not a plea for inaction, but a basis for understanding how to proceed. The metaphor of the integrated circuit is a way to examine our simultaneous complicity and our agency.

Peg leg, black patch, the pirate image is also one of the body dismembered. This fragmentation is polysemic. It indicates the fate of the body in our culture in territories such as science, medicine, advertising and labour. It resonates with memories of my grandmother's fingers, cut to the bone from her work on a factory line. It acts as a line to the life of other women in the electronic circuit, women whose lives and labour are exchangeable in the economic trade zones that are netherworlds often located along coastal waters. These human beings labour to produce the silicon chips, the superconductors in the global information circuit. Their bodies absorb the toxic substances so carefully wrapped in a plastic skin. I am reminded that I can turn on my computer and plug in my machine because of this hidden contribution.[19]

Here I think Patrick Ready's installation, *Radio and Beans,* covers crucial ground: radio and beans, radio and beams, radio and beings. How is this electricity affecting our bodies? What digital diseases are transforming our genetic structure? My mother complains of numbness in her fingertips. Her doctor says her work with a computer terminal at a bank causes this condition.

I have been a producer and a consumer of the products of the information made possible by the machines assembled in these factories. I have translated speech into the punctuated digital language of numbers to be fed into computers. I have squatted for hours in front of a terminal feeding numbers into the computer, to chart the movements of the Canadian consumer population. My phone now reads my hydro meter. I eat my lunch in Banff and I am bombarded by messages on a computer terminal. I walk through a door to be zapped by surveillance, and I listen and participate in the growing electromagnetic field of technological communication.

Should I unplug myself? Could I even survive without all these connections?

What space could exist outside of this pervasive electromagnetic field? Wherever we are the new satellite technologies ensure that these beams are travelling over our heads and through our bodies.

I remain hopeful, perhaps naïvely. There are more and less contaminated areas and a growing need to conceptualize a techno-ecology. And here I return to radio and its possible use in this current situation of psychasthenia. Let me give you a recent Montréal example of one effective short-circuiting tactic.

operator

Play tape: Trish Kearns voice (approximately 63 seconds).

"My feeling when I perform it . . . it's exciting for two things. One that it's being transmitted from this transmitter that she's built. So it really is for me the idea of taking the power into your own hands, you know, using technology and airwaves in a way that I've never thought about doing. It's like pirate radio. It's fun. It kind of opens up the possibilities, you know, what can you do. The idea of pirate radio has always been connected for me to a sort of revolutionary agenda."

storyteller

In honour of International Women's Day, The Chouer Maha, an all woman, thirty-member choir under the direction of Kathy Kennedy, upset the normal working routine in selected local sites of capitalism and patriarchy – Hydro Québec, the Palais de Justice and L'Église Notre Dame.

operator

Turn on tape of choir on other cassette. Keep it playing low in the background.

storyteller

The choir entered into these ostensibly public spaces, in reality carefully monitored by a vast security system that controls disruptions, while singing. "So what," you say. "Aha," I reply, it was not simply what they sang, but the way they sang, and manoeuvered through these architectural sites. Their first intervention brought the media to the doors of Hydro Québec – home to both the provincial premier and the national corporation responsible for the creation of ecological and social havoc through an ill-conceived megaproject that involves the damming of several northern Québec rivers for – you guessed it – the sale of electricity; their second intervention into the Palais de Justice beautifully demonstrated the subversive potential of easy-to-build technologies. Carrying beat boxes on their shoulders tuned to a station that picked up a pirate radio signal broadcasting the orchestration, choir members sang a peaceful yet haunting series of notes, as they meandered throughout the building. Because of the transmitter, built by Kathy Kennedy herself, they were able to disperse (rather than simply be displaced) yet remain unified. They entered washrooms, corridors, elevators, to the puzzled smiles of the employees and the consternation of the building's security guards who demanded they leave. United by their shared knowledge of the musical score, and wired together electronically via their radios and a pirate transmitter, they were able to maintain a tentative collective cohesion despite their dispersion. Their entry interrupted the circulations and flows of a normal working day that leaves little time for pleasure or play at the Palais. Their final intervention at L'Église Notre Dame was less an intrusion *into*, than a liberation of the possibilities of the space. Not wanting to disturb those praying, they simply sang at the back of the building, their voices a ghostly presence within the church. Same choir, three spaces, different tactics, in accordance with the moment.

operator

Turn off tape.

storyteller and alter ego

IDENTITY IS A PERFORMATIVE, POLITICAL ACT NOT A FACT.

storyteller

We need to think of creative radio strategies to work with our deterritorialization.

One of PoMoCoMo's more successful public projects, for example, was to reclaim noise.[20] The amplified sounds of the low-flying jets of the Canadian military continues to interrupt the hunting life of the Innu people in Labrador with grave consequences for this community. The timing of "Noise Day," an event to protest this policy, coincided with the arrival of the Odeyak brought by the Cree and Inuit to Montréal to travel down the Champlain River to New York to protest the Québec government's scheme to dam James Bay and sell hydroelectricity to the United States.

Cree, Inuit, Innu, French, English, we gathered in front of one of the benefactors of government contracts, the engineering firm Lavalin, and made noise in anger and in celebration on their steps and on the air. We became simultaneous, and asked all radio listeners scattered throughout Montréal, bound to their jobs, to join us. Like the participants in this event, we created a temporary community using radio, constituting a double community, one on location, connected with those in the studio and throughout the airwaves.[21]

Later, we gathered for a feast.

alter ego and storyteller

Struggles linked both spatially and temporally through the radio.

operator

Play tape with sound of water.

storyteller

In the sixteenth century rivers and seas were channels for transporting goods and messages over long distances. Today these currents generate electricity to carry information. Unstable, fluid, in kinetic motion, rivers are in between, bordering the technological and the organic. Water, the conductor of sound and electricity and bodies. We must ask how water has served colonization and remember that water, in its multiple states, is a source of life.[22]

Modern day feminist techno-pirates depend on the flow of these currents.

operator

Continue taped sound of water: this fades out after approximately two minutes.

Notes

* Presented at the Walter Phillips Gallery, the Banff Centre for the Arts, February 11, 1992, with Colette Urban as Alter Ego and Colin Griffiths as Operator in the radio booth. "Pirate Writing" was scripted as a radio text, a performance piece, and a written work with several audiences in mind: visitors in the gallery space, the broadcast audience around the Banff Centre, radio listeners in the town of Banff and readers of the book.

1 Identity as performative is an idea borrowed from Judith Butler, *Gender Trouble: Feminism and the Subversion of Identity* (London: Routledge, 1990). The strategic importance of parody has been inspired by the performance work of Guillermo Gómez-Peña and the writings of Coco Fusco.

2 For more on feminism and technology see Sally Hacker, *Doing it the Hard Way: Investigations of Gender and Technology*, ed. Dorothy Smith and Susan M. Turner (Boston: Unwin Hyman, 1990) and *Power, Pleasure and Technology* (Boston: Unwin Hyman, 1990). See also Judy Wajcman, *Feminism Confronts Technology* (University Park: Pennsylvania State University Press, 1991). In this paper I am consciously working against the inherent equation feminine/nature, masculine/technology. Daniel Defoe's *A General History of the Robberies and Murders of the Most Notorious Pyrates, and Also Their Policies, Discipline and Government*, first published in 1724, remains the most comprehensive history of the English pirates. See Daniel Defoe, *A General History of the Pyrates*, ed. Manuel Schohorn (Columbia: University of South Carolina Press, 1972).

3 This is the process of interpellation, according to Louis Althusser, "Ideology and Ideological State Apparatus," *Lenin and Philosophy and Other Essays* (New York: Monthly Review Press, 1971). I emphasize that image is related to the word "imaginary" however what we term the imagination is not simply visual but audiophonic. Althusser's notion of subjectivity as interpellation is a decidedly audiophonic word.

4 Constance Penley and Andrew Ross, "Cyborgs at Large: Interview with Donna Haraway," *Technoculture*, ed. Constance Penley and Andrew Ross (Minneapolis: University of Minnesota Press, 1991), 4.

5 Celeste Olalquiaga, *Megalopolis: Contemporary Cultural Sensibilities* (Minneapolis: University of Minnesota Press, 1992), 4.

6 For a history of early Ukrainian settlement in western Canada see Myrna Kostash, *All of Baba's Children* (Edmonton: NeWest Press, 1992).

7 Christina Kubisch, "About My Installations," in *Sound by Artists*, ed. Dan Lander and Micah Lexier (Toronto and Banff: Art Metropole and Walter Phillips Gallery, 1990), 72.

8 Norbert Wiener, *Cybernetics: Control and Communication in Animal and Machine* (Cambridge: MIT Press, 1948), 15.

9 Gregory Bateson, "Cybernetics and the Self," *Steps to an Ecology of Mind* (New York: Ballantine, 1972).

10 Ibid., 19.

11 Timothy Leary, "The Cyberpunk: The Individual as Reality Pilot," in *Storming the Reality Studio*, ed. Larry McCaffery (Durham: Duke University Press, 1991), 245–258.

12 Wiener, 19.

13 Donna Haraway, "A Cyborg Manifesto: Science, Technology and Socialist Feminism in the Late Twentieth Century," *Simians, Cyborgs and Women* (New York: Routledge, 1991).

14 This is a direct paraphrase from Meaghan Morris, *The Pirate's Fiancée: Feminism, Reading, Postmodernism* (London: Verso, 1988), 51–69. See Kim Sawchuk, "Medusa's Revenge," *The Panic Encyclopedia*, Arthur and Marilouise Kroker (London: Macmillan Education, 1989). This was presented as the installation piece *There's a Mirror at the End of my Bed* in collaboration with Nell Tenhaaf, SAW Gallery, 1990.

15 For a defense of bodily noise, even amongst the dead, see Gregory Whitehead, "'Principia Schizophonia': On Noise, Gas, and the Broadcast Disembody," *Social Discourse* III:3,4 (Fall/Winter 1991), 121–126.

16 Jorge Louis Borges, *A Universal History of Infamy*, trans. Norman Thomas di Giovanni (New York: Dutton, 1972), 41.

17 In particular I have been inspired by the work of Genvième Heistek, Margo and Julia Loktev; programs such as *Hersay*, *Dykes on Mikes*, *Cuts*, and *Cups and Cakes;* and *PoMoCoMo* participants Kathy Kennedy, Kelly Hargraves, Nell Tenhaaf, Aimee Rankin, Sandra Buckley, Renee Baert, Marie Annhart Baker, Gail Scott, Marilouise Kroker and Nancy Krywonis.

18 Borges, 44.

19 Annette Fuentes and Barbara Ehrenreich, *Women in the Global Factory* (London: South End Press, 1983).

20 Deriving its name from the term "postmodern commotion," PoMoCoMo was a group of artists and academics in Montréal who wrote and presented a weekly radio show and other public activities.

21 Kim Sawchuk, "Audio Terrorism: Low Level Flights Over Nitassinan," *Public* "Sound" 4/5 (1990).

22 Sean McCutcheon, *Electric Rivers: The Story of the James Bay Project* (Montréal: Black Rose Books, 1991).

Photo courtesy the author

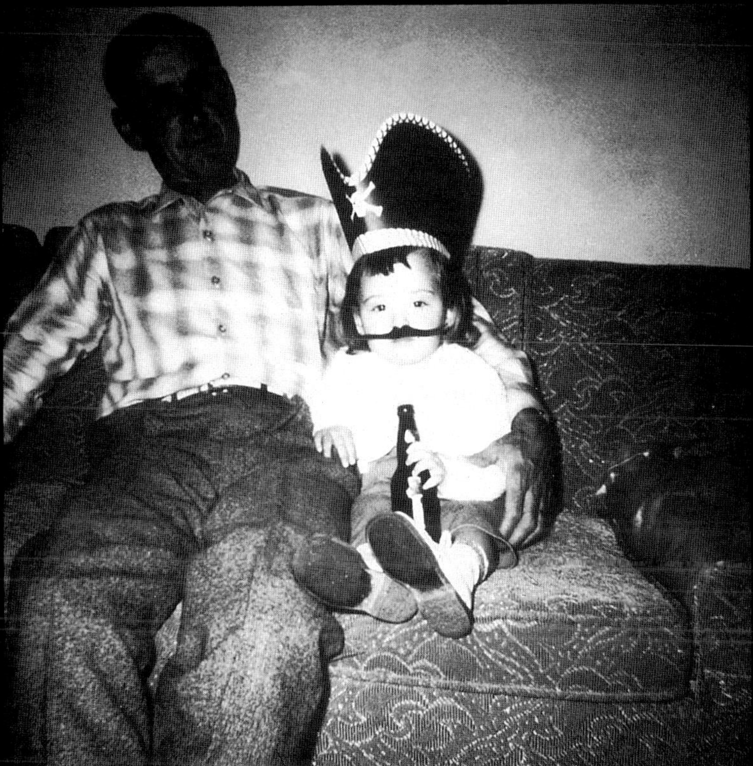

New World Radio

dialogues between Coco Fusco and Guillermo Gómez-Peña

Since 1989, interdisciplinary artists and writers Coco Fusco and Guillermo Gómez-Peña have collaborated on a variety of experimental art projects that deal with the redefinition of "American" culture and with current debates on cultural pluralism and the Columbian legacy. One of their first collaborations was Norte-Sur *(1990), which combined multimedia, visual arts, performance and radio in an attempt to understand the ongoing dynamic between the United States and Latin America as expressed through popular culture. They also developed* The Year of the White Bear, *a counter-quincentenary effort that involved radio and other communications media, an installation, publication and performances throughout the United States and Europe.*

The following two dialogues were composed by the artists in February and March, 1992. The one on the left was recorded during the Radio Rethink *symposium and revised for publication. In it, Fusco and Gómez-Peña discuss their interests in and use of radio, the role that radio plays in intercultural relations, and its potential as a medium for social change. The one on the right is a fictional conversation about the quincentenary, parts of which appear in the radio script of* The Year of the White Bear.

Guillermo Gómez-Peña In the mid-1980s, performance artists in the United States began to talk about the need to make radical ideas more accessible and to step outside of the art world in order to participate in the national debates about American culture and society. Some of us realized that radio was an ideal vehicle to broadcast our ideas beyond the boundaries of art and we found some possibilities in public radio. My own involvement with performance radio includes my participation in *The Territory of Art*, a series of radio art programs produced by Julie Lasar at the Museum of Contemporary Art in Los Angeles and a long-term involvement with *Crossroads*, the Miami-based national program produced by Elizabeth Perez-Luna. This extraordinary weekly audio magazine enables Latino, black, Asian and native American writers and performance artists to have a national voice in a country where intellectuals and artists are, for the most part, confined to academic or alternative spaces and permitted only to have opinions about our own métiers or our very specialized concerns. For three years, I covered United States-Mexico relations for *Crossroads*, but always from the perspective of a performance artist. My shows were layered with poetical voices, bizarre musical juxtapositions and sound effects. In fact, they very much resembled my live performances, with the difference that the programs were heard by thousands of people.

ANNOUNCER Good morning friends, and welcome to MPR's "Voyage to the American Zone," radio for the New World Border – I mean Order – 1992 megahertz above reality. Each week, we bring you fascinating people who are guaranteed to expand your horizons without having to leave the comfort of home. My name is Dwight Christian Windbag, and I'll be your host for our special program on the five-hundredth anniversary of Christopher Columbus' discovery of America.

As you listeners know, artists and writers around the world are creating fascinating works to commemorate this historic occasion. Two of them are with us today in the studio.

Nuevoo Latinoo artists Gwermo Gomez-Pina and Coocoo Fuscoo are going to key us into the Hispanic perspective on the encounter.

CF Desencuentro, I'd say.

GGP (with an exaggerated accent and emphatic manner) We see this as an important opportunity to

"Authentic Cuban Santena and El Aztec High-Tech advertise Latino products as part of the Free Art Agreement" (1990)

Photo Cristine Noschese

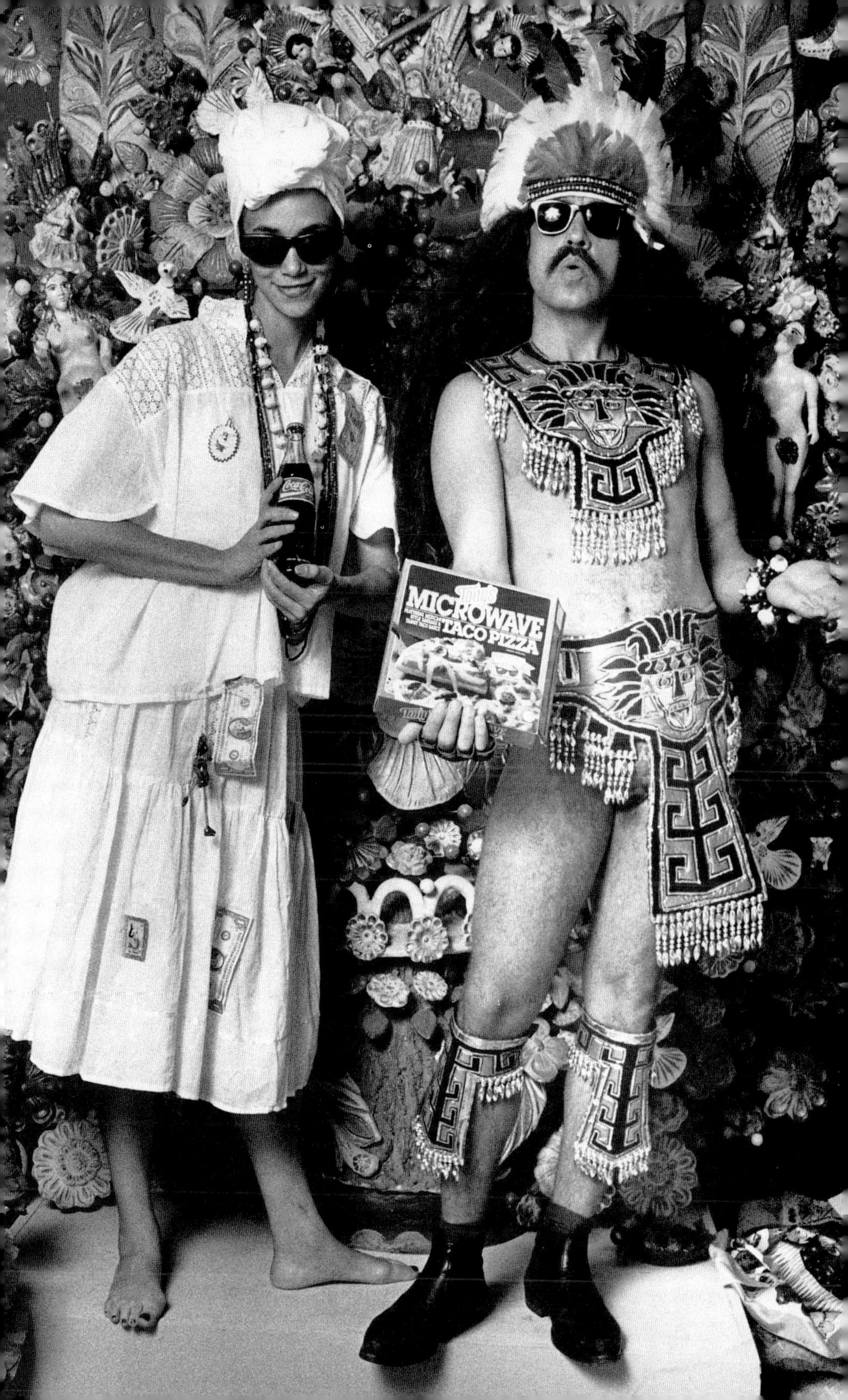
MICROWAVE
TACO PIZZA

When I first started, it was hard for me to find this border zone between performance and social chronicle because in United States' culture, these territories are extremely separated. Performance artists are allowed to have frantic and fractured voices but journalists are supposed to be "objective," logical, measured and non-ideological. In my work, both of these voices constantly invade one another. Julie and Elizabeth were patient and daring enough to allow me to experiment in a national context. My goal was to do highly experimental pieces that were also socially, politically, linguistically and anthropologically meaningful to larger sectors of society, and not just to specialized art audiences.

Coco Fusco My involvement in radio comes out of my interest in popular culture and oral forms of language, and also because of my interest in the very important role that radio plays in Latin America and in Latino communities in the United States. It also comes from my seeking out communicative strategies that allow me to address a larger audience than the specialized readership of small art publications and print media in general. As a cultural critic, I have concentrated primarily on analyses of the media arts, and am very sensitive to the fact that despite certain prejudices and traditions in academia that privilege the written over oral, it does not make sense to limit one's understanding of language to its written form. Most language that we use, experience, learn from, get information from, and take pleasure from is not written

question First World expansionist behaviour and Bush's New World Order. Like many other artists across the continent, we are conducting a series of counter-celebratory activities.

MPR (annoyed) Did I hear you say ca-ca-counter-celebration? What's going on, my press release here says you two are from the Walker Art Center in Minneapolis. You know, fine art, good taste. I thought you guys were . . . Who are you?

CF I am a multi-culti pop semiotician from Cuba York. Guillermo is a post-Mexican MacCabron authentic genius. We're excavating contemporary material culture in search of signs of the persistence of the Great Columbian Myth.

GGP It is everywhere – Seiko "Discovery" watch ads, Sears "Discovery" credit cards, PBS "Discovery" specials – these phenomena express a deep anxiety about white America's place in this hemisphere.

MPR Oh my God. It's the gringostroika warriors – you always manage to

anymore but rather is either visual or is conveyed orally. It seems to me that this situation demands some reflection as to what strategy constitutes an effective and appropriate creative response to radio as it exists in the world. Composing a written commentary *to be read* on radio as an oral form may not always be the best way to analyze it. And what I have been most interested in doing in recent years is developing a radio language that can reflect, critique and expand the medium from within.

I also like to remind myself of the politically emancipatory uses of radio throughout history. My research on the emergence and development of alternative media in progressive political movements – particularly those in Latin America – has also led me to a rich history of examples of artists, writers and activists who use radio and other mass media forms to communicate radical ideas, to disseminate critical information and to strengthen a sense of community in times of repression, violence or under other less overt forms of duress, such as immigration. Every Third World nationalist movement in the last four decades has used radio and used it extremely effectively. It is often easier to produce and to disseminate than visual media such as film and video, making it a perfect populist communications device.

Guillermo and I developed *Norte-Sur* to look at ways that cultures live and breathe outside their country of origin. In the process I became even more sensitized to the role radio plays in places like the

spoil the fun of holding certain things about this country sacred. Just like our president said – you are like Puritans who can't sleep at night because some big guy out there might be having fun.

GGP Pendejo –

(sound of censoring noise)

CORPORATE VOICE This is the voice of Airheadedness and Nationalism in Media speaking. We are interrupting this program to delete inappropriate language for radio broadcast – this station does not permit the use of Spanish, Spanglish, or any other inferior language. Continue.

GGP Pinches bigots.

(horn noise)

MPR Please, let us return to our topic.

CF Fine. As far as I'm concerned, Columbus is just another one of this country's disposable Icons – he's being wheeled out to stand for everything the powers that be would like to defend against cultural transformations taking place. People are afraid of . . .

GGP Of minor problems like racial divisions, economic depression, spreading homelessness.

Latino immigrant communities of the American southwest and on the east coast. I am currently working on a radio script about the "latinization" of New York (*Son de Nueva York*) that deals specifically with this phenomenon. While many immigrant communities in the United States lose a written relationship to language very quickly, an oral relationship to the mother tongue of an ethnic group is not lost as quickly. As a child of immigrants I developed a very strong relationship to spoken Spanish and a very weak one to the written language. I could understand more than I could speak and speak more than I could write. As a result, I began to think about how a sound-dominated relationship to language had affected my sense of who I was or what that language was. I want to be able to play with that experience and recognize the importance of radio in having helped to create a sound environment in my home that broke the hegemony of English from outside.

GGP For many United States-based Latin Americans, radio has helped to expand the notion of the role of the artist. It provides us with a mode of address that is very common in Latin America, but very uncommon for artists in the United States. This medium is capable of containing the complex voices of the artists who see themselves as social critics and popular philosophers. One of my main interests in the past ten years has been to experiment with the fluctuating boundaries that exist between the realm of art and the rest of society. The notion of the artist as a

Add to that the fact that whites will soon be a minority here, and that spells big trouble for some.

MPR (nervous) Let's try to keep it light folks, this is the culture hour after all. How about telling our listeners about your art exhibit at the Walker? It has such a wonderful title – isn't it *The Year of the White Bear*? 1992 is just the perfect time to explore the links between native Americans and their Asian ancestors – we must remember that even the American Indians were immigrants, right? So when was the White Bear dropped from the Chinese calendar?

GGP That has nothing to do with it. The White Bear was the name the Paez Indians of Columbia gave to the Spaniards when they first saw them.

CF Nowadays, we tend to forget that both cultures developed myths about the other – the thing is that the indigenous peoples based their ideas on their experience of violence at the hands of Europeans – while the Europeans propagated myths about the Indians that justified enslaving them and taking

solitary image-maker or a marginal genius is no longer operative. We live in a time of crisis. In light of this, we must seek clarity through dialogue and attempt to be active participants in the shaping of public reality. When I talk about "public reality" I refer to the civic realm, the place where the citizen intersects with community and country. And this is precisely the space that radio occupies.

CF Our way of working always begins with ideas that we want to communicate. From there, we choose what we feel to be the most effective strategy for presenting them. That is one reason why the radio programs that we have done integrate into larger interdisciplinary projects. While the other media we use might be more confined to an art context, radio has offered one way to take the work outside the gallery and in that sense cross the boundary between the gallery and the rest of the world, and this appeals to us. A critic who wrote about *Norte-Sur* said that the radio show acted as a kind of catalogue and that it was very democratic because of its accessibility to anyone who tuned in. I really like that idea of radio as a friendly freebie.

GGP I would like to call this strategy the culture of recycling – the idea that an artwork can be continuously recycled, reformatted and recontextualized. In this sense, a radio art piece can become a soundtrack for an installation and later on, a partial soundtrack for a live performance. It can also be distributed as an audio book or it can be cut and re-edited to become

their lands.

GGP Yes, the Amerindians in Surinam called the Europeans the *parakitis*, or the "people who kill their kind." The Aztecs called the Spaniards *teules* meaning "arrogant outsiders." Nowadays their descendants call North Americans *gringos* because of the I-can-buy-anything-in-this-greasy-country attitude they bring to Mexico.

MPR (exasperated) Charming.

CF Those who got caught in the middle of these conflicts were often the Indian women concubines and their mestizo children. They became the first bicultural translators.

GGP They were the original borderologos. Or the primeval pochos.

CORPORATE VOICE Watch it pal, your English is slipping. What is your resident alien number?

GGP Uh, 224 33 5670.

CORPORATE VOICE Just checking . . .

MPR You still haven't answered my question – what is your show about?

GGP It's about western mythologies about "otherness" and how they are used to further political

part of an audio magazine. It can even be presented as ritual. One of the things we like to do is ritual radio presentations. We put lots of candles in the presentation space, people sit on the floor and we ritualize the sound experience, which is the way we presented our work at the Walter Phillips Gallery.

CF Participating in the symposium at Banff, I think we both became aware that what we are doing is slightly different from the work of many of the other artists involved. I am not arguing that there should be one kind of radio practice. Nonetheless, our social, political and cultural concerns take us in a different aesthetic direction from that of work dealing with the specificity of sound or of radio technology.

In programs such as *Norte-Sur* and *The Year of the White Bear*, we explore a set of issues that have to do with how radio shapes, defines and contributes in many different ways to cultural identity. We try to find ways to use radio to present or represent our sense of the multiplicities of identities that operate within American culture and even within Latino or Latin American culture. We develop bilingual, bicultural programs as a way of reflecting on the processes of cultural hybridization that we experience in our lives. Radio is an extremely critical and important tool for creating a simulated sense of what North America is like for Latin Americans. Radio is an important medium for maintaining a sense of cultural identity by constantly recycling and recreating an image of what

ends. Like the weird explanation you made up for the title of our show. People who don't want to deal with racism in this country have a vested interest in pushing the notion that everyone's migration was essentially the same –

CF And this makes it easier to propagate the fiction that Columbus' saga stands for everybody's.

MPR But that's the point. Why can't Columbus' legacy be something we can all share? Sure, no one is perfect, but we can't turn the clocks back now so we might as well celebrate our connection to the bold spirit of rugged individualism he stands for.

CF Look let's get something straight here. Columbus never arrived in the United States. He never discovered anyone here. But he did begin the European invasion that led to the mass killings of indigenous peoples in the name of God and kicked off the African slave trade in the New World. Did you know that he got so out of hand that Queen Isabella put him in jail for his mistreatment of the Arawaks?

MPR That's an awfully one-

Latin America is for Latinos outside Latin America. Those messages about culture are transmitted through news, radio soaps, cultural programs, advertising, and even jingles and background noise. This ongoing cultural exchange is an intercultural dynamic that is constantly taking place.

GGP We are interested in "disorienting" the audience through unexpected sound and language. By making them experience a kind of cultural vertigo and by shattering their sense of "the familiar," we aim to erase the borders between "us" and "them." This experience could sensitize our audiences to accept a kind of otherness that they might otherwise see as a threat. Americans are extremely intolerant of non-Anglo European cultures. Many Americans still do not want to acknowledge the fact that they already live in a fully multiracial and multilingual country. The Bush administration did everything possible to rescue a mythical monocultural America that never really existed in the first place. In this sense, multilingual radio and multi lingual performance can be very effective forms of activism. We want to push the limits of tolerance of American culture for multilingualism. Our pieces contain Spanglish, Ingleñol, various dialectical forms of English and Spanish tongues. We also use very thick accents and very stylized colloquial textures. We want to "borderize" the centre, so to speak. A Chicano friend of mine once said that what we really want is to "infect" the

Photo Rachel Slavinsky

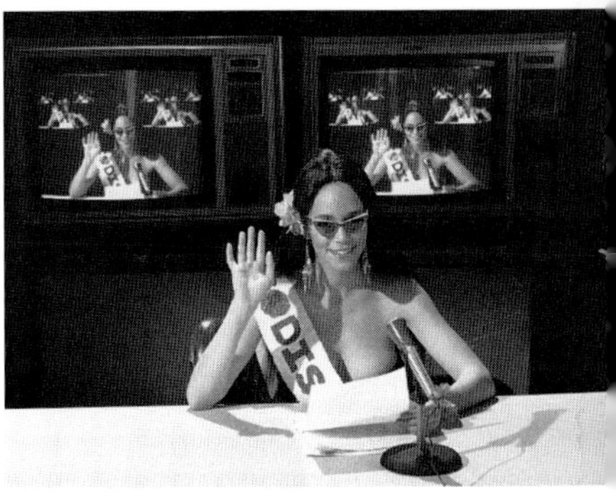

"Miss Discovery 92 as newscaster" from *The Year of the White Bear* (1992)

sided view. You're just like that cranky wet blanket Kirkpatrick Sale.

CORPORATE VOICE I'm sorry – that enemy agent has been banned on the airwaves by the Defense Department as hostile to national interests. Repeated use of his name will lead to your removal from the station.

MPR Oops, sorry . . .

CF What we have now is a mass-scale historical fiction that draws a direct line from Columbus to the District of Columbia, from the New World to the New World Order. See, the United States is at a critical juncture. Its sense of self is very fragile and its future as a world leader is uncertain. It's at times like these that we need self-

English language. What we are actually doing is healing the language by forcing it to open its structures. In my opinion the most interesting literature currently written in English is coming from writers of colour: for many of these writers English is not their first language.

CF One of the first repressive gestures undertaken by colonizing forces has always been the censoring of languages and the imposition of one language over other languages. This is a process we are attempting to disrupt with our use of radio. We try instead to create a utopian space of linguistic pluralism. We dispense with the conventional hierarchy that designates English as the proper language of radio, making any other language on the radio somehow marginal. Even in documentary pieces about Latin Americans, their "difference" must be conveyed through background sound, while the English-speaking voice of the outsider dominates. We, on the other hand, propose a space in which all languages are purveyors of information and disinformation and otherness.

GGP There is also a clear hierarchy of tolerance for linguistic otherness in the United States. English is the one and only *lingua franca*, but there is a general acceptance of French and a few other European languages. At the bottom of the list are the languages of the immigrants of colour. Spanish is seen as *lingua poluta*, as the language of the colonized, the criminals and the undocumented. It also stands for the memory of the American southwest before 1848. Because of this, an American

aggrandizing myths.

MPR I disagree. Columbus has always been meaningful to us. There are more places in this country named after him than anyone except George Washington.

GGP Actually, Americans didn't start celebrating his ventures until 1892, when this country was beginning to assume the status of a world power.

MPR Is there anything I can say that you two won't find a political answer for? I think it's time for all of us to shed our anger.

GGP You mean, it's time to forget history, right?

MPR Yeah. I mean no.

CF Well we think it's time to take a critical look at the past instead of stroking Euro-American egos.

GGP We're not suggesting that all European-descended people be deported. We recognize that most of us on this continent are the product of a mixing of the Old and New Worlds. And I don't only mean culturally, I also mean mixed genetically, even though most white Americans have a hard time acknowledging that they probably have some

audience will accept the experience of watching an experimental theatre troupe from France, Germany or Italy, they will also accept opera in a foreign tongue, but if a Chicano poet or performance artist performs in Spanglish for more than twenty minutes that same audience gets very upset. This extremely disturbing phenomenon is the reason why I am interested in confronting my audience and making them aware of their ethnocentrism. If they want dialogue with the American south, they have to get used to not being able to understand everything. Partial misunderstanding is part of the deal.

This brings us to the question of privilege. I think that the notion of reproducing the marginality and isolation of a modernist art world within radio, is an expression of class and ethnic privilege. For many in the north, marginality is often a privilege precisely because it is a voluntary decision. But for communities that have been marginalized and denied access to public expression for five hundred years, marginality is not a privilege. It is a painfully imposed condition.

CF Romanticizing marginality is to a certain extent a sign of privilege. It is also part of a Euro-American image of a bohemian avant-garde as a marginal underclass. This romanticism evokes an artist-centred model of innovation, in which experimentation is understood as primarily formalist. I find this model problematic for a number of reasons. One of the fundamental characteristics of radio is that it transmits to someone – it is not

black or native American ancestry.

MPR I beg your pardon?

CF What are we supposed to be celebrating? The survival and flourishing of Europe thanks to the gold, silver, corn, potatoes and sugar that was taken from the Americas? Or is it the fact that England, Spain and Holland made a mint off the slave trade, contraband and piracy?

MPR Well if it weren't for those deeds, we wouldn't be around today, so I suppose the end justifies the means. There's also a lot to be excited about when it comes to the New World Order. The world is becoming more connected then ever – and, as a result, more intercultural. Now that should appeal to you Nuevoo Latinoos. Soon there will be no reason for you to fight, because we will all buy the same, eat the same and think the same.

GGP Okay, you can dream about the future – that's America's favourite pastime. We, on the other hand, are more interested in how the present resembles the past. In 1492, international trade

simply a practice that begins and ends with the artist. Radio exists in the world, and it exists principally outside the realm of art, so to pretend to create something completely distinct from those overshadowing realities seems a bit ludicrous. Because of this, we look for strategies that take into account radio's social function and its place in the world. We are experimenting but we are also trying to communicate to other people and to engage them in the process of rethinking radio. A very specialized artistic activity that revolves around sound's intrinsic qualities for me simply leaves out half of what radio is about. We continue to work on programs that present utopian visions of cultural interplay and parodies of radio conventions. By doing so, we can comment on radio as an institution and as a purveyor of ideology and social and political ideas. We also establish that there is a common language between ourselves and the audiences that are listening because, like the audience, we learn those languages from radio.

GGP Our strategy is to take popular and populist cultural forms and make them more overtly reflexive through humour and experimentation. In Latin American performance art, humour performs a very subversive function: the dismantling of dominant cultural forms. This humour often depends on the strategy of creative expropriation. We steal the dominant cultural forms sent from the north and subvert them. Through parody and mimicry we turn this material into a political vehicle of empowerment.

was based on gold. Now it's based on oil but the fight for control of non-European natural resources is the same.

CF Yes, and back then these ventures were presented as religious crusades, with sanctions from the Holy Office of the Pope. We've spent the last forty years invading countries to save the world from communism with a mandate from the inner sanctum of the CIA.

GGP Way back then the Spanish Crown's hold on the New World economy was constantly threatened by illicit trade of tobacco, tea and rum. Now the United States' hegemony is disrupted by competition from the illegal sale of cocaine and marijuana. The problem with the druglords is that they're bigger than the government.

CF Not much about labour has changed either. Latin America used to have encomiendas. Now they have maquiladoras.

CORPORATE VOICE Translation please!

GGP Back then, there was the Holy Inquisition that suppressed dissent.

CF These dominant cultural forms are also demystified. We want to denaturalize what is understood as the truth as it is conveyed through radio or the absolute quality or absolute nature of things as they are presented in radio. It is still hard to resist that radio news is telling us the "truth" about what is happening in the world, or that what seems like a democratic interview conveys significant information about the people who are in the studio. By stressing the formulaic aspect of radio, our parodies bring out the process of mediation through which we are able to understand information at all. We want to expose this process to scrutiny in a playful way, to show the seemingly benign models which generate ideas and misinformation and misperceptions and stereotypes about culture, particularly about Latin American culture in the United States. They are generated through the news which circulates stereotypes; they are generated through nice-sounding national public radio interviews with nice "others" who just sit there and reveal intimate details about themselves, and then once they are done it is time to move on to basket-weaving, so to speak.

GGP Another important conceptual strategy that we often apply to radio is that of playing around with historical "contingencies," with the "what ifs": what if suddenly the continent turned upside down; what if Spanish was English; what if Spanglish became the official language in the American southwest; what if the *gringos* crossed the border to work illegally

CF Now it's the American Family Association and Pat Buchanan.

GGP Back then the colonial governments outlawed native languages.

CF Now the United States is pushing English only.

GGP A la chingada con el inglés oficial.

UNKNOWN VOICE One more unAmerican word and you'll be on a plane back to Mexico. We don't mess around with your kind. You've proven to be excessively resistant to assimilation.

MPR Please, this is getting out of control. I just can't accept that things are as bad as you say. We have more liberties now. More democracy. The Columbian legacy has led to the founding of the greatest democracy on earth.

GGP What you call a Columbus-derived democracy we see as a complex system based on divisions according to race and sex. We're still struggling to overcome the American legacy of segregation and racist immigration policies.

MPR And we're getting much, much better.

CF Who says things are

in Mexico; what if there was a *Gringostroika* movement in America; what if the New World Order turned into a New World Border, and so on. This allows us to create out-of-sync "socialscapes" of contemporary America in which things are pushed two or three degrees beyond reality. This is a very useful strategy especially when it is accompanied by humour. We believe large audiences are more willing to accept extreme behaviour and radical thinking if it is presented humorously. For example, this year we are engaging in a series of performances in which we will present ourselves as "undiscovered aborigines" from an island that was overlooked by Columbus. We are actually making a reference to a former European and American practice of displaying indigenous people from Africa, Southeast Asia and the Americas in zoos and public parks and freak shows. In a kind of extended joke, our aborigines go north and to the Old World to be discovered. Even though these aborigines had technically not been discovered, they always had an understanding of what "the west" was. Our aboriginal characters are postindustrial beings. Their rituals include operating a lap-top computer, a VCR and a telephone. They observe the west through television and radio. This piece will be presented at politically sensitive public sites in California, Washington, Madrid and London. We would love to have a little radio transmitter inside the cage. I call this experimental trouble-making.

CF One of the commentaries that will better? And for whom? For the hundreds of undesirable immigrants who get deported daily? For the hundreds of thousands of people living in the streets? There are more than a few people in this country who believe that a full-scale participatory democracy is just too damn expensive and risky.

MPR You guys are really just a couple of downers. The New World starts to sound like five hundred years of genocide.

GGP Actually, I did a show with that title last year in Barcelona. Did you see it?

MPR No.

CF Well, there is some good news.

MPR I can't believe it. Please share it with us. We need some balance here.

CF People have never stopped fighting back since the invasion started. pre Columbian languages are still spoken. Non-western religions are still practised. Runaway slaves rebelled and formed maroon states across the Americas. Indigenous people continue to argue for land rights. Many of those who have been colonized have managed to find a way to

Photo Peter Barker

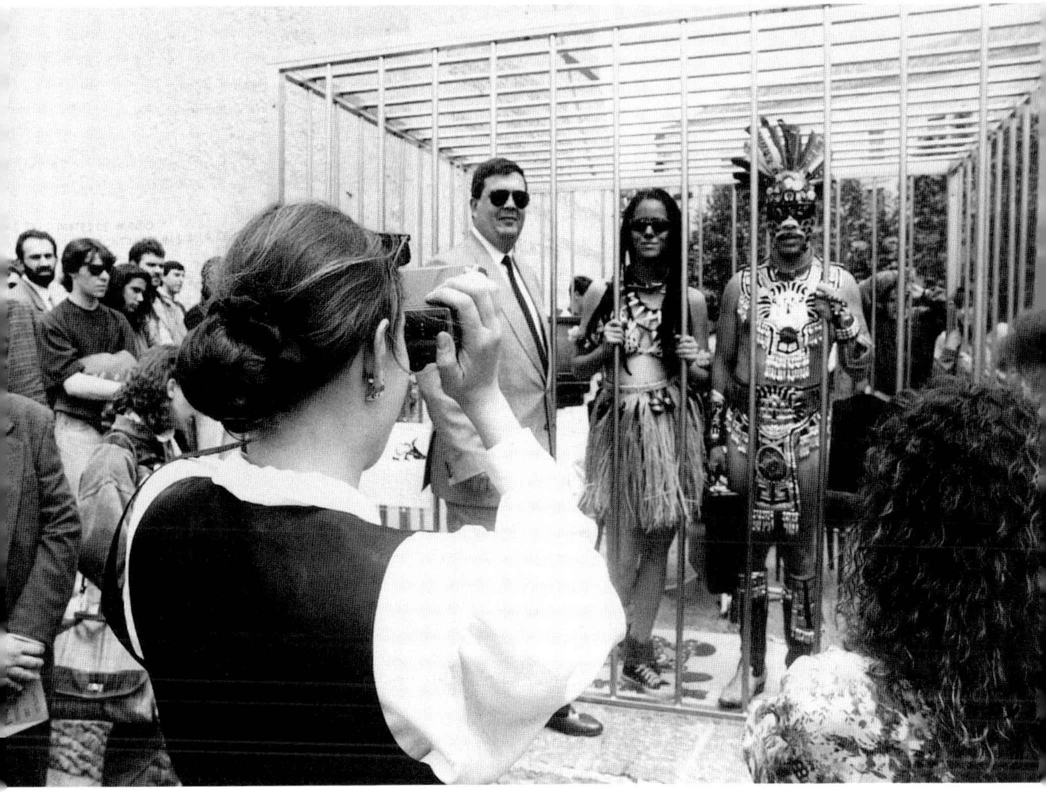

"Two Undiscovered Amerindians visit Madrid" (1992)

run through *The Year of the White Bear* radio program and other elements of the project is a reflection on how five hundred years of history is being collapsed into neat, marketable tidbits of history for pleasurable consumption. Arbitrary chronologies are constructed to justify the needs of the present in this process. Precisely because institutions such as museums and galleries and radio are involved in this process of flattening cultural differences to create global histories, our program offers a very interesting space in which to deal precisely with the problems that conventional radio has in dealing with historical and ideological complexity.

We will once again parody radio genres to make our point. The disembodied voices of radio make it very easy to propagate fictions. We can play with that and parody it and revel in its possibilities by using radio in that way. Radio is also a tool for discovery in that it has the ability to create a sense of being in contact with every place in the world at the same time. The listener thus feels empowered by being able to access the whole world. In our programs we can manipulate these conventions to make apparent how the listener is set up as discoverer of the foreign and as a discoverer of otherness by creating pseudo-documentaries, by presenting information and disinformation side by side, or fictions as truth.

GGP There is a very interesting hidden history of radio: the history of border radio. From the 1920s to the 1960s, outcasts of different sorts – political radicals, bilingual poets, ranchero and

throw off the yoke, even if only through irreverent humour.

GGP These are the kind of stories that have been suppressed by the dominant culture. They want us all to forget that anyone ever thought colonization wasn't the natural order of things.

MPR (defensive) You just want to blame Europeans for everything. What makes you think that everything was so hunky-dory in the Aztec Empire? I've read that most societies in Mesoamerica were pretty decadent by the time that we arrived.

CF I think it's stretching it to say that pre-Columbian societies were decaying. Mesoamerica was socially advanced enough to sustain the largest population in the world at the time of the encounter.

GGP Yeah. At the time that Shakespearean English had twenty-four thousand words, Nahuatl had twenty-seven thousand. So there!

MPR Oh, quiet Gwermo. So Coocoo, wouldn't you at least concede that there was some internal conflict in the Americas?

CF Sure, but Europe was also at war with itself. It

cowboy singers, charlatan doctors and religious freaks – crossed the border into Mexico and broadcast from the Mexican side without restrictions. Mexico had very lenient regulations for radio at the time. These stations were called "border blasters." They were equipped with extremely powerful transmitters that could literally reach the rest of the planet. There were wild border disc jockeys broadcasting from Nogales, Piedras Negras and Tijuana all the way to Sweden, Brazil and Alaska. They created a very exciting era of radio. Their formats were very fluid, eclectic and unconsciously "experimental." Even Wolfman Jack in the sixties was able to broadcast United States counterculture worldwide from one of these tiny little pirate radio stations located in Ensenada, Mexico. These people created a fascinating border milieu that was eventually brought down by American governmental authorities. Two years ago I did a project in England in homage to border radio. I was participating in EDGE 90, the bi-annual British festival of experimental art in Newcastle. In addition to presenting my performance work, I collaborated with two British radio pirates on a series of clandestine broadcasts from artists' lofts. For five days, we broadcast multilingual performance poems comparing the Chicano experience in the United States to that of the British "minorities." While pirate radio is difficult in the United States due to harsh restrictions, I have managed to persuade some daring producers to allow me to simulate pirate interventions. For example, a month before the National

was already overcrowded and overrun with diseases. The Conquest was driven by competetiveness, and by a scramble for wealth. It's just that even though everyone was looking for a way out, nobody really knew where they were going.

MPR So what's wrong with utopia and competition? Sounds very American to me.

GGP Are you ever going to accept that there might have been something wrong? I can't understand the resistance that many white Americans show to dealing with the darker aspects of the Columbian legacy. You are always worried that someone is going to pin the blame on you.

MPR Isn't that the way Latin Americans feel too?

GGP No. People aren't really talking about Columbus in Mexico, for example. There is a clear understanding that the official celebrations organized by government agencies are just publicity ploys to attract tourism and trade.

MPR Well at least somebody in Latin America is taking advantage of an

plug into them, your artwork is reproduced and distributed all over Latin America. This has happened to some of my tapes. In 1985, I made a bilingual radioart program called *Border-X-Frontera*. I sent it to several artists in Latin America and three or four years later I was still receiving news from Buenos Aires, São Paulo and Bogotá. Many artist groups had received a third or fourth generation copy. This network throughout Latin America has created a kind of "unofficial avant-garde," and sound and radio art are very much a part of it. For me a truly binational artist is fully aware of all these possibilities and takes advantage of them.

CF Even though we must take account of the invasion of national cultures via the airwaves, we must also realize that these are unfortunate indications of a reality that may not be entirely bad. National boundaries and notions of cultural purity that go along with maintaining them in very strict or even paranoid ways just do not work anymore. The models of cultural hybridity that we present in our work might be disturbing for those who have a tremendous investment in having the world or this hemisphere be entirely English or Spanish or French. Instead, we must deal with a reality in which there are multiplicities of languages in cultures operating in the airwaves – all of which create a sense of being inside and outside of a culture at the same time.

chaos. So Columbus gets called back to bring order to the new wild urban jungles of contemporary America.

MPR Every time I think I've finally got a handle on what you're talking about you step back into all that political stuff. I'm tired of it. You're uncontrollable – so I'm going to cut you off. Take that!

(static sound)

VOICE You've been listening to "Voyage through the American Zone." Stay tuned for next week's program on how to communicate with your maid without breaking the English Only law.

"La Miss Discovery y El Aztec High-Tech" (1992)

Photo Glenn Halvorsen

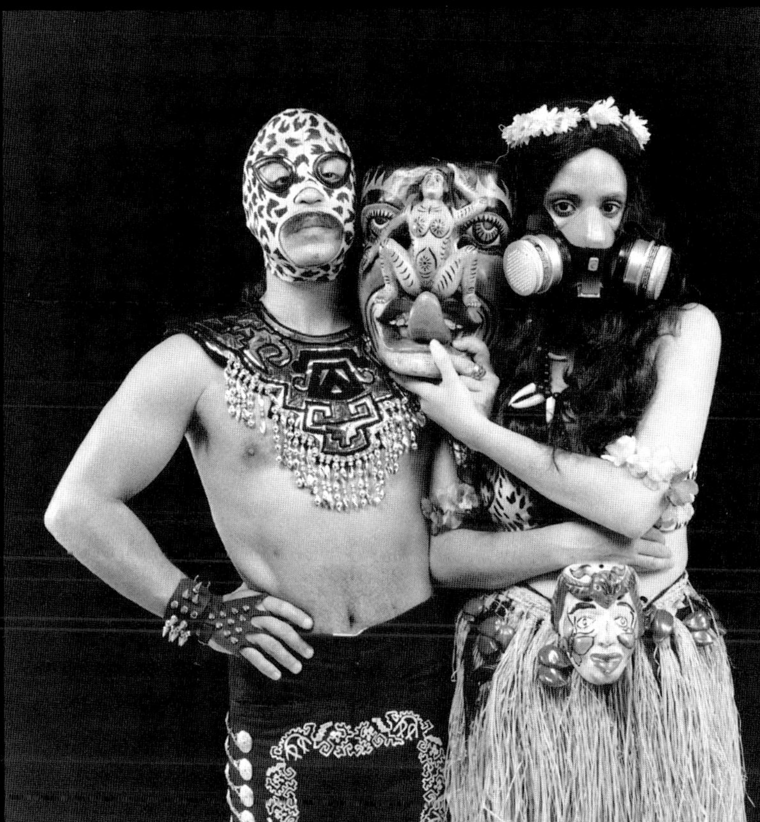

Women and Radio

"LIVE" LETTERS TO PRODUCERS . . . OR THREE NOISY RECIPES FOR COOKED SPEECH

Carol Laing

PREFACE

To speak before others speak. Before speaking about others who are recorded, speaking . . . (she clears her throat, bites her lip, swallows hard). Trying to say something about speaking and sound in the silence that is writing, where ambient sounds play – unrehearsed and unrecorded – across a limited range brushing my thoughts: the irregular traffic outside, sounds of (invisible) birds, a lawnmower, the computer's hum and the rush of tapping as my fingers strike keys so these thoughts can become visible, though not audible (you won't hear the sound of *my* voice in this text – or not that voice my body speaks, for my tongue is quiet, writing: this text is *not* an order of speech. Instead, it is an order of language gauged for printing, geared to the reading of words, not the hearing of words (and so to the difference between having and losing them). Are you with me? Where are *your* words? Should we not talk? Because this text is about *a kind of talk* – about talking back to three works by women artists whose medium is radio. Saying, clearly, from the beginning – this is still the preface, remember – that sound is not my field but, like most people, I am in its fields. Trying, here, to think about radio. Trying then to, *re*think radio. Trying to hear what has been recorded. Listening. Keeping my tongue quiet. Screening out other sounds, other tongues. When I am listening *in* I mean . . .

Asking, for the first time, what can be voiced to the void?
What patterns radio speech?
What are the relations of radio speech to, say,

speech habits or speech organs?
What does not belong to the voice or to words?
What does one call *that*?

Thinking about *invisibility*:
the sound studio, and talking to walls
the unpicturable audience, dispersed, uncollectable
the speakers heard, but unseen
voices that hang by a thread
Thinking about radio as *public* speech:
withdrawing, redrawing speaking boundaries
scripting and pacing and playing
(a *rhetoric*, then?)
situating sounds, and silence
Thinking what recording means, what editing means:
correctability, repeatability, erasure
layering, mixing, distorting, changing speeds, pitch

Understanding that *desire* elicits speech
Understanding the illicitness of some speech
Understanding that the word arrives within us from outside
that it returns *there*
this displacement, one's voice outside oneself
as the flesh becomes disembodied word . . .
audible, receivable, retrievable, stable, sentient
this re-embodied word bound to time . . .
capable of summoning others
whose origins are *not* recoverable

. . . this *mimicry* . . .

Dear Helen. Dear Susan. Dear Julia and Nancy . . . Let's talk. Let's talk about rhetoric and desire and mimicry. Let's taste your radiowork. Cite it. Recite it. Tongue it. Mouth it. Ear it, remembering how listening – if we track *its* etymological origins – blended lust and hearing. Pass the ears, won't you? Wet your lips . . . I'm at the end of the beginning.

I. A RHETORIC OF STICKY SPEECH AND OTHER VISCOUS FLUIDS

ENTRÉE — *Building a Universe: Rifts, Absences and Omissions* by Helen Thorington

DESCRIPTION — *XX XX XY XX XX XX XY XX . . .*
This recorded piece for broadcast is an experimental work focusing on new reproductive technologies, based on texts taken from actual statements of doctors and researchers. Alternating male and female voices seem to represent voices of authority: the announcing voice, the controlling voice, the instructing voice, the analytical voice. Sounds of music, cows, clicks, birds, and so on are intercut.

SELECTED EXCERPTS

FEMALE VOICE — And one and two and three and four stre- [word interrupted] . . . and [sound of scratch] stretch, stretch, stretch [pause] . . .

FEMALE VOICE (*British accent*) — **Course Book One, Technical Discussion A. Reproductive Interests: When To Engage In Female Infanticide.** Here are some methods that have proved successful . . .

FEMALE VOICE — [music] And stretch, stretch, stretch [sound of scratch again, like a stylus drawn across a record] . . .

FEMALE VOICE (*young, breathy*) — Hello, me again, I'm smiling at you. I'm young and slender. And so very happy. I have a cute little pout, overwhelming confidence [voice fades] . . .

FEMALE VOICE — Stretch. And lean, and lean, a lean ma-chine [sound of scratch]. Hello, hello. I'm smiling at you. I'm young and yes, impossibly slim. My dress hangs well, clings a little here, a little there. My breasts are forever pert, as if a cold wind is blowing. Or perhaps, just perhaps, it's you [sounds of interference] . . .

MALE VOICE — It's ten o'clock. Do you know where your children are? [sounds of music, birds, then, the rasping stretched repetition of the word "love," heard against the background of music, birdsong] . . .

MALE VOICE	The childbearing process still has about it a sense of prehistory. It's sort of savage and elemental but we're changing it. Medicine and technology are changing it. We're denaturing the reproductive process . . .
MALE VOICE	You could be using her eggs even when she's dead . . .
MALE VOICE	The new reproductive technology. It will benefit women [click]. It will benefit women [click]. It will benefit women, no doubt about it – . . .
MALE VOICES (*alternating*)	It's great, a whole new science. It will benefit women, I'm so sure – my research – *my* research – with surgery and hormones – my research. My research. My research. My research. My research. My research. It's great. My research. My research. I will get a Nobel. I will – . . .
MALE VOICE (*very patronizing)*	Thanks to the devotion of thousands upon thousands of men around the world, maternity is no more mysterious than paternity. And the delivery of a child no more awesome than the emptying of a jar. Thank you. And Good Night.

CREDITS: *Building a Universe: Rifts, Absences and Omissions* (29:00), created and produced by Helen Thorington, with the voices of Pamela Tyson, Sarah Montague, Regina Byer, Art Kemp, Jack Davis, Richard Mann, Stephen Eldridge, Bob Buckley and George Zar. Commissioned in 1987 by New American Radio.

GLOSSOGRAPHY

1.1 Jill Dolan: "Cultural feminist ideology is based in female biology . . . so, the importance of giving birth . . . "[1]

1.2 Jill Dolan: "The 'sense of the documentary' – the one-to-one correlation between art and life – rests on an unchallenged assumption about the way meaning is generated . . . how it assumes a stable system of representation."[2]

1.3 Judith Butler: "Gender is in no way a stable identity or locus of agency from which various acts proceed; rather, it is an identity tenuously constituted in time – an identity instituted through a stylized repetition of acts. Further, gender is instituted through the stylization of the body and must be understood as the mundane way in which bodily gestures, movements, and enactments . . . constitute the illusion of an abiding gendered self."[3]

1.4 John Bender and David E. Wellbery: "Rhetoricality designates the thoroughgoing impropriety of language and action . . . and the partial and provisional character of every attempt to know it."[4]

1.5 Marysia Lewandowska: "The impossible task . . . to untie the knot of a language/voice/power relationship . . . "[5]

1.6 Michel de Certeau: "[R]hetoric . . . not a descriptive catalogue of tropes, but instead a logic of 'displacements,' 'distortions' which its destination (i.e., the audience) elicits, in its Otherness . . . this produces a 'swerving' trickery . . . a truth which is not the opposite of error, but a lie itself, a symbolization of the impossible, impossibility at play . . . "[6]

1.7 Frances Dyson: "the body caught in the web of technologies which transform it . . . "[7]

1.8 Frances Dyson: "[T]he transmitter body also repeats the rhetorics of the future. In its vacillation between the transmitter and receiver, body and instrument, matter and machine, origin and outcome, it complements technophilic projections of what the body and reality might one day become."[8]

*****

Dear Helen;

This is not a letter, exactly, because although I've listened to your work, Building A Universe, *I'm not quite sure who I'm addressing here. Are you a mother, for instance? If so, we could talk about that: fill in the names, ages, sexes of who's been born to us, compare experiences, bring out the pictures, fill in with narratives what your "discussion" intentionally leaves out: what having and inhabiting a female life in a female body sometimes means. And what that meaning is in this culture – what is represented by the nymphic lean-and-stretch, the coy posturings in your piece. That some "researchers" seem intent on eliminating: all the leakages, and indecisions, the sheer labour and the mess of everyday life . . . it makes me wonder where/how they live, exactly, what they feel – now that you've filled in some of how they think. The shockingly disembodied and utterly alienated sounds of their desires makes me want to ask not,*

"Do you know where your children are," but, "Do you know children?" Do you talk to your children? Touch your children? This hygiene of children, so far from the real bodies and lives of children. This disguised – for you can never quite say what you mean – hatred and contempt for female bodies, this arid jealousy of their capacities and the sterility (ironically, in the name of fertility) of their proposed alternatives. Their terrifying research . . .

. . . performed inside their labs, where language seems not to enter. Or what perhaps is more true, never exits. Why we never quite know what is going on in there, or what is coming . . . although it will benefit women, we are assured. Why then is theirs not a universe I want to live in? This we agree on. This is what your work so eloquently says. But I have to say, as the mother of a son, I do not like the "us" and "them" distinctions in it – even if I am endlessly tired (and angry) with what so often still seems to come from "their" research. It makes me wonder if we might all need other ways to speak . . .

Yours across distance, time and media,
admiringly, and with best wishes,

Carol

II. DESIRE, OR, THE SYNCHRONIC PULSE OF NARRATIVE

ENTRÉE — *Viscera* by Susan Stone

DESCRIPTION — This work for radio is a portrait of passion. A man and a woman are linked by emotions that pull them together and drive them apart, conveying sensations of longing, possession and "primitive" need – where an unexpected gesture of love proves fatal. There are sounds of voices, ambient noise, music (winds), a heartbeat.

SELECTED EXCERPTS

FEMALE VOICE — I am the movement of my mouth. I lie. I lie in wait. I lie on the throat of my own voice . . . I whisper. I whisper that I don't really know. I whisper that I cannot scream . . . I am a sequence of letters across my face . . . I feel, I feel a long time off. I feel like a drowned thing, reached from behind [sounds of a flute, a heartbeat].

MALE VOICE

This is a story of conquest and capture. Of danger and desire. It has been written down here in order to give shape and substance to the couple pictured in this frame.

They do not have much time now because he is leaving first . . .

This is how it all begins. It is some time in the past. He wants to walk her home. She is a woman in her thirties. She lives alone in a small town. He speaks . . . She does not look at him . . .

But soon she begins to meet him in the security of a locked garage. They make love amid the parts of dismantled cars. She does not take him to her home. And he does not take her to his . . .

FEMALE VOICE

I watch.
I watch black and white [sounds of ticking].
I watch black and white turn blue.
I turn into blue.

MALE VOICE

He takes her to an apartment . . .
At night he tells her stories . . .
They create fiction together, but her images never fit at any one point. At night, they are lit by an erotic phosphorescence. Their desire is violent and primitive. They press upon each other like a mouth over a bottle. They collapse only when they share one pulse . . .

FEMALE VOICE

He is not a part of her fiction, or fact.
He is thinking now that he has not lost her:
he simply has never had her [sounds of a flute].

MALE VOICE

Now he becomes cruel. At the bottom of her eyes lies a deep sadness, an admission of defeat . . .
She cannot intellectualize her hunger . . .
Her writing is delirious . . .
But in seeking clarity, she creates further illusion.
What does become clear is that her only refuge is in her writing . . .

It has been decided that he will leave first [sounds of ambient noise, a dog barking, traffic, then sounds of wind, human pleasure – stretched over time] . . .

Now he turns and enters the building again. He enters the

room . . . Slowly, he kneels by her side. He wills her to look at him. She looks past him. Now his hands close about her neck . . . He thinks: sometimes love is mistaken for crime . . .

FEMALE VOICE I lie. I lie in wait. I lie on the throat of my own fear . . . I whisper. I whisper that I don't really know . . .

CREDITS: *Viscera* (22:40) was conceived, written and produced by Susan Stone, performed by Christopher Hastings and Susan Stone. Commissioned in 1989 by New American Radio.

GLOSSOGRAPHY

2.1 Roland Barthes: "the erotic component the voice carries – which is not subjective . . . "[9]

2.2 Michel de Certeau: "[Radio, like psychoanalysis, is] an ascetic practice – [inside erotic, aesthetic and technological frameworks] – for supporting a desire that cannot be identified with an act . . . this fictiveness, this rebelliousness; this trickery . . . "[10]

2.3 Patricia Mellencamp: "Feminist artists turn to narrative as a means of incorporating and critiquing the problem of female identity and history . . . interrupting those processes . . . "[11]

2.4 Patricia Mellencamp: "the subject's entry into language which inaugurates the condition of desire where desire persists 'as an effect of primordial absence': regardless of the object chosen, desire refers to the impossibility of satisfaction, to the endless displacements impelled by an originary loss . . . desire circulates . . . voices incapable of assuming a stable narrating position . . . react fearfully, helplessly, anxiously, erotically, both to what they witness and to what they partially remember . . . "[12]

2.5 Patricia Mellencamp: "The narrativizing consumption of the female is a constant cultural activity, an aspect of human history."[13]

2.6 Marysia Lewandowska: "Technology presents us with a promise of record keeping, of retaining memory, the privilege of truth. But we no longer live in the world of the original . . . the reading of reality becomes a terrain for the reflection of our own uncertainty."[14]

2.7 Daina Augaitis: "Sounds have the ability to flood the mind with striking visualizations, just as images often resonate acoustically. This crossing of senses seems natural, yet within the sphere of creativity, visual and aural traditions have remained fundamentally separate."[15]

2.8 Christof Migone: "The spatiality and temporality of the radiophonic field inscribes an intimacy of experience. Measuring our bodies invisibly creates a sensual fiction, a poetic virtuality, creating a space where we can describe ourselves and still not know who we are . . . 'the intimacy of the voice betrays a body out there, warm to the touch . . . this sort of alienated intimacy' . . . There's no language of radio, just tongues . . . "[16]

* * * * *

Dear Susan;

How can I speak back to Viscera *(which is who you are to me) – to the poignant and terrifying fabric, the fiction, that you've pieced together there? I begin by wanting, even needing, to respond to events in the relentless building of your narrative: I want to change the ending. I don't want to be left with another dead woman, dead because she lived past the limits of desire, but not dead by her own hand. How can I save her? By picking up the marine thread that weaves (waves?) its way down your story? To try to bring her back, alive, I will need help and it may come from someone else I've never met (but I have heard her live, lecturing) – Luce Irigaray. It does not come from what I heard her saying when I heard her speaking but from something of hers I read. I am risking translation here so I can give you back a text, one that has the potential, I think, to revive your female character.*

So, here is Irigaray. The Irigaray of Amant Marine (de Friedrich Nietzsche). *It's another story about the sea, but not about any particular sea – about the sea as metaphor (so we're staying inside what's literary, not literal). It's the littoral ground I need beneath my feet, up against the telos of your narrative. So this is Irigaray, mouthed by me to you, a translation and a letter, both:*

> *Yes, I come back from very far away. And my crime is, for now, my candor. I am no longer your double – faithful. The echo of your joys and pains, of your fears and resentments. This mirror of you that you have always made of me. I have steeped it in the waters of forgetfulness – what you have named life. And from farther than there, where you began to be,*

> *I am returning. Washed free of your masks and disguises, cleansed of your projections and many-coloured plans, stripped of your pretences and the clothes hiding the shame of your nakedness. It has been necessary to disencrust my flesh of the insignias and markings that you have engraved there.*
>
> *Let me go. Yes, let me go elsewhere . . . I don't want to come back inside you anymore . . .*
>
> *. . . whoever entrusts the sea with their fate is in rapture always. Rising or falling, the sea's ecstasy is the same. For whether she rises or falls, nothing changes this being engulfed by life, this motion of one's self, endlessly . . .*

Sometimes, crime is mistaken for love. I'm mirroring back to you the reversals that your work suggests. Interestingly, I don't feel at all that this puts us in opposite places: in fact, Viscera *confirms many things I also know: why resistance is important, why a fictive death is only that – a metaphor for "real" life. I'll remember the sound of your work for a long time: it is very moving.*

Turning your blue back to black and white,
returning a speaking silence to your sounds,
imagining you might write back,
yours,

Carol

P.S. The text by Irigaray was translated by me from "Dire d'eaux immémoriales" in Amant Marine, *published in French, by Éditions de Minuit (Paris, 1980), pages 10, 17 and 19.*

III. MIMICRY, OR EVERYTHING BY MOUTH: HOT TIPS FOR (FOOD) LOVERS

ENTRÉE	*Eating In Tongues* by Julia Loktev and Nancy Steadman
DESCRIPTION	This collaborative recorded work for radio pseudo-seriously focuses on cooking procedures for certain foods

– meat, fowl, pasta and eggs – playfully blurring the boundaries between the pleasures of eating, forms of popular language use (including limericks, tongue twisters and ads) and *desire*. Male and female voices, sighs, laughter, singing, ambient household noise are heard.

SELECTED EXCERPTS

[music, percussion, collective laughter, sighs]

MIXED VOICES
There was a man who lived on the air,
lived on the air,
lived on the air;
There was a man who lived on the air,
and his name was Achin' Tongue.
[laughter] . . .

FEMALE VOICE (*confidingly*)
But, you know, you don't have to talk about it, if you don't want to talk about that sort of thing. I guess I can tell you, I mean, it's something I haven't been very open about for a long time. You know, it's about the way I cook chicken . . .

SAME VOICE
Sometimes when I'm cutting beets, you know they'll stain my hands completely blood-red and sometimes – uh – I like to keep the stain on.

FEMALE VOICES (*alternating*)
Secret secretionary traces –
I guess they're all secrets, aren't they?
Secret secretionary traces –
I guess they're all secrets, aren't they?
Secret secretionary traces . . .

FEMALE VOICE
But it doesn't have to be just plain spaghetti or anything. You know, I mean it could be linguine – little tongues, in Italian; lin-gu-ine. Or orecchie – little ears . . .

FEMALE VOICE
Let's try eating one of these tongues . . .

FEMALE VOICE
Would you like to partake in a little ear? But you have to bend down and suck it off the plate [laughter] . . .

FEMALE VOICE
Ah. Aaah – I can flip it all the way over. Aah. No. Imagine if your tongue was in my mouth, and I did that: wouldn't you be

impressed? Aah, aah, flip, flip, and all the veins come up. Aah – [sounds of smacking, chewing] . . .

FEMALE VOICES (*alternating*) I guess they're all secrets, aren't they?
Yeah. Secret secretionary traces.
Yeah. Secret secretionary traces.
Yeah. Secret secretionary traces.
[sighs, laughter]

FEMALE VOICE You know marinades have a lot of uses [general laughter]. They can tenderize the tough [laughter].
I know they moisten the dry. And they can sure enliven the bland, if you know what I mean . . .

If I went over for dinner and I was just served a shank – without any kind of marinade, nothing, no kind of intense flavouring, I would feel hurt. I'd be hurt. You know, I'd think my friends didn't care.

This is where marinades can make a big difference: they can improve your friendships, your palette, your repertoire of ideas. I really think they're crucial [laughter] . . .

FEMALE VOICE I don't expect everyone to eat like I do. Anyways, I'm bored by most foods, except for this one fabulous recipe I've been making for myself these past three weeks. It's – uh – absolutely delicious – sweet and sour tongue.

FEMALE VOICES (*alternating, then together*) I wish you could touch my tat with your tongue. I wish you could tit my tat with your tongue [sighs, laughter].

FEMALE VOICE If you didn't like the strawberries or cherries, I mean, you could just pick them out; if you didn't like them, you could just pick them out.

CREDITS: *Eating In Tongues* (23:00) by Julia Loktev and Nancy Steadman (1991), with voices by Loktev, Steadman and a host of diners.

GLOSSOGRAPHY

3.1 Patricia Mellencamp: "Popular culture, which is 'free, full of ambivalent laughter . . . disparagement and unseemly behavior, familiar contact with everybody and everything' with respect for the intimate, the familiar, 'the repertory of small, everyday genres' – women's culture – is preferred to official culture . . . 'monolithically serious and somber, beholden to strict hierarchical order.'"[17]

3.2 Patricia Mellencamp: "Bakhtin's concept of dialogical culture . . . a trio of voices – author, text, and listener – with personal *and* historical 'images of language,' with shared 'social horizons.' Against the centripetal notion of 'common language,' Bakhtin prefers dispersion, plurality, and decentring, without closure or identification . . . "[18]

3.3 Patricia Mellencamp: "Bakhtin's valuation of intonation – which is 'always at the boundary between the verbal and the nonverbal, the said and the unsaid . . . Intonation is the sound expression of social evaluation' . . . intonation is directed toward life and the listener, in his or her capacity as ally or witness . . . "[19]

3.4 Judith Butler: "As a given temporal duration within the entire performance, 'acts' are a shared experience and 'collective action.'"[20]

3.5 Donna Haraway: "Feminism loves another science: the sciences and politics of interpretation, translation, stuttering, and the partly understood . . . Feminism is about a critical vision consequent upon a critical positioning in inhomogeneous gendered social space. Translation is always interpretative, critical, and partial. Here is a ground for conversation, rationality, and objectivity – which is power-sensitive, not pluralist, 'conversation . . . '"[21]

3.6 Frances Dyson: "The meaning of voice . . . a surrender to the non-semantic meaning which the voice generates in speaking language . . . The *meaning* of the voice lies in its *movement*, its ability to occupy different symbolic niches within different cultural-historical epochs . . . the best analogue for this is the circuit . . . The circuitry is as much metaphorical as material or technological . . . "[22]

3.7 Julia Loktev: "We are the language here. The language of radio is polyglot, articulated by a multiplicity of tongues speaking from a wired mouth. Intimate and public in the same breath, the technology offers a plethora of possibilities. It is simultaneously tactile and impenetrable, inviting and elusive, here and gone."[23]

3.8 Julia Loktev: "The Body as Organ is neither a conquest nor a transcendence of the body. It is the pleasure of it. The freeplay of the flesh . . . corporeal, finite, and musical. The Body as Organ is entirely noisy."[24]

*****

Dear Julia and Nancy;

I really enjoyed Eating in Tongues: *it was pretty – tasty. Dan told me what a great cook Nancy is, how you put on a dinner and taped the proceedings, using some of that commentary here (I listened for his voice, but wasn't quite sure I heard it – somewhere in the "pass the ears . . . I paid for ears . . . any noses?" sequence). What he didn't tell me was what was on the menu. Tongue, by any chance?*

Well, I fished around for something that might seem appropriate by way of a response here. And what I came up with was perch, bullheads, carp and eel: you know, that's what lives off my shore down in South Bay. This local culture has its own way of preparing carp. So I thought I'd share that secret with you. Here is how it goes: make a very hot fire, outdoors. Then take your cleaned carp and nail it to a board. Place the board in the coals of the dying fire. Let it cook. When the flesh is firm – but not dry – take it out of the fire. Throw away the carp, and eat the board. Which means, as you can imagine, that the waters at the head of South Bay are not exactly crowded with people fishing, though they're full of carp.

Maybe that's not a fair exchange. Not being anything you can really eat, I mean. So I asked my friend Diana if she could help me out: she's a much better cook than I am, though we both like Italian food best. Anyway, she came up with this great recipe for car-pac-cio: you know, marinated raw fillet of beef. Yeah, it's a bit pricey I suppose – a lot more so than shanks or tongue. But for that special occasion, when you're a little short of time, or the oven element is burned out, it'd be perfect, don't you think? This is how it goes:

> *Put five ounces of lean fillet of beef in the freezer, until it firms up. Then, slice it paper thin using a slicing machine.*
>
> *Put these thin slices in a marinade (slowly add olive oil to a mixture of lemon juice and Dijon mustard, whisking constantly in the same direction until the oil is well blended. Then, add salt and pepper to taste).*
>
> *Refrigerate for at least thirty minutes.*
>
> *Serve with freshly ground black pepper, and toasted bread. Serves two.*

Let me know if you try it. I forgot to say that if you haven't got a slicing machine, you can get the butcher to slice it.

Well, it's time to wrap this up, I guess. In closing, I just thought you might like to know that I'm not one of those people who picks out the strawberries and cherries: I like them both. But when I was a kid I used to pick the raisins out of raisin buns – after I licked off the sugar glaze. It seemed important to eat the raisins last . . .

I look forward to hearing your next work. It would be great to get a letter too, but – hey – who has time these days to write? I know, it's pretty impossible, so don't worry about it. Really. And thanks for the piece. It made me hungry for more. Why, I hope you'll go on passing the ears. And as far as I'm concerned – if you want me to tell the truth – you can hold the Spam . . . Yeah, hold the Spam, but not your tongues . . .

Yours, from the kitchen, where I'm testing the carpaccio recipe,
and keying in this text,
buon appetito, and warm regards,

Carol

AFTERWORD

Approaching the ending, what is there to say now? I want to say what I think I have heard – that with these works particularly, it is yet possible to imagine radio as a "theory of desire,"[25] grounded in both the necessity and limits of speech, one that often reaches for the classic trickeries of both the narrative and the documentary, insisting however on the impossibility which it materializes. It is still possible that one's sounds, separated from the originating body, might survive that body, that for radio, speakers speak, *because* they die. In this sense, at least, radio speech is continuous with literature, for it operates by doing without the very things it signifies,[26] acting as a mode of reference but not of simple reference. Instead, radio allows referentiality traversed by the figuring power of language, and by the suggestibility of sounds, which means, by a *poesis* . . .

For not utterly disembodied, but re-embodied differently, the voice is that "slippery thing . . . 'between body and language,'"[27] stubbornly present and absent simultaneously and inflected always by the culture from which it speaks. It is memorable but not visible, a mouth to the cultural body that is its own. So, numbers and numbers of bodies and voices, noisy – "fleshy bodies, bodies of sound, electronically reproduced bodies and bodies of thought"[28] – all somehow fluid within a continuum that has no edges, intended for that particular mode of listening that is still tuned to an ideal, interior – impossible – space.[29] Tasty, to the imaginary tongue . . .

Notes

1 Jill Dolan, *The Feminist Spectator As Critic* (Ann Arbor: UMI Research Press, 1988), 90.

2 Dolan, 96.

3 Judith Butler, "Performative Acts and Gender Constitution: An Essay in Phenomenology and Feminist Theory," in *Performing Feminisms*, ed. Sue-Ellen Case (Baltimore and London: Johns Hopkins University Press, 1990), 270.

4 John Bender and David E. Wellbery, "Rhetoricality: On the Modernist Return of Rhetoric," in *The Ends of Rhetoric*, ed. John Bender and David E. Wellbery (Stanford: Stanford University Press, 1990), 39.

5 Marysia Lewandowska in conversation with Caroline Wilkinson in "Speaking, the Holding of Breath," in *Sound By Artists*, ed. Dan Lander and Micah Lexier (Toronto and Banff: Art Metropole and Walter Phillips Gallery, 1990), 55.

6 Michel de Certeau, *Heterologies*, trans. Marie Rose Logan (Minneapolis: University of Minnesota Press, 1986), 53.

7 Frances Dyson, "Transmitter Bodies: Aurality, Corporeality, Cuts and Signals," *New Music Articles* (1990), 17.

8 Dyson, 17.

9 Roland Barthes, *Image-Music-Text*, trans. Stephen Heath (New York: Hill and Wang, 1977), 186.

10 de Certeau, 61.

11 Patricia Mellencamp, *Indiscretions* (Bloomington and Indianapolis: Indiana University Press, 1990), 94–5.

12 Mellencamp, 102.

13 Mellencamp, 104.

14 Lewandowska, 56.

15 Daina Augaitis, "As Told To," in *Sound By Artists*, ed. Dan Lander and Micah Lexier (Toronto and Banff: Art Metropole and Walter Phillips Gallery, 1990), 147.

16 Christof Migone, "Language is the Flower of the Mouth," *Musicworks* 53 (Summer 1992), 47.

17 Mellencamp, 183.

18 Mellencamp, 182.
19 Mellencamp, 183.
20 Butler, 276.
21 Donna Haraway, *Simians, Cyborgs and Women* (New York: Routledge, 1991), 195.
22 Frances Dyson, "Circuits of the Voice," *Musicworks* 53 (Summer 1992), 6–7.
23 Julia Loktev quoted by Dan Lander in "Radio Art: The Pubescent Stage," *Musicworks* 53 (Summer l992), 22.
24 Julia Loktev, "The Body As Organ," *Musicworks* 53 (Summer 1992), 42.
25 There has been considerable theoretical writing about "desire" in the last decade, such as the Institute for Contemporary Art in London's first publication of its Documents series, called simply *Desire* (London: ICA, 1984). Other important sources that have informed my own concept of a specifically "female" desire include *Powers of Desire*, ed. A. Snitow, C. Stansell and S. Thompson (New York: Monthly Review Press, 1983); *Pleasure and Danger*, ed. Carole S. Vance (Boston: Routledge and Kegan Paul, 1984); *Sex, Power and Pleasure* by Mariana Valverde (Toronto: The Women's Press, 1985); *The Straight Mind* by Monique Wittig (Boston: Beacon Press, 1992); and *Sexing the Self* by Elspeth Probyn (New York: Routledge, 1993).
26 See de Certeau, 51–52.
27 Augaitis quoting Guy Rosolato, 159.
28 Dyson, 14.
29 Dyson, 17.

The Time Has Come for the Neo-Nativist Generation: Leonard Fisher's *Earth Police*

Paul Wong

> Legend has it that the shamans, who predicted the arrival of the white man and the near-destruction of the Indian people, also foretold of the resurgence of the native people seven lifetimes after Columbus; we are that generation.[1]

INTRODUCTION

The radio work produced by Leonard Fisher for *Radio Rethink* is a dense and haunting, passionate work, composed of snags of natural sounds, snips of white man's history and accounts of other histories – such as his grandfather's. The work opens with emotive drumming and singing, followed by the violent clash of thunder and lightning, then rain, the sound of wood being chopped, a player-piano, approaching trains, the grinding whine of chain-saws, the creak of falling trees, the ding of cash registers, the buzz of low-flying aircraft and the bass reverberations of a detonated bomb.

> Technology is here to serve mankind. Who? What? Mankind? Whitemankind motherfucker? . . . In the time of neo-fascism, you have to be neo-nativist.
>
> Leonard Fisher, *Earth Police* (1992)

A year after creating this work, Leonard Fisher is again living in Chilliwack, in the Fraser Valley, an hour's drive from Vancouver. He is back in the community in which he grew up, close to family and friends, after five years of active involvement with cultural, social and political issues and the contemporary art world. This was an intense period filled with discovery and contradiction – attending art college, working in the predominantly white commercial film and professional art worlds, confronting urban and rural lifestyles, and getting to know himself – all in tandem with a re-awakening of First Nations spirituality and political awareness.

Over the course of this journey, Leonard Fisher has embraced media technologies such as film, video, audio and other contemporary art forms including performance, storytelling and collaborative projects, making several trips across Canada to visit different native nations. In 1991 he videotaped the Sacred Run, a three-month trip that started on Vancouver Island and concluded at Kahnawake, just outside of Montréal, on the first anniversary of the Oka crisis. The Sacred Run was realized on a modest budget, and consisted of several dozen runners and support vehicles visiting dozens of native communities and reservations from British Columbia to Québec. Native and non-native participants from as far away as Europe and Asia joined the runners for an hour, a week or the full three months and were fed, sheltered and hosted by the different nations they visited across the country.

I had the privilege of witnessing both the sendoff on the west coast and the arrival in Kahnawake, where the runners were welcomed at the end of the extraordinary trip. For me, to be among these runners, supporters and the Mohawk community was a powerful experience. Just one year earlier, when this community had been under siege by provincial police forces and the Canadian army, I was a helpless observer at the peace camp outside Oka. Now, the longhouse was filled to the rafters; respected elders called out the dances to the singers and the drummers; proud youths, the next generation, strutted their stuff; I was surrounded by an empowered and healthy community.

In 1992, Fisher again set out across Canada to revisit many of those communities he met during the Sacred Run. From June to September, he travelled and worked on the *Earth Police* concept that had been incubating. Although he produced a performance as part of the Vancouver Mayworks Festival in 1992, he has remained isolated for the most part from the downtown scene, avoiding association with recognized groups of people or artistic forms of activity. I see this as a refusal to be a "career-track Indian" and a rejection of "middle-of-the-road" success stories. During a conversation with me in Vancouver, Fisher elaborated on his motivations shaping

Photo Paul Wong

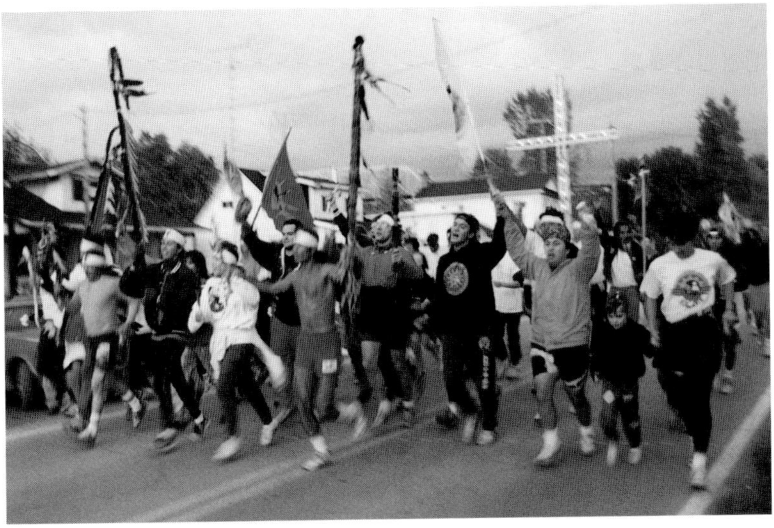

Sacred Run at Kahnawake, Québec, in 1991

Earth Police. This artwork took the form of a twenty-minute performance in the Walter Phillips Gallery using pre-recorded tape, which was later edited to seven minutes for the *Radio Rethink* compact disc.

Paul Wong What is your reaction when listening to the edited version of *Earth Police*? What comes to mind?

Leonard Fisher The piece was condensed from about two and half hours of free thinking or free association on tape. When I hear it now, I think of all the issues in there that I was pre-conceiving and pre-visualizing, and they are all things that are happening around me now. It frightens me because I feel like I have already lived it. Now I am watching it happen with Clayoquot Sound and wondering what is going to happen with Gitksan Wet'suwet'en.[2] *Earth Police* is a concept I have been mulling over as a conceptual explanation of what aboriginal people are doing right now in the defense of their homelands and territories. They are being *Earth Police*, monitoring industrial expansion and resource development. You could even go so far as to call it "cultural cross-hybrid-nation" with the incorporation of native people in logging and other resource-based industries.

PW I found the opening of the tape extraordinarily chilling – the sound of singing and drumming followed by the almost inaudible sounds of generations gone by.

LF In that three-minute segment, I am trying to compress technology as it has been compressed in aboriginal understanding in a historical context, so it goes from the chop chop of the axe to the train whistles, to chain-saws and other environmental sounds that I grew up knowing. Barely audible, in the background, are the *sieg heils* of the neo-Nazis, which in my mind represents the way industry moves through aboriginal communities or aboriginal space.

PW With the heavy breathing, there was a real sense of aliveness to it. Actually, it reminded me of the journalist who was out on Mount St. Helen's when it exploded, walking around with his camcorder. "It's getting dark, I can't breathe . . ."

LF Do you think that has an association?

PW It did occur to me. Another thing came to me while listening to the tape, and thinking about you and your art practice. Because of the many times we have spent together during which you have gone into a free-flowing rant, I wondered if radio – live radio, talk-show radio – would be a perfect forum for you? Does the idea of a live radio show with a fully native agenda appeal to you?

LF (laughs) What, just so I could blow off steam? Or just so I could voice my opinion? After doing the piece at the Walter Phillips Gallery, a Japanese artist, Tetsuo Kogawa, taught us how to build little radio transmitters. I thought, "Here is something to put together, to tour around with on the rez [reservation], broadcasting to a local audience with feedback about what is going on, about how I feel in their community, what I am reading from their community," and stuff like that. But other than that, it never occurred to me to pursue anything like a radio show.

PW Did you feel that *Radio Rethink* was an interesting venue, format or process?

LF Absolutely. It was a lot of fun because of what I was doing or what I tried to do. I was rethinking radio in terms of waves and energy. I did not tell anybody about my ideas of parapsychological communication or becoming a radio wave, but that is what I was doing in the studio. I was opening up to the spirits about who I was, what I was about, and trying to receive messages from what was around me. The *Radio Rethink* project was a performance as well, so it offered the chance to incorporate, if I wanted to, elements of drama or production elements that were not oriented towards audio. When I was dealing with *Radio Rethink* and the institute that it was held in, I was coming to a wall as far as I was concerned but it was great to have the opportunity to do it, and it was fun to have the liberty to experiment and expose myself to all this other technology. But it also represented a certain system that I was not about to subscribe to or anything like that. That is why I did my piece as a performance. What I was thinking was, "Okay, what I'm going to do here is reduce all my frustrations or all my really heavy emotional feelings into a project." I was not going to give everything to that audience but I was going to begin there and then take the rest out to the community that I come from and begin the process of unfolding.

It was a transformational project. I had to dial a trickster to get my buddy Archer Pechawis to Banff. Basically Archer and I are both venturing into the realm of the trickster, and sometimes we find ourselves in there and sometimes we do not. He helped to filter and frame the sound and idea structure so I could see through his eyes what I looked like and thereby have a better understanding of who I might be to different people. So that was the collaborative process for us. Radio is a tool and a place but it is also a transformational thing.

PW Do you see radio as a vehicle for what you have to say?

LF It is *one* of the vehicles. It is *one* media that I want to involve myself with. I don't want to restrict myself to just one format or one medium. I don't want to be an expert in all of them but I want to be versed in several. That is why I have chosen to dip my toes into all these pools of technology. Now I have been kind of washed in all of them, in a manner of speaking, I have been baptized in electronic media and now I am ready to re-emerge from that immersion with my ideas or my opinions, my perspectives. I have opened my world to many influences and an enormous number of people from all spectrums of society, all different cultures, and at different levels. It has been a self-edifying period of understanding that I am a part of history and I am making history.

PW In the last section of the work, when you say,

> I spend time swimming in my mind. I spend time flying the terrain I've walked many times, I see visions of people I've met along the way. I see a young man holding a drum in the middle of a great circle talking about his pains, his anger, all the things he feels, all the things he's felt,

do you see yourself? Is this autobiographical?

LF I am old enough to experience certain levels of prejudice and certain degrees of dispossession yet I have not completely been exposed to the kinds of dispossession and marginalization my predecessors have experienced. I recount the story of my grandfather in the closing portion of the piece. My grandfather is the example that I use, but the driving force behind this part was an attempt to understand what my grandmother went through – holding up, propping up or helping him get through all these periods of conscious deconstruction of identity. What I am trying to do, I guess, is get things centred and balanced in my own life, in my own mind, so that I can carry their story forward but without the self-righteousness, or the indignation, that makes it sound like it happened directly to me because it did not. I have the fallout of it.

> In the time of my grandfather, when he was a young man, my grandfather went off to fight in the Second World War for the things he believed in and for the things he wanted to do. He thought he was saving his country. Believing in his country he went off and enlisted in the army and came back from overseas after the war and realized that in joining the army he had given up his identity, and had given up his status. When he came back he expected all the benefits that veterans would receive and he received a closed door. They told him he was not their responsibility, they told him he was the responsibility of the Indian Department. So he went to talk to them. They told him they had no allocation, nothing for him. They had no land like other veterans had received. He was sent back to the Veterans Department. Without his status, without his identity, with nothing, he had risked his life.
>
> Leonard Fisher, *Earth Police* (1992)

PW I see the devastating effects of generations of displacement on native people. It is referred to as the Residential School Syndrome and the Foster Child Syndrome – young children forcibly taken from their families and their culture to live in a horrific racist world of abuse and alienation.

LF I have a very different foundation than a lot of other people, a lot of urban Indians and a lot of my contemporaries. I grew up in my family, with both grandparents still alive. Both my parents were with me. I had a very organic upbringing and exposure to all the social, cultural and spiritual activities that we are capable of as autonomous individuals or as an autonomous community.

Over the past five years, I have been learning how power works, how it unfolds, how influence unfolds and how to prepare yourself for potential initiatives that will either be directed at you or that you will be subjected to. I do not want to sit around and wait for things to pop up. I want to move away from being a reactionary artist; that is counterculture, sixties, seventies stuff. I think what we are involved in now is conscious culture. Conscious culture is something that knows it can make a difference if it makes a commitment to making a difference.

PW As a young native person who has been part of contemporary analysis and contemporary action, and someone who has had the opportunity to participate in and outside the art world, the media world, the commercial world, urban life, family life, and having travelled across this country involved in several projects in various capacities, where do you see the future of the First Nations?

LF The contact period just ended no more than one hundred and fifty years ago on the west coast – where the adventure from east to west culminated. Travel further and you are in the east again. So, now that we have all contacted one another, we can start communicating. But the frame of mind brought on by popular mediums like television, radio and film, has created a certain mindset that understands a little bit about everything but lacks the ability to interconnect it. So now we are working on the interconnection. We have got all the parts to a wonderful machine that we are

Page 270: Archer Pechawis in *Earth Police* (1992) at the Walter Phillips Gallery
Page 271: Leonard Fisher in *Earth Police* (1992) at the Walter Phillips Gallery

Photos Cheryl Bellows

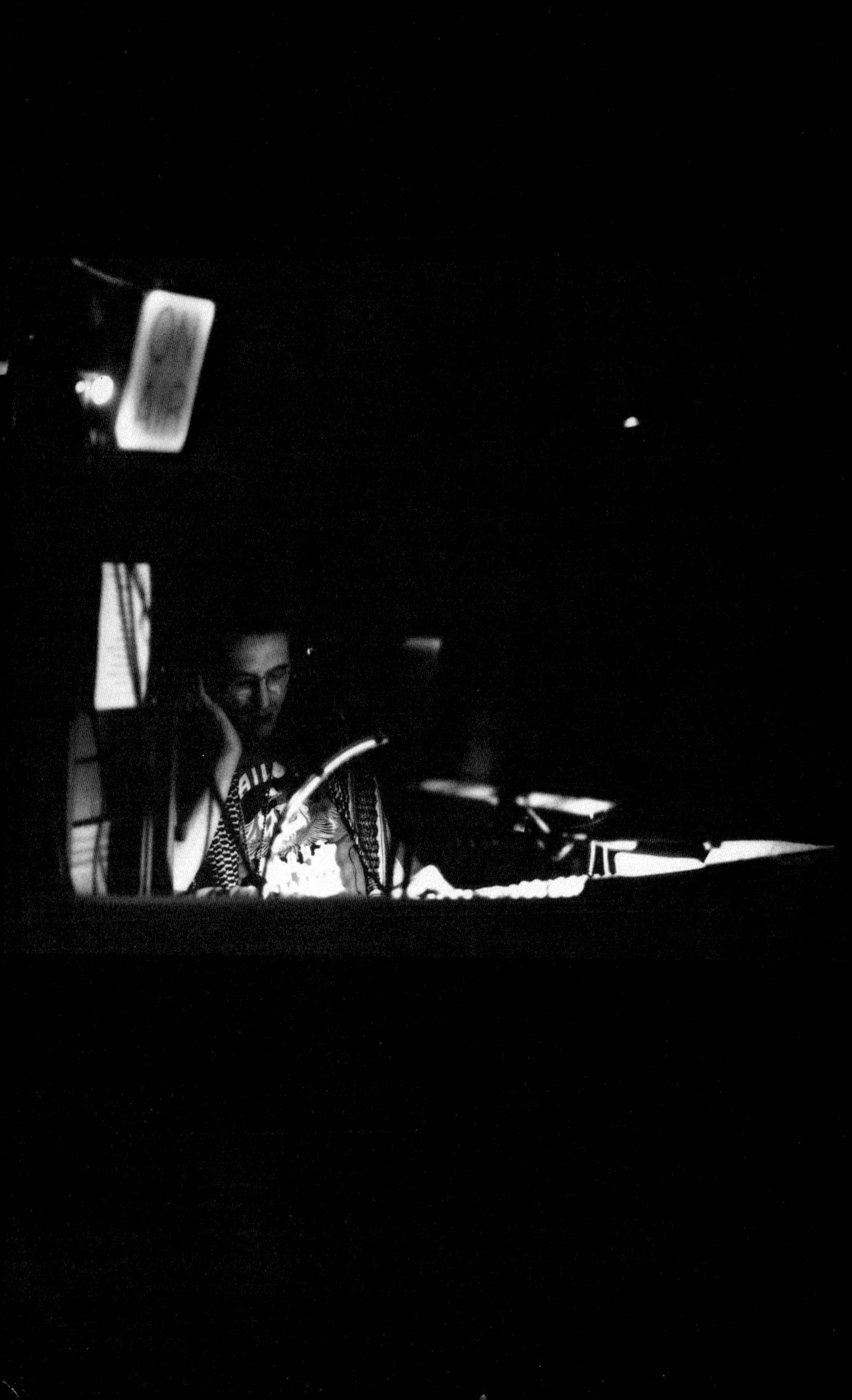

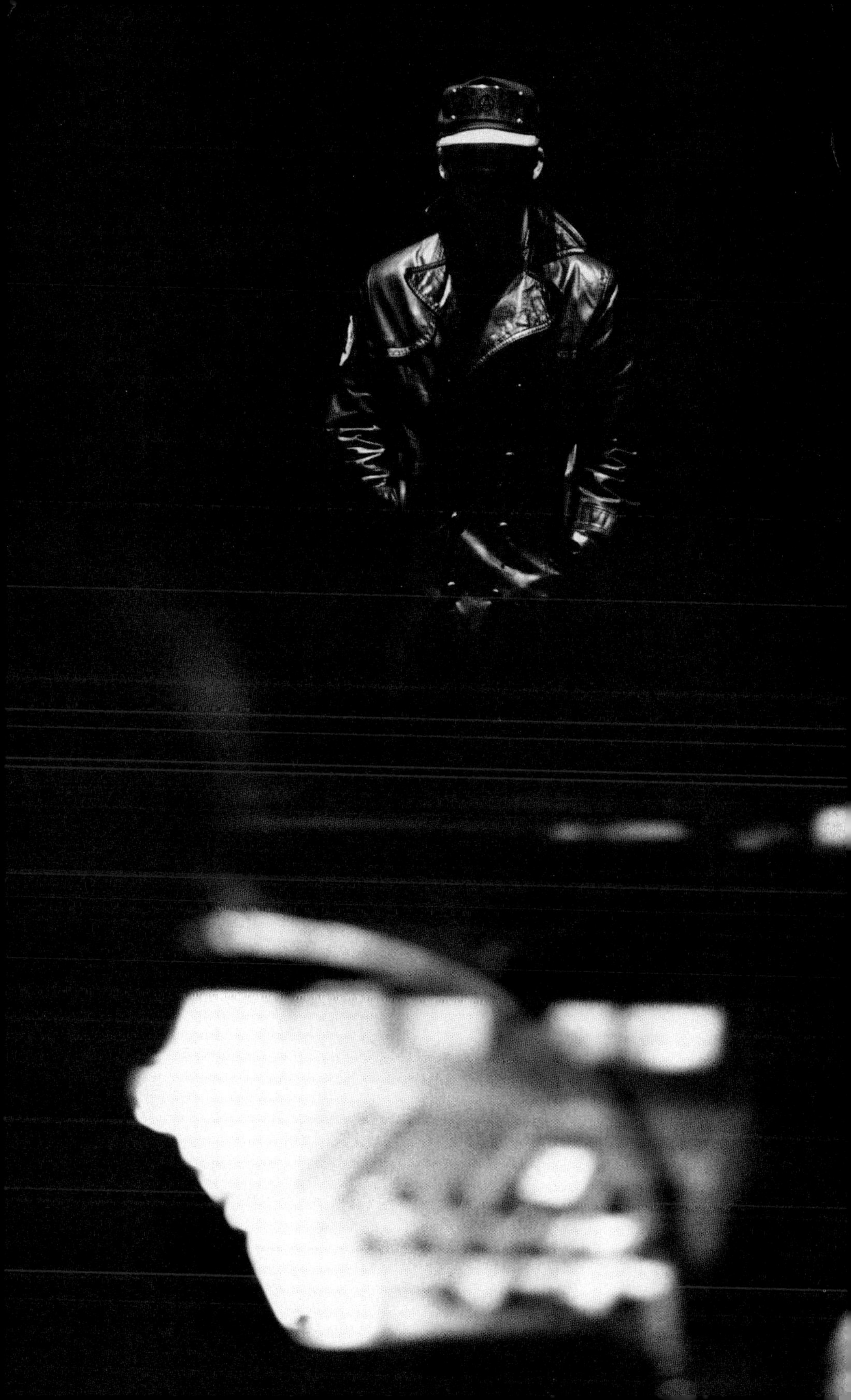

going to design to bring us into the twenty-first century: it will be a completely internalized creation – we just have to link it all up and attach it to different parts of ourselves.

I did this thing called *DisInformation*. It was a performance poem at the original Neo-Nativist show. I think about disinformation a lot, when I am out hitchhiking, doing my own thing, doing meditation in various locations. We are at a different plateau here in the nineties, with the end of colonial empires around the world and the acknowledgment that the discovery of North America was something other than the discovery of a pot of gold at the end of a rainbow. So, if that is the reality of the situation then I can be a linchpin between that disinformed society and the information it requires. As techno-Neo-Nativists, we are the ones who will maintain links between ancient history, postmodernism today and the future. That future is what we are creating as individuals working in whatever mediums and on whatever issues that we feel we are capable of controlling or understanding.

DisInformation is coming to you,
DisInformation is troubling you,
DisInformation says that we're no good,
But walk in my shoes if ya think ya could.

DisInformation means telling lies,
Too many people won't open their eyes,
Right across the country, as the crow flies,
is a Native nation with fire in their eyes.

This information is z knowledge of roots
I got spurs of terrafirms attached to my boots,
I got dignity in my own land
When I beat the drum I put thunder in my hand.

Leonard Fisher, *DisInformation* (revised version) (1989–93)

In 1989, I made a conscious decision to do something before the turn of the century and said to myself that I am not going into the next century suppressed or under the influence of anybody other than my own community. That was a personal, conscious decision and I started to undertake and initiate certain activities that I felt would help me get to that point as an individual. And, as I am trained to be and do, I wanted to immediately include other people of like-minded spirits and ideas. So that was the impetus for creating an idea called Neo-Nativism and pursuing that. I am not proclaiming to be the founder or the instigator of this whole Neo-Nativist spirit; I coined the term that helped me understand what it was and what it is in terms of larger society, a historical, postmodernist society, if you want to call it that. Then 1990 hit, and the confrontational things took place in eastern Canada at Oka and in southern Alberta at the Oldman Dam. It was like a validation of my frustration because I was feeling it, they were feeling it. We were of a like mind in that period of the disinformation campaign; the whole attempt at extinguishing native identity had reached the boiling point. When I saw all those people and felt their spiritual frustration, I knew that everything I had to do was in front of me and that I had to pursue it on whatever level I felt comfortable with. I feel comfortable doing it in an artistic or creative capacity.

PW I think of you as someone who wants to be recognized, a messenger, yet you are not calculating, your ambitions are not determined. You are not caught up marketing your works or your ideas in an organized and professional way. You also have several uncompleted works in progress such as *Personal Success Stories*.

LF I shot that video in 1990. I have not felt compelled to complete it although that has been changing over the last little while. *Personal Success Stories* is a political satire, a comedy on televangelism and cultural identity. It has been delayed because it has not steeped or matured. But now, as the warm arms of inclusion begin to surround us, I think it is time to let something like that go because it acts like a torpedo among all this benevolence of opinion and attitude. It is not fired out of aggression, it is fired in the hopes of suspending people from their over-anxious embrace or their over-enthusiastic acceptance of who we are and what we are. It is not because I do not want them to accept us or that I want to remain at loggerheads with people. I do not like this idea of this binary opposition, but I want people to come forward with a conscious understanding that they can be ingratiating and that they can be patronizing even though they are allegedly open-minded.

In our community, it is not that you do not speak until you are spoken to; it is that you do not talk unless you have something to say.

That is an important lesson for the non-native community to understand when they deal with us. That is what is missing right now in the dialogue or the exchange of ideas that is taking place between us and society at large.

PW In your opportunities, good, bad and indifferent, to immerse yourself in various conversational technologies, which I will call here the media arts, who has been your audience?

LF Primarily my audience is young native people – who might believe that they have a cross to bear or have this same feeling of dispossession. When I started, my purpose was to give aboriginal kids an avenue for expression in the world of technological possibility, to provide that voice for myself and others to understand and identify themselves in a very rapidly evolving society – one that may not understand that certain developments are creating frustration, anger and fear, especially fear of the devolution of life forces. We are the generation that my grandparents have been waiting for, you know, the ones to turn it around.

> I hear that young man standing in the middle of that circle
> . . . the time has come
>
> Leonard Fisher, *Earth Police (*1992)

Notes

1 From the back of a t-shirt produced by the Native Theatre School, a project of the Association for Native Development in the Performing and Visual Arts. Other natives have also referred to this as the 7th Fire, which is also the name of a group of musicians recording under the label Technawbe Sound.

2 In 1993, logging was scheduled to begin on Clayoquot Sound, one of the last unlogged rainforests on Vancouver Island. Plans for logging Gitksan Wet'suwet'en, also on the west coast, have also been strongly contested. These projects have attracted considerable media attention due to the opposition and debate surrounding the provincial licence to clear-cut these areas.

In the Noise of the Signals

Richard Kriesche

ONE

as a consequence of the total aestheticization of our entire life sphere, art seems to have become superfluous for the first time. art is only stylized anymore as a contradiction to everyday life. kept out of life, it is guaranteed "freedom" in the dead matter. the public, that is the social space for art, is the "free space of what is dead." the artist has nothing to do anymore with life itself, just as she or he has stopped being useful in the society of the living. however since genetic technicians have started replacing doctors there has been a paradigmatic change. the creation of life out of dead matter as the ultimate rationale of technological art – a metaphor of the creating person – has called art, which had already been declared dead, back to social reality.

TWO

with the increasing industrial dynamization of the body, freedom of the mind was suggested. this freedom, in the information sense, was followed by the evacuation of bodies into dead spaces. there were attempts at once to manifest in artwork the mind which was already separating itself from the dynamized body. the manifestation of freedom demanded dead objects. but the repeatedly propagated death of art in industrial modernity has been replaced by the art of death in informational modernity. death, as a contradiction to the dynamization and aestheticization of everyday life, is the result of the exponential acceleration in the information environment. in it, the content of art is its own disappearance, the art form is background noise.

THE PUBLIC SPACE

the sphere of the "public space" – and thus of "public art" – is that of the "publication of traffic"; of communication, information, telephone, radio, television, transmitting, broadcasting, of car, train and satellite networks, of global and cosmic traffic. in the dynamized state, within the lines of communication, the bodies begin to dissolve in accordance with their designation and make any visibility of the bodies appear reactionary. the body as a data carrier disappears in the intersection of accelerated data, as the car disappears in traffic.

the free dynamic subject is therefore no longer measured and determined by its shape or form but rather by the degree of its disintegration. disintegration is the self-expression of the subject that has become technically mobile.

but it is only with the electrification of the dynamized subject that the movement of subjects in space also initiates a disintegration. an eloquent testimony for this transition from "mobile subject" to "mobile background" is provided by the development from radio to car radio. i will even go so far as to state that it was only with car radio that radio found its real definition and designation. this history of radio accompanies the section of history covering a technological society that has been set into motion. from the stationary box to transistor and ultimately car radio, from the stationary to the mobile and ultimately to the dynamic object. dynamic because the "apparatus radio" becomes so "interconnected" with the "machine car" that the dynamics of the machine and the statics of the apparatus raise each other to a higher level of power. as the moving car sets the radio in motion, the radio heats up the body that is now motionless – tied down with belts. (television on the other hand has accompanied the technically travelling body since its emergence.) car television is replaced by collages on the car window. the tv screen is replaced by the wind screen. driving along, whether along the highways or in urban rush-hour traffic, corresponds increasingly to the collage technique of the dadaists. concrete dirt on the window panes, mixed up with fragments of landscape, melt together to become an inseparable unity. video clip technology with its extremely short cuts and sounds continues the trip at highest speeds in the mental space, beyond all visible speeds and laws of perception.

the special significance of car radio lies in its unique fusion of the industrial and the informational communication levels. the car radio is the transitory sign of the change from the mobile object to the mobile symbol. for no one but the travelling subject are radio frequency tables erected along the communication paths (highways) as visible signs of non-visible frequencies. these signs however must be read as an expression of the transition from industrial to informational communication and of the society based on it.

it thus becomes clear that the mobile subject, once set into motion, dissolves increasingly into a noise of the signals. in the car radio, the data of the channels blur with the sound of the motor and the temporal collages of the car windshield to become a synaesthetic perception of the world. the faster the movement, the more this background emerges. the higher the speed, the harder it gets to filter "stationary data" from the data background, that is to follow the program, pick out information. the multidimensional data background becomes the actual program. in it, the speed of the moving body is proportional to the noise of the signals, until at last it melts inaudibly into the background releasing only one piece of information, that of the background. the interest in news programs is heated up by the fact that the data background, which means loss of information, is artificially supplied along with the program. in the space age this noise does not suggest distance between the scene of the action and the receiver, as it did at the beginning of the radio age, but rather a compressed speed for the subject that remains in immobility (rigor mortis!).

RADIOMAN

the electric man no longer listens to the radio – he himself is radio: set at the same time on reception and transmission. as a sign of his existence he thus leaves his marks on the data background. the drawing of marks is the basis of his existence (on video, banking card, telephone, fax, personal computer and so on). as if in recognition of the electric circuits in his own body, the "radioman" charges himself up with mobile electronic calculators, watches, data and dictating machines, Walkmans, cellular telephones, electronic locators, laptops, notebooks. supported by batteries, he creates around himself the postmodern aura of an omnipresence. his exterior is radiant like the detergent "radion," his interior is embedded in the electronic community of the data background. he himself is a light spot (pixel) in the space of surfaces, the "computer planes," of foregrounds, backgrounds and image planes. into them he plunges, to disappear and then emerge in another place as someone else. as a light spot the "radioman" has permanently taken on the form of the vanishing point.

and even more: "radioman" has fused with the vanishing point. "radioman" has overcome Renaissance space, with its absolute authority of the vanishing point and the unequivocal rules connected with it regarding representation and contemplation. in that space the vanishing point itself was invisible, nevertheless it was present in every single thing. one could also say that in the space of objects and things the vanishing point dissolved itself by concretizing space above the visible and unequivocal order of objects. this vanishing point was not visible but it was present in every single thing. this invisible and infinitely remote point, that vanishes from the eye, puts the viewer into an unequivocal relation to the world and creates control over the world. at the same time, above the invisibility of the vanishing point that is within the finite world, infinity interweaves with space. it is this invisible power of the vanishing point in the finite world that, in the "technifestation" of photography, imparts to each single photo its very splendour, that speaks to us from infinity.

in the cameraless zooming of the computer-generated data images, the vanishing point itself is dynamized. every pixel is its own infinity, its own vanishing point. vanishing point and electronic subject – "radioman" – meet in the light spot on the surface of the screen in order to unite indissolubly in the noise of the signals. the vanishing of the objects in infinity, or the dissolution in the noise of the signals, leads to the vanishing of all differences in the finite world.

the once aural vanishing point, which as a symbol also represents social hierarchy and referred to the infinity of space, takes shape in the "radioman" as a light spot in the space of surfaces. in this space the spaces and objects, which were once subject to the vanishing point, dissolve to become their own vanishing points, in order to shine in the infinite data background. the vectors in the data background, or according to communication theory in the network, then point into all directions and times.

OMNISCIENCE

if in the industrial societies it was said that "knowledge means power" then translated into the electric society it should be said that "the sole power is 'knowledge about knowledge'" thus "the human dream of omniscience, which is also part of the history of fascination with information technology, enters into a qualitatively new phase. it is probably no coincidence that omniscience means an ability and privilege that was mostly reserved for the gods."[1] omniscience touches upon the background of all knowledge which has its place and time in the omnipresence, which has found its technical base in the communication network of information technology. knowledge no longer has anything to do with information in networks and systems, but with the noise of the signals and its systems. "whoever is omniscient breaks through the limitations of space and time and knows what there is to know about each time and about each place. it is exactly this grand gesture that is becoming manageable, in a very humanly secular fashion, due to the communication networks and computers with their almost inexhaustible data of knowledge."[2] telecommunication networks overcome all natural obstacles like mountains, oceans, rivers, but also all historically determined social, cultural ones and all dividing lines between private and public (an art-in-public-space must find its legitimation here). in this telecommunicative space of time, "city, country, mountain, river, animal, plant, boy's name, girl's name – the objects of our childhood in the old children's game – must congeal to become data in order to enter into the infinity horizon of omniscience, at which point the causal connection with outer space or the universe as the basis of knowledge or data background becomes effective.

INFINITY

in the context of the data background any appearing object is an arbitrary manifestation of the infinity syndrome of vanishing points and periods of time. the objects in the universal machine that are designed for infinity, with their fleeting stores and screens, are designed for the infinite place, from where they speak to us with infinite time. the machine, like its objects, is a paraphrase of the infinity of the universe. as a universal machine, it is the child of the same universe hypotheses in modern science that is mentioned by, among others, the American astronomer Frank

Wilczek: "at the point of the big bang – as the theory of the beginning of the universe accepted by all scientists – the universe was not only infinitely dense, but also infinitely hot."[3] this state of infinitely high density dates back billions of years. the vanishing point in space has dissolved in the infinity of density. the American astrophysicists David L. Meier and Rashid A. Sunyaev allow at least in theory for the possibility of being able to find temporal infinity, for "if we could look at objects which are so far away that their light takes 16.5 billion years to reach the earth, then we would see these objects in the state they were in just after the beginning of the universe."[4]

VANISHING

with the one vanishing point in the Renaissance making things disappear, the objects arose in the foreground in their order. with the vanishing points in the electronic context making things appear, the objects disappear in the background. as the Renaissance was characterized by its universal order of objects in their uniqueness of space and time, so the informational design is characterized by making objects disappear. the beginning of this process is the indistinguishability of the concrete world, which at the same time is able to be anything and everything.

the resigned design in its postmodern arbitrariness and colourfulness demonstrates very clearly the long lost fight against the vanishing of objects. the actual design decision has already been made in the microelectronic circuit, where the distinguishing criterion is unimportant, not because it in itself provides nothing more to see but because nothing may be seen that makes any difference. (in the next chip generation a pea by comparison will prevent the chip from functioning in an area the size of five soccer fields. the present technology with its microdesign has reached the atomic limitations of the material. it gets below the dimensions of light waves so that in absolute terms as well, seeing anything is impossible.) thus the absolute dissolution of the vanishing point, which points into infinity, has been carried out. once the one vanishing point has disappeared into space the innumerable light spots of the surface come into being. this constitutes the intoxication of signals, beyond any acoustic or visual information values. "here space disappears in a new sense of time," according to Julian Halliday at a communication conference in Montréal in 1987. "the new space is semantically defined as a surface for games and diversion, divided into fear and promise, a surface through which existence and objects exhibit and repress their materiality . . . a space that is perceived and shown in a superficial and empty fashion does not reveal anything but only exhibits, as all surfaces do . . . the archetypal illustration of Walt Disney's film *TRON*, whose space is not a real but a virtual one that is literally spread out in the computer circuit."[5]

the vanishing of space and time in favour of a permanent mutation was mentioned as early as 1920 by Hermann Weyl, who worked closely with Einstein and stated the following to explain Einstein's theories: "we totally deny the existence of matter filling space by merely being there; if, according to the theory of relativity, it does not make sense anymore to speak of the same point in space at different times, or of the same point in time at different places, then this also eliminates any meaningful possibility of recognizing 'the same point of substance' and following it through its history. there are no unchangeable corpuscles that the force field only grasps from the outside, pushing them back and forth."[6]

Einstein himself even mentioned "a field of ghosts . . . where the waves only had the purpose of guiding the way for the corpuscular light quanta . . . this guiding field determines the probability of a light quantum, the carrier of energy and impulse, taking a certain path."[7] although this theory by Einstein is no longer valid today, there is talk of fields again in the context of the macrocosmic. they are now called "background radiation" of outer space and "their uniformity suggests that this radiation was produced at the beginning of the universe (big bang) and has since cooled down to 2.9 Kelvin (2.9 above the absolute zero point) due to the expansion of the universe," with "the intensity of the background radiation – except for deviations of less than one per million – creating an even distribution all over the sky."[8] finally, the recently discovered Röentgen background makes it necessary, according to its discoverer Bruce Margon, "that the astronomers get used to the fact that up to now they may have ignored ninety-nine percent of the matter in the universe. the known galaxies and the shining objects within them would then be no more than impurities of the intergalactic mediums."[9]

all of this would not be so interesting if these theses did not coincide with a new perception of the world in the social context which, as a background of life, appears to be carrying our lives. grasping this background is difficult to us because it cannot be communicated, because mutual communication is based on it or takes place through it. what cosmic background radiation is for the universe, according to astrophysics, is equivalent to "common sense" in terms of the functioning of societies. we seem to know that it exists, however, it has not been possible so far to describe it, as the state of artificial intelligence research shows very clearly. "the problem of common sense has prevented any progress especially in the theory of artificial intelligence in the past twenty years . . . because understanding natural language depends on humans and computers having a general communication context (common sense). it is necessary to solve the problem of what common sense means and what it comprises."[10] without knowledge of "common sense" as the background of knowledge there cannot be any progress in artificial intelligence research, as in astronomy nothing will happen without the "background radiation," as in the new culture nothing will happen without the "noise of the signals," as the background constitutes the signals themselves.

THE DEAD DATA BACKGROUND

while telegraph, radio, television, telephone, for example, were still reporting to us from far-away spaces, we are now preparing for the report from beyond these spaces. those are dead spaces, spaces of the dead, that we will be confronted with.

a presentiment of this is provided by the radio voice. the distance between transmitter and receiver, which was technically overcome but also technically cut out or eliminated, is, metaphorically speaking, a dead space that, as we should never forget, always resonates in the technical voice. the technical voice is the mood of the eliminated spaces and times, and it makes absolutely no difference whether the voice comes to us live or from storage. live is now only a sentimental technological lie. it is only the elimination, the cancellation of space and time that makes it possible for storage technologies to make their appearance in order to realize their own characteristic competence: vitalizing what is dead. storage technologies are the harbingers of vitalization technologies, which require the killing of what is alive in space and time so that they can vitalize what is space – and timeless. if it could be imagined that Zeuxis, when he simulated grapes in an alleged mural, so perfectly outdid this world that even birds were fooled, then it is much easier to imagine that in radio – immanently present technically dead spaces – "the beyond" speaking to us is simulated. (in the "virtual reality" of computer spaces these dead spaces have already received their first name.) now we must learn to exclude the vitalization of what is dead in the information of the technically transmitted messages, in the noise of the signals. so begins the "resurrection from the dead" in a qualitatively new state. in the beginnings there were shapes, patterns, forms, rhythms that spoke to us from the three-dimensional space and found their input, output and shape in the apparatuses. now it is the entire data background, the data storage of otherworldly spaces and times, heaven and hell, speaking to us, but it does not put our bodies into motion anymore, rather it puts us into synchronous vibration with the noise of the data background. as "radioman" we are the mental resonating bodies of omniscience, of the dead spaces, of the universe.

this completes the circle: the accelerated radio provides us with a presentiment from the realm of the data-dead. nothing is more alarming in a radio transmission than an interruption in broadcasting because it makes the dead space between transmitter and receiver come alive. in the broadcasting interruption, the dead space, for a few moments potentially coincides with the death of the "radioman."

"radioman" oscillates like an electric body between the "dead data background" and the "technosphere" as the foreground. in this way, in the after-era of postmodern times, he breaks the beaming of the technosphere and the beaming away of the social side, as practised up to that time. as in the "radioman," the aestheticization finds perfection in the total beaming of the technosphere which, as many people think, has made art in its political, social and aesthetic function a nice memory. in the place of this "fine," socially disconnected, art-historizing material art of the museums, there is now the futurizing pendant of an "electronic kitsch art." in contrast to the former, which still pretends to be political, the latter, in its ostensibly unpretentious spectacle, is the most political art in the history of mankind – as the ejection of the data background.

it goes without saying that with the aestheticization of technology in technological societies those very societies aestheticize themselves, and that this leads to an anestheticization in the political sense. another commonplace observation is that technologies reinforce trends, that they can force freedom as well as power, death as well as life. if one considers that information technology is a military technology, then "the generalization of technologies – especially of information technologies – creates the danger for the civil and inner concerns of the state of carrying the total military machinery, including projective driving controls, into all areas of society."[11] in this way the eminently political role of a "technical media art" as kitsch art receives a new importance: it is to transfigure the "technological death urge" of society as an "art of beauty," using the technical means inherent in it.

VIBRATION, OSCILLATION, NOISE

the intoxication with drugs at the beginning of the sixties is followed by the technological data intoxication of simulation. in the noise of the signals the increasingly paralyzed body receives its frequency impulses. this noise is not motion in a conventional space, it is the synchronization with the vibrating body of society. from the noise of the signals "radioman" arises. in the noise, space and time are connected as are zero and one in the chip. in the noise of the signals death and life meet. this noise is the oscillation between the grounds and the surfaces without depth between which "radioman" diffuses back and forth. noise is the vibration, the continuous massage as the only message. noise is the stimulation of mental sensorics, the informational pendant to the vibrator. in the noise, the hitherto dead background will shine. in the noise of the signals, time in its infinity returns. noise is the frequency of infinity.

those who will be tied up in this data background will also be the ones who will determine the actions of all those who still make their decisions based on the traditional times and spaces, therefore, they will decide over dependence and independence, freedom and domination.

Translated from German by Anna Lausch

Notes

1 Doris Janshen, "Bilder von Menschen," *Computer und Kultur*, ed. H. Schauer, M.E.A. Schmutzer (Vienna: R. Oldenbourg, 1987).

2 Ibid.

3 Frank Wilczek, "Materie und Antimaterie," *Kosmologie* issue of *Spektrum der Wissenschaft* (German edition of *Scientific American*) (1986).

4 David L. Meier and Rashid A. Sunyaev, "Galaxien im Fruehzustand," *Kosmologie* issue of *Spektrum der Wissenschaft* (German edition of *Scientific American*) (1986).

5 Julian G. Halliday, "Co-opting the Future," paper presented to the International Communication Association Conference, Montréal, 1987

6 Hermann Weyl, "Die Einsteinsche Relativitaetstheorie," *Gravitation* issue of *Spektrum der Wissenschaft* (German edition of *Scientific American*) (1987).

7 Walter Greiner, "Elementare Materie," *Vakuum und Felder* issue of *Spektrum der Wissenschaft* (German edition of *Scientific American*) (1986).

8 John D. Barrow and Joseph Silk, "Raum und Zeit," *Spektrum der Wissenschaft* (German edition of *Scientific American*) (1987).

9 Bruce Margon, "Der Kosmische Roentgenhintergrund," *Kosmologie* issue of *Spektrum der Wissenschaft* (German edition of *Scientific American*) (1987).

10 Hubert L. Dreyfus, "Menschliche Sprache versus Computer Code," *Computer und Kultur*, ed H. Schauer, M.E.A. Schmutzer (Vienna: R. Oldenbourg, 1987).

11 Janshen.

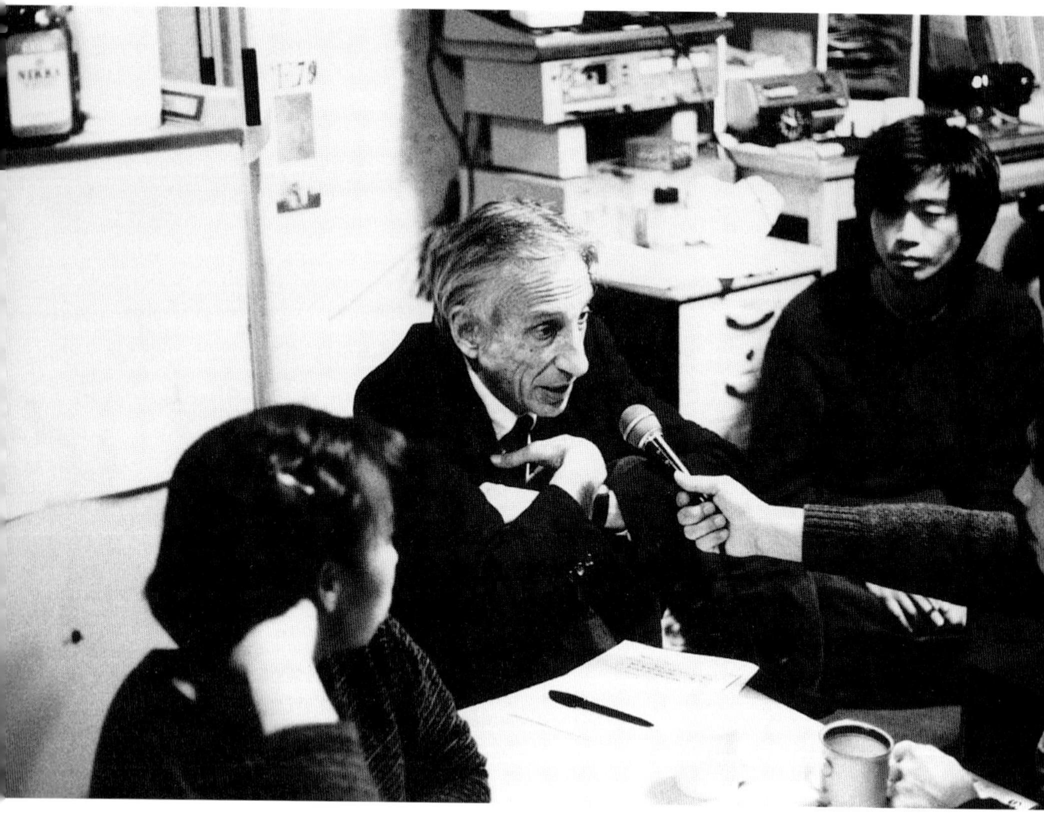

Ivan Illich in 1986 at *Radio Home Run*, a mini-FM station in Tokyo

Toward Polymorphous Radio

Tetsuo Kogawa

> We understand the end of something all too easily in the negative sense as a mere stopping, as the lack of constitution, perhaps even as decline and impotence, the end suggests the completion and the place in which the whole of history is gathered in its most extreme possibility.[1]

Throughout its history, despite efforts by the Futurists in the 1920s, radio has been considered largely a means of communication rather than an art form. Therefore, it is ironic that just as traditional forms of radio are in decline, its possibilities as an art form are reaching extreme potentials. If, as Heidegger suggests, extreme possibilities are reached at the end of something, what then ends with radio? What is radio's "most extreme possibility?" In order to rethink these questions, I will talk about my experiences in Japan with free radio, which developed out of the mini-FM movement.

The term mini-FM was first used in a mass-circulation newspaper in 1982, when a very low-watt FM-station movement started. Mini-FM stations have very little power judged by any standard – usually less than a hundred milliwatts. Although such a weak signal may seem to be of no use for broadcasting, the purpose was *not* broadcasting but *narrowcasting*.

The birth of mini-FM is related to the peculiar situation of radio in Japan. When mini-FM originated in the early 1980s, most cities in Japan had only one FM station, if any at all, because only government-operated stations could obtain licenses; station administrators tended to be retired government officials. The situation is not so different today, although

Photo courtesy the artist

there are seven stations in Tokyo now instead of two. In this constricted atmosphere many people wanted more open programming. Throughout the late 1960s and 1970s, we had become familiar with American popular and countercultures, since American films and records were easy to obtain. People were longing for diversity in culture yet there were no radio or television stations in Japan covering subcultures. When mini-FM started, therefore, it became a cultural craze.

In addition to a desire for diverse culture, there was another motivation for those of us who started the free radio movement – to resist the commodification of subculture. Political activists for alternative culture in Japan had been involved traditionally with underground newspapers and magazines rather than electronic media. When youth subcultures started to develop mini-FM there was no immediate concern among political radicals since radical political groups tended to critically dismiss youth culture. However, certain industries began to develop new commodities for the subculture market and targeted young people as the new consumers. This created a dilemma for radical activists because we were aware of the tendency of postindustrial institutions to co-opt diverse culture and society. The Italian free radio movement and Félix Guattari's approach to it presumably solved our dilemma.[2] It provided thrilling examples in which politics and culture creatively worked together and gave us hope with which to cope with the dismal state of Japanese mass media. Guattari stressed the radically different function of free radio from conventional mass media. His notions of transmission, transversal and molecular revolution suggested that, unlike conventional radio, free radio would not impose programs on a mass audience, whose numbers have been forecast, but would come across freely to a molecular public, in a way that would change the nature of communication between those who speak and those who listen.[3]

Based on these events, friends and I began experimenting with radio transmission in the early eighties. At that time we intended to establish a pirate FM station with a leftist perspective. However, there were few people who could help us build an appropriate transmitter and it was difficult to find a ready-made transmitter at a reasonable price. Even a techno-freak friend, instead of giving me the instructions, warned me that within half an hour of breaking the radio regulations, the Ministry of Post and Telecommunication would discover it. This negative attitude had resulted largely from the psychological stigma attached to breaking the law

Photo Toshiyuki Maeda

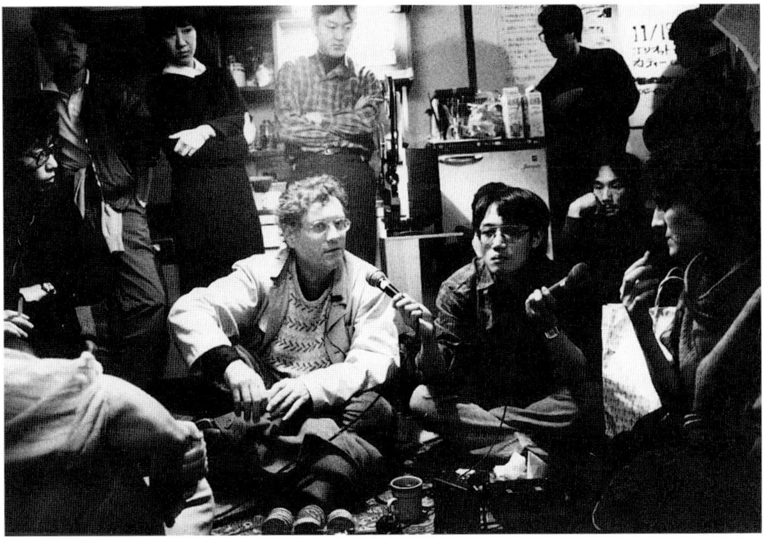

Félix Guattari, *Radio Home Run* (1985)

during World War II when the authorities strictly banned the use of short-wave radio receivers, to say nothing of transmitters. Still now, there is a general feeling that the airwaves belong to the government. In fact, Japanese mass media always use the term *national resource* to describe the airwaves. However, we had a different idea about airwaves – that they should be public resources, not monopolized by the state. Nevertheless, the fact remained that it was difficult for us to get a transmitter. As a result, I embarked on an independent study of transmitter technology.

In the meantime, an interesting thing happened: I stumbled upon Article 4 in the Radio Regulations Book. It permits transmitting without a license if the power is very weak and is intended to accommodate wireless microphones and remote-control toys, for example. Under this regulation, quite a few wireless transmitters were sold in toy stores and electronic markets. Also, several audio-parts makers sold the wireless stereo transmitters to link amplifiers to speakers without wires. My idea was to use this type of tiny unit for radio transmitting.

At the beginning, I was dubious about the power of this level of transmission. During several tests of small ready-made FM transmitters, however, we found that some of them could cover a half-mile radius. Presumably, the sensitivity of radio receivers had increased beyond the Ministry's estimation when they established the regulation in the 1950s.

I started to make this idea public in various kinds of periodicals using the opportunities that I had in popular magazines. My book *This is Free Radio*[4] provoked strong responses. The next stage transpired quickly and dramatically. In late 1982, my students and I started *Radio Polybucket*, a station using a small transmitter on the university campus. At the same time, a group of young musicians, advertising agents, designers and so on, started a station called KIDS, intending to promote their new businesses – shops selling goods for the young. They were so eager to advertise themselves to the mass media who looked for new youth cultures that the news about the radio station was widely published and televised. This news had a strong impact on young people and the media.

Whenever popular journalism addressed this kind of news item, the number of mini-FM stations increased. Many stations with a similar aim as KIDS appeared. Even major advertising agencies tried to open mini-FM stations. The exact number is unknown, but it can be estimated from the number of small transmitters sold that, in a year, over one thousand stations appeared in Japan. People on college campuses, in housing complexes, coffee shops and bars, stalls at street fairs and even local offices started mini-FM stations. More than ten companies, including Mitsubishi, Panasonic, Hitachi and Sony, sold a transmitter labelled "For mini-FM use."

The boom was fantastic, in a sense, but it puzzled us. We had intended to establish a free radio station, not to transmit a one-way performance that disregarded listeners as most stations did. During the boom, most mini-FM stations were able to communicate to a handful of people only. Many of these stations seemed to us to be naïvely copying professional radio studio work. To the contrary, we paid attention to constant and serious listeners. We wanted to provide a community of people with alternative information on politics and social change.

The radio station that my students and I had started on the campus re-established itself in the centre of Tokyo when the students finished school in 1983. The new station was called *Radio Home Run*. Every day, from 8 PM to midnight, one or two groups aired talk or music programs. Themes depended on who was host and who were guests. The members always invited new guests who were involved in political or cultural activism. Also, listeners who lived close to the station hesitantly began to visit. To repeat the telephone number during each program was our basic policy. Guests sometimes recorded cassette tapes of our programs and let their friends listen. *Radio Home Run* quickly became a meeting place for students, activists, artists, workers, owners of small shops, local politicians, men, women and the elderly.

Theoretically, I had argued that mini-FM stations might be linked together to extend the transmission/reception area. Since the cost of each unit is cheap, one could have a number of radio sets and transmitters to relay to each other quite inexpensively. *Radio Home Run* was not so eager to do this but some stations succeeded in establishing a very sophisticated network to link together and extend their service areas.[5] Through a number of experiments to remodel the transmitting system, create programs and pursue a new way of getting together, we came to the conclusion at *Radio Home Run* that we must work within a half-mile service area. Tokyo is densely populated so even a half-mile area has at least ten thousand inhabitants. This meant that mini-FM could function as community radio. Moreover, we realized that in the process of transmitting we were more conscious of our members than (possible) listeners. The action of transmitting together changed our relationships and feelings in a way that seemed distinct from the effects of other collective actions that did not involve transmitting. Further, we surmised that relationships differed because we were narrowcasting rather than broadcasting. We decided it had something to do with the limited area of our transmission signal.

We tried to think about radio in a different way, as a means to link people together. To the extent that each community and individual has different thoughts and feelings, we believed there should be different kinds of radio – hundreds of mini-FM stations in a given area. If you had the same number of transmitters as receivers, your radio sets could have completely different functions. Thus radio transmission technology could be available for individuals to take control of their transmission and reception. This block radio could reactivate diverse cultures and politics, "micro-politics," in the words of Félix Guattari. Guattari once expected "des millions et des millions d'Alice en puissance."[6] However, I think that if you expect molecular revolution via radio, size is important. In my opinion, even *Radio Alice*[7] in Bologna, the symbol of the free radio movement in the 1970s, was too large.

Conventional radio and television is generally eager for as large a service area as possible: from nation-wide to global networks. According to these models, communication is considered as a way of conveying infor-

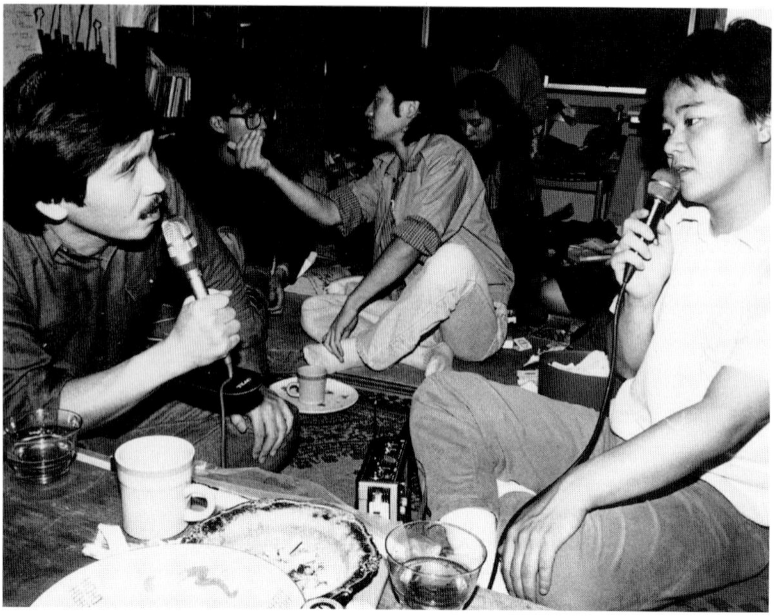
Photo Toshiyuki Maeda

Typical scene at *Radio Home Run*, a mini-FM station in Tokyo

mation as a material entity from one place to another. Mass media has functioned (and still does) as a strong catalyst of industrialization, characterized by the transportation of solid material, integrated homogeneous grouping and an industrious work ethic. However, as Humberto Maturana and Francisco Varela have argued, such a notion of communication is forced and distorted. Human communication is not based on tube conveyance but on structural coupling.[8]

It is in this context that I gradually understood the meaning and potential of mini-FM. Radio could serve as a communication vehicle not for broadcast but for the individuals involved. Even if they have few listeners, these stations do work as catalysts to *reorganize* groups involved in mini-FM. Those who were familiar with conventional radio laughed at mini-FM because it had only a few listeners, listeners within walking distance of the station, and no consistent style. However, even if one overlooks the dramatic effect on society, one must admit that mini-FM has a powerful therapeutic function: an isolated person who sought companionship through radio happened to hear us and visited the mini-FM station; a shy person started to speak into the microphone; people who never used to be able to share ideas and values found a place for dialogue;

an intimate couple discovered otherwise unknown fundamental misunderstandings. At that time nobody talked about such a psychotherapeutic function, however, given the number of people involved in mini-FM, it must have been understood unconsciously. Indeed, the 1980s in Japan saw the transition from conventional *banzai* collectivity to electronic individuality, where people needed different media and locations in which to replace traditional togetherness like eating and drinking with family and friends, in schools and workplaces.[9]

Mini-FM is idiosyncratic to Japanese society, especially that of the 1980s. When you consider a unit of a social and cultural idiosyncrasy, the size will be equivalent to the size of mini-FM's transmitting area – it has something to do with geography and culture. In an Australian city like Canberra, the size of an idiosyncratic unit would be relatively large. Even if you wanted to narrowcast, you would need at least a ten-kilometre radius for the service area. On the other hand, in Manhattan, even one block would constitute a mini-FM unit.

In my experience, the standard power of mini-FM has been one watt. The area that a one-watt transmitter covers is within walking or bicycling distance, which is ecologically sound. Also, there is airwave pollution to consider – the twenty-first century pollution. As Paul Brodeur and Stephan Steneck have warned,[10] electromagnetic pollution is strong but it is not made public because it is connected with the economic interests of corporations and states. Electromagnetic radiation from the antennae of microwaves, radars, broadcasting stations and satellites may damage genetic codes. Many people admit feeling strangely tired after using a cellular telephone or transceiver for extended periods of time. By the twenty-first century, it may not be possible to use strong transmitters like those used by large radio stations. At any rate, it is easier to deal with a one watt transmitter. You can even build one yourself, although, in the last ten years of mini-FM, I have learned that even the simple technology of a one-watt transmitter is monopolized by specialists and institutions. In accordance with the fact that free transmission on the airwaves is prohibited in most countries in the world, there is very little information on transmitters and therefore few parts available at radio shops popular with the public. If you can get the parts, though, building a transmitter is as easy as building a radio receiver today. My performance workshop at the Walter Phillips Gallery was an attempt to illustrate this.[11]

Although I have been involved in the free radio movement of mini-

FM and also pirate stations in Japan since the early 1980s, I now doubt if radio, when developed to its most extreme potential, can be appropriately called free radio. My experiences have led me to imagine therefore what ends with radio: we are now in the process of surpassing radio as a communication means and as a form of self-expression for artists. Both of these models belong to modernity, the same matrix that adopted terms such as freedom and democracy. We might in the 1990s have to consider retiring the expression "free radio." Even mini-FM is not within the descriptive framework of free radio. The signal is too weak or too special to provide an "alternative radio" to mass media like community radio.

However, this does not mean that mini-FM is not relevant to discussions of free radio. Mini-FM has changed our communications procedures and has offered examples of new types of communication. For as long as radio has been considered as a means of communication, as a means for the circulation of information from one place to another, mini-FM has been different. How can you define radio that reaches a small audience in a very limited area? It could be possible to define it as a kind of performance art. Perhaps radio art might be a more appropriate term for mini-FM. But it is not quite adequate because mini-FM is still radio.

In light of history it is regrettable that a word such as free is still used as we approach the end of the twentieth century. Whether *free* is interpreted as *freedom* or *free of charge*, it remains a word whose consequences were seen during the French Revolution. One would think a new direction or framework for human self-fulfilment that does not rely on notions of freedom would have been found. Yet over the past two hundred years, it has not happened. Perhaps now, though, the era of freedom as an ideology has ended. This does not mean that freedom was an illusion or that we enter a new age of non-freedom. Rather, it means that other concepts completely different in character from freedom are emerging. Compared to technologies using steam and springs which are based on compression and release, radio is a medium always beyond freedom in the sense that it is based on electronics, a post-freedom technology. When radio was first developed, there was no inherent need to separate transmitters from receivers. However, at that time, freedom was still a valid political ideology, so transmission and reception were strictly separated to allow for contrasts between the free and the not free: transmission was monopolized by the broadcast stations and "unfree people" called "listeners" were created artificially.

Photo Gon Nanashi

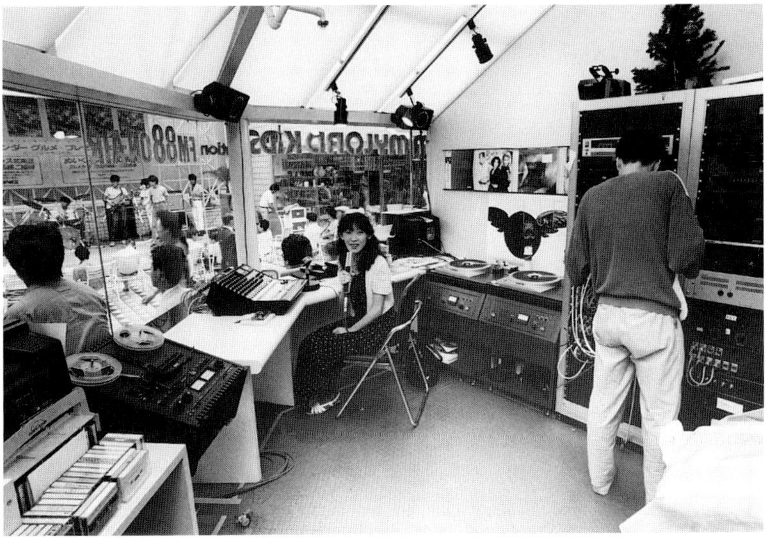

Mini-FM sometimes made a profit

It was under those circumstances that demands and fights for media "freedom" began. When Marconi, the "father of wireless communication," succeeded in establishing transatlantic wireless communication in 1901, radiowaves were already reserved by the British Navy: he was engaging in pirate communication. After numerous pirate broadcasting attempts since then, "free radio law" was established in Italy finally in the 1970s, allowing anybody to become a transmitter, for all practical purposes (actually, the supreme court merely acknowledged that radio waves comprised a medium for expression permitted to everybody). A new horizon was opened, outdating the separation of transmission and reception that had been forced upon electronic media.

This horizon, however, has been put into action in television more effectively than in radio. In the seventies in the United States, a new movement, demanding "public access" to television began, led by George Stoney and video activists like Dee Dee Halleck, one of the founders of Paper Tiger Television. This led to the creation of public access channels within cable television and, in the 1980s, even to the opening of some satellite channels for the public.[12]

The Deep Dish Project, started experimentally in 1985 by the public access cable station Paper Tiger Television, attempted to satellite-cast programs by public access stations like Paper Tiger Television, which had only been seen in some parts of Manhattan up to that point. The project received strong positive response and this method of linking public access cable television and satellite became organized, namely as Deep Dish TV. This organization has a small office in the same building as Paper Tiger Television but is active on a national scale. Deep Dish TV does not have an integrated central function like organizations such as Cable News Network (CNN). It is not a broadcast station but a "network organization," which initiates projects according to certain themes, and realizes them by asking American television stations (mostly public access) to participate. Gulf Crisis TV Project is a typical example of this. It was not a program created by the station Deep Dish TV but a "video collaboration" which, via satellite, edited and linked documents and works created by various American stations – including public broadcasting, community television and public access stations.

The main difference between public access television and traditional television is that while the latter contains only programs made by its own company, in the former, a number of "stations" share the same channel. For example, Paper Tiger Television is a "station" that only exists every Wednesday night for thirty minutes. When this station's programming ends, another station's begins. In this case, there is no collaboration; the different stations merely share space and tools. Among those who broadcast in this way, some hope to own their exclusive channel in the future. In contrast, the Gulf Crisis TV Project emphasized the communal aspect of public access channels. It provided an opportunity for media to be recognized, not as remote and inaccessible platforms, but as sites for the continuous exchange of polymorphous elements. The importance of Deep Dish TV is that it put an end to the ideas of centralization and concentration which have been associated with "broadcast" (to cast broadly). Communication satellites are no longer seen as antennae, 36,000 kilometres high, which can centralize information on a global scale. Satellites are not global hyper-mass media instruments, but networking devices which create polymorphous circuits. They are "polymedia" devices.

The question in the age of satellite media is no longer whether television or radio is "free" or not but whether it is "polymorphous" or not. Whether a station can become a place of polymorphous "chaos," obtaining "order through fluctuations," in the sense of Ilya Prigogine,[13] depends on how many heterogeneous autonomous media units can be created. Such units are not likely to be large. A "chaos unit," which could be sensed easily, might be relative to the human body. Radio stations which can only cover areas within walking distance might already exist as a form of a particular unit of polymedia, a chaos unit. Polymedia are not intended simply to link smaller units into a larger whole: instead they involve the recovery of electronic technology so that individuals can communicate, share idiosyncrasies and be convivial. The satellite presents possibilities for polymedia but it does not create it. Polymedia must be based on self-controlled tools, otherwise, advanced technologies like satellites will remain as tools for the manipulation of power.[14]

Notes

1 Martin Heidegger, *On Time and Being*, trans. Joan Stambaugh (New York: HarperCollins, 1972), 56–57.

2 See John Downing, *Radical Media: The Political Experience of Alternative Communications* (Boston: South End Press, 1984), 296–297. There sprang up in Italy, beginning in the mid-seventies, a host of "wildcat" alternative and political stations including Radio Città Futura (Radio City of the Future) in Rome, Radio Alice in Bologna, Controradio in Florence and Radio Popolare (People's Radio) in Milan. Downing devotes an entire chapter to Radio Popolare. "Radio Popolare made the attempt to communicate outside the left wing ghetto in its broadcasts after 11:00 pm when as Pedrocchi put it, 'we used to discuss many things: the family, sex, death, what the future holds.' One device they used involved watching television with the listeners and asking them what they thought of the program or watching a movie with the sound off, and substituting Radio Popolare's own spontaneous commentary. In another format, they would ask a woman and a man to phone in and then to ask them to role-play: 'You've been living together for ten years, but things are going badly between you now. What would you say to each other if you were talking about this together?' Often there would be as many as five or six 'takes' of this conversation between different people."

3 For a classic English document of the Italian radical movement called Autonomia see *Italy: Autonomia – Post-Political Politics*, the special issue of *Semiotext(e)* 3:3, 1980. For the relationship between the movement and radio see John Downing, *The Media Machine* (London: Pluto Press Limited, 1980) and *Radical Media: The Political Experience of Alternative Communications* (Boston: South End Press, 1984). Guattari's contribution to radical radio in *La révolution moléculaire* (Paris: Éditions Recherches, 1979) is still provocative.

4 This was published in Japanese only in 1983. Some of the contents can be read in my English articles: "Free Radio in Japan" in *Cultures in Contention*, ed. Douglas Kahn and Diane Neumaier (Seattle: The Real Comet Press, 1985),

116–121; "New Trends in Japanese Popular Culture" in *The Japanese Trajectory: Modernization and Beyond*, ed. Gavan McCormack and Yoshio Sugimoto (Cambridge: Cambridge University Press, 1988).

5 The following articles written in English are valuable: Steve Usdin, "We've Got Radios, So Where's the FM?" *PHP INSPECT* (March 1988), 30–35.

6 *La révolution moléculaire*, 143–52.

7 Franco Berardi, alias Bifo, "Anatomy of Autonomy," in *Italy: Autonomia, Post-Political Politics*, 156. "The movement for free radio spread widely. In every city, neighborhood and village the young proletarians, together with students and communications workers, used the occasion of a legislative vacuum (the result of which was that the State monopoly on information lapsed and was not replaced by any other sort of regulation) to give life to a network of small "wildcat" stations. The radio stations were operated with luck and very little money, but they could cover a territorial space adequate for the organizational forms and communication needs of the emerging proletarian strata. Through this channel circulated an uninterrupted flood of music and words, a flood of transformations on the symbolic, perceptive and imaginative planes. This flood entered every house, and anyone could intervene in the flow, telephoning, interrupting, adding, correcting. The design, the dream of the artistic avant-garde – to bridge the separation between artistic communication and revolutionary transformation or subversive practise – became in this experience a reality. The brief, happy experience of Radio Alice – which from February 1976 to March 1977 transmitted from Bologna – remains the symbol of this period, of that unforgettable year of experimentation and accumulation of intellectual, organizational, political and creative energies."

8 See Humberto Maturana and Francisco Varela, *Autopoiesis and Cognition: The Realization of the Living* (Norwell, Massachusetts: D. Reidel, 1980).

9 For the changing situation of Japanese society in the 1980s, see my account "Beyond Electronic Individualism," *Canadian Journal of Political and Social Theory* 8:3 (Fall 1984), 15–19, and a series of my discussions with Douglas Lummis, "What the World Looks Like Through the Japanese Mass Media" in *Japan-Asia Quarterly Review* 16:4 (1984), and 17:4 (1985).

10 See Paul Brodeur, *The Zapping of America* (New York: W. W. Norton and Company, 1977) and Nicholas H. Steneck, *The Microwave Debate* (Cambridge: MIT Press, 1984).

11 My piece also tried to remove conventional differentiation to evaluate body actions between performance artists and electrical engineers.

12 For detailed information, see an excellent video document by New Decade Productions, "Everyone's Channel" produced by David Shulman, Paper Tiger Television, New York, 1990. For information on Deep Dish TV, see Martha Wallner,"Tigers Sprout Wings and Fly!" in *ROAR! The Paper Tiger Television Guide to Media Activism* (San Francisco: Paper Tiger Television, 1991), 33–34. This book is also a self-history of ten years of Paper Tiger Television.

13 See Ilya Prigogine and Isabelle Stengers, *Order Out of Chaos: Man's New Dialogue with Nature* (New York: Bantam Books, 1984) especially pages 167ff. and 177ff.

14 Ivan Illich used conviviality as a postmodern umbrella concept for living, work, art and technology. See his *Tools of Conviviality* (New York: Harper and Row, 1973).

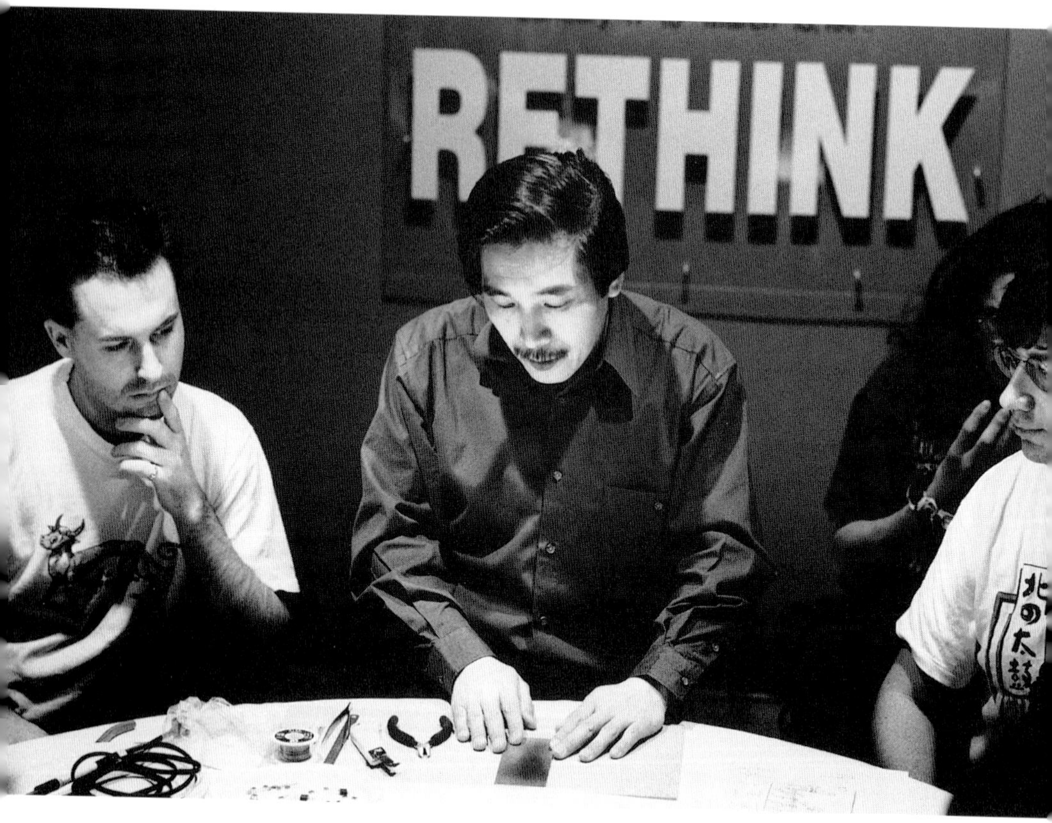

Tetsuo Kogawa (centre) during a workshop on how to build a one-watt FM transmitter at the Walter Phillips Gallery during *Radio Rethink* (1992). Tim Westbury (left) and Mike Ewanus (right)

How to Build a One-Watt FM Transmitter Based on a Workshop by Tetsuo Kogawa

Rob Kozinuk

The following instructions provide the information required to build a one-watt mono FM transmitter. Tetsuo Kogawa provided the original plans for this polymorphous transmitter during his visit to Canada for *Radio Rethink*. Although the text proceeds roughly in the order the transmitter should be assembled, you should read the entire text before starting. The first step is to assemble the tools and parts listed here. For each of the parts required, two drawings are provided, one physical (left) and one electrical (right).

NOTE: The building of a low-power transmitter is not illegal however the operation of it may be. In certain situations, low-power transmitters may cause "harmful interference," defined as an adverse effect on safety-related radio communication systems, or radio-sensitive equipment such as that used by hospitals. Information on certification, licensing and exemptions in Canada is available from Industry and Science Canada.

TOOLS REQUIRED

- soldering iron
- blade knife
- small needle-nose pliers
- small wire cutters
- plastic TV tuning tweaker
- volt/ohmmeter

Photo Cheryl Bellows

PARTS LIST FOR THE ONE-WATT RADIO TRANSMITTER

COPPER PLATE

Base	two sided	8 x 16 cm
6 mm squares		15
5 minute epoxy		

RESISTORS

180	Ω	1
300	Ω	1
1	kΩ	1
4.7	kΩ	1
22	kΩ	1
27	kΩ	1

CAPACITORS

3.3	pF	ceramic	1
10	pF	ceramic	4
15	pF	ceramic	1
22	pF	ceramic	1
33	pF	ceramic	2
68	pF	ceramic	1
100	pF	ceramic	2
0.01	μF	ceramic	3
47	μF	electrolytic	2

RADIO FREQUENCY CHOKES

1	μH	1
2	μH	2
4.7	μH	1

TUNING COILS (all coils about 6mm diameter with ferrite core)

3.5 turn	1
5.5 turn	1
8.5 turn	1

DIODES

No. 2 VCD	Variable Capacitance Diode, aka Tuning Diode	1
8.2 Volt Zener		1

TRANSISTORS

2SC1906	1
2SC2053	1
2SC1970	1

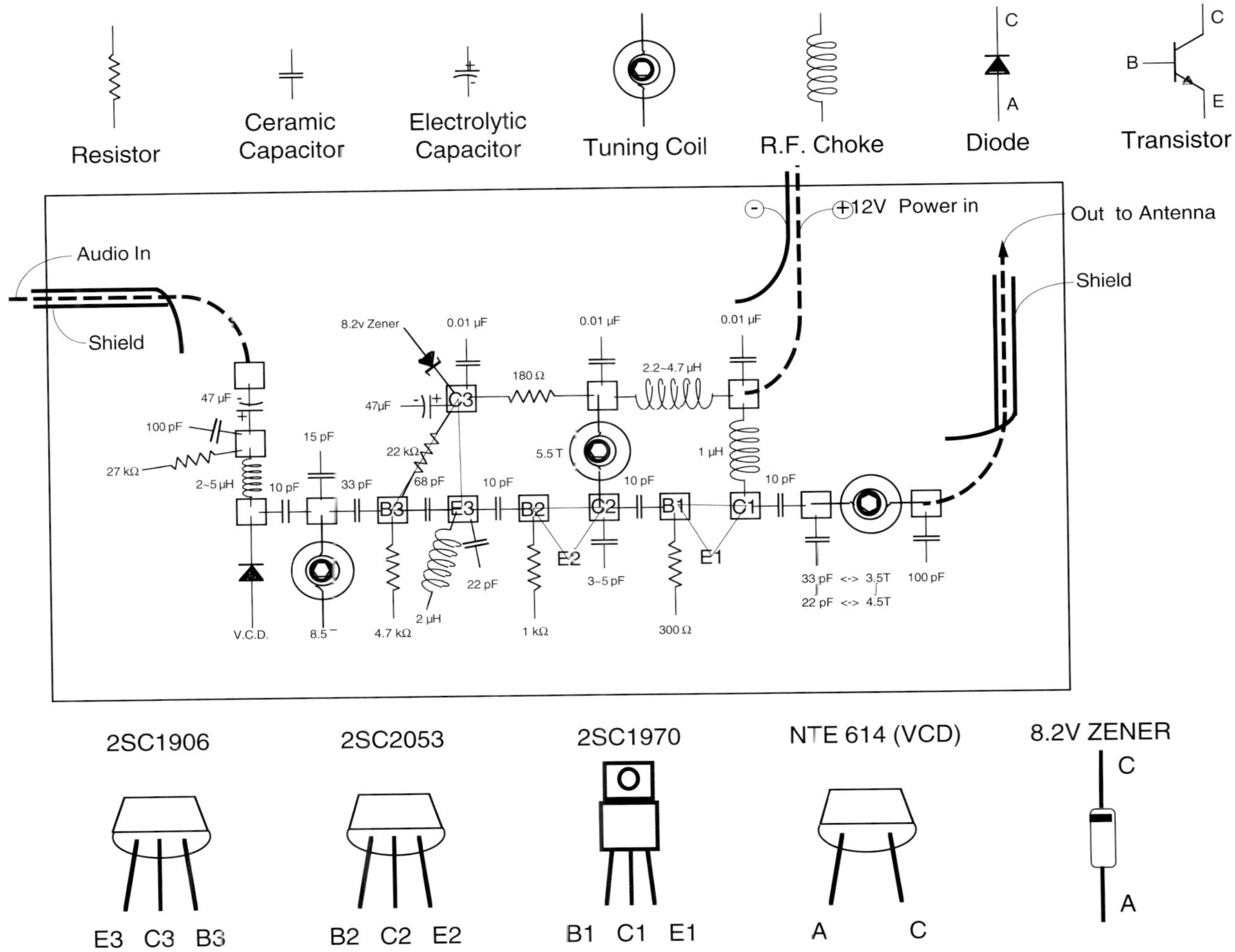

Resistor
Ceramic Capacitor
Electrolytic Capacitor
Tuning Coil
R.F. Choke
Diode
C
A
Transistor
B
C
E
Audio In
Shield
-
+12V Power in
Out to Antenna
Shield
8.2v Zener
0.01 µF
0.01 µF
0.01 µF
47 µF
47µF
180 Ω
2.2~4.7 µH
100 pF
15 pF
22 kΩ
5.5 T
1 µH
27 kΩ
2~5 µH
10 pF
33 pF
68 pF
10 pF
10 pF
10 pF
B3
E3
B2
C2
B1
C1
C3
E2
E1
22 pF
3~5 pF
33 pF <-> 3.5T
22 pF <-> 4.5T
100 pF
V.C.D.
8.5
4.7 kΩ
2 µH
1 kΩ
300 Ω
2SC1906
E3 C3 B3
2SC2053
B2 C2 E2
2SC1970
B1 C1 E1
NTE 614 (VCD)
A C
8.2V ZENER
C
A

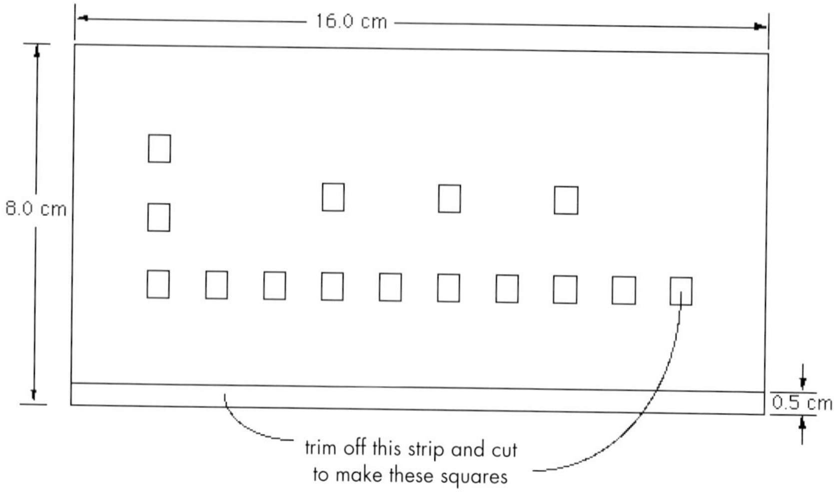
16.0 cm
8.0 cm
0.5 cm
trim off this strip and cut
to make these squares

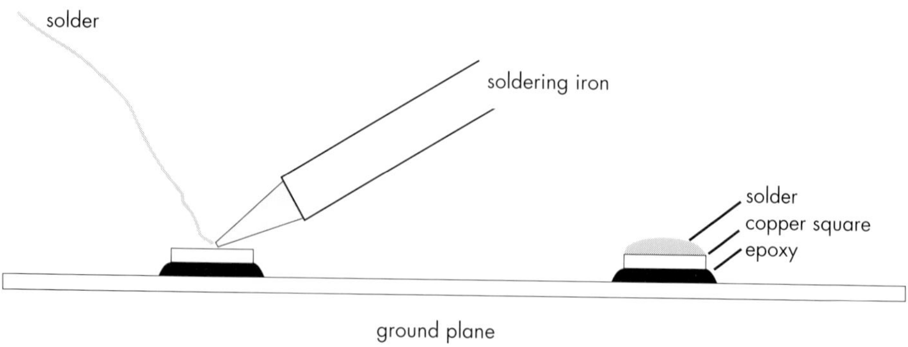
solder
soldering iron
solder
copper square
epoxy
ground plane

WHERE TO BUY PARTS

Although most of the required parts can be found at any electronics store (such as Radio Shack) you will need to find a specialty shop for the inductors, diodes and transistors. In most cities there can be found a small shop that caters to ham radio operators with shelves piled high with electronic parts. They will be able to supply the tuning diode and transistors that operate at the correct frequency. They will probably be willing to order in the tuning coils for you and sell the individual parts. You can also order directly from Electrosonic or one of the other big electronic parts distributors but they will have minimums on what you can order, partwise and pricewise. The list prices are very high on single parts, so make sure you negotiate as much as possible, and make sure you get the quoted price when you pick up the parts.

CIRCUIT BOARD

Start with a piece of two-sided copper plated circuit board, 8 cm by 16 cm. This will form the ground plane. Rub the oxidation off the copper surface with steel wool or rough cloth so that it shines. The board can be cut by scoring both sides several times with a razorknife. Cut a 5 mm strip off the long edge, in the same manner. Using wire cutters, cut the strip into 5 mm squares. Glue them onto the circuit board with five-minute epoxy in the pattern on the diagram opposite.

After the epoxy dries, try to pry the squares off to make sure that they are solid. Re-glue any that come off. Test again. When they are all solid, use a hot soldering iron to melt a pool of solder about 2 mm deep onto the top of each point (see example opposite). Next check that they are all electrically isolated from the ground plane – use an ohmmeter to check for ∞ resistance between the point and the main board.

RESISTORS

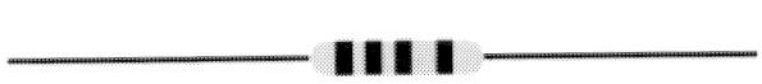

resistor

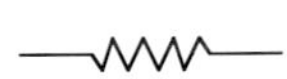

resistor

Resistors are fairly heat resistant, and also the least expensive parts, so you can learn to solder at this stage without risking much. First, choose the resistor by the code and then wipe the leads with a rough cloth to remove the oxide. This will make it easier to solder but be careful not to bend the leads. Put the resistor in place on the circuit board according to the main diagram on page 303 and push the lead into the pool of solder on the square (not too hard). You may need to prime the tip of the soldering iron with a bit of fresh solder to make the heat transfer to the pool. As soon as the lead melts into the pool, remove the iron, holding the resistor until the solder rehardens. A pair of needle-nose pliers is needed as the other lead will often get quite hot and burn your fingers.

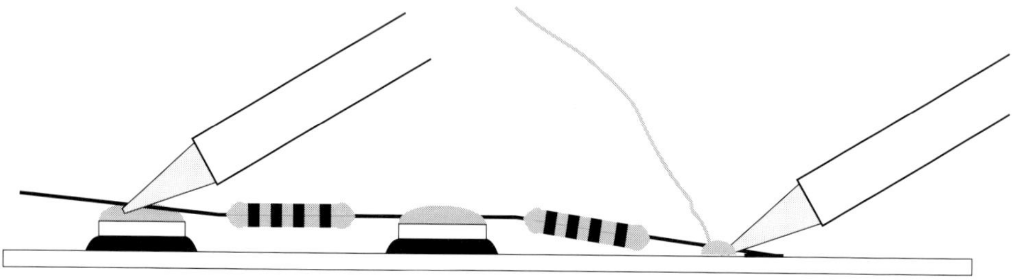

Next, solder the other lead into another point following the connections on the diagram. If the lead is not connected to another point, push the lead into the ground plane and apply solder to the junction (see diagram above). When there is a small pool around the lead, remove the iron and hold the lead in the pool until it hardens. Cut the excess leads off as short as possible, so that they will not form tiny antennas. You may also cut (and bend) the leads before you solder if you are careful not to make them too short. To bend a lead, hold it close to the component with needle-nose pliers and bend the leads outwards from that point to avoid breaking the connection within the component. When you have put on all the resistors, use an ohmmeter to check that the resistance is correct across the points and that you have not soldered any points to ground.

Something to watch out for is cold solder joints. These occur when the solder melts around the lead or onto the ground plane and seems to stick but does not make a solid electrical contact. The joint will have a high and possibly variable resistance when it should have no resistance. If

RESISTOR AND INDUCTOR CODE

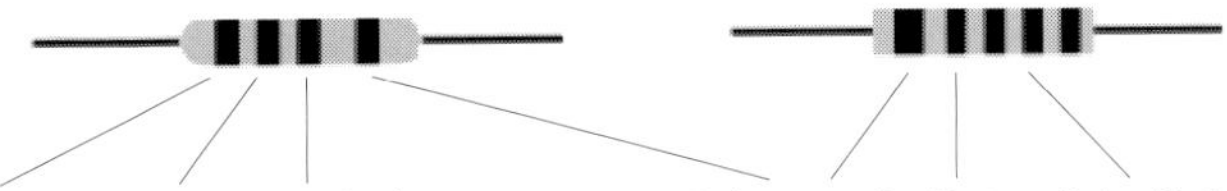

Colour	1st Digit	2nd Digit	Multiplier	Unit	Tolerance	1st Digit	Point Digit	Unit
Black	0	0	X1	Ω		0	.0	μhenrys
Brown	1	1	X10			1	.1	
Red	2	2	X100			2	.2	
Orange	3	3	X1,000	kΩ		3	.3	
Yellow	4	4	X10,000			4	.4	
Green	5	5	X100,000			5	.5	
Blue	6	6	X1,000,000	MΩ		6	.6	
Violet	7	7	X10,000,000			7	.7	
Grey	8	8	X100,000,000			8	.8	
White	9	9				9	.9	
Gold					5%			
Silver					10%			
No Band					20%			

you find one, you have to reheat the joint and add new solder until the solder makes a good connection with all leads and the plane. To prevent cold solder joints from happening, you can wipe the lead to remove the oxide (solder will stick better to clean leads) and then pre-tin the lead. Hold the lead against the iron and hit them with fresh solder until the lead has a thin coat of solder. The flux in the centre of the fresh solder helps to make a good connection.

CAPACITORS

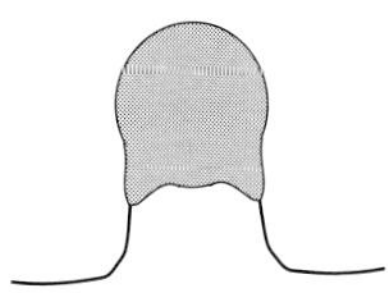

capacitor

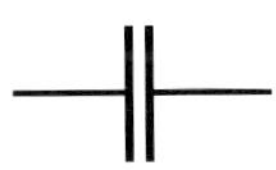

capacitor

Two types of capacitors are used: the smaller disc caps (above) and the "can" electrolytic (next page). Start with the disc caps, which have two radial leads and are covered in epoxy. The first two digits (with point) of the printed numbers on the side give the capacitance in picofarads (pf or 10^{-12} farads). The third digit is the X10 multiplying factor. Solder these disc capacitors on in the same manner as the resistors, wiping the leads first and then pushing one of the leads into the point. Again, put the other lead to another point or to the ground plane according to the connections on the diagram. Cut the point leads short enough so that they will not contact the ground plane if the capacitor is bent. You may need to add a bit of electrician's tape under some leads to isolate them from ground.

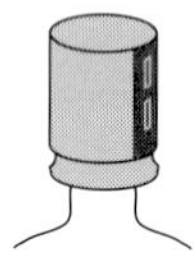

electrolytic capacitor

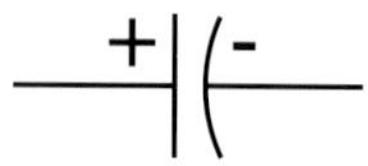

electrolytic capacitor

So far all the parts have been non-polarized, meaning that the leads are equal so it does not matter in which direction the part is connected in the circuit. The electrolytic capacitors are polarized, which means that one of the leads is positive, one is negative and you must be careful to solder the correct lead to the correct point. On the capacitor you will notice that the negative lead is nearest a black line with a negative sign. This is the cathode (-). The other lead is the anode (+) and must be connected to the point on the board that is marked positive on the diagram. Once the two electrolytic capacitors are soldered on you can again check for short-circuits to the ground plane and cold solder joints.

INDUCTORS

Two types of inductors are used in the transmitter: Radio Frequency

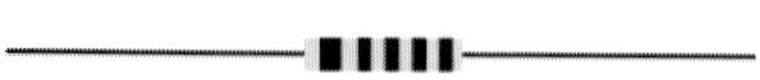

Radio Frequency Choke

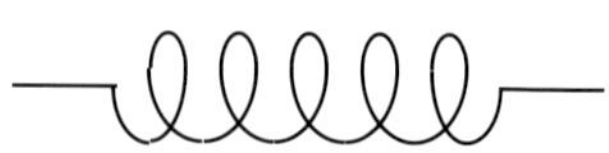

Radio Frequency Choke

Chokes (RFC) and tuning coils. Both are non-polarized. The RFCs look like resistors with sharper ends and coloured stripes that give the value in μhenrys using the same code as resistors. The tuning coils are visible coils of wire set in plastic with a ferrite core that can be screwed in and out of the coil. You must count the number of turns of wire to get the rough value and then adjust the ferrite core to set the exact value when you are tuning the transmitter.

Apply the RFCs in the same manner as resistors.

Now is a good time to check your handiwork. Most of the parts added so far are quite sturdy and will not be destroyed if the iron is left on the point a little too long. We will be moving to the more fragile parts next so you should check that there are no cold solder joints and reheat any that are not smooth. Some of the points get quite crowded so you should check that there is enough solder on each to allow for a quick connection with the remaining parts. Cut off any leads that are sticking out of the solder. Check that the parts are the correct value in the correct place according to the diagram.

The radio frequency circuits react with the ground plane and a more massive ground plane will help to stabilize them. To make a better ground plane use the cut-off leads to connect the top ground plane to the bottom at several points around the outside of the circuitboard. Solder them first to the top and then bend them around to the bottom. Once you are satisfied, move on to the tuning coils.

TUNING COILS

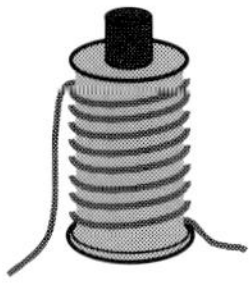

tuning coils

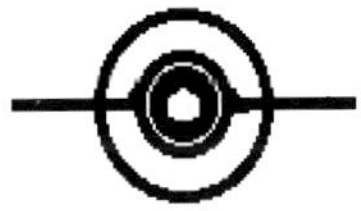

tuning coils

The tuning coils are soldered on by pushing the leads into the solder points as before but be careful that you do not hold the iron on the lead too long as the heat will travel up it and melt the plastic. Pre-tinning the leads may help make a quick connection. These parts need a solid joint as they undergo physical stress when the transmitter is tuned. They can be glued down in place when the unit is up and working but be careful not to get any glue into the centre of the coil or touching the ferrite core. Hot glue works well for this.

DIODES

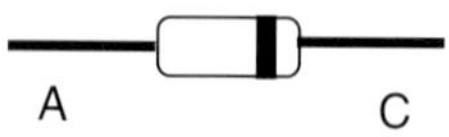

Zener Diode

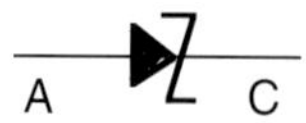

Zener Diode

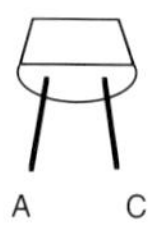

Variable Capacitance Diode

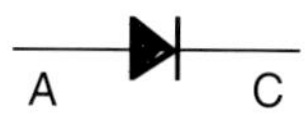

Variable Capacitance Diode

Two diodes are used, both polarized. The first is a Zener diode rated at 8.2 volts which holds the point where the cathode is connected at 8.2 volts (at most) above the anode (which is connected to ground). This biases the first transistor. It looks like a regular diode with a black bar marking the lead from the cathode. The other diode is a Variable Capacitance Diode (VCD), also called a Voltage Controlled Diode or a tuning diode. It is used to help select the transmitting frequency. It looks more like a small transistor with only two leads. Solder these into place, taking care that the cathode goes to the point as in the diagram.

TRANSISTORS

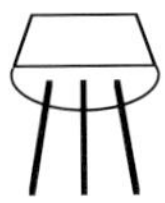

transistor
2SC1906
2SC2053

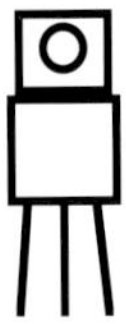

transistor
2SC1970

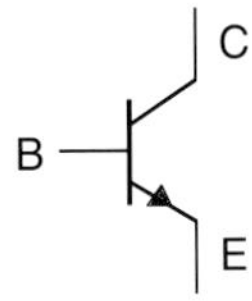

transistor

A transistor is used to amplify the signal. It has three leads - the Base, the Emitter and the Collector – each of which must be connected properly for it to work. A small current or voltage is applied as an input to the Base. The current is then amplified, which allows a larger current to flow from the Emitter to the Collector. On the circuit diagram, transistors are shown as triangles with each corner labeled B, C or E. If you do not get the exact ones shown in the diagram you will have to check the layout of these pins as they are not all the same.

Transistors are the most fragile of the components so be very careful when soldering them in. Bend the leads and make sure all three leads will contact the correct points before applying any heat. Do not hold the iron on each lead more than ten seconds as you will overheat the transistor and possibly destroy it. Prime the tip of the iron to ensure a quick connection.

Each of the transistors corresponds to a stage of amplification. Starting at the left end where the audio comes in, each transistor increases the power until the maximum power goes to the antenna. You should start at the left side, testing each stage as it is added. You should have your power supply ready to turn on and off and an FM radio tuned to an empty spot below 90 MHz. When you have the first transistor soldered into place, carefully power up the transmitter. Adjust the first tuning coil until you hear the radio go from white noise to silence. This shows that the first stage is working. Do not leave the unit powered up for too long.

When the first stage is working go on to the second. When the unit is powered up with the next transistor added you should notice a gain in power on your receiver's signal-strength meter. You can also test the output of each stage with a signal-power meter. Again, when you are satisfied this stage is working, move on to the next transistor. Continue until all three transistors are added. Caution: do not power up the completed transmitter without an antenna attached.

CONNECTORS AND CABLING

There are three connections that need to be made to the transmitter: power input, audio input and antenna output. The easiest to accomplish is the power. It is connected with two separate wires: ground to the ground plane and +12 volts to the first point. A power supply with clip leads is acceptable for testing but is dangerous for regular use. It is useful to have a switch and fuse in your power line. A four-pin XLR can be used as a connector (especially if you have an old 12-volt camera power supply that uses them). Also good is a regular post/sleeve type as used in many electronic devices with external power supplies. Be careful to check the polarity of any connectors, as reversing the power can result in blown components.

The audio must be connected with audio coaxial cabling right to the board. The shield goes to the ground plane and the centre wire goes to the marked point. A mini plug (that is, a mono headphone) can be used as a connector or a pair of RCA jacks with the tips connected to combine left and right signals to a mono signal.

The output is connected with video type coaxial cable (50 to 75 ohms impedance). Small diameter coaxial is good to connect the circuit to the connector but use as large a diameter as possible to make the run to the antenna, especially if it must go more than a few feet. Regular F-type (cable TV) connectors will do if you are using ordinary RG59 cable. Better are the large UHF connectors with RG58 or even the giant RG213 coaxial.

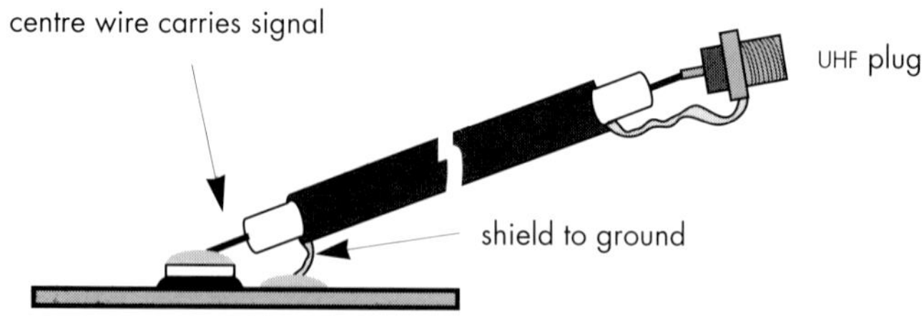

POWER SUPPLY

The transmitter requires 12 volts DC to operate. This can be supplied by a regular plug-in-the-wall transformer but they usually will add a large sixty-hertz hum to the signal. A computer-grade power supply could also be used. The preferred method is a battery which gives an absolutely smooth voltage. You will need one that can provide a sustained 200 mAmp current for as long as you want to transmit. A rechargeable gelcel is ideal for this but remember to never discharge the gelcel completely before recharging. Even an old car battery that cannot start a car will work if it will hold a charge. You should put a 250 mAmp fuse in the power line to protect the transmitter from any supply that can put out more current than that.

TUNING

The transmitter is designed to work at the low end of the FM dial (from 88 to about 91 MHz) because at lower frequencies the radiowaves will travel farther. You will need a good receiver that has a signal-strength meter. Scan the low end of the dial for an empty frequency. On the FM band only the strongest station at any frequency can be heard. Therefore, the farther you can get from the other broadcasters on the dial, the less they will interfere with your narrowcast. When you tune your radio to your chosen frequency you should hear white noise. Then, with the antenna attached, power up the transmitter. Using a plastic TV tool, adjust the ferrite core of the first tuning coil up and down until you hear the noise cut to silence. You are now transmitting at that frequency. While watching the signal-

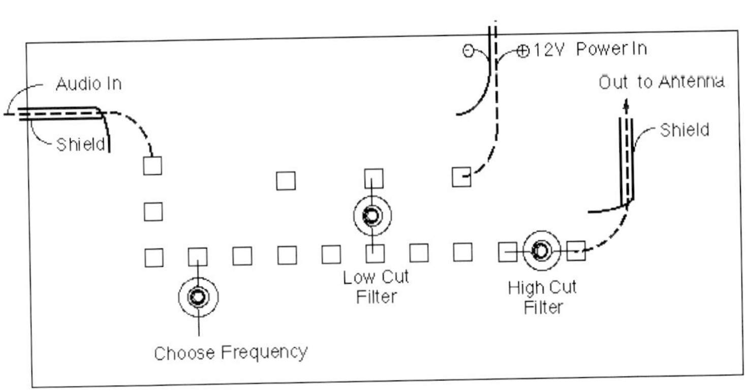

strength meter, adjust the second coil to maximize the strength. If you move the core up or down from the optimal position, the signal strength should decrease. This coil helps to cut out the higher frequencies and the more they are cut out, the more power is put through at the desired frequency. Adjust the third coil in the same manner, as it is cutting the lower frequencies. You are now ready to connect your audio source. Readjust the second coil and then the third until your audio signal is optimized. When the transmitter is properly adjusted, a radio receiver that is positioned at least 50 metres from it should pick up the signal only at the desired frequency.

ANTENNA

The simplest antenna is a monopole for which you can use a regular telescoping antenna. The signal (the centre conductor) is attached to the base of the antenna, while the ground (shield) just ends at the connection point. This antenna gives roughly equal power in all directions. To maximize the power given off, the length of the antenna should be adjusted to a quarter wavelength ($\lambda/4$) as given by the formula:

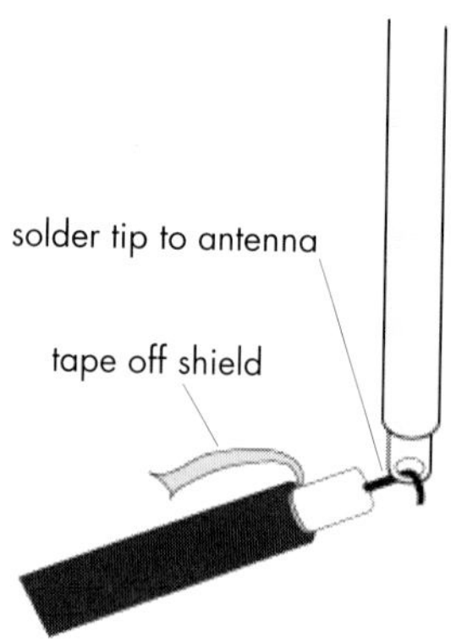

wiring detail

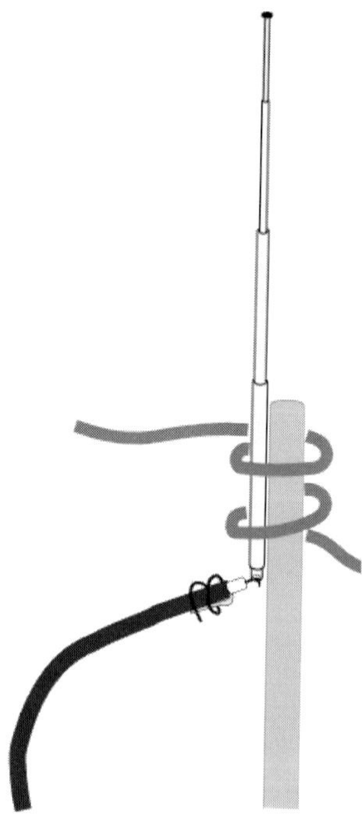
monopole antenna

$$\text{length} = \lambda/4 = (1/4)(3 \times 10^8 \text{m/s}) / \text{frequency}$$

$$\text{length (in centimetres)} = \lambda/4 = 7500 / \text{frequency (in megahertz)}$$

This length should be eighty to ninety centimetres for the frequencies this transmitter will produce. The antenna should be mounted vertically as high as possible (on top of the house?) on a non-metallic support. Keep it at least one wavelength, λ (four times the antenna length) away from other metal structures.

DIPOLE ANTENNA

A more effective antenna is a dipole, for which a pair of rabbit ears works well. The two ears are pointed directly away from each other with the signal going to the side pointing up and the shield connected to the side pointing down.

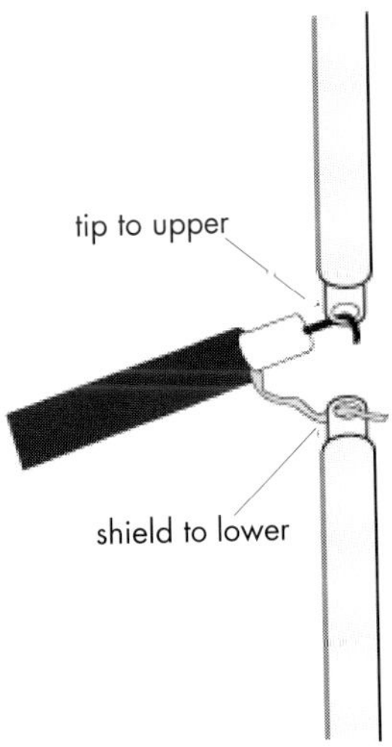

wiring detail

The length of each end is given by quarter wavelength formula. This antenna concentrates the power in the plane perpendicular to the two ears so that if it is mounted vertically most of the power goes out horizontally and not into the ground or sky. Again, it should be mounted as high as possible and away from metal structures.

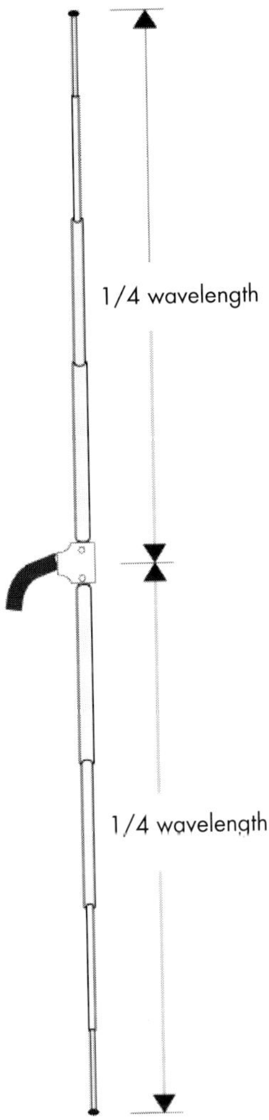

dipole antenna

RECEIVING THE NARROWCAST

In early days of radio most station transmitters had relatively low power so receivers had to be well designed in order to pick up the signal. However, as it became more and more expensive to get a license, more and more money was spent on increasing the transmission power to reach a larger audience. As the big stations raced to increase their power output, receiver manufacturers realized that radios could be made more cheaply by simplifying the design. This means that the radios can pick up the high-powered signals but they will not pick up low-powered stations very well. Just try any average car radio at night, and you will not get as many faraway stations as you previously could.

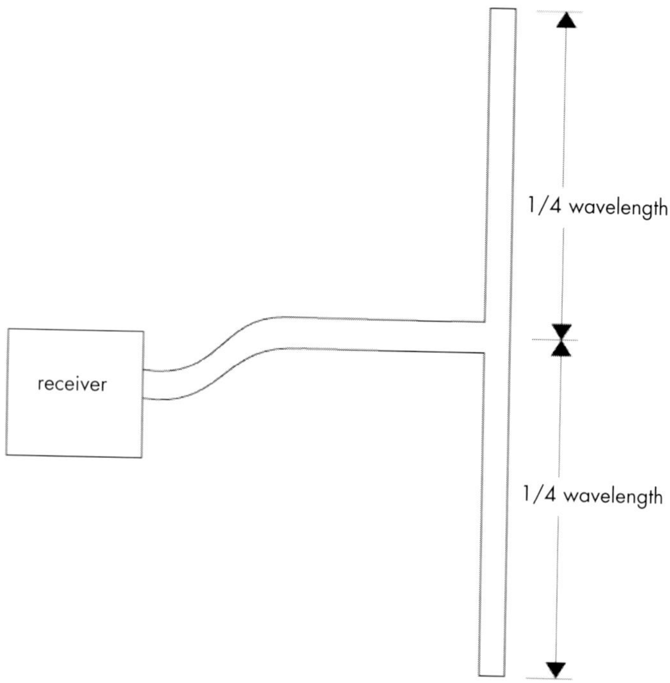

I am not just waxing poetic about the good old days, I am telling you this to explain why you must educate your audience so that they will be able to pick up your low-powered station. The best way to receive the narrowcast is to use a half-wavelength-loop dipole antenna, the type you get with a home stereo. The idea is to tune it to your frequency by making each arm one quarter wavelength as given by the formula above for transmitter antennas. This will work best for your frequency and quite well for the rest of the FM band. If you are using a dipole antenna oriented vertically to narrowcast, the signal will be polarized vertically and the top of the T of the receiving antenna should be mounted vertically as well, not horizontally as is usually the case. A good receiver with a proper antenna should be able to pick up your signal three kilometres away.

Thanks to Don Chow for his help with the drawings

Playing in the Airwaves

Margaretta D'Arcy

LANCASTER UNIVERSITY, UNITED KINGDOM, 5 APRIL 1990 – I am going to start off with a very bigoted assertion. That the theatre (by which I mean any form of dramatic entertainment that involves an audience passively watching performer or "participating" under the control of performers), instead of changing society, has actually copperfastened the unequal distribution of wealth and the unequal distribution of power.

If we take a global perspective, the inequality is greater than ever before particularly between the First and Second Worlds and the Third World; and even within the so-called First World the gaps are growing wider. When I talk about gaps I do not only mean gaps between classes but gaps between the genders. This is now common knowledge and widely quoted: women do two-thirds of the world's work, own five percent of the world's assets, and earn one percent of the world's income.

The very structure of theatrical form, I believe, contributes to this. In general, time, place and membership are controlled for both preparation and performance. And yet it is exactly the rigidity of time and place that prevents the majority of women from taking part, in contrast to the fluidity of life, birth and death, with which women throughout the world primarily have to cope. In my own experience, I have had eight pregnancies and given birth to five children. This radically altered my availability for the theatre and therefore my perception of the usefulness of theatre. Over the past thirty years I have had to look towards other forms of communication to find the most flexible. After twenty-seven year's search and breaking through my conditioning, I have come to the conclusion that radio is the answer.

One minor problem! All the airwaves are controlled, and it is illegal to use this form of communication without being employed by a licensed station or getting a license for oneself. The pioneers of radio were developing not so much an art form as a convenience for military and commercial pursuits, which necessarily involved the interests of the state, and the licensing laws in every country today still have state security as their first priority.

(A suggestive digression. The first real BROADCAST – that is, the first time radio messages were sent out at large for anyone to pick up who cared to do so – was in Morse code from Sackville Street, Dublin, on 25 April 1916, by the Irish Volunteers in rebellion *against* the British state. They proclaimed the establishment of a new Irish Republic.[1])

I am not very ambitious. I believe in doing things in a small way in small groups. Only in small groups can there be the full exploration of the three Fs: freedom to receive and give information, freedom of expression, freedom of speech. I believe the three Fs are the pivot of human development, essential if we are to share, analyze, understand, and move forward. And yet these three Fs are continually under attack, and not only from governments. Kevin Boyle, professor of law at the University of Essex, has pointed out that:

> The control of all communications technology in industrialized nations, and of its content, will rest in the hands of as few as six large media corporations by the end of this decade . . . To replace the classic era of state censorship with private monopoly power is not to usher in the era of universal enjoyment of freedom of expression . . . The growing use of new technology in developed countries is widening the gap between the "information rich" and the "information poor" in the world . . . Technological literacy now has become just as important as the ability to read and write.[2]

Of late in Britain, with the new curtailments of broadcasters' freedom in regard to spokespeople for Sinn Féin ["We ourselves," the political wing of the Irish Republican Army] and positive representation of homosexuality – and in my own country of Ireland, with very strict political control of the airwaves (Section 31 of the Broadcasting Act restricts the voices of the members of Sinn Féin from being broadcast on radio or television in the Republic of Ireland) and new legislation preventing any information about obtaining an abortion – it has become impossible to take freely to the airwaves and to talk and to listen at large about all issues of life and death without becoming a criminal.

Why don't they want us to talk, listen, show, or see these things? Because if we can do that we can take their control away from them. If there is one thing more frightening to society than a rival society, it is the threat of chaos: a threat made immediate by the very existence of the three Fs.

I have been reading the advance brochure for this conference [this article is based on a speech given at a conference on theatre and ideology held in Lancaster, United Kingdom, in April 1990]. It talks about: "ideology," "political power," "influence," "public policy" – I am reading words from the program, and very important, profound words they are too. But what is the reality of them when we try to apply them? These words are the words used by any group that wants to maintain its own power and neither share it nor give it to anyone else. I have no interest in using these words. But there is one word which is omitted: the word *play*!

When you are playing, you know what you're doing, but to the outsider it often appears as though other people's play is very little better than chaos. Play is recognized as an aspect of human development, but it is chiefly associated with children, and attempts are always made to control play and to turn it into competitive games which are a model of adult society. Because our play has been processed and controlled we ourselves are processed and controlled. When I was young I used to go to *plays*, I used to be in *plays* and I used to be part of a group that made up *plays*. Four hundred years ago there were *playhouses* and *players*. Now in 1990 – if our conference brochure is anything to go by – the word "play" is eliminated altogether (except just once, in the specialized sense of playwright). We must bring that word back. It is not a controller's word, it is a word that he has always fought against. If we use his words we become his mirror image. He controls women's communications by constructing a mystique of technology and theoretical science and making us frightened of it.

I see no mention in the brochure of the airwaves. We all know that when a government feels threatened they impose extra controls on the airwaves, and when the opposition seizes power the first thing they go for is the airwaves. And yet the use of airwaves is technically accessible to all of us, and the idea of using them for *playing* rather than for an active/

passive relationship between skilled communicators and unskilled audience has hardly been thought about.

But this is how we should be thinking for the future. Building up networks of small transmitters, learning how to make the transmitters for ourselves and passing the skills on, learning how to run our own radio and TV stations, where all our skills can be shared and passed on, where we can play over the airwaves in the community, the city, the housing estates, the countryside. The technology is now available, and it is cheap. But the controls over it are strong and they have to be broken.

A group of women in Galway (where I live) has just finished an international women's radio festival on what is known as a "pirate" radio station. Over fifty women participated live – either actually at the microphone or over the telephone. We broke Section 31 and also we broke the laws against giving information about abortion. Only one of these fifty women has a full-time job; she works in the local supermarket, and is a trade-union activist. Fifty women broke the law and we were prepared to accept the consequences. The transmitter (with a radius of two miles) operated from my small terrace-house in a working-class area. The cost was only the electricity we consumed – the same as using a record player, a cooker, or a washing machine. The transmitter cost no more than £25 ($40). But the penalties imposed by the Irish government are two years in jail and a fine of £20,000 ($32,600).

Objectively speaking, it could be looked at as a ridiculous bit of play because in all probability more women were talking on the radio than were actually listening! (Just like Dublin, 1916.) But it did prove one thing: the sense among women of starvation, of never being listened to, overcame their fear of being penalized for talking or singing into a microphone. Our activities were pointedly ignored as irrelevant by local liberal intelligentsia and feminist groups. Or – put it another way – such people had too much to lose by being associated with a small and uncontrolled outfit of marginalized women not attached to any specific organization. The only form of control we imposed on our broadcasting was our agreed upon rule-of-procedure that any woman could express herself in any way she wanted, and while women could disagree with what she said, they could not stop her.

But we did have enormous international support from women's radio stations in three continents; they sent tapes and made telephone linkups. In fact through these linkups millions heard us. Thanks to WINGS

(Women's International News-Gathering Service) in America, AMARC (World Associations of Community Radio Broadcasters) in Canada, Women on the Line in Australia, Air Libre in Belgium, Air Libertaire in France. All these groups entered into the spirit of our play.

We had a little advertising jingle which we used to sing in the streets and over the air:

> Hey, Pirate Woman, what you cookin' today?
> I'm airing subversion the radio way.
> Excuse me, Galway woman, play a pirate this day,
> Join the craic[3] on the free airway!

To deny knowledge is to deny freedom, to deny freedom is to deny power.

We play again on the airwave on 24 May, Women's Disarmament Day. Whether women will be as brave this time is yet to be seen, because of the yelpings from the local consortium (patriarchal triumvirate – church, sport, education – that controls the ideology of Galway's licensed commercial radio station) demanding immediate action against us from the authorities of the state. We may have to play hide-and-seek (quite literally) in the hills.

Notes

1 See Peter Mulryan, *Radio Radio* (Dublin: Borderline Publications, 1988).
2 Kevin Boyle, lecture given at Dublin City University, reported in *The Irish Times* (11 May 1990).
3 "Craic," pronounced "crack" means a jolly time, a friendly chat.

Index

Contributors

DAINA AUGAITIS has been a curator of contemporary art for ten years. She has organized numerous exhibitions exploring relationships between art and technology and is currently Director of Visual Arts at the Banff Centre for the Arts and Chief Curator of the Walter Phillips Gallery.

JODY BERLAND is a professor in the Department of Humanities, Atkinson College, York University. She has written numerous articles on radio, sound and the media and is corresponding editor of several magazines (*Border/Lines*, *New Formations* and *Popular Music*). She has recently written several of the entries pertaining to broadcasting in the *Encyclopedia of Music in Canada.*

HANK BULL has lived in Vancouver and worked at the Western Front since 1973. He became involved in radio and television in 1975. In collaboration with Patrick Ready, he produced a weekly show of original radio art which ran for eight years. He has been active as an organizer of international artists' projects using electronic networks and continues various pursuits as a "TOTALmedia" artist.

MARGARETTA D'ARCY lives and works experimentally with women in the west of Ireland. She was part of the late 1950s Royal Court era in London and in 1982 founded *Galway Women's Entertainment* as a forum for theoretical and practical work to develop radical participatory/celebratory form. In 1987 she started Galway Women's Scéal Radio. Her latest published works include a book of essays,

Awkward Corners (1988) and *Whose Is the Kingdom?*, a book of radio plays (1988), both co-authored with John Arden.

FRANCES DYSON is an Australian writer and multimedia artist, currently living in the United States, who specializes in sound theory and audio art. Her radio works have been aired in Australia, North America, Canada and Europe and she has written numerous articles on sound within media theory, mass media, philosophy, music and technology.

LEONARD FISHER is an independent video producer and a member of Neo-Nativists, a performance art group in Vancouver which interprets current events from a native perspective.

COCO FUSCO is a Los Angeles-based writer, curator and media artist. Her articles have appeared in numerous publications including *The Los Angeles Times*, *The Village Voice*, *The Nation* and *Third Text*. She recently completed a video documentary about her cage performances with Guillermo Gómez-Peña entitled *The Couple in the Cage: A Guatinaui Odyssey*.

GUILLERMO GÓMEZ-PEÑA is an interdisciplinary artist whose work focuses on border culture and United States/Mexico relations. He is a founder and co-editor of the bilingual arts magazine *The Broken Line/La Linea Quebrada*, and founding member of the bi-national Border Arts Workshop. He was a regular contributor to the national public radio program *Crossroads* from 1987 to 1990 and now contributes to *Latino USA*.

HEIDI GRUNDMANN has worked for over twenty years in radio as a journalist and editor specializing since 1975 in the visual arts and news media. As producer and curator she developed *KunstRadio/RadioKunst*, a weekly program in Vienna which broadcasts and commissions original artworks for radio. In 1991 she organized Geometry of Silence, a symposium on radio art for the Museum moderner Kunst Stiftung Ludwig Wien in Vienna.

DOUGLAS KAHN is associate professor of media arts at Arizona State University West and author of *John Heartfield: Art and Mass Media*

(1985). He is co-editor of *Cultures in Contention* (1985) and *Wireless Imagination: Sound, Radio and the Avant-Garde* (1992) and is on the executive committee of SoundCultures, a Pacific region initiative for the production and discussion of the sound arts. His essays have appeared in *October*, *Public*, *Musicworks*, *Music Today* (*Tokyo*), *Sound by Artists* and *In the Spirit of Fluxus*.

FRIEDRICH KITTLER is a professor of German philology at Ruhr University in Bochum who has written extensively on radio theory.

TETSUO KOGAWA teaches communications at Tokyo Keizai University and is director of the Goethe Gallery in Tokyo. A specialist in free radio, he has performed extensively throughout the 1980s and is the author of *This is Free Radio* and *Confusion of Babel*, among other important books.

ROBERT KOZINUK experiments with electonics from building circuitry to using software. He worked as the technician at the Western Front in Vancouver for several years where he is currently Head of Media. Although his interest in low-power radio had been simmering for several years, it was brought to a boil when he met Tetsuo Kogawa. He has since been teaching others to build their own FM transmitters.

RICHARD KRIESCHE lectures at the Technical University of Vienna on "Aesthetics of Scientific-Technical Operations," and is a professor at the College of Design in Offenbach, Main. He is active internationally as an artist and curator and writes regularly on art and technology including radio art.

CAROL LAING is an Ontario artist/writer who divides her time between South Bay and Toronto. She teaches women's studies, contemporary Canadian art and art criticism at the Ontario College of Art.

DAN LANDER is an independent editor and artist living in Toronto. He is co-editor of *Sound by Artists* (1990), a guest editor for *Musicworks* (1992) and producer of *The Problem with Language* (1987–91) aired on CKLN-FM. Recent recorded works for radio and loudspeaker include *City Zoo/ZooCity* (1992) and *Room* (1993).

PAULA LEVINE is a Canadian/American visual artist currently working in the Bay area and teaching at San Francisco State University and the California College of Arts and Crafts. Her video, installations and photography have been exhibited widely and her articles have appeared in *Vanguard*, *West Coast Review*, *Photo Metro*, *Arts Atlantic* and *Cinematograph*.

RITA MCKEOUGH is an installation artist, musician and former disc jockey who has worked in radio, written an opera and incorporated audio into her work in integral ways. A retrospective of her influential feminist work was exhibited at the Glenbow Museum in Calgary in 1993.

CHRISTOF MIGONE lives in Montréal and is the instigator of the *Centre for Radio-Telecommunications Contortions* (CRTC). He is the producer of *Danger in Paradise* (CKUT FM) and is a founding member of the Association de création et diffusion sonores AVATAR. His writing can be found in *Musicworks* and *Radiotext(e)*.

MARY ANNE MOSER is a writer and editor interested in science, technology and culture. She also works as a designer and is the Publications Editor at the Walter Phillips Gallery in Banff.

ROBER RACINE is a writer, broadcaster and artist who has produced innovative programming for Radio-Canada and collaborated with dance choreographers. His work has been exhibited widely and, in 1992, was in *Documenta 9* in Kassel, Germany.

PATRICK READY is a Vancouver-based writer, inventor and radio artist who hosted *The HP Show* with Hank Bull for eight years. His collaborative radio plays, were first produced in 1973 and have since been performed in galleries in Toronto and Vancouver. In 1989, he invented the "water radio," as artist-in-residence at the Banff Centre.

KIM SAWCHUK is a professor of communications at Concordia University in Montréal. She is a member of the PoMoCoMo, a Montréal-based collective involved in performance and radio art. She is also a writer and contributor to *Impulse*, *Border/Lines* and the *Canadian Journal of Social and Political Theory*.

COLETTE URBAN has performed and exhibited her work throughout Canada and in Europe. She has been an instructor in art at the University of Victoria (1983), Emily Carr College of Art and Design (1985–88), and the University of Saskatchewan (1988–89), as well as a visiting artist at several artist-run centres. She is currently teaching at Memorial University in St. John's, Newfoundland.

TIM WESTBURY is an artist and musician currently living in Canmore, Alberta, whose work addresses popular culture and scientific rationalism. He has worked as a media associate, production coordinator and curatorial assistant at the Banff Centre for the Arts.

HILDEGARD WESTERKAMP grew up in postwar Germany and emigrated to Canada in 1968. She is a freelance composer/audio artist and has taught courses in acoustic communication at Simon Fraser University in Vancouver. She has given many lectures, workshops and seminars on sound, noise and music – locally and internationally. Most of her work during the last twenty years has centred on environmental sound and acoustic ecology.

GREGORY WHITEHEAD has produced over fifty radio features, earplays, voiceworks and conceptual talk shows. He has written extensively on subjects relating to language, technology and "the public," and co-edited *Wireless Imagination: Sound, Radio and the Avant-Garde* (1992).

PAUL WONG lives in Vancouver where, since the mid-seventies, he has been active as an artist, community activist and curator. Primarily known for his video work, he was the 1992 recipient of the Bell Canada Award for outstanding contribution to the field of video art in Canada. He is a co-founding director of Video In and On Edge Productions.